Equality
and Achievement
in Education

Social Inequality Series
Marta Tienda and David B. Grusky, Series Editors

Equality and Achievement in Education, James S. Coleman

Ethnicity and the New Family Economy:
Living Arrangements and Intergenerational Financial Flows,
edited by Frances K. Goldscheider and Calvin Goldscheider

FORTHCOMING

Getting Started: Transition to Adulthood in Great Britain,
Alan C. Kerckhoff

Social Stratification: Class, Race, and Gender
in Sociological Perspective, edited by David B. Grusky

Equality
and Achievement
in Education

James S. Coleman

Westview Press
BOULDER, SAN FRANCISCO, AND LONDON

mc

Social Inequality Series

Published in 1990 in the United States of America by Westview Press, Inc., 5500 Central Avenue, Boulder, Colorado 80301, and in the United Kingdom by Westview Press, Inc., 13 Brunswick Centre, London WC1N 1AF, England

Library of Congress Cataloging-in-Publication Data
Coleman, James Samuel, 1926–
    Equality and achievement in education / James S. Coleman.
        p.   cm. — (Social inequality series)
    ISBN 0-8133-7791-9
    1. Educational equalization—United States.   2. Academic
achievement.   3. Education—Social aspects—United States.
I. Title.   II. Series.
LC213.2.C63   1990
370.19′34′0973—dc20   89-48344
                                                                                        CIP

Printed and bound in the United States of America

The paper used in this publication meets the requirements of the American National Standard for Permanence of Paper for Printed Library Materials Z39.48-1984.

10   9   8   7   6   5   4   3   2

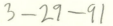

Contents

Foreword

At the start of the 1990s, the issues of educational achievement and inequality of educational opportunity remain as salient as they were in the mid-1960s, the era of the Great Society. In some ways, these issues are even more conspicuous because of the changed skill demands of the work force and because of mounting evidence that educational inequities have increased for some groups. While race, ethnic, and gender differentials in average attainment levels have narrowed since 1960, high school noncompletion rates are alarmingly high among Hispanics and blacks, and college enrollment rates of blacks have begun to decline. Moreover, there are signs of widening differentials in educational outcomes between private and public schools, between schools located in inner cities and those located in affluent suburbs, and between those whose student body is largely minority and those whose student body is largely majority. The state of American schooling is problematic enough that a recent report characterized us as a "nation at risk"—one ill-prepared to face the close of the current century let alone the challenges of the next century.

There is, of course, an important difference between the 1960s and the present: We now have a reasonably large amount of empirical evidence that sheds light on the processes that generate and maintain educational inequities and that can inform policy bodies about appropriate strategies to reverse these troubling trends. This was not the case in 1964, when James S. Coleman began his distinguished research career focused on educational achievement. His pioneering study, *Equality of Educational Opportunity*, served as a benchmark in multiple ways: It marked a turning point in redefining the domains of social policy research and the relationship between the federal government and private research institutions; it broadened the conception of school quality and the ways in which we measure and assess educational inputs and outputs; and it redefined the domains of inquiry by asking new questions and by insisting on scientific evidence as a basis for decision-making.

That social policy can be informed in useful ways by empirical social science research is a generally accepted, if not a well-defined, tenet in both academic and policy circles as the 1990s begin. Some twenty-five years ago, when the federal government initiated massive social change programs, this was not the case. Hindsight aids in appreciating that the relationship between social sciences and policy research has matured, and Coleman's role in shaping this relationship testifies that the maturation process was rocky. Always controversial initially, his work has withstood the test of time and replication, setting a new agenda for research and public policy time and again.

The history of how we came to know as much as we currently do about the social forces that generate educational inequities is well known only by those who have followed Coleman's voluminous scholarly works and government reports over the past thirty years. The current volume traces this history by compiling several of his contributions from the first (1966) to the third (1981) Coleman Report and by providing a context for interpreting the evidence. This volume is a unique resource for students of social inequality and public policy, for educators, and for those engaged in the formidable task of restructuring educational opportunities in America. It is an appropriate flagship for a series on social inequality.

Marta Tienda
University of Chicago

David B. Grusky
Stanford University

Preface

The essays and analyses in this book might be said to have had their origins in a telephone call I received on a day in February 1965 from Alexander Mood. Mood was assistant commissioner for statistics of the United States Office of Education (OE), and shortly after the telephone call, he asked if I would direct a survey of the lack of equality of educational opportunity for OE. Section 402 in the Civil Rights Act of 1964 directed the commissioner to carry out such a survey and to report the results to Congress and the president by July 2, 1966. I agreed to do so and enlisted Ernest Campbell, a sociologist from Vanderbilt University, to serve as codirector. This was the beginning, for me, of research into equality and achievement in education. It was also the beginning, or nearly so, of a new relation of social science to government policy, and the beginning, or nearly so, of a new orientation to research on the quality of education provided by schools. The work reported here, spanning more than twenty years, covers the period of these extensive changes in the relation of social science to social policy and in research on education. This volume covers three areas of research in Parts 2–4, each involving a major report that has both evoked extensive controversy and initiated extensive policy debate on equality and achievement in education. Part 1 contains an examination of the concept of equality of educational opportunity, and Part 5 concludes the book with an examination of the relations between equality and achievement and between families and schools.

The chapters of this book are reprinted without change from the originals, with the following exceptions:

1. All misspellings and grammatical errors have been corrected.
2. The term "Negro," used in those selections written when that term was a standard convention, has been replaced by "black."
3. Chapters 7 and 12 consist of excerpts from the original longer reports. Deleted text and footnotes have been indicated with ellipses.

James S. Coleman

Introduction

In 1964, Section 402 of the Civil Rights Act directed the commissioner of education to carry out a survey on the lack of equality of educational opportunity. Previously, governmental social policy (other than economic policy) had incorporated very little social science; what little there was consisted principally of consultation with leaders in the social science disciplines. Policymakers usually aimed to obtain the advice of "wise men" in the field on a specific topic. For some years, social scientists had been doing applied research in education, mental health, and other areas that were subject to government policy, and some of this research was funded by government agencies. The research, however, was initiated by social scientists and focused on problems that interested them; the results made their way into the disciplines of social science but seldom into social policy. The congressional request in Section 402 was, or at least could be interpreted as, the beginning of a new mode of interaction between social science and social policy: the initiation of "social policy research," as it has been called, designed to inform government policy in specific areas.

This new social policy research had forerunners, principally in the form of audience research and market research carried out to inform product and marketing decisions. But with few exceptions (one of which was survey research carried out in the U.S. Army during World War II and reported in Stouffer et al. [1949]), there had not been large-scale, policy-related research initiated at government request. Since that time, of course, an industry has bloomed, comprising policy research of numerous forms: evaluation research, social experiments, longitudinal studies of cohorts and of specific population groups, large-scale sample surveys, and still other forms. In 1964, however, none of this existed.

The direction that social policy research took constituted also the beginning of a new attitude toward research on the quality of education provided by schools. School quality had been characteristically measured by inputs: per pupil expenditure, teachers' degrees, age of textbooks and of buildings, numbers of library books, and other tangible inputs. Educational practices were included as well: In the 1940s and 1950s, Paul Mort, at Teachers College, Columbia, had devised a whole set of such practices that taken together were regarded as a measure of a school's adoption of modern educational practice.

In our design of the research called for in Section 402, however, we refused to accept an input-only definition of educational quality. We measured inputs, to be sure, but we measured outputs as well, in the form of achievement on standardized tests. It was this paradigm shift in research on school quality that made possible the impact of the resulting report, *Equality of Educational Opportunity*, sections of which are reprinted in Chapter 7. Without this shift, the hard questions would have remained: Which school inputs make for differences in outputs? What difference does the school a child goes to make in the child's achievement? How much do schools overcome the inequalities with which children come to school?

One might wonder why educational researchers had not asked these questions long ago, why they had not always focused on outputs of schools in assessing their quality. My conjectural answer is that there had been an unspoken, almost subliminal, gentlemen's agreement: School administrators, for their part, were no more eager to be tested on their actual achievements than children are, and unlike children, school administrators were not under the control of others who demanded that they be tested. Educational researchers, for their part, could be safe from the attacks of other researchers who challenged their results as long as they made no research-based statements about the relative effectiveness of different educational practices. The implicit agreement seems still to hold at another level: Researchers characteristically do not study the effectiveness of teachers by measuring what teachers do and comparing their activities to what children learn.[1] Instead, they carefully study what teachers do but seldom examine what their students learn. There are many reasons researchers will give for this practice, but the simplest is that studying teachers requires their cooperation, which is easier to obtain if the teachers are not evaluated through their students' performance. As a result of this polite agreement, children's minds are left to wander aimlessly, untaught because the lessons that might be learned about teaching effectiveness remain unlearned.

Beginning with the publication of the *Equality of Educational Opportunity* report, the first hurdle was cleared and schools' effectiveness could be measured by the performance of their students. However, it was not in order to help bring about this change that I agreed when Alexander Mood invited me to direct this research. I agreed in part because I saw the opportunity to help move the interaction between social science and social policy away from consultations with wise men and toward providing systematic sociological information useful to social policy. Also, I was interested in the content of the policy issue, which I took to be how best to increase educational opportunity for black children still subject to inequality of opportunity in education. The five parts of this book constitute a partial history of the succession of activities to which that initial decision led. The five parts are all concerned with education, with policy in education, and with issues of achievement in education and equality of opportunity in education.

Among these five parts, three (Parts 2, 3, and 4) deal with research that violated three gentlemen's agreements by asking questions that were ordinarily left unasked. Subsequently, all three have become conventional research questions. I have already referred to one of these agreements: not to use the outputs of education as a criterion for measuring the effectiveness of school inputs and school quality. The use of achievement outputs to measure school quality has subsequently become conventional wisdom.[2]

The research I present in Part 3 violated the second gentleman's agreement. That agreement, a strong one when the first results were reported in 1975, was that a researcher could only question desegregation policy on the grounds that it did not provide rapid enough or complete enough racial integration of schools. The research in Part 3 dared to ask whether the policies of rapid and complete school integration in large cities did not defeat their very purposes by provoking resegregation through the loss of white students from the central city school districts.

This gentleman's agreement is no longer in force, and it is now conventional wisdom that ill-designed policies that create immediate integration of schools can create extensive white flight. Both research and policies are now designed to discover how to reduce racial segregation in schools in ways that produce long-term stability.

The research in Part 4 violated the third gentleman's agreement by asking whether private schools (even religiously based ones) might not be more effective than public schools for comparable students. That agreement was based on the general premise that public schools were democratic, and private schools were undemocratic and divisive. Therefore, research that could show greater effectiveness of private schools was necessarily anti-democratic, a contributor to divisiveness, and vulnerable on methodological grounds. The assumption that the self-selection of children in private schools made it impossible to compare schools' effectiveness aided this agreement.

This gentleman's agreement too is now a thing of the past. Not only the potential dangers but also the potential benefits of private schools—even religiously based ones—to society are openly discussed and examined in research. The answers have provided insights into ways that public schools might change to benefit their students.

The lessons in all this for the researchers in education, or in social policy research generally, are straightforward: There are policy-related questions that remain unasked because of implicit agreements to leave them untouched. Advances may be made quite simply by breaking the agreements and refusing to leave the questions unasked.

Notes

1. An exception is research by Barr and Dreeben (1983); their focus is on the relation of material covered by the teacher (in elementary reading instruction) to the amount learned by the students. This design, simple and unusual, is responsible for the well-deserved attention that research has received.

2. Reactions to this "input-output" research have taken the form of studies of "process." This in turn carries with it the danger of reinstating the old gentleman's agreement to ignore outcomes of schooling.

References

Barr, Rebecca, and Robert Dreeben. 1983. *How Schools Work*. Chicago: University of Chicago Press.

Stouffer, Samuel A., E. A. Suchman, L. C. DeVinney, S. A. Star, R. M. Williams, Jr., A. A. Lumsdaine, M. H. Lumsdaine, M. B. Smith, I. L. Janis, and L. S. Cottrell, Jr. 1949. *The American Soldier*, Vols. I and II. Princeton: Princeton University Press.

PART ONE

The Concept of Equal Educational Opportunity

One view of the ideal state of social science is that questions of fact and cause flow from theoretical, philosophical, and normative discourse. The wisdom from such discourse would guide and inform subsequent empirical research. This intellectual enrichment is especially important for the inherently normative issues surrounding the concept of equality of educational opportunity.

If this ideal state had characterized the work on equality of educational opportunity reported in Parts 1 and 2 of this book, it would have been impossible to extricate the one from the other into two separate parts. The empirical work would have flowed quite naturally from the juxtaposition of philosophical and policy questions. But it was not quite that way. The positions of research and theory in the image were reversed; the empirical research informed the theoretical work. The results of the empirical research exerted a continuing pressure to address certain theoretical and normative questions that had not been apparent in the absence of the research. It was the needs imposed by the policy questions that forced serious examination of just what might be meant by equality of educational opportunity. And, as indicated in the latter part of Chapter 2, it was the research results that forced a further refinement of the concept itself and exposed the naivete of the earlier theoretical position. Chapter 2 might, in fact, be seen as an exercise in conceptual clarification through empirical research.

One of the conclusions of Chapter 3, forced by the empirical research results, is that "complete equality of opportunity can be reached only if all the divergent out-of-school influences vanish, a condition that would arise only in the advent of boarding schools." This conclusion, confronting John Rawls'ss *Theory of Justice*, pits empirical research results directly against *a priori* principles of moral philosophy. Rawls'ss vision of a just society assumes that "there is fair (as opposed to formal) equality of opportunity . . . either by subsidizing private schools or by establishing a public school system" (Rawls 1971:275) He does not envision removing the child from the family at an early age; but the research results show that actions short of this, whether carried out in a public school system or in private schools, are insufficient.

The research results show the excessive simplicity of Rawls'ss assumption and make apparent what an abstract philosophical argument can miss: The achievement of a just society (in Rawls'ss sense) entails the sacrifice of other values (such as the value of nurturance provided by a child's parents) that may be held at least as strongly. Thus, it becomes clear that the achievement of justice, at least in Rawls'ss sense, requires not merely that the good forces overcome evil ones, but that one quality regarded as good overcome others also regarded as good.

Chapter 4 shows a somewhat different relation between the real world and theoretical positions in moral philosophy. Here the relation does not involve empirical research, but rather a concrete policy problem: the problem of racial desegregation in the schools. The nature of the relation is also different: Seen through the lenses of Rawls'ss work on justice and Robert Nozick's answer to Rawls, the nature of the rights at issue in the policy question becomes more transparent.

Again it becomes clear that to realize one value regarded as desirable, other values, also held strongly, must be sacrificed. In this case, the conflict can be conceived in terms of a balance of rights: the rights of parents and the rights of the state. But not only is the policy problem of school desegregation clarified by viewing it through the lenses representing two philosophical positions; the character of these positions, and the nature of the rights involved, is clarified through the implications of the philosophical positions for the real world.

Chapter 5, really only a brief comment, can be seen as a continuation of the attempt in Chapter 2 to clarify the concept of equality of educational opportunity. Written several years after Chapter 2, and after the juxtaposition of empirical results, policy issues, and moral philosophy presented in Chapters 3 and 4, Chapter 5 contains a further distillation, which arrives at a view of "equal educational opportunity" shaped by policy issues, empirical results, and philosophical argument.

Finally, back to the beginning: The placement of Chapter 1, which was written last, as the first essay is a further indication of the inductive character of the philosophical and theoretical enterprise. Chapter 1 provides the broadest theoretical perspective of all the chapters of this part. In the exposition, this chapter serves as an appropriate starting point because of its broad view. This broad view arose only through the continued focus on the theoretical-philosophical questions, a focus that itself was generated by the policy questions and empirical results. Chapter 1 raises the meta-normative question of what the social conditions are under which a norm of equal opportunity is likely to arise and be strongly held. This is an empirical question, about which I have no systematic data, but I examine the question with conjectures about what empirical data would show, together with a small amount of illustrative data. With this chapter, the interrelation between empirical research and normative philosophy comes full circle, from empirical to normative to empirical: We begin with empirical questions (generated by policy issues); these lead to philosophical and normative questions. Then there arises an empirical question about the norm itself. The empirical question is not designed to help bring about a moral relativism, to free the society from the norm of equal opportunity. It is, rather, to help us understand when and where the norm will wax strong, and when and where it will weaken or vanish.

Altogether, Part 1 of this book provides a conceptual and philosophical background for the value that has been dominant—the value of equal opportunity in education—in educational policy throughout the period covered by the research in this book. Thus the essays of Part 1, though mostly written after those of Part 2, serve as a philosophical and theoretical introduction to Part 2.

References

Rawls, John. 1971. *A Theory of Justice.* Cambridge, Mass.: Harvard University Press.

1

Norms of Equal Opportunity
When and Why Do They Arise?

I begin with a quote from the British economist, Lionel Robbins: ". . . I am not clear how these doubts first suggested themselves; but I will remember how they were brought to a head by my reading somewhere— I think in the work of Sir Henry Maine—the story of how an Indian official had attempted to explain to a highcaste Brahmin the sanctions of the Benthamite system. 'But that', said the Brahmin, 'cannot possibly be right— I am ten times as capable of happiness as that untouchable over there'. I had no sympathy with the Brahmin. But I could not escape the conviction that, if I chose to regard men as equally capable of satisfaction and he to regard them as differing according to a hierarchial schedule, the difference between us was not one which could be resolved by the same method of demonstration as were available in other fields of social judgement. . . ."

The context of Robbins' comment was a dispute with Roy Harrod over the question of whether the repeal of the Corn Laws in Britain could be held to be beneficial, although the losses were experienced by one set of persons and the gains by another. As Robbins' comment indicates, such a judgement implies interpersonal comparison of utility, and there is no way that such comparisons can be made on positive, rather than normative grounds.

Although the context for Robbins' comment was a specific economic policy, it is relevant as well to questions of social policy that involve benefits to certain persons at an expense to others. In particular, it is relevant to the question of equal opportunity. Just as there seems no justification, other than a normative one, for deriving societal happiness from a particular combination of the Brahmin's happiness and the untouchable's happiness, there seems no justification, other than a normative one, for policies that promote equal opportunity or those that promote unequal opportunity.

Perhaps this point would be of less relevance if a goal of equal opportunity were always and everywhere held. But the Brahmin-untouchable example

Reprinted with permission from *Angewandte Sozialforschung* (Vienna), vol. 13, no. 1 (1985): 55–60.

is a reminder that it is not. Nor do we need to travel so far to find it not held. In the United States, there is much discussion of equal educational opportunity, as if this were held as an absolute goal. Yet any careful examination of the policies that would be necessary to achieve this shows that it implies steps that no one is willing to take: Removing the child from the family, the single institution that provides opportunity most *differentially* and *unequally*, and placing that child in another social environment, the same for all children (see Coleman 1974). In fact, there are many policies toward equal educational opportunity that could be taken in the United States which are not—precisely because they would severely harm other values that are strongly held.

It thus seems of sociological interest to treat a norm or goal of equal opportunity not as something to be attacked or defended, but rather as a norm that arises in certain times and places, and to examine what characterizes those times and places.

To address the question of when and why such a norm arises, I turn to John Rawls's *Theory of Justice*. Rawls derives principles of justice which contain inherently the notion of equal opportunity. Rawls's second principle states as its second part that any social and economic inequalities be "attached to offices and positions open to all under conditions of fair equality of opportunity" (1971, p. 83). The question I want to ask is how Rawls can arrive at a presumptively universal principle of justice that is so much at odds with the principle which Sir Henry Maine's Brahmin would have arrived at?

Perhaps the most attractive part of Rawls's theoretical structure is that the two principles are regarded as chosen by rational individuals behind a "veil of ignorance". Behind this veil, "no one knows his place in society, his class position or social status, nor does anyone know his fortune in the distribution of natural assets and abilties, his intelligence, strength, and the like" (p. 12). The attractiveness of this aspect of Rawls's theory lies in the fact that it appears to derive the principles of justice purely on rational grounds without importing value premises. In effect, what Rawls has done through use of the veil of ignorance is to convert *interpersonal* comparison of utility into *intrapersonal* comparisons. Each of the prospective members of the society is acting self-interestedly, but because none knows his future position, each favors a policy which he sees as most beneficial over all the ups and downs he will confront over his lifetime.

I will not examine the question of whether such a veil of ignorance would lead rational persons to choose the two principles that Rawls arrives at. Rather, what is of interest here is the kind of society within which Rawls's original position behind a veil of ignorance is reasonable. It would hardly be conceivable to the Brahmin, nor to the untouchable, because in the system in which they lived, such caste distinctions were taken as a starting point. Is this to say, then, that "justice" is incompatible with a differentiated social system of the sort that caste India was? I think this is hardly so: There are notions of justice within a society having highly differentiated institutions with fixed internal boundaries, just as there are within societies without this differentiation, and without the fixed internal boundaries.

Rather, I think we must say, that Rawls's theory of justice is a product of a particular kind of social structure, one in which *each person can reasonably visualize himself as exchanging places with any other person in society*. It is only to persons in such a social structure that Rawls's original position would even appear worth taking seriously. In other social structures, such a conception of justice would have no rationale.

This begins to suggest a first condition for the rise of a norm of equal opportunity. The condition might be stated this way: that all persons among whom the norm is held be able easily to imagine themselves exchanging positions with anyone else covered by the norm.

Perhaps the example of the Brahmin and untouchable is not sufficiently persuasive. There are many others, some of which may be more persuasive:

1. There exists within the state of Israel a strong norm of equal opportunity, a norm which can be traced back to before the founding of the state, in the socialist ideology that was part of Zionism, and the socialist institutions in Palestine that predate the state. Yet this norm of equal opportunity does not, in all its aspects, include Israeli Aarbs. Why not? Further, I will venture a prediction that twenty years hence, the norm of equal opportunity *will* include Israeli Arabs. If so, what conditions will bring about the change?

2. In the United States, the democratic and egalitarian foundations have meant that a norm of equal opportunity has always been held, though of course not as the single overriding social value. That norm has led, throughout at least the period of industrialization roughly coinciding with the 20th Century, to great concerns with poverty and to legislation, particularly in the 1930s, to increase opportunity. Yet until sometime in the late 1950s or early 1960s, most discussions of alleviation of poverty were confined to poverty among whites. Since that time, black Americans have come to be included in the set of persons to whom the norm of equal opportunity applies. Why has there been this change?

3. Norms of equal opportunity are widespread today in most developed countries. These norms are widespread among the general population in these countries. Yet the norms are peculiar in one sense: They stop at national boundaries. For example, the norm of equal opportunity in the United States includes U.S. citizens or residents, but not Mexicans residing in Mexico. (Mexicans residing in the United States constitute an interesting intermediate case, for some persons in the U.S. holding equal opportunity norms include them, while some do not.) Nor are the natives of New Guinea included. Why do these norms stop at national boundaries? Why do they reach that far?

These examples should be sufficient to illustrate the point that norms of equal opportunity are highly time-and-place specific, highly restrictive as to coverage, and far from ubiquitous. The variations presented in these examples also seem to be compatible with the condition stated earlier: that all those holding the norm be easily able to imagine themselves exchanging positions with anyone else covered by the norm.

Another way of getting a sense of the time-and-place specificity of norms of equal opportunity is to consider two conceptions of democracy. One conception characterized the British political system before the entrance of the Labour Party, and continues to characterize a segment of the Conservative Party as well as some individuals within the Labour Party. It is a conception of a certain class of persons having both rights and responsibilities beyond those of another class. Candidates for office are chosen from the former class, and when they come to govern, they are expected to govern not in terms of their interests or those of their class, but with a responsibility for the society as a whole, and especially for those who are their "dependents", that is, those who are, and will always be, the governed. Policies are arrived at (or at least seem to be arrived at) not through the clash of interests, but through the judgement and wisdom of those who have this special responsibility for the society as a whole. The conception arises from the traditional class structure that characterized precapitalist Europe. From that structure arose the conception of "noblesse oblige" and the principle that is inculcated in trainees for the officer corps of most military services: "Rank has its privileges; rank has its responsibilities." It is the conception of democracy that arises out of, and is compatible with, a hierarchial society.

The second conception of democracy is one that more nearly characterizes the American political system, especially since the Jacksonian Revolution. Every citizen has the opportunity to run for office, and the political contest is a contest between differing interests. There is no noblesse oblige, no conception that those who govern have a special responsibility for a permanent governed class, but a conception that policies arise in the day-to-day functioning of government through the struggle of interests that results in legislation. These policies represent a balance among the interests who are affected by them. It is a conception of government more compatible with Congressional system and a weak party structure than with a Parliamentary system where policies are arrived at by the Cabinet and ratified by a Parliament controlled by party discipline. This difference is described at length and in vivid detail by Moise Ostrogorski (1902) in his two volumes on English and American democracy. The conception I have described for American democracy was brilliantly described by Arthur F. Bentley (1908) with the political system as a market in which political resources are employed by various interested parties leading to policies that reflected the balance of these interests in the society as a whole.

Norms of equal opportunity are compatible with a democratic political system of the second sort, but not that of the first. The reason appears to be that in the first of these two conceptions of democracy, the society stratified by rank is not one in which each member can easily imagine himself changing positions with anyone else in the society.

There is another way of looking at a norm of equal opportunity that may give some insight into the conditions under which such norms arise. I introduce this only tentatively, because I see no direct evidence for it. It arises from a general conception that I have proposed elsewhere, of the condition under which norms arise (Coleman 1984). The argument goes as follows: Norms arise when one actor's action imposes negative externalities on a set of others, who then come to hold the proscriptive norm. Prescriptive norms, to encourage the action, arise when the action imposes positive externalities on those who come to hold the norm.

A norm of equal opportunity is a prescriptive norm, dictating that government and other public or semi-public bodies act to provide equal opportunity to all who are subject to their actions. Thus if this norm arises, as I have argued that prescriptive norms do generally, because such governmental action will make those who hold the norm better off, what must be explained is why citizens generally, including not only those who are worse off than others, but also those who are better off, regard such a norm as making them better off.

Holding of the norm by those who are worse off than most others can, of course, be directly explained, for equal opportunity policies help improve their lot. What is not so easily explained is the holding of this norm by those who are better off than most. For them, the principle I stated earlier may operate: that norms of equal opportunity arise when each person holding the norm is easily able to imagine himself exchanging positions with anyone else to whom the norm applies. If those who are better off than most can imagine such an exchange, then, following the general ideas of Rawls about why persons in the original position would choose only inequalities that made the least advantaged better off, they may regard themselves as helped more by a policy of equal opportunity, when they were made worse off than most by such an imagined exchange, than they are hurt by an equal opportunity policy in their current position. (This implies that money has declining marginal utility for persons, with a decline sufficiently great to overcome the discount applied to the post-exchange position.) Further, since such policies are ordinarily dissociated by governments from the source of the resources necessary to put them into effect, the costs of these policies to those who are better off may be less visible to them than are the potential benefits under the imagined exchange.

If this argument does have validity, then we should find that those policies of equal opportunity which require extensive resources should not be as fully supported by those who are better off than most as are those equal opportunity policies that require few resources, but consist primarily of equal treatment before the law. Similarly, for two policies requiring equal resources, the one for which the benefits for the worse off are more closely linked to costs for the better off should be less fully supported by the better off.

If we return for a moment to the debate between Harrod and Robbins about an economic justification for repeal of the Corn Laws, there is a further development which has relevance for the present discussion. Accepting Robbins' general position about the incomparability of different persons' utilities, Nicholas Kaldor (1939) nevertheless came up with a principle that could give an economic justification for a policy that helped some and harmed others. This was a compensation principle: If those who were made better off by the policy were sufficiently benefitted by it to compensate all losses of those who were harmed and even so remained better off, then the policy was justifiable on grounds of economic efficiency. If not, the policy was not justifiable on efficiency grounds.

An analogue to Kaldor's compensation principle might be devised as a principle to describe the conditions under which a norm of equal opportunity will be held by all in a system as "generally beneficial". If those who see themselves as losing under a policy that follows such a norm see that loss as more than compensated by the benefit they would experience under the imagined exchange, and those who are benefitted see themselves as benefitted more than is necessary to compensate their losses under their imagined exchange, then the norm is held by all as generally beneficial. This would provide, as Kaldor's principle provides, a pseudo-Pareto optimality. I call this "pseudo-Pareto optimality" because not everyone is better off than in the absence of the policy, but because, by virtue of a thought experiment, each is potentially better off.

There is another, somewhat different, analogue to Kaldor's principle that involves the political system. If those who see themselves in their current position as losing under the policy cannot or will not muster sufficient resources to defeat it against the forces of those who see themselves as gaining, then the policy is passed even though the norm is not universally held. It can be regarded as "politically efficient" under the given distribution of political resources (a qualifier that is analogous to a qualifier about economic efficiency that is necessary for Kaldor's compensation principle). This, however, would not be a condition under which the norm of equal opportunity would be held by all, even though the policy was in effect. The norm of equal opportunity would, in this case, be held only by those who were made better off by it, not by those who were made worse off.

There is another principle that seems to govern the scope of equal opportunity norms. I will introduce it through use of an example. I attribute this to James Dusenberry, though I have not found the specific reference, and details may be in error. In New York City, the subways which had been owned privately, were taken over by the city. Before that time, subway motormen in New York were earning more than city firemen and policemen. After the city became owner and operator of the subway system, firemen and policemen immediately struck for higher wages, for parity with the subway motormen.

It appears that the bringing of subways under city jurisdiction was the event that precipitated the strike. The policemen and firemen did not strike for higher wages on the basis of some absolute level of need, but on the basis of the relative size of their wages and those of the subway motormen. Yet they did not invoke the subway motormen's wages as a yardstick so long as they were under separate management. It was only when they came under city management, paid from the same overall budget as the policemen and firemen, that their wages became a yardstick that was seen as relevant. To use a sociological concept, the subway motormen became for the first time a reference group for the policemen and firemen.

This example is directly relevant to the question of when and why norms of equal opportunity arise. The central element of this example does not have to do with imaging exchange of places, but rather with being subject to the policies of a single authority. This principle that could be stated as a generalization of this case would be something like this: The scope of the population covered by norms of equal opportunity is defined by the limits of the population subject to actions of the same authority. This defines the limits of comparison, to determine who are the appropriate referents for an equal opportunity norm.

Returning to the earlier argument that norms arise when there are externalities of action, this principle fits well with that. When two subgroups (subway motormen and policemen) are subject to the actions of the same actor, and one is favored over the other, then the latter is clearly experiencing negative externalities of the authority's action. But if these two groups are subject to different authorities, their differences in opportunity are not seen to be produced by a particular actor's action, but by impersonal forces.

For example, when schools were primarily financed at the local level, based on local property taxes, norms of equal educational opportunity were limited to the local school district. But in the past few decades, financing of public education has shifted greatly to the state, with about half of school costs borne at the state level, averaged over the country (about 8 or 9% coming from the Federal government, and about 41% from local taxes). During this same period, there has been a considerable growth of educational opportunity. Lawsuits have been brought to create financial equalization throughout the state.

There is another aspect of equal opportunity norms that is important in giving some understanding of when and why they arise. Norms of equal opportunity are characteristic of a highly individualistic society. If there is very high collectivity orientation, norms of equal opportunity are secondary to norms about what is best for the community. For example, in a very familistic society, like those of earlier periods in America or those in Arabic societies of the Middle East today, the individual's opportunity is subordinate to the demands and needs of the family—for the individual is, at the extreme, merely the agent of the family, with the task of carrying it forward undiminished into the future.

Religious communes show this collectivity orientation especially well. The history of such communes (see Zablocki 1980, for an historical discussion of communes as well as empirical study of contemporary communes) shows that many have a highly centralized structure of governance, and a high degree of acceptance of differences in rank. In such social systems, individual rights to have equal access to all opportunities are subjugated to collective needs. Even in communes such as Israeli kibbutzim, founded on the principles of socialist ideology, tasks are generally allocated with less regard for individual opportunity than for kibbutz needs. It is the young women who care for infants in the infants' houses, not the young men, and it is the women who carry out the tasks of communal kitchen, while the men work in the fields. This is not to say that there are not norms of equal opportunity in these and other communes; they fulfill more than do larger societies the condition stated earlier that individuals can imagine themselves exchanging places with anyone in the system. But the strength of collectivity orientation means that any such norms must operate within the confines of what is judged to be best for the collectivity.

Zablocki's work on communes shows another element of their functioning which confirms this general principle. He asks the question, when and why does charisma arise in a commune, with all members vesting extensive authority in a single leader, and giving up large amounts of individual rights? He finds that this occurs at times when the commune is literally falling apart, dissolving, with so little attention to the public good that the collectivity's existence is threatened. The "demand for charisma" arises as a demand for subordinating private interests to the public good. The conception that arises from this work is one in which these small social systems go through periods of individualism followed (for those that are successful) by a sudden rush to vest all authority in a single person, imbuing that person with a sort of mystical charisma.

It may well be the case that such a cyclical pattern is characteristic not merely of small closed communities but of larger societies as well. If so, then based on the general principle that I have expressed, norms of equal opportunity are especially characteristic of the individualistic portion of these cycles. It may, in fact, be that the current period in American society is one following an extreme burst of individualistic orientation in the 1960s and 1970s, and that now, rather than during that period, is a time at which it becomes possible to even raise a question about the norm of equal opportunity.

Conclusions

I have stated three principles about the conditions under which a norm arises concerning equal opportunity.

1. Equal opportunity appears to become a norm when each member of the social system is easily able to imagine himself exchanging places with anyone else in the system.
2. The scope of equal opportunity norms appears in many cases to be determined by the scope of the authority whose policies are at issue.

If the scope of that authority widens to include additional persons, the norm expands to cover those persons.

3. Equal opportunity norms arise in a social system that is highly individualistic. In a system in which collectivity orientation is high, equal opportunity norms are overridden by needs of the collectivity.

For none of these principles have I offered evidence beyond illustrations. Thus these principles must remain regarded as suggestive, but not conclusive. Yet they indicate a potentially fruitful area of intersection between normative work in moral philosophy and positive work in sociology.

References

Bentley, A.F. (1980), The Process of Government. Chicago.

Coleman, J.S. (1974), Inequality, Sociology, and Moral Philosophy. American Journal of Sociology, Vol. 80, No. 3, pp. 739–764.

Coleman, J.S. (1984), Norms As Social Capital. Unpublished paper. University of Chicago.

Kaldor, N. (1939), Welfare Propositions of Economics and Interpersonal Comparisons of Utility. Economic Journal, Vol. 49, pp. 549–552.

Ostrogorski, M. (1902/1964), Democracy and the Organization of Political Parties VI England, VII the United States. Chicago.

Rawls, J. (1971), A Theory of Justice. Cambridge.

Robbins, L. (1938), Inter-personal Comparisons of Utility. Economic Journal, Vol. 48, pp. 635–641.

Zablocki, B. (1980), Alienation and Charisma. New York.

2

The Concept of Equality of Educational Opportunity

The concept of "equality of educational opportunity" as held by members of society has had a varied past. It has changed radically in recent years, and is likely to undergo further change in the future. This lack of stability in the concept leads to several questions. What has it meant in the past, what does it mean now, and what will it mean in the future? Whose obligation is it to provide such equality? Is the concept a fundamentally sound one, or does it have inherent contradictions or conflicts with social organization? But first of all, and above all, what is and has been meant in society by the idea of equality of educational opportunity?

To answer this question, it is necessary to consider how the child's position in society has been conceived in different historical periods. In pre-industrial Europe, the child's horizons were largely limited by his family. His station in life was likely to be the same as his father's. If his father was a serf, he would likely live his own life as a serf; if his father was a shoemaker, he would likely become a shoemaker. But even this immobility was not the crux of the matter; he was a part of the family production enterprise and would likely remain within this enterprise throughout his life. The extended family, as the basic unit of social organization, had complete authority over the child, and complete responsibility for him. This responsibility ordinarily did not end when the child became an adult because he remained a part of the same economic unit and carried on this tradition of responsibility into the next generation. Despite some mobility out of the family, the general pattern was family continuity through a patriarchal kinship system.

There are two elements of critical importance here. First, the family carried responsibility for its members' welfare from cradle to grave. It was a "welfare society," with each extended family serving as a welfare organization for its own members. Thus it was to the family's interest to see that its members became productive. Conversely, a family took relatively small interest in whether someone in *another* family became productive or not—merely because the mobility of productive labor between family economic units was relatively low. If the son of a neighbor was allowed to become a ne'er-do-well, it had little real effect on families other than his own.

The second important element is that the family, as a unit of economic production, provided an appropriate context in which the child could learn the things he needed to know. The craftsman's shop or the farmer's fields were appropriate training grounds for sons, and the household was an appropriate training ground for daughters.

In this kind of society, the concept of equality of educational opportunity had no relevance at all. The child and adult were embedded within the extended family, and the child's education or training was merely whatever seemed necessary to maintain the family's productivity. The fixed stations in life which most families occupied precluded any idea of "opportunity" and, even less, equality of opportunity.

With the industrial revolution, changes occurred in both the family's function as a self-perpetuating economic unit and as a training ground. As economic organizations developed outside the household, children began to be occupationally mobile outside their families. As families lost their economic production activities, they also began to lose their welfare functions, and the poor or ill or incapacitated became more nearly a community responsibility. Thus the training which a child received came to be of interest to all in the community, either as his potential employers or as his potential economic supports if he became dependent. During this stage of development in eighteenth-century England, for instance, communities had laws preventing immigration from another community because of the potential economic burden of immigrants.

Further, as men came to employ their own labor outside the family in the new factories, their families became less useful as economic training grounds for their children. These changes paved the way for public education. Families needed a context within which their children could learn some general skills which would be useful for gaining work outside the family; and men of influence in the community began to be interested in the potential productivity of other men's children.

It was in the early nineteenth century that public education began to appear in Europe and America. Before that time, private education had grown with the expansion of the mercantile class. This class had both the need and resources to have its children educated outside the home, either for professional occupations or for occupations in the developing world of commerce. But the idea of general educational opportunity for all children arose only in the nineteenth century.

The emergence of public, tax-supported education was not solely a function of the stage of industrial development. It was also a function of the class structure in the society. In the United States, without a strong traditional class structure, universal education in publicly-supported free schools became widespread in the early nineteenth century; in England, the "voluntary schools," run and organized by churches with some instances of state support, were not supplemented by a state-supported system until the Education Act of 1870. Even more, the character of educational opportunity reflected the class structure. In the United States, the public schools quickly became the common school, attended by representatives of all classes; these schools provided a common educational experience for most American children—excluding only those upper-class children in private schools, those poor who went to no schools, and Indians and Southern blacks who were without schools. In England, however, the class system directly manifested itself through the schools. The state-supported, or "board schools" as they were called, became the schools of the laboring lower classes with a sharply different curriculum from those voluntary schools which served the middle and upper classes. The division was so sharp that two government departments, the Education Department and the Science and Art Department, administered external examinations, the first for the products of the board schools, and the second for the products of the voluntary schools as they progressed into secondary education. It was only the latter curricula and examinations that provided admission to higher education.

What is most striking is the duration of influence of such a dual structure. Even today in England, a century later (and in different forms in most European countries), there exists a dual structure of public secondary education with only one of the branches providing the curriculum for college admission. In England, this branch includes the remaining voluntary schools which, though retaining their individual identities, have become part of the state-supported system.

This comparison of England and the United States shows clearly the impact of the class structure in society upon the concept of educational opportunity in that society. In nineteenth-century England, the idea of *equality* of educational opportunity was hardly considered; the system was designed to provide *differentiated* educational opportunity appropriate to one's station in life. In the United States as well, the absence of educational opportunity for blacks in the South arose from the caste and feudal structure of the largely rural society. The idea of differentiated educational opportunity, implicit in the Education Act of 1870 in England, seems to derive from dual needs: the needs arising from industrialization for a basic education for the labor force, and the interests of parents in having one's own child receive a good education. The middle classes could meet both these needs by providing a free system for the children of laboring classes, and a tuition system (which soon came to be supplemented by state grants) for their own. The long survival of this differentiated system depended not only on the historical fact that the voluntary schools existed before a public system came into existence but on the fact that it allows both of these needs to be met: the community's collective need for a trained labor force, and the middle-class individual's interest in a better education for his own child. It served a third need as well: that of maintaining the existing social order—a system of stratification that was a step removed from a feudal system of fixed estates, but designed to prevent a wholesale challenge by the children of the working class to the positions held for children of the middle classes.

The similarity of this system to that which existed in the South to provide differential opportunity to blacks and whites is striking, just as is the similarity of class structures in the second half of nineteenth-century England to the white-black caste structure of the southern United States in the first half of the twentieth century.

In the United States, nearly from the beginning, the concept of educational opportunity had a special meaning which focused on equality. This meaning included the following elements:

1. Providing a *free* education up to a given level which constituted the principal entry point to the labor force.
2. Providing a *common curriculum* for all children, regardless of background.
3. Partly by design and partly because of low population density, providing that children from diverse backgrounds attend the *same school.*
4. Providing equality within a given *locality*, since local taxes provided the source of support for schools.

This conception of equality of opportunity is still held by many persons; but there are some assumptions in it which are not obvious. First, it implicitly assumes that the existence of free schools eliminates economic sources of inequality of opportunity. Free schools, however, do not mean that the costs of a child's education become reduced to zero for families at all economic levels. When free education was introduced, many families could not afford to allow the child to attend school beyond an early age. His labor was necessary to the family—whether in rural or urban areas. Even after the passage of child labor laws, this remained true on the farm. These economic sources of inequality of opportunity have become small indeed (up through secondary education); but at one time they were a major source of inequality. In some countries they remain so; and certainly for higher education they remain so.

Apart from the economic needs of the family, problems inherent in the social structure raised even more fundamental questions about equality of educational opportunity. Continued school attendance prevented a boy from being trained in his father's trade. Thus, in taking advantage of "equal educational opportunity," the son of a craftsman or small tradesman would lose the opportunity to enter those occupations he would most likely fill. The family inheritance of occupation at all social levels was still strong enough, and the age of entry into the labor force was still early enough, that secondary education interfered with opportunity for working-class children; while it opened up opportunities at higher social levels, it closed them at lower ones.

Since residue of this social structure remains in present American society, the dilemma cannot be totally ignored. The idea of a common educational experience implies that this experience has only the effect of widening the range of opportunity, never the effect of excluding opportunities. But clearly this is never precisely true so long as this experience prevents a child from pursuing certain occupational paths. This question still arises with the differentiated secondary curriculum: an academic program in high school has the effect not only of keeping open the opportunities which arise through continued education, but also of closing off opportunities which a vocational program keeps open.

A second assumption implied by this concept of equality of opportunity is that opportunity lies in *exposure* to a given curriculum. The amount of opportunity is then measured in terms of the level of curriculum to which the child is exposed. The higher the curriculum made available to a given set of children, the greater their opportunity.

The most interesting point about this assumption is the relatively passive role of the school and community, relative to the child's role. The schools' obligation is to "provide an opportunity" by being available, within easy geographic access of the child, free of cost (beyond the value of the child's time), and with a curriculum that would not exclude him from higher education. The obligation to "use the opportunity" is on the child or the family, so that his role is defined as the active one: the responsibility for achievement rests with him. Despite the fact that the school's role was the relatively passive one and the child's or family's role the active one, the use of this social service soon came to be no longer a choice of the parent or child, but that of the state. Since compulsory attendance laws appeared in the nineteenth century, the age of required attendance has been periodically moved upward.

This concept of equality of educational opportunity is one that has been implicit in most educational practice throughout most of the period of public education in the nineteenth and twentieth centuries. However, there have been several challenges to it; serious questions have been raised by new conditions in public education. The first of these in the United States was a challenge to assumption two, the common curriculum. This challenge first occurred in the early years of the twentieth century with the expansion of secondary education. Until the report of the committee of the National Education Association, issued in 1918, the standard curriculum in secondary schools was primarily a classical one appropriate for college entrance. The greater influx of noncollege-bound adolescents into the high school made it necessary that this curriculum be changed into one more appropriate to the new majority. This is not to say that the curriculum changed immediately in the schools, nor that all schools changed equally, but rather that the seven "cardinal principles" of the N.E.A. report became a powerful influence in the movement toward a less academically rigid curriculum. The introduction of the new nonclassical curriculum was seldom if ever couched in terms of a conflict between those for whom high school was college preparation, and those for whom it was terminal education; nevertheless, that was the case. The "inequality" was seen as the use of a curriculum that served a minority and was not designed to fit the needs of the majority; and the shift of curriculum was intended to fit the curriculum to the needs of the new majority in the schools.

In many schools, this shift took the form of *diversifying* the curriculum, rather than supplanting one by another; the college-preparatory curriculum remained though watered down. Thus the kind of equality of opportunity that emerged from the newly-designed secondary school curriculum was radically different from the elementary-school concept that had emerged earlier. The idea inherent in the new secondary school curriculum appears to have been to take as given the diverse occupational paths into which adolescents will go after secondary school, and to say (implicitly): there is greater equality of educational opportunity for a boy who is not going to attend college if he has a specially-designed curriculum than if he must take a curriculum designed for college entrance.

There is only one difficulty with this definition: it takes as *given* what should be problematic—that a given boy is going into a given post-secondary occupational or educational path. It is one thing to take as given that approximately 70 per cent of an entering high school freshman class will not attend college; but to assign a *particular child* to a curriculum designed for that 70 per cent closes off for that child the opportunity to attend college. Yet to assign all children to a curriculum designed for the 30 per cent who will attend college creates inequality for those who, at the end of high school, fall among the 70 per cent who do not attend college. This is a true dilemma, and one which no educational system has fully solved. It is more general than the college/noncollege dichotomy, for there is a wide variety of different paths that adolescents take on the completion of secondary school. In England, for example, a student planning to attend a university must specialize in the arts or the sciences in the later years of secondary school. Similar specialization occurs in the German gymnasium; and this is wholly within the group planning to attend university. Even greater specialization can be found among noncollege curricula, especially in the vocational, technical, and commercial high schools.

The distinguishing characteristic of this concept of equality of educational opportunity is that it accepts as given the child's expected future. While the concept discussed earlier left the child's future wholly open, this concept of differentiated curricula uses the expected future to match child and curriculum. It should be noted that the first and simpler concept is easier to apply in elementary schools where fundamental tools of reading and arithmetic are being learned by all children; it is only in secondary school that the problem of diverse futures arises. It should also be noted that the dilemma is directly due to the social structure itself: if there were a virtual absence of social mobility with everyone occupying a fixed estate in life, then such curricula that take the future as given would provide equality of opportunity relative to that structure. It is only because of the high degree of occupational mobility between generations—that is, the greater degree of equality of *occupational* opportunity—that the dilemma arises.

The first stage in the evolution of the concept of equality of educational opportunity was the notion that all children must be exposed to the same curriculum in the same school. A second stage in the evolution of the concept assumed that different children would have different occupational futures and that equality of opportunity required providing different curricula for each type of student. The third and fourth stages in this evolution came as a result of challenges to the basic idea of equality of educational opportunity from opposing directions. The third stage can be seen at least as far back in 1896 when the Supreme Court upheld the southern states' notion of "separate but equal" facilities. This stage ended in 1954 when the Supreme Court ruled that legal separation by race inherently constitutes inequality of opportunity. By adopting the "separate but equal" doctrine, the southern states rejected assumption three of the original concept, the assumption that equality depended on the opportunity to attend the same school. This rejection was, however, consistent with the overall logic of the original concept since attendance at the same school was an inherent part of that logic. The underlying idea was that opportunity resided in exposure to a curriculum; the community's responsibility was to provide that exposure, the child's to take advantage of it.

It was the pervasiveness of this underlying idea which created the difficulty for the Supreme Court. For it was evident that even when identical facilities and identical teacher salaries existed for racially separate schools, "equality of educational opportunity" in some sense did not exist. This had also long been evident to Englishmen as well, in a different context, for with the simultaneous existence of the "common school" and the "voluntary school," no one was under the illusion that full equality of educational opportunity existed. But the source of this inequality remained an unarticulated feeling. In the decision of the Supreme Court, this unarticulated feeling began to take more precise form. The essence of it was that the *effects* of such separate schools were, or were likely to be, different. Thus a concept of equality of opportunity which focused on *effects* of schooling began to take form. The actual decision of the Court was in fact a confusion of two unrelated premises: this new concept, which looked at results of schooling, and the legal premise that the use of race as a basis for school assignment violates fundamental freedoms. But what is important for the evolution of the concept of equality of opportunity is that a new and different assumption was introduced, the assumption that equality of opportunity depends in some fashion upon effects of schooling. I believe the decision would have been more soundly based had it not depended on the effects of schooling, but only on the violation of freedom; but by introducing the question of effects of schooling, the Court brought into the open the implicit goals of equality of educational opportunity—that is, goals having to do with the *results* of school—to which the original concept was somewhat awkwardly directed.

That these goals were in fact behind the concept can be verified by a simple mental experiment. Suppose the early schools had operated for only one hour a week and had been attended by children of all social classes. This would have met the explicit assumptions of the early concept of equality of opportunity since the school is free, with a common curriculum, and attended by all children in the locality. But it obviously would not have been accepted, even at that time, as providing equality of opportunity, because its effects would have been so minimal. The additional educational resources provided by middle- and upper-class families, whether in the home, by tutoring, or in private supplementary schools, would have created severe inequalities in results.

Thus the dependence of the concept upon results or effects of schooling, which had remained hidden until 1954, came partially into the open with the Supreme Court decision. Yet this was not the end, for it created more problems than it solved. It might allow one to assess gross inequalities, such as that created by dual school systems in the South, or by a system like that in the mental experiment I just described. But it allows nothing beyond that. Even more confounding, because the decision did not use effects of schooling as a criterion of inequality but only as justification for a criterion of racial integration, integration itself emerged as the basis for still a new concept of equality of educational opportunity. Thus the idea of effects of schooling as an element in the concept was introduced but immediately overshadowed by another, the criterion of racial integration.

The next stage in the evolution of this concept was, in my judgment, the Office of Education Survey of Equality of Educational Opportunity. This survey was carried out under a mandate in the Civil Rights Act of 1964 to the Commissioner of Education to assess the "lack of equality of educational opportunity" among racial and other groups in the United States. The evolution of this concept, and the conceptual disarray which this evolution had created, made the very definition of the task exceedingly difficult. The original concept could be examined by determining the degree to which all children in a locality had access to the same schools and the same curriculum, free of charge. The existence of diverse secondary curricula appropriate to different futures could be assessed relatively easily. But the very assignment of a child to a specific curriculum implies acceptance of the concept of equality which takes futures as given. And the introduction of the new interpretations, equality as measured by results of schooling and equality defined by racial integration, confounded the issue even further.

As a consequence, in planning the survey it was obvious that no single concept of equality of educational opportunity existed and that the survey must give information relevant to a variety of concepts. The basis on which this was done can be seen by reproducing a portion of an internal memorandum that determined the design of the survey:

> The point of second importance in design [second to the point of discovering the intent of Congress, which was taken to be that the survey was not for the purpose of locating willful discrimination, but to determine educational inequality without regard to intention of those in authority] follows from the first and concerns the definition of inequality. One type of inequality may be

defined in terms of differences of the community's input to the school, such as per-pupil expenditure, school plants, libraries, quality of teachers, and other similar quantities.

A second type of inequality may be defined in terms of the racial composition of the school, following the Supreme Court's decision that segregated schooling is inherently unequal. By the former definition, the question of inequality through segregation is excluded, while by the latter, there is inequality of education within a school system so long as the schools within the system have different racial composition.

A third type of inequality would include various intangible characteristics of the school as well as the factors directly traceable to the community inputs to the school. These intangibles are such things as teacher morale, teachers' expectations of students, level of interest of the student body in learning, or others. Any of these factors may affect the impact of the school upon a given student within it. Yet such a definition gives no suggestion of where to stop, or just how relevant these factors might be for school quality.

Consequently, a fourth type of inequality may be defined in terms of consequences of the school for individuals with equal backgrounds and abilities. In this definition, equality of educational opportunity is equality of results, given the same individual input. With such a definition, inequality might come about from differences in the school inputs and/or racial composition and/or from more intangible things as described above.

Such a definition obviously would require that two steps be taken in the determination of inequality. First, it is necessary to determine the effect of these various factors upon educational results (conceiving of results quite broadly, including not only achievement but attitudes toward learning, self-image, and perhaps other variables). This provides various measures of the school's quality in terms of its effect upon its students. Second, it is necessary to take these measures of quality, once determined, and determine the differential exposure of [blacks] (or other groups) and whites to schools of high and low quality.

A fifth type of inequality may be defined in terms of consequences of the school for individuals of unequal backgrounds and abilities. In this definition, equality of educational opportunity is equality of results given *different* individual inputs. The most striking examples of inequality here would be children from households in which a language other than English, such as Spanish or Navaho, is spoken. Other examples would be low-achieving children from homes in which there is a poverty of verbal expression or an absence of experiences which lead to conceptual facility.

Such a definition taken in the extreme would imply that educational equality is reached only when the results of schooling (achievement and attitudes) are the same for racial and religious minorities as for the dominant group.

The basis for the design of the survey is indicated by another segment of this memorandum:

Thus, the study will focus its principal effort on the fourth definition, but will also provide information relevant to all five possible definitions. This insures the pluralism which is obviously necessary with respect to a definition of inequality. The major justification for this focus is that the results of this approach can best be translated into policy which will improve education's effects. The results of the first two approaches (tangible inputs to the school, and segregation) can certainly be translated into policy, but there is no good evidence that these policies will improve education's effects; and while policies to implement the fifth would certainly improve education's effects, it seems hardly possible that the study could provide information that would direct such policies.

Altogether, it has become evident that it is not our role to define what constitutes equality for policy-making purposes. Such a definition will be an outcome of the interplay of a variety of interests, and will certainly differ from time to time as these interests differ. It should be our role to cast light on the state of inequality defined in the variety of ways which appear reasonable at this time.

The survey, then, was conceived as a pluralistic instrument, given the variety of concepts of equality of opportunity in education. Yet I suggest that despite the avowed intention of not adjudicating between these different ideas, the survey has brought a new stage in the evolution of the concept. For the definitions of equality which the survey was designed to serve split sharply into two groups. The first three definitions concerned input resources: first, those brought to the school by the actions of the school administration (facilities, curriculum, teachers); second, those brought to the school by the other students, in the educational backgrounds which their presence contributed to the school; and third, the intangible characteristics such as "morale" that result from the interaction of all these factors. The fourth and fifth definitions were concerned with the effects of schooling. Thus the five definitions were divided into three concerned with inputs to school and two concerned with effects of schooling. When the Report emerged, it did not give five different measures of equality, one for each of these definitions; but it did focus sharply on this dichotomy, giving in Chapter Two information on inequalities of input relevant to definitions one and two, and in Chapter Three information on inequalities of results relevant to definitions four and five, and also in Chapter Three information on the relation of input to results again relevant to definitions four and five.

Although not central to our discussion here, it is interesting to note that this examination of the relation of school inputs to effects on achievement showed that those input characteristics of schools that are most alike for blacks and whites have least effect on their achievement. The magnitudes of differences between schools attended by blacks and those attended by whites were as follows: least, facilities and curriculum; next, teacher quality; and greatest, educational backgrounds of fellow students. The order of importance of these inputs on the achievement of black students is precisely the same: facilities and curriculum least, teacher quality next, and backgrounds of fellow students, most.

By making the dichotomy between inputs and results explicit, and by focusing attention not only on inputs but on results, the Report brought into the open what had been underlying all the concepts of equality of educational opportunity but had remained largely hidden: that the concept implied *effective* equality of opportunity, that is, equality in those elements that are effective for learning. The reason this had remained half-hidden, obscured by definitions that involve inputs is, I suspect, because educational research has been until recently unprepared to demonstrate what elements are effective. The controversy that has surrounded the Report indicates that measurements of effects is still subject to sharp disagreement; but the crucial point is that *effects* of inputs have come to constitute the basis for assessment of school quality (and thus equality of opportunity) in place of using certain inputs by definition as measures of quality (e.g., small classes are better than large, higher-paid teachers are better than lower-paid ones, by definition).

It would be fortunate indeed if the matter could be left to rest there— if merely by using effects of school rather than inputs as the basis for the concept, the problem were solved. But that is not the case at all. The conflict between definitions four and five given above shows this. The conflict can be illustrated by resorting again to the mental experiment discussed earlier— providing a standard education of one hour per week, under identical conditions, for all children. By definition four, controlling all background differences of the children, results for blacks and whites would be equal, and thus by this definition equality of opportunity would exist. But because such minimal schooling would have minimal effect, those children from educationally strong families would enjoy educational opportunity far surpassing that of others. And because such educationally strong backgrounds are found more often among whites than among blacks, there would be very large overall black-white achievement differences—and thus inequality of opportunity by definition five.

It is clear from this hypothetical experiment that the problem of what constitutes equality of opportunity is not solved. The problem will become even clearer by showing graphs with some of the results of the Office of Education Survey. The highest line in Figure 1 shows the achievement in verbal skills by whites in the urban Northeast at grades 1, 3, 6, 9, and 12. The second line shows the achievement at each of these grades by whites in the rural Southeast. The third shows the achievement of blacks in the urban Northeast. The fourth shows the achievement of blacks in the rural Southeast.

When compared to the whites in the urban Northeast, each of the other three groups shows a different pattern. The comparison with whites in the rural South shows the two groups beginning near the same point in the first grade, and diverging over the years of school. The comparison with blacks in the urban Northeast shows the two groups beginning farther apart at the first grade and remaining about the same distance apart. The comparison with blacks in the rural South shows the two groups beginning far apart and moving much farther apart over the years of school.

Which of these, if any, shows equality of educational opportunity between regional and racial groups? Which shows greatest inequality of opportunity? I think the second question is easier to answer than the first. The last comparison showing both initial difference and the greatest increase in difference over grades 1 through 12 appears to be the best candidate for

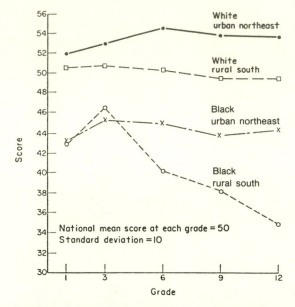

FIGURE 1 Patterns of Achievement in Verbal Skills at Various
Grade Levels by Race and Region

the greatest inequality. The first comparison, with whites in the rural South, also seems to show inequality of opportunity, because of the increasing difference over the twelve years. But what about the second comparison, with an approximately constant difference between blacks and whites in the urban Northeast? Is this equality of opportunity? I suggest not. It means, in effect, only that the period of school has left the average black at about the same level of achievement relative to whites as he began—in this case, achieving higher than about 15 per cent of the whites, lower than about 85 per cent of the whites. It may well be that in the absence of school those lines of achievement would have diverged due to differences in home environments; or perhaps they would have remained an equal distance apart, as they are in this graph (though at lower levels of achievement for both groups, in the absence of school). If it were the former, we could say that school, by keeping the lines parallel, has been a force toward the equalization of opportunity. But in the absence of such knowledge, we cannot say even that.

What would full equality of educational opportunity look like in such graphs? One might persuasively argue that it should show a convergence, so that even though two population groups begin school with different levels of skills on the average, the average of the group that begins lower moves up to coincide with that of the group that begins higher. Parenthetically, I should note that this does *not* imply that all students' achievement comes to be identical, but only that the *average* for two population groups that begin at different levels come to be identical. The diversity of individual scores could be as great as, or greater than, the diversity at grade 1.

Yet there are serious questions about this definition of equality of opportunity. It implies that over the period of school there are no other influences, such as the family environment, which affect achievement over the twelve years of school, even though these influences may differ greatly for the two population groups. Concretely, it implies that white family environments, predominantly middle class, and black family environments, predominantly lower class, will produce no effects on achievement that would keep these averages apart. Such an assumption seems highly unrealistic, especially in view of the general importance of family background for achievement.

However, if such possibilities are acknowledged, then how far can they go before there is inequality of educational opportunity? Constant difference over school? Increasing differences? The unanswerability of such questions begins to give a sense of a new stage in the evolution of the concept of equality of educational opportunity. These questions concern the *relative intensity* of two sets of influences: those which are alike for the two groups, principally in schol, and those which are different, principally in the home or neighborhood. If the school's influences are not only alike for the two groups, but very strong relative to the divergent influences, then the two groups will move together. If school influences are very weak, then the two groups will move apart. Or more generally, the relative intensity of the convergent school influences and the divergent out-of-school influences determines the effectiveness of the educational system in providing equality of educational opportunity. In this perspective, complete equality of opportunity can be reached only if all the divergent out-of-school influences vanish, a condition that would arise only in the advent of boarding schools; given the existing divergent influences, equality of opportunity can only be approached and never fully reached. The concept becomes one of degree of proximity to equality of opportunity. This proximity is determined, then, not merely by the *equality* of educational inputs, but by the *intensity* of the school's influences relative to the external divergent influences. That is, equality of output is not so much determined by equality of the resource inputs, but by the power of these resources in bringing about achievement.

Here, then, is where the concept of equality of educational opportunity presently stands. We have observed an evolution which might have been anticipated a century and a half ago when the first such concepts arose, yet one which is very different from the concept as it first developed. This difference is sharpened if we examine a further implication of the current concept as I have described it. In describing the original concept, I indicated that the role of the community and the educational institution was relatively passive; they were expected to provide a set of free public resources. The responsibility for profitable use of those resources lay with the child and his family. But the evolution of the concept has reversed these roles. The implications of the most recent concept, as I have described it, is that the responsibility to create achievement lies with the educational institution, not the child. The difference in achievement at grade 12 between the average black and the average white is, in effect, the degree of inequality of opportunity, and the reduction of that inequality is a responsibility of the school. This shift in responsibility follows logically from the change in the concept of equality of educational opportunity from school resource inputs to effects of schooling. When that change occurred, as it has in the past few years, the school's responsibility shifted from increasing and distributing equally *its* "quality" to increasing the quality of its *students'* achievements. This is a notable shift, and one which should have strong consequences for the practice of education in future years.

3

Inequality, Sociology, and Moral Philosophy

The theoretical enterprise of moral philosophy has deep roots in both Continental and British philosophy. In Germany Hegel and Kant; in France Rousseau and Les Philosophes; in Scotland the moral philosophers, Frances Hutcheson, Adam Ferguson, and Adam Smith; and in England Locke and Mill, aspired to express normative principles for the organization of society.[1] Sociology began much later, with aspirations to be a positive science of society, and, befitting such goals, the discipline started as not only a theoretical enterprise but also an empirical one.

Despite the differences in their aspirations and modus operandi, moral philosophy and sociology have shared a subject matter, the functioning of society, and the relation of the individual to society. Consequently, it is surprising that except for readings in moral philosophy assigned to students in courses on the historical background of social theory, and for casual reading of modern sociological theory by moral philosophers, sociology and moral philosophy have remained wholly apart, with no interchange of ideas.

The same cannot be said of the relation between economics and moral philosophy, for the origins of economic theory may be found in one branch of moral philosophy: classical utilitarianism, as expressed by Jeremy Bentham and John Stuart Mill. Along with its aspirations as a positive science economics as a discipline has maintained a parallel set of aspirations as a normative science, principally in the branch of economics known as welfare economics, which continues to hold, perhaps in a narrower context than does moral philosophy, the aim of expressing normative principles for the organization of society.[2] In turn, moral philosophy as a theoretical enterprise has often made extensive use of the economist's paradigmatic rational man to serve as the foundation for a particular system of moral philosophy. That, indeed, is the foundation used by Rawls (1971), whose work I shall examine more closely below. Several circumstances have combined over the past few years

Reprinted with permission from *American Journal of Sociology*, vol. 80, no. 3 (November 1974): 739–764. Copyright © 1974 by The University of Chicago. All rights reserved.

to make possible a much more direct confrontation between sociological research and theory on the one hand, and moral philosophy on the other. One of these has been the empirical investigations by sociologists into the character, levels, and sources of inequality in society. Social essayists—in particular Michael Harrington (1963)—drew attention in the 1960s to the degree of inequality within and between races in the United States, and a number of empirical investigations attempted to study the amount and causes of inequality. A large body of this work centered around inequality of opportunity in education, including a congressionally mandated study of inequality in the schools (Coleman et al. 1966) and a large number of works that used this study as a starting point (Mosteller and Moynihan 1972). Another body of work has focused on inequalities of school financing between rich and poor districts (see Coons, Clune, and Sugarman 1970; Levin 1972). Both of these directions of work were inextricably woven into the political fabric of society: numerous administrative decisions, legislative actions, and court cases concerned with school desegregation and school financing used these growing bodies of research results.

Some research on inequality focused on income (Duncan 1968), and at least one (Jencks 1972) covered comprehensively both problems of inequality in education and inequality in income. In addition, work in which sociologists have participated, though economists have been the initiators, has been addressed to issues related to income inequality both empirically and normatively. In particular, the income-maintenance experiments have dealt with questions of the incentive effects of certain kinds of income-redistribution plans: that is, examination of the empirical consequences of reduction of income inequality.

This paper is not the place to ask what in the 1960s led to this surge of interest—not only among sociologists, but in society at large—in issues of inequality. Rather, my point is that sociologists did carry out extensive empirical research on the extent and sources of educational inequality— and to some degree other inequalities—that has begun to amass data bearing on some of the fundamental issues of moral philosophy.

A second circumstance that conspires with others to bring together work in sociology and work in moral philosophy is the fact that, in this empirical research, sociologists have been led to examine the conceptual foundations of "inequality," to attempt to discover the senses in which it exists in society, and to discover in which of these senses "inequality" is held to be illegitimate or at least undesirable in society. Although there are many variations, two strong polar concepts, "equality of opportunity" and "equality of results," have been identified (see Coleman 1968, 1973; Jencks et al. 1972). Along with that conceptual examination have come initial forays into what has been the province of moral philosophy: normative expressions concerning the elimination or reduction of inequality. For example, Jencks, after examining the extent of income inequality in this country and its impermeability to changes in the distribution of education, proposes income-redistribution schemes which would reduce greatly the level of income inequality; in Mosteller and Moynihan these issues are considered as well.

Thus sociologists, though beginning from an empirical base, have begun to address normative issues of the "appropriate" or "proper" or "optimum" levels of inequality or arrangements to bring about equality. It is true that these attempts are ad hoc rather than founded on an explicit philosophical base; nevertheless, definite movement toward problems traditionally in the domain of moral philosophy has taken place. A third circumstance that has helped bring together these two modes of inquiry has been a massive change in social organization. The total amount of income redistribution through government in American society to reduce inequality that arises from economic activity has increased enormously over the past decades. This situation probably has arisen from the urbanization of society, which has greatly increased economic interdependence and made impossible subsistence living by families with almost no money income, as is possible in a rural setting. Whatever the cause, the increased necessity for income redistribution through government has created policy questions about how much of such redistribution should take place, how it should take place, and what resources can be employed to reduce the dependency of those who now receive income through redistribution. These policy questions focus the attention of research sociologists on just those issues of inequality that moral philosophy has long addressed.

Finally, a fourth circumstance that has brought a confrontation between sociology and moral philosophy is the publication of a single book, John Rawls's *A Theory of Justice* (1971). This book constitutes the culmination of a long preoccupation of Rawls with the question of how one can characterize, in principle, a just society, one in which the dual problems of preserving individual autonomy and rights and obtaining the benefits that arise from a social order are solved. This is the fundamental question of the tension between the individual and society which Hobbes posed, and which many, including Hobbes, Rousseau, Locke, Kant, and many others have attempted to answer. Such attempts have not characterized modern sociology as a discipline, however, for sociologists have regarded such normative questions as being outside their province as they sought a "value-free" science. I believe this has been a mistaken orientation of the discipline. As I shall attempt to show before the end of this paper and in more detail elsewhere, I believe that one approach to social theory, a particular branch of the theory of action, is capable of addressing normative questions surrounding the relation between the individual and society.[3] The lack of attention to this issue in sociology, in contrast to continued interest in it in political science and economics, is illustrated by the relative absence of references to sociological works in Rawls's book. There are three references to works by contemporary sociologists (two in one footnote to Homans and one in in another footnote to Runciman) and three to classical sociologists, but there are hundreds to economists and dozens to political scientists. Clearly, in the literature which forms the discourse of moral philosophy, sociological research and theory have not played an important part.[4]

Rawls's attempt to lay out a set of principles for a just society does not in itself bring moral philosophy into contact with the recent developments of sociology I have described. What does do so is the content of his principles, for one of Rawls's two central principles concerns the conditions under which inequalities may properly exist in a just society. It is with the enunciation of this principle (which, to be sure, he first described in an earlier form in a paper in 1958 [pp. 185–87]) that Rawls brings moral philosophy into full position for direct confrontation with recent developments in sociological research and theory. In some respects, Rawls's theory can be seen as an attempt to establish a philosophical base for overriding the principle of efficiency, which is the governing principle of classical economic theory. In recent years, the defects of elevating efficiency to the governing principle of social and economic institutions have become increasingly apparent because the criterion of efficiency is oblivious to issues of distribution, and, in recent years, inequalities of distribution (e.g., income distribution) have not come to be reduced through market forces. This has led to increasing attention, both in policy and in theory, to problems of distribution.

I have described a number of circumstances that have conspired to bring sociology and moral philosophy into contact, a contact that will provide, I believe, benefits to both. But the contact and its implications are not self-evident, and in this paper I want to show the points of contact. In particular, I will use empirical results from sociological research to question the structure of Rawls's theory of justice. Then I will propose an alternative formulation, one which begins from a social contract and uses the rational-man paradigm (as does Rawls), but does not run afoul of the sociological evidence in the way that I believe Rawls's theory does.

To accomplish this, I will first describe the central principles of Rawls's theory. Second, I will point out some of its aspects as they relate to sociological theory, in order to provide a sociological framework within which to view the theory. Then I will examine critically two points in the theory before examining the sociological evidence. Fourth, I will examine recent sociological evidence relating to inequality and attempt to show the points of incongruity of Rawls's perspective with that evidence. Finally, with this confrontation and its results as a background, I will present the initial steps of what I believe to be a proper beginning for a theory of moral or political philosophy.

The Central Principles
of Rawls's Theory of Justice

Although Rawls describes his theory as only a theory of justice, it is in part a normative theory of the social order. It is in the grand tradition of the contract theorists of the 18th century, and it addresses the fundamental problems of a social order. Thus it is not to be taken lightly, for its aims are to enlarge upon, and indeed to complete, a theoretical direction that was initiated by the contract theorists. Whether it turns out to be largely successful or largely a failure, it constitutes the first major attempt in a very long time to fashion a theory of the social order from contract theory.

The starting point of Rawls's theory, unlike that of most sociological theory, is the individual—the rational man—determining whether to enter into a social contract with others for mutual benefit, and, if so, what kind of contract to establish. It is essential to recognize the implications of this starting point. It is a most difficult starting point for a theory of society for it assumes no social institutions, and it must make the great leap from the individual to the social order. Rawls's concern is to devise a starting point such that the institutions that emerge from it are fair to all persons who enter the contract.

Thus for him the original position from which persons contract into the social order is crucial. If the resulting contract is to be fair, Rawls argues, the rational men who establish the contract must do so behind a veil of ignorance—and the particular ignorance that concerns us here is ignorance as to what their positions will be after the contract is complete and the institutions are established. No one should select principles that favor a certain position through knowledge that he himself is likely to occupy that position.

As Rawls makes clear, the theoretical starting point is sharply distinct from classical utilitarianism, which is the one major theoretical framework other than contract theory that derives a social order from the individual choice of rational actors. In utilitarianism, each person acts from the particular position in which he actually finds himself, pursuing his own interest. This pursuit of self interests, combined with the fact that interests are interdependent, causes desirable social institutions to develop, not through anyone's willing them, but, following Adam Smith's famous phrase, through the action of the "invisible hand."[5] To the degree that utilitarian theory addresses itself to the appropriate institutional structure of society it says only two things: that the institutional structure should be as open as possible to the free exercise of these interests, a condition which will lead to the maximum possible good; and that the only proper restraint in the exercise of these interests is the sympathetic identification with the interests of others (either on the part of all members of society, as in Smith, or for most utilitarians, on the part of an ideal observer who takes the interests of all into account), which will lead to the establishment of fair and impartial rules.[6]

In part, the difference between the social-contract theorists and the utilitarians is that of a different stage: the contract theorists, including Rawls, would allow the play of self-interests once the initial rules were established via a proper social contract. In this sense, Rawls's theory can be regarded as a modification of utilitarianism, prefacing the interplay of self-interests by a social contract made behind a veil of ignorance about what one's interests will be once the rules are established. Rawls indicates this at many points. For example, "I assume . . . that the economy is roughly a free market system" (p. 66), and, "It is necessary to note the distinction between the constitutive rules of an institution, which establish its various rights and duties, and so on, and strategies and maxims for how best to take advantage of the institution for particular purposes" (p. 56). But, as in

Rousseau's theory, the rules of the contract may be highly restrictive, such that most resources are regarded as collectively held, or at least subject to a collective will, rather than individually held. This is incompatible with utilitarianism, for it largely precludes that individual action which, according to utilitarian theory, produces individual and social benefits.

In Rawls's theory, once the original position of equality or ignorance is established the rational persons are to decide on those principles that will govern their social institutions. Rawls postulates that rational persons in such a position will choose two principles, and these are the principles that form the basis for his just social order. The two principles stated in their simplest forms are: "First: each person is to have an equal right to the most extensive basic liberty compatible with a similar liberty for others. Second: social and economic inequalities are to be arranged so that they are both (*a*) reasonably expected to be to everyone's advantage, and (*b*) attached to positions and offices open to all" (p. 60). Rawls further indicates that the first principle has priority: liberty can be restricted only for the sake of greater liberty, not for the sake of increased social gains. In effect, this means that the liberty of one can be restricted only for the sake of increasing the liberty of another with lesser liberty.

Rawls elaborates these principles in many ways in order to draw out their implications, but for the purposes of the critique I wish to make it is sufficient to give only a few and introduce them at points where I will use them. He says: "As a first step, suppose that the basic structure of society distributes certain primary goods. . . . For simplicity, assume that the chief primary goods at the disposition of society are rights and liberties, powers and opportunities, income and wealth. . . . Imagine, then, a hypothetical initial arrangement in which all the social primary goods are equally distributed—everyone has similar rights and duties, and income and wealth are equally shared. This state of affairs provides a benchmark for judging improvements. If certain inequalities of wealth and organizational powers would make everyone better off than in this hypothetical starting situation, then they accord with the general conception" (p. 62).

This passage suggests what I believe is Rawls's fundamental aim: to describe those conditions in a society in which one can say that a given set of inequalities is just. Rawls does not by any means aim to establish a set of rules such that inequalities in society are ruled out. Rather, he aims to establish a set of rules that determine which inequalities are just, or fair, and which ones are not. To put it roughly but simply, those inequalities are fair or just which by their existence make everyone better off (in particular, the least advantaged, he says at several points [e.g., p. 15]); those which do not meet this criterion are not fair or just. It is not immediately apparent how an inequality might make the less advantaged better off, but the idea is roughly this: an unequal distribution of resources or a given system of hierarchical authority may lead to greater productivity in a social system than an equal distribution or the absence of authority. If, and only if, that greater productivity brings to those on the lowest level more than they would have had under an equal distribution of resources or a wholly egalitarian authority system, the inequality is justified. This is a stronger constraint than the efficiency criterion of utilitarianism, in which the inequalities are justified if, and only if, they lead to greater productivity.

It is useful to note as an aside that welfare economists have attempted to abrogate the efficiency principles of utilitarian economics, not for the establishment of a "just" social order, but for "maximization of social welfare." Pigou argued, from the fact that the marginal utility of any normal good is declining, that the marginal utility of all a man's resources taken as a whole is declining, so that the addition of a dollar to a rich man's wealth gives less utility than the addition of a dollar to a poor man's wealth. It then follows that, at any point in time, social utility (i.e., social welfare) will be increased by a transfer of wealth from the rich man to the poor man. The maximization of social utility can then occur only when no more transfers can take plce, that is, at a point where all resources are equally distributed.

Thus we see that Rawls is focusing on the same general problem as that of the sociological research I referred to earlier: the problem of inequality in society. While that research addressed itself to measuring the extent and inferring the causes of inequality in society, Rawls is addressing himself to the normative question: when is inequality justified?

The paragraphs above show the central core of Rawls's theory. Before examining it in the context of empirical research results on inequality, it is useful to do two things: first, to mention a logical problem that arises from the structure of the theory itself, and then to relate Rawls's just society to conceptions in sociological theory. In doing the latter, some of the special characteristics of the theory will become more evident.

First, there is a defect in the logical structure of the theory. Rawls creates a hypothetical starting point of individual choice behind a veil of ignorance, the "original position" of persons establishing the contract. One might then say that this is the fundamental postulate of the theory—but then Rawls postulates the actual content of the choice that these persons in their original position would take. This content cannot be deduced from the original position; it is an independent postulate. Rawls justifies this content by arguing that a rational person behind a veil of ignorance would choose these two principles. But this is an a priori psychological argument which is subject to empirical falsification.[7] And it is very easy to imagine that it might be falsified. For example, one can ask what degree of progressivity in income tax would be preferred by a set of rational persons voting early in their lifetime without knowledge of what their future incomes will be (that is, behind a veil of ignorance). A reasonable conjecture might be that each rational voter would weigh the burden of taxation he would experience in those future years when his income was high against the burden of taxation he would experience in those future years when his income was low. He would then vote for that degree of tax progressivity which he felt would equalize those future burdens. This conception of what a rational man would do in devising a tax rate bears no hint of Rawls's principles of justice, and raises doubt that rational men behind a veil of ignorance would arrive at the principles which Rawls lays down.[8]

Consequently the two starting points, the original position and the principles for a just society, must be regarded as alternatives that cannot be simultaneously held because they are not logically independent, nor is one logically derivable from the other. Thus we may regard these double starting points in one of two ways: (1) the conception of rational persons establishing a social contract behind a veil of ignorance is not to be taken seriously; it is to be regarded as merely a way of creating a plausible background and thus encouraging assent by the reader to what would otherwise be two wholly a priori principles; (2) the two principles are not to be taken as central but as subject to change if it can be shown that this original position does not lead to such a choice on the part of rational persons. I will take the first of these interpretations, assuming that Rawls wants to hold to the content of these principles for a just society, however they may have been arrived at.

The Just Society and Sociological Theory

What is most striking as one examines Rawls's conception of justice as fairness is how special is the kind of society he proposes. Parsons characterizes societies according to four polarities, two of which are universalism versus particularism in the relations that characterize institutions and achievement versus ascription in the access of persons to positions or resources in society. Rawls's just society could not be particularistic; it could not be ascriptive. For example, in his preliminaries, in his discussion of "formal justice" which he sees as prior to and assumed by the substantive justice provided by his two principles, he says: "For if it is supposed that institutions are reasonably just then it is of great importance that the authorities should be impartial and not influenced by personal, monetary, or other irrelevant considerations in their handling of particular cases" (p. 59); and again: "Let us also imagine . . . that institutions are impartially and consistently administered by judges and other officials. That is, similar cases are treated similarly, the relevant similarities and differences being those identified by the existing norms." And in describing the formal constraints of the concept of right, which are constraints on the persons in Rawls's "original position," he describes the constraint of generality: "It must be possible to formulate them [the principles of justice] without the use of what would be intuitively recognized as proper names, or rigged definite description" (p. 131).

In this and other places Rawls makes clear that the institutions of a society governed by his principles of justice are characterized by universalism rather than particularism. Equally intrinsic to his principles is the criterion of achievement rather than ascription in the access of persons to derived positions in the society. This is explicitly stated in part (*b*) of his second principle and reiterated elsewhere. For example: "As earlier defined fair equality of opportunity means a certain set of institutions that assures similar chances of education and culture for persons similarly motivated and keeps positions and offices open to all on the basis of qualities and efforts reasonably related to the relevant duties and tasks" (p. 278). This passage could well be a joint definition of universalistic and achievement-oriented institutions, or alternatively, of Weberian ideal-type bureaucracy.

These passages and others make clear that the institutions of Rawls's just society, characterized by universalism and achievement, are bureaucratic in form. This may be an inevitable consequence of the search for a just society; on the other hand, it may merely signal a kind of myopia about the varieties of forms that justice might take. It denies that the caste society of India could be just, for example, no matter how extensive the system of obligations and responsibilities that hold among castes. And it denies that a close community, in which most relations are particularistic rather than universalistic and in which many positions are ascribed rather than achieved, could be a just society. It denies that familistic societies, in which one's social location is ascribed largely on the basis of the family's position in a larger structure and the person's position in the family, could be just societies. Yet close communities and familistic societies often are believed to have a humane quality lacking in modern, impersonal, universalistic, achievement-oriented societies.[9]

I will not pursue the point here, but it is important to recognize that the conceptions of justice that Rawls holds are highly specific to the impersonal *Gesellschaft* which modern society has become. Only if we want to deny at the outset that primitive tribes and other *gemeinschaftliche* social systems can constitute just systems can we accept a definition of justice as circumscribed as that which Rawls sets forth. Yet we know from a great deal of social research, if not from personal experience, the psychic costs of living in an impersonal universalistic, achievement-oriented social system. What is lost in such societies is the personal care, personal attention, warmth, and sense of responsibility each person has for particular persons. When these elements are weighed against impersonal justice, as Rawls's theory of justice forces them to be, is it clear that they are less necessary to us?

But while social theory should sensitize us to the possible culture boundedness of Rawls's theory of justice, it does not address the question of whether the theory is satisfactory within societies of the type for which it is developed: modern industrial society. To examine that question requires recourse to recent sociological research in inequality.

Sociological Research on Inequality and Its Relations to a Theory of Justice

As I have described above, Rawls's theory can be regarded as an attempt to express the conditions under which inequalities are compatible with a just society. Intrinsic to the theory is the principle of "fair equality of opportunity," as expressed, for example, in the passage quoted earlier from page 278. More explicitly, Rawls says at another point: "I assume that there is fair (as opposed to formal) equality of opportunity. This means that, in addition to maintaining the usual kinds of social overhead capital, the government tries to insure equal chances of education and culture for persons similarly endowed and motivated either by subsidizing private schools or by establishing a public school system" (p. 275). This assumption brings the theory into direct contact with recent sociological research on inequality, for that research has been confronted with precisely the question of what constitutes equality of opportunity in education. The problem was created by the mandate to the commissioner of education in the Civil Rights Act of 1964, which directed the commissioner of education to carry out "a survey of the lack of availability of equal educational opportunity." One of the principal problems in carrying out that mandate lay in the interpretation of the term "lack of equality of educational opportunity." It was clear from the legislative history of the act and from the expressions of interest groups that at least five distinct definitions of equality of educational opportunity were held, and that these five were sharply separated into two groups: a set of more or less conventional definitions in which equality of educational opportunity is defined in terms of the input resources to the schools, without regard to the effect of these resources on the outcomes of education, and one in which the criteria are outcomes of education with the inputs evaluated solely in terms of their effects on these criteria (Coleman 1968).

The results of the research showed several things which create a dilemma for Rawls's theory (Coleman et al. 1966). First, they showed that there was a sharp difference between the level of inequality of opportunity according to the two groups of definitions. According to the conventional definition, in terms of input resources provided by boards of education, the degree of inequality of educational opportunity by race was relatively small (when compared, say, with the inequality by geographic region or by urbanism). But according to the definition in which inputs are evaluated by their effects on academic achievement, there was high inequality of opportunity by race. (For example, there was a high degree of racial inequality in teachers' verbal skills, which was of some importance for students' achievement.) Thus the choice of definitions is not merely important in principle, but in actuality as well. Second, and more crucial, when inequality of educational opportunity was defined according to the effects of input resources on educational achievement, those resources under the control of the school were considerably less important than those which were intrinsic to the child's family background. That is, the resources brought to education from the home were considerably more important for achievement than those provided by the schools. Extensive further analysis of that research (see for example, Mosteller and Moynihan 1972) as well as research in other countries (Purves 1973; Comber and Keeves 1973; Thorndike 1973) confirm and strengthen this result. Less important, but still more important than most school resources, were those inputs to a student's educational opportunity provided by the level of background of other students in his classroom (see McPartland and Sprehe [1973] for further analysis of those effects). That is, the social composition of his classroom was an important input to educational opportunity.

It is clear from these research results that the very conception of inequality of educational opportunity in Rawls's theory is not appropriate. The privately held resources located in the family are unequalizing, while the publicly held resources provided by the school board are equalizing, since they are already distributed rather equally. Thus, inequality of opportunity is the starting point, brought about through the unequal family resources available to different children. Effective reduction in inequality of opportunity can come about only by increasing the ratio of public to private resource inputs to education, since the public inputs are equalizing and the private ones are unequalizing. Consequently, the crucial question that arises is not the passive one suggested by the phrase, "equality of opportunity," but rather the very active one: just how much collective resources are to go into education? The answer must be given with full realization that, whatever it is, the result will not be equality of educational opportunity but rather a reduction in the inequality, simply because the private resources continue to be unequalizing forces, provided differentially by different families.

Viewed in this way, these results create a dilemma for Rawls's theory. To resolve it in one direction, he may accept the conventional definition of equality of educational opportunity as the passage quoted earlier from page 278 suggests. That definition accepts the level of motivation it finds in the child and appears to imply that equal opportunity lies merely in provision of equal facilities, with no societal responsibility for the child's use of them.

But to do that implies, as these results show, that although formal equality of opportunity will exist by definition, little substantive or effective equality of opportunity will exist in fact. The difficulty of this resolution, however, does not end here. For the question arises: how much educational resources, equally distributed, are to be supplied? Five hours per day per child? One hour? Ten hours? Does equality lie merely in the equal distribution of resources or in the level of resources supplied as well? The question would be unimportant if all children began from a point of equality, but they do not. Consequently, insofar as school resources are effective in providing substantive educational opportunity, the degree of substantive equality of opportunity depends not merely on the equality of distribution of collectively held resources, but on the level of these resources as well.

If the dilemma is resolved in the other direction, with equality of education opportunity evaluated by the effectiveness of the inputs, that is, the results, then a just society requires equalizing all these inputs. Yet it is clear that the most effective inputs are those that reside in the most intimate elements of a student's environment: the gentle encouragement of his mother, the painstaking hours that parents—some parents—spend in nurturing reading and spelling skills, the discussions that take place in some homes which stretch the child's mind. If Rawls's just society is to equalize educational opportunity in this sense, the equalizing institutions must invade the home, pluck the child from his unequalizing environment, and subject him to a common equalizing environment. It is difficult to believe that Rawls would intend the dilemma to be resolved in this way. Yet there are many passages that suggest this resolution. Throughout, his imagery concerning distribution of primary goods (rights, liberties, powers, opportunities, income, wealth) implies that their source is central, not dispersed among a set of sovereign persons. For example: "The justice of a social scheme depends essentially on how fundamental rights and duties are assigned" (p. 7); "Once we decided to look for a conception of justice that *nullifies the accidents of natural endowment* . . . we are led to these principles" (p. 15; my italics); "All social values—liberty and opportunity, income and wealth, and the bases of self-respect—*are to be distributed equally unless* . . ." (p. 62; my italics); "As a first step, suppose that the *basic structure of society distributes* certain primary goods. . . . For simplicity, assume that the chief primary goods *at the disposition of society* are . . ." (p. 62; my italics); and in his final statement of the principles, he states as the "general conception" of the theory of justice: "All social primary goods—liberty and opportunity, income and wealth, and the bases of self-respect—*are to be distributed* equally unless an unequal distribution of any or all of these goods is to the advantage of the least favored" (p. 303; my italics).[10] It is true that Rawls assumes the existence of markets and private property. In his discussion of the four branches of government the transfer branch reallocates only a portion of privately held income to establish a given minimum income for all, and the distributive branch allows the existence of private property (p. 274–84). Nevertheless, the overall conception which Rawls has is that of a centralized agency established by the social contract, with unlimited power to establish institutions and to tax and reallocate, constrained only by that central agency's interpretation of the principles of justice that Rawls proposes. There is no residue of sovereignty remaining to the members of this society once they have established their social contract, nor is there any mechanism to insure that whatever person or persons acting as their agents in executing those centralized powers will not use that power for their own ends. Yet since Michels, and perhaps since Acton, we have known that such an assumption is naive in the extreme. In short, in Rawls's theory, persons, via a social contract, give up their rights and resources and vest them in a central agency which, in a disinterested and dispassionate way, redistributes these rights and resources, including the basic liberties, to the members of society.

Given Rawls's conception, that the social contract places in the hands of a disembodied central agent all primary goods, it is difficult to see how that agent could do less, in following Rawls's principle of equality of opportunity, than to remove the child from the family and place him in an environment that will be effectively equal, and not only formally so. One might argue that taking the child from his parents violates the priority of Rawls's liberty principle; but if parents' liberty is being decreased, that of the child is being increased, since he is being liberated from the constrictions of the parental home.

These research results, in juxtaposition with Rawls's principles, bring us back to the discussion of Rawls's just society in relation to sociological theory. As indicated there, Rawls's theory implies a society with wholly bureaucratic institutions governed by universalism. Particularistic institutions are incompatible with the theory of justice. The family is perhaps the supremely particularistic institution in society, so it is no accident that an effective, rather than formal, interpretation of the principle of equality of opportunity would lead to the destruction of the family as a socializing institution.

Thus these results of research in educational opportunity leave Rawls's theory, and for that matter any theory which gives equality of opportunity the highest place, in a dilemma. Long ago I concluded, after considering these research results at some length, that the only viable approach to inequality of educational opportunity is to recognize that full equality of educational opportunity is not a proper collective goal; instead, the proper goal is either establishing some minimum level of effective educational opportunity for all—the minimum to be collectively decided—or reducing, through educational institutions, the amount of inequality of opportunity. If the second goal is chosen, a collective decision must be made to determine the amount of resoures to be devoted to this collective goal, not to "nullify the accidents of natural endowment," but to reduce their impact on subsequent opportunities.

Another aspect of these research results presents a further difficulty for Rawls's theory. The results show that one resource which leads to educational achievement, and thus toward equality of educational opportunity if equally distributed, is the social backgrounds of classmates. If we assume for a moment that there are no constraints on freedom of movement among schools, due to discrimination or low income, then all families will have equal and high liberty in the choice of schools for their children. But this choice may lead to socially homogeneous schools, leaving some chldren with lower effective educational opportunity than others. Indeed, this has been the position of many of this country's courts which have mandated busing to create racially heterogeneous schools.[11] Yet Rawls's priority of the liberty principle would restrict the state from interfering with those choices, because that would reduce the liberty for all only to increase the equality of opportunity. Thus Rawls's principles could lead us to acquiesce in this voluntary segregation, for to do otherwise would reduce liberty. Such segregation could lead, as indicated above, to very different levels of educational opportunity for different children, to say nothing of the potential for splitting society into hostile self-segregated subgroups. This again seems a case in which moral principles must be balanced off against each other in terms of the costs and benefits, without giving one or another absolute priority. Each of us has an interest in decreasing the inequality of educational opportunity; each of us has an interest in maintaining our freedom of choice of school; and each of us has an interest in maintaining a cohesive society. We should each weigh those interests within ourselves and reach a collective decision based on the outcome of these private calculi, rather than binding ourselves to an ordered set of principles that can create results which no one desires.

The overall impact of these research results is not that Rawls's theory gives the wrong answer. It is rather that it asks the wrong question—it poses the problem in the wrong way. Rawls's second principle, stated in its final form is: "Social and economic inequalities are to be arranged so that they are both (a) to the greatest benefit of the least advantaged, consistent with the savings principle; and (b) attached to offices and positions open to all under conditions of fair equality of opportunity" (p. 302). Posing this issue in this way implies that there is collective or at least central control of social and economic inequalities—that those inequalities are arranged by "the society" (perhaps "the society" in the sense of Rousseau's general will) in order to satisfy parts (a) and (b) of the principle. But the research results show that this is not the case at all: inequalities arise through individual activity, like dandelions sprouting in a lawn. As with the dandelions, the question is not how to arrange them, but rather just how much effort, how many resources, are to be devoted to reducing their number, and which ones are beneficial to eliminate? Resources used to reduce inequalities are resources that have an opportunity cost, since they can be employed elsewhere. Perhaps a principle could be devised that would capture the essence of this point. But Rawls's second principle does not. That principle is based upon the conception that some inequalities are bad for the least advantaged and some are good, and the principle is designed to discriminate between them. But the principle does not recognize that eliminating the first set of inequalities or encouraging the second set costs resources. It costs resources since most inequalities sprout up among individuals, and modifying them requires the collection and centralized use of resources that have an opportunity cost. Unless these resources are included in the calculations, and unless the distributional effects of the collectivization of these resources are noted, there can be no answer to the question, now properly posed: what amount of resources ought to be used in the reduction of inequalities of the first set and encouragement of those in the second? Rawls's principle implies either merely a formal rather than a substantive elimination of inequalities or no limitation upon the collective use of resources to arrive at the objective. If the former, the principle is emasculated and virtually meaningless. If the latter, the principle implies full collective ownership and control of resources.

It is this last implication that brings the imagery behind Rawls's second principle forcefully to bear. For at issue is not only the question of just what quantity of resources ought collectively to be devoted to reduction of inequalities, but also the balance between the rights that men hold collectively and those they hold individually. And this brings us full face to consider the two conceptions of a democratic society: the individualistic conception, resulting from Locke and Mill, in which men hold their rights individually, and the collectivist conception, held by Rousseau, in which all persons' rights are held collectively, capable of disposition through the general will. It is the difference between two conceptions of government described by Ullmann (1966) as "the ascending theory of government," in which rights and resources are held individually (i.e., at the bottom) to be selectively vested in government, and "the descending theory of government," in which all rights and resources are held collectively (i.e., at the top) to be delegated to persons below.[12]

If we conceive of a social structure in which men gain their resources through the individual effort of wresting a living directly from nature, the totalitarian character of collectivist democracy becomes most apparent. For resources in such a society are quite clearly gained directly by individuals in a contest with nature. By what justification, then, are these resources, individually gained, appropriable by the collectivity to serve its ends? The only proper justification is a collective decision in which each of those persons takes part and which itself establishes the degree to which each person shall give up his individual rights to the collectivity: in effect, a constitutional decision. The outcome of that constitutional decision cannot be determined on a priori grounds, as Rawls has attempted to do. Furthermore, it is very unlikely that it will be one in which all rights and resources are given over to the collectivity, as Rawls's theory implicitly requires. It will depend on the needs that persons have that they feel can best be satisfied through individual action. It is inappropriate to discuss the properties of a just collectivity—as if persons had already given up all their rights to the collectivity—without knowing first the degree to which persons choose to vest resources and rights in the collectivity. The collectivity is an actor created by the social contract. Only those actors that we can take as given, with resources of their own, can be evaluated by a principle of justice. Those actors which must gain their resources from others—that is, all collective or corporate actors, of which the state is an important case— must first of all gain their particular degree of being, before questions can be asked about their degree of justness, or of any other moral virtue.

From this point of view, Rawls is guilty of the error of misplaced concreteness: he regards a collective actor as concrete, full-blown and in fact implicitly in control of all resources, in order to establish a criterion of "justice" for that actor. The prior question is exactly what resources have individuals vested in the corporate actor?

An Alternative Starting Point
to That of Rawls's Social Contract

As the examination of Rawls's theory of justice in the context of sociological theory makes evident, it is not at all clear that a theory of justice should be developed independently from a general theory of society, or at least independently from a general moral philosophy. But whether one sets out on the more specialized enterprise, as Rawls has done, or on the more general enterprise, as 18th-century philosophers did, it is useful to give some attention to the general framework that is used.

The 18th-century philosophers can be divided into two groups, according to their solutions to the problem Hobbes posed, that is, the problem of how man can be not engaged in a war of all against all. Both groups held what was a new conception—that ultimate rights are inherent in persons as individuals, that all persons were endowed with a set of "natural rights." Furthermore, both groups began with a conception of man as self-interested, using his sovereign rights to implement his interests—though in various ways and by various theorists these interests were modified. In one group were the utilitarians, whom I have mentioned earlier and need not examine again. It is the second group that is of interest because it is with this group that Rawls locates his theory: the contract theorists, with Hobbes and Rousseau as the two most extreme representatives. These theorists solved Hobbes's problem by positing that persons entered into a social contract because each saw it to be to his long-term advantage to do so and thus to experience social order. The contract constrained his pursuit of short-term interests by imposing on him certain duties and obligations, or by withdrawing from him certain rights and resources to be held and used collectively. Both Hobbes and Rousseau took the second, extreme solution, so that rights and resources came to be held collectively. Rousseau provided a philosophical foundation for socialism and in some respects for the modern forms of totalitarianism, all of which have acted in the name of "the people," or in other words, Rousseau's "general will" (see Talmon [1952] for further discussion).

The difficulty of a contract theory is precisely that encountered by Rousseau. Once the natural rights are given over to a central agent they are no longer held individually by the persons, and those persons as individuals possess no resources with which to oppose the use of the collectively held resources against them. Rawls's theory has no protection against this difficulty: in the social contract, men give over their sovereign rights to a central agent, with only Rawls's principles of justice to protect them from further aggrandizement and misuse of the resources by the central agent.[13]

As evidenced by Hobbes's Leviathan, Rousseau's general will, and Rawls's principles of justice, social-contract theories do contain the danger of denuding sovereign persons of rights and resources, which become collectively held. Yet in all societies something like a social contract is made, either in the form of an explicit constitution or in the form of a set of common laws, generally accepted. Of course this may be a social contract in a much more individualist sense insofar as very limited powers are given over to the state, with many rights and resources still held individually. In some form, however weak, it seems likely that if a social theory is to mirror the functioning of actual societies, a social contract must appear in the theory of anyone who begins from a position of analytical individualism (as Parsons [1965] terms the starting point of the natural rights philosophers).

I want to sketch, in a few paragraphs, the outlines of a social theory which does include a social contract yet does not contain the dangers of the loss of sovereign rights by persons to a central source. I have touched upon elements of this theory in earlier publications (1966, 1974). In the more recent of these I have introduced the concept of "corporate actor," closely corresponding to the legal definition of a corporation (whether profit or nonprofit, and for whatever purpose organized) but somewhat broader, to include both those bodies that act corporately, though they are not legally chartered by the state (e.g., the family), and the state itself.

All resources reside in natural persons, and corporate actors gain their resources through resource investments of one sort or another by natural persons. In doing so they establish implicitly or explicitly a constitution, which may well be regarded as a social contract among them. The social contract is one in which each party contracts to invest certain rights and resources in the corporate actor, for which he receives two things in return: partial control over the actions of the corporate actor and an expectation of more beneficial consequences from the corporate actor's actions than he would have had from his own individual actions.

The general framework is intended to be equally valid for financial investments in a business corporation and for psychic and other investments in a commune, to mention only the extremes. In the first case, only a single kind of resource is invested, and the person keeps most of his rights to himself; in the second, nearly all his rights and resources are invested in the commune, and he withholds almost none, giving the commune as a corporate actor not only rights to use alienable resources, such as money, but also rights to control his time and his actions and to punish him if he acts against the interests of the commune. In the extreme (see Durkheim's altruistic suicide [1951]), he gives up to the corporate actor his very right to live, his very control over life and death.

Because this theory bears a kinship to contract theories of society, it is rather simple to examine the theory's implications for the 18th-century philosophers' social contract, which natural persons implicitly can be said to make when they agree to live together under rules and institutions in a society.

In the present theory, as distinct from classical social-contract theories and as distinct from Rawls's theory, there is no single social contract, no single pact that each person can be said to make with others, covering all the institutions of society. There are instead a number of social contracts into which he enters, one for each of the corporate actors of which he is a member. One of these corporate actors, however, has a special character, for it establishes and enforces the laws which natural persons and all corporate actors within its jurisdiction must obey. In modern societies, this actor is the state. The contract with the state is somewhat different from that with other corporate actors, for a person gives over to the state a larger set of rights than he ordinarily does to other corporate actors of which he is a member—such as rights to incarcerate him, inflict punishment and even death upon him, according to certain rules.[14] It is the contract with this corporate actor to which the social contract of Locke and other political philosophers most closely corresponds. Yet it is not identical, for they conceived of society as a single fabric of institutions which one made a single contract to join, while conceive of society as consisting of distinct corporate actors, only one of which is the encompassing state. Their conception was more appropriate to their time because they were closer to the closed and monolithic societies of the Middle Ages, in a social structure that was less pluralistic, had fewer independent loci of power, and in which natural persons were not so fully recognized as endowed with natural rights as is the case today. Indeed, their theories helped bring us to the pluralistic and differentiated societies of today. All these "single contract" theories, as I shall call them, are more appropriate to something like (though more voluntaristic than) states characterized by "state socialism" than to the pluralist societies of Western democratic states.[15] Before proceeding to examine the nature of the state contract a person makes, it is useful to emphasize once again that the form of a social theory must differ as the social structure for which it is designed differs. In particular, in the Middle Ages, a person was not simultaneously a member of a family, city, and kingdom. First, he was a member of the family, which had complete jurisdiction over him; then the family was a member of the city; and the city a member of the kingdom. In the social structure, the social contracts to be made were not, as at present, all made by natural persons as members—rather, only the lowest-level contract was made by persons. Those at higher levels can be best conceived of as contracts made by the corporate actor at the next lower level: families making a social contract as members of a city, etc.[16]

The General Properties of the Investment Decision

The overall conception is this: all resources reside individually in natural persons, and these persons make investment decisions. The investments are investments in corporate actors, ranging from a corporate actor that has only one other member (such as a married couple, or a pair of friends)[17] to the encompassing corporate actor of the state. Intermediate between these extremes are the various corporate bodies through which much of the action in society takes place. All these corporate actors receive their resources ultimately from natural persons, although for some the resources do not come directly from persons, but through other corporate actors. The resources that are invested are resources of all sorts, ranging from the most alienable, such as monetary wealth, to the most inalienable, such as the right to control one's time or speech. These corporate actors, most of which are single-purposed or narrow-purposed bodies, have interests the same as natural persons and pursue those interests through agents, using the resources invested in them. Their interests are, just like those of natural persons, sometimes in accord, sometimes in conflict; and at times they are in conflict with personal interests of their members. What protects the members, however, is the very multiplicity of the corporate actors in which the investment is made. It is this multiplicity of intermediate corporate actors that protects the person's interests from the actions of that special and most powerful corporate actor, the state. It should be evident that this is little more than a restatement of a pluralist conception of society, using the conception of corporate actors and of the social contract. It is not in this form a normative theory, except insofar as the investments are so distributed to insure protection of natural persons from the arbitrary exercise of power by any one of the corporate actors in which they have made investments, and in particular, the state.[18] Thus it does not address the problems of inequality, or more generally the distributional problems that arise in a market society, as Rawls's theory does. The next stages in the theory, however, begin to do so, not by beginning with a theory of justice, but by establishing a theory of political structure through which investments are made and withdrawn. I will not discuss that here; I will only point out that in such a political structure persons have the capability, through ease of shifting of resource investments, to increase or decrease the relative importance of different interests, and thereby of different moral virtues, including justice. The power given to the agency pursuing the goal of reducing inequality will differ from time to time. I believe this is appropriately the case, as individual needs and public or collective needs differ at different times.

The brief sketch of an alternative starting point to Rawls's is designed merely to show that a social-contract theory which attends to distributional problems in society need not contain the dangers inherent in powers collected in a central locus, as I believe Rawls's theory does. It is useful to point out, however, that this formulation eliminates the need that exists in Rawls's theory of justice to precede a principle of distributive justice (his second principle) with a prior principle that guarantees maximum and equal liberties. With the starting point I have outlined, liberty is guaranteed by the structure itself: by the rights and resources withheld from the state, many of which are invested in corporate actors that can oppose the state on behalf of the natural person. To insure equal liberty, it is necessary in the constitution only to insure that one person's actions do not reduce another's liberties: that is, only to protect persons from infringement of liberties by others. There is no danger that liberties will be preempted by the state (except through the use of force or fraud, if the state gains too great a set of resources in toto) because they hever have been vested in the state; they have been retained by persons.

It is also useful to point out that the starting point I have sketched does not lead to a dilemma about inequality of educational opportunity as does the theory of justice. First, it does not pose a requirement of absolute equality of opportunity as does the theory of justice. Thus it does not establish a goal that must either be satisfied in a purely formal way or else is unachievable. Instead, via a theory of variable investment in the state, and in the different agencies of the state, the question is posed in the appropriate way: what is to be the level of investment of collective resources in the reduction of inequality of educational opportunity, to counterpose against the private unequalizing resources? There is in this theory no conception that all the resources are centrally gathered to be redistributed. Instead, the issues of moral philosophy revolve around the question of how much public resource investment there will be toward equalizing what private enterprise has made unequal. Since this is a quantitative question, as it must appropriately be, rather than a question of absolutes, the resulting answers relevant to moral philosophy must also involve balancing different principles rather than establishing absolute priorities, as Rawls's theory does.

A Partial Veil of Ignorance

In addition to the theoretical structure outlined above, it is useful to modify the conception of a social contract (whether single or multiple) made behind a veil of ignorance about one's future position relative to that corporate actor. For is such a theory is to be useful, it must recognize that social contracts or constitutions are made and modified by persons, each of whom has expectations about his future positions, expectations that differ to some degree from those of other persons. Thus he is behind a "partial veil of ignorance," not a complete veil, about his future position. We can expect each person to vote, or otherwise act, from the point of view of his long-range interests, which are based on these expectations about the future.[19]

Now if a community is homogeneous in terms of the life chances of its members, either because it is currently homogeneous with stability or because persons can reasonably expect high mobility during their lifetimes, there will be a high degree of consensus on the properties of the social contract or constitution, or on amendments to the constitution. If the community is heterogeneous in its expectations about future positions, there will be low consensus on the properties of the contract. The degree of consensus of the community can be said to be a consequence of the homogeneity of future expectation streams.

When we have a constitutional proposal to be voted on there will not be identical opinions, so there is not complete consensus (as would exist if rational men were acting behind a complete veil of ignorance about their future positions and thus held identical expectations). But the sensitivity of the result of a vote to differences in initial power of different persons will be low insofar as the difference in expectation streams is low. It will not matter much what the initial allocation of votes among different persons is. The vote outcome will be insensitive to differences in initial power if the difference in expectation streams is low. It will not matter much what the initial allocation of votes among different persons is. The vote outcome will be very sensitive to differences in initial power if the difference in expectation streams is high. If, for example, the issue is one of the degree of progressivity in income taxes, there will be high consensus on the degree of progressivity if different persons expect roughly similar income profiles over their lifetimes: that is, if they expect to spend similar amounts of time at low levels of income and similar amounts of time at high levels. If they do not, then there will be little consensus in the degree of tax progressivity, and different initial allocations of votes among different persons will lead to very different outcomes.

One may thus begin to conceive of the viability of a society in these terms: a potential collectivity, to be created through a social contract, is highly viable if different allocations of power to determine the terms of the contract lead to much the same resulting contract, and of low viability if different allocations lead to very different resulting contracts. The degree of sensitivity of the resulting contract or constitution to initial power allocations can thus be used as a measure of the viability of a potential corporate actor to be created or modified through the contract.

Conclusion

Sociological theory and research have remained almost wholly out of contact with theories of moral and political philosophy. Recent research into levels and sources of inequality in society, together with the recent publication of John Rawls's *Theory of Justice*, which addresses inequality normatively, provide the basis for some contact. In this paper, I have tried to examine Rawls's theory in the context of this recent sociological work and also to sketch the outlines of a sociological theory that can address the questions of distributive justice in a somewhat different way than does Rawls's theory.

Notes

1. A critic of an earlier draft argued that "political philosophy" is a more appropriate term for describing this work. I will continue to use "moral philosophy," because this is how John Rawls, whose work I shall discuss in detail below, describes his work. Otherwise, this general direction of effort is better described as political philosophy, an enterprise which has begun a resurgence recently (see, for example, Laslett [1956], Laslett and Runciman [1962, 1967], and Laslett, Runciman, and Skinner [1972]).

2. In the 20th century, the development of welfare economics began with Pigou in the 1920s, continued through Bergson in the 1930s, and then, in the 1950s, was brought up short by Arrow, who showed that any method for deriving a social optimum from individual preferences was destined to fail unless one assumed an interpersonal comparison of utility, which was implicitly what the classical utilitarians did. Since then, welfare economics has been hung on this one point, despite extensive forays into the theory of social choice by economists and political scientists.

3. I begin this attempt in Coleman (1974). In a larger work that is not yet completed, I spell out the details of the theory.

4. One might argue that Rawls is atypical, and that argument is to some degree well taken. Rawls, by his very acceptance of the social contract framework as a starting point and his use of the rational-man paradigm from economic theory, is from the start closer to economics than to sociology, which begins from other points.

5. Perhaps the earliest pure expression of this theoretical position was that of Mandeville's Fable of the Bees. In Mandeville's fable, so long as the bees were motivated by altruism, the tasks of the hive did not get done, and only when the bees attended each to his own selfish interests did the hive thrive, to the benefit of all.

6. This sympathetic identification is found most fully developed in Adam Smith's *Theory of Moral Sentiments*.

7. At another point he rejects Kant's use of such arguments: "*A priori* psychological argument, however plausible, is not sufficient to abandon the principle of toleration" (p. 215).

8. This means of arriving at an "appropriate" level of progressivity in income tax was suggested by James Buchanan in a personal communication.

9. One colleague has remarked that when he read Rawls, he kept thinking of the kinds of Orthodox Jewish communities portrayed in *Fiddler on the Roof*, which clearly could not measure up to Rawls's criteria of a just society. Yet such societies have a kind of humane justice that the bureaucratic form required by Rawls could never have.

10. In his section 79, The Idea of Social Union (pp. 520–29), Rawls goes to some pain to distinguish his just society from a "private society" in which men have no common ends. There he emphasizes common ends and the communal or collective aspects of his just society.

11. The parallel is not exact since blacks and other minorities do have lower liberty to attend a school of their choice, due to discrimination or income. But this does not invalidate the point made in the text.

12. It is true that Rousseau's conception of democracy begins with rights held individually. But once the social contract is made, those rights are given over to a central agent to implement the general will. Thus Rousseau's theory is not a pure case of Ullmann's descending theory of government. The political philosophy of the late Middle Ages, in which all power was seen to be held either by the king or the Church, is an example of a pure descending theory of government (see Gierke 1900).

13. It is useful to note that in the shift from "Justice as Fairness" published in 1958 to a *Theory of Justice* in 1971, Rawls has become in effect collectivized. Justice as fairness began, in 1958, as a modification of utilitarianism designed to remedy utilitarianism's lack of attention to distributional problems. It perhaps arose as a natural extension into moral philosophy of economists' increasing use of the principle of Pareto optimality and recognition of the impossibility of interpersonal comparison of utility, the latter undermining the utilitarians' conception of aggregating utilities of different persons. As such it is a natural extension: if one person could become better off than at present, even if he was already better off than his fellows, and if by so doing this would not hurt others and perhaps even help them, then this was a Pareto-optimal move and should obviously be made. Further, if the original starting point for all such moves is equality, then the society would already appear to be a just one. But over the years Rawls "collectivized" his principles as he developed them into a fully developed theory, and the end result is a collectivist theory closer to Rousseau's general will than to Locke's political economy.

14. There is no sharp distinction between the contract a person makes as a member of a state and the contract he makes as a member of other corporate actors, for there are cases in which he gives over rights to the corporate actor which are just as extensive as the rights he gives over to the state. Certain communes can inflict severe punishment upon their members, even death; certain religious orders and secret societies are accorded similar rights by their members. The distinction made above in the text is one that separates the state from most other corporate actors in society, though not all. Those others, like certain communes or religious and secret orders that are not distinguished from the state by this definition, are subject to the same theoretical statements as those I shall shortly make about the state.

15. The term "state socialism" is used to refer to Eastern Europe, USSR, and China.

16. It is true, of course, that the option of an actor's withdrawing from the corporate actor was much less under those conditions, whether the actor was a person, a family, or a village. But the point of interest here is the structural difference between interlocking sets of corporate actors, with the person as the investor in all cases versus a nested set of corporate actors, with the person making only the lowest-level investment decision.

17. At first glance, it would appear that a "relation between two friends" cannot be a corporate actor by any stretch of the imagination. However, the definition of a corporate actor implies that whenever actions are taken corporately, a corporate actor can be appropriately defined. Thus, insofar as the pair of friends does act corporately, it is a corporate actor. The set of activities or events it covers may very well be small; nevertheless, in those activities or events it can be conceived as a corporate actor, replacing the action of its members.

18. The character of the theoretical framework, in which natural persons make investments in a set of corporate actors, provides the basis for a kind of "portfolio theory" analogous to the portfolio theory for financial investments, in which the investor can maximize certain objectives through carrying an appropriate portfolio. I have not, however, begun to develop such a portfolio theory for investments of rights and resources.

19. I have excluded here consideration of the identification of persons with others' interests, which is another source of cohesion, particularly strong in small communities. Such identification can produce a high degree of consensus in communities in which expectation streams are very diverse. This is very likely the principal source of cohesion in particularistic, ascriptive communities.

References

Coleman, James S. 1966. "Individual Interests and Collective Action." Pp. 49–62 in *Papers on Non-Market Decision Making*, edited by Gordon Tullock. Charlottesville: Thomas Jefferson Center for Political Economy, University of Virginia.

———. 1968. "The Concept of Equality of Educational Opportunity." *Harvard Educational Review*, 38, no. 1 (Winter): 7–22.

———. 1973. "Equality of Opportunity and Equality of Results." *Harvard Educational Review* 43, no. 1 (Winter): 129–37.

———. 1974. *Power and the Structure of Society*, New York: Norton.

Coleman, James S., et al. 1966. *Equality of Educational Opportunity*. Washington, D.C.: Government Printing Office.

Comber, L. C., and John P. Keeves. 1973. *Science Education in Nineteen Countries*. New York: Wiley.

Coons, J., W. H. Clune III, and S. Sugarman. 1970. *Private Wealth and Public Education*. Cambridge, Mass.: Harvard University Press.

Duncan, O. D. 1968. "Inheritance of Poverty or Inheritance of Race." Pp. 85–110 in *On Understanding Poverty*, edited by D. P. Moynihan. New York: Basic.

Durkheim, É. 1951. *Suicide*. Glencoe, Ill.: Free Press.

Gierke, Otto von. 1900. *Political Theories of the Middle Ages*. Translated by F. W. Maitland. Cambridge: Cambridge University Press.

Harrington, Michael. 1963. *The Other American*. New York: Macmillan.

Jencks, C. 1972. *Inequality*. New York: Basic.

Laslett, Peter. 1956. *Philosophy, Politics, and Society: First Series*. Oxford: Blackwell.

Laslett, Peter, and W. G. Runciman. 1962. *Philosophy, Politics, and Society: Second Series*. Oxford: Blackwell.

————. 1967. *Philosophy, Politics, and Society: Third Series*. Oxford: Blackwell.

Laslett, Peter, W. G. Runciman, and Quentin Skinner. 1972. *Philosophy, Politics, and Society: Fourth Series*. Oxford: Blackwell.

Levin, B., et al. 1972. *Paying for Public Schools*. Washington, D.C.: Urban Institute.

McPartland, James, and J. Timothy Sprehe. 1973. "Racial and Regional Inequalities in School Resources Relative to Their Educational Outcomes." *Social Science Research* 2, no. 4 (December): 321–32.

Mosteller, F., and D. P. Moynihan. 1972. *On Equality of Educational Opportunity*. New York: Random House.

Parsons, Talcott. 1965. "The Interpretation of Action in the History of Social Thought." Pp. 85–97 in *Theories of Society*, edited by T. Parsons, E. Shils, K. D. Naegele, and J. R. Pitts. New York: Free Press.

Purves, Alan. 1973. *Literature Education in Ten Countries*. New York: Wiley.

Rawls, John. 1958. "Justice as Fairness." *Philosophical Review* 67 (April): 164–94.

————. 1971. *A Theory of Justice*. Cambridge, Mass.: Harvard University Press.

Talmon, J. L. 1952. *The Origins of Totalitarian Democracy*. London: Secker & Warburg.

Thorndike, Robert L. 1973. *Reading Comprehension Education in Fifteen Countries*. New York: Wiley.

Ullmann, Walter. 1966. *The Individual and Society in the Middle Ages*. Baltimore: Johns Hopkins Press.

4

Rawls, Nozick, and Educational Equality

Two recent treatises on moral philosophy have attracted far more general attention than is ordinarily given to works in academic philosophy: *A Theory of Justice*, by John Rawls, and *Anarchy, State, and Utopia*, by Robert Nozick. Together, they offer a framework for considering the difficult problems of inequality in education. Rawls's theory of justice directly addresses the question of what is a just distribution in society—or, put differently, whether inequalities are justified in society, and if so, what kinds and amounts of inequality. Rawls's answer is that only those inequalities are justified which are to the benefit of the least advantaged. Because some inequalities of position or of resources may bring greater productivity and thus greater benefits to all, they may be justified by this principle—though only those such inequalities are permissible.

Nozick's book is in part a response to Rawls. He points out that most inequalities are not created by some central authority, but arise because of individuals' innate or acquired differences in skills, capabilities, and other resources. Thus, he argues (correctly, I believe) that Rawls's principle presupposes that these resources and their products are collectively held, and that individuals have no rights to them. Nozick's own theory is diametrically opposed to this principle. Beginning with the assumption that each person has a set of natural rights, Nozick argues that justice demands neither equality nor an inequality that must benefit the least advantaged, but rather the full entitlement of each person to what he has justly acquired. Whereas for Rawls, a central authority is entitled to distribute the fruits of everyone's labor, for Nozick, only the individual is entitled to the fruits of his own labor, and he has full rights to the use and disposal of them.

Although these are merely the positions of two philosophers, they express both the principal argument for regarding equality as the only just distribution, and the principal argument for regarding inequalities as justified and equality

Reprinted with permission from *The Public Interest*, no. 43 (Spring 1976): 121–128. Copyright © 1976 by National Affairs, Inc.

as an artificially imposed state. The equality position begins with an imagery of a set of benefits held by a central authority; and the question is then raised: How shall these benefits be distributed? Isaiah Berlin has expressed well this position in his answer to that question:

> . . . no reason need be given . . . for an equal distribution of benefits—for that is "natural"—self-evidently right and just, and needs no justification. . . . If I have a cake and there are 10 persons among whom I wish to divide it, then if I give exactly one tenth to each, this will not, at any rate automatically, call for justification; whereas if I depart from this principle of equal division I am expected to produce a special reason.

The inequality position begins with a very different imagery: a set of individuals each having produced certain goods through his own skills and efforts. The question is then asked: Who has the right to these goods? the answer is as self-evident as the answer to the parallel quesiton raised by the equality position: Each has the right to the product of his labor until and unless he chooses to transfer some portion of it to another (or perhaps to a central authority for redistribution). According to this position, imposition of equality in benefits constitutes a significant loss of rights, not only for the "haves," but also for the "have nots" (for after redistribution, they must be restrained from market transactions that would destroy the pure equality and reinstate inequality).

Now what do these two positions imply for education? Rawls's position implies erasing all the "accidents of birth" which give one person more opportunity than another, and thus creating a full equalization of opportunity for each child. As political philosophers have long noted, this necessitates removing the child from all influences of his family—because families provide differential opportunity—and raising him as a ward of the state, subject to precisely the same conditions as any other child.[1]

Nozick's position implies, in contrast, no system of public education at all. For public education is redistributive, and by Nozick's "entitlement" principles each child is entitled to the full untaxed benefits of his family's resources, insofar as it chooses to use those resources for his benefit. Thus for Nozick, all education is private, paid for individually by each family according to its resources and preferences.

These are extreme positions; few persons would assent to the educational structure implied by either. And it is clear from the extreme educational structures they imply that neither position can be a correct expression of a just society. For if justice in society requires a Rawlsian solution, then justice must also bring many undesirable consequences in its wake. And if justice in society requires no more than a Nozickian solution, then the sins of the fathers are indeed visited on the sons, with no outside alleviating influence to mitigate the inheritance of advantage or disadvantage.

Yet these two extreme positions are useful, because they show the different ends toward which each philosophical position points, and they sensitize us to what is gained or lost by moving in either direction. By moving in the direction of equality, we lose individual liberty in a central authority which imposes equality; and by moving in the direction of individual liberty, we lose equality to the accidents of birth reinforced by the market and the institution of private property.

The existence of the family is a negation of Rawls's position; the existence of the public school is a negation of Nozick's position. But the balance of power between the family and the school, and the balance of power among the forces that control the school, reflect the balance in society between these two positions. As the latter balance shifts, then there will be a shift in the relative power of family and school, and a shift in the character of the school itself. Before examining the principal issues of equality and liberty that have arisen in the schools, it is useful to examine some general processes that have changed American public educaiton since its inception, processes that have implications for these issues.

Public education in America from the outset had two properties: It was locally financed and controlled, and it was egalitarian. Local communities set up, ran, and oversaw their own schools, with only slight aid, encouragement, or interference from the state, and none from the federal government. But because this country had no remnants of the hierarchical feudal society which spawned a two-tier public school system in Europe, but had instead an egalitarian ethic, the public schools were *common* schools—one school for children from all walks of life. To be sure, there were private schools used by some, particularly in the less egalitarian East, but as the public school movement grew, the single, common public school became the overwhelmingly dominant institution in American education. The schools showed some homogeneity, because different communities and, in the cities, different neighborhoods had different populations. Yet, in general, the banker's son and the laborer's son went to the same school, because their fathers lived and worked in the same community. (The dual school system of the South was an aberration, a persistent residue of slavery.) I don't mean to imply that the "common school' was highly egalitarian in practice: The very social diversity of its population led to practices within it designed to preserve the advantages of some and to reproduce, without too much reshuffling, the social structure of the preceding generation. Yet the school remained a common school, in which children from all social levels mixed—and in smaller communities of that early period, social levels were not as far apart in social style as they are today. If a family was strongly opposed to anything about a child's school, but without the money for private school, it could move to satisfy its educational tastes; or in some cities with optional attendance zones or city-wide schools, it could choose another school without changing residence. But these choices were highly constrained, because limitation in transportation kept residence, workplace, and school physically close.

However, in more recent years, particularly since World War II, several developments have greatly altered the patterns of the early public shools. One is the great growth of metropolitan areas and the concomitant decline of the independent small town. For the first time, most American children were attending school in a city of some size or the suburbs surrounding it. Parallel with this was the growth of a remarkably flexible and adaptable transportaion system based on the automobile. These two changes, together with a general increase in affluence for all—and thus a greater range of economic options—made possible the separation of workplace from residence, and the development of large socially homogeneous residential areas served by socially homogeneous schools. In principle, the possibilities of choosing a school by choosing residence had not changed; but in practice, the possibilities had expanded greatly, as residence anywhere in the metropolitan area became a practical possibility for many persons in many cities. The result was a much greater social homogeneity of the population within each school, and an erosion of the egalitarian principle that underlay the common school. These possibilities coincided with the large-scale movement of blacks to large cities in the South and particularly in the North. This accelerated the residential homogenization and the choice of school by choice of residence.

At the same time, there were more subtle changes taking place in the control and financing of schools. School districts became larger and more removed from the effective control of parents in the community. State governments substantially increased their financing of schools and began to exercise more control over school policy and operations; and in 1965 the federal government began for the first time to add to general school finances— and with this financial wedge gained the possibility of some control. At present, over the country as a whole, just about half of school finances are provided by state and federal funds: about 41 per cent provided from state government and about nine per cent from the federal government.

Thus at the same time that schools were homogenizing—increasing the separation of social classes and races through residential choice—the localism of school control was giving way to large districts and a financial structure appropriate for the exercise of state and federal power. What had happened was two movements in opposing directions: on the one hand, a movement toward greater local differentiation and greater social homogeneity of individual schools; and on the other hand, a movement away from local finance and control of schools and toward increasingly centralized finance and control. The first movement was a movement away from the egalitarian principle of the common school; the second was a movement that placed more power in centralized hands that could attempt to reinstate the egalitarian principle, or to impose new, even more stringent, egalitarian measures.

The impasse to which these two movements have led is the impasse that currently confronts schools. There has been an increased exercise of residential choice of school, a right which most persons regard as a natural right (in Nozick's sense), and at the same time attempts by government agencies at the district, state, and federal levels, to impose equality of opportunity through restriction or withdrawal of this right. There are two major issues in education where this impasse has occurred; school finance and school desegregation.

The most direct clash of two principles of liberty and equality has occurred over the imposition of compulsory busing within school districts; and an even more intense clash appears ahead with the possibility of compulsory busing across school district lines within a metropolitan area. I am not discussing here school desegregation that rectifies the discriminatory actions of school boards and school administrations. But by definition, nearly all busing seeks to rectify that school segregation which arises from residential segregation—that is, from individual choice. By compulsory busing I mean the assignment of children by a central authority to schools at some distance from their homes to insure that all schools have a similar racial composition.

It is useful to pause for a moment and ask just how the issue of compulsory busing relates to the positions of Rawls and Nozick regarding equality versus liberty. Compulsory busing of children within a jurisdiction involves two ideas: first, that different children, because of their differing backgrounds, constitute resources for the learning of other children; and second, that a central authority has the right to redistribute such "resources" equally among all children. Opposition to compulsory busing accepts the first idea, but rejects the second: If there is to be redistribution, opponents of busing hold that this is a matter to be left up to individual parents who, through their choice of residence, decide where their children go to school. The advocates of compulsory busing (whether within the city, within the metropolitan area, or within some differently defined jurisdiction) subscribe to the premise underlying the arguments for equality: Resources or benefits are under the legitimate control of a central authority, not of individuals. Opponents subscribe to the premise underlying the arguments for liberty and against equality: Resources or benefits are under the legitimate control of the individuals who generate them (the family—or at a later age, the children themselves), not of a central authority.

Much can be said against both positions. The first is obviously a violation of individual rights as they have existed in this country. The second is blind to one fact: Exercise of individual rights under reduced external constraints (i.e., reduced constraints on contiguity of workplace and home) can lead to great increases in inequality. When the physical constraints that ensured the diversity of the common school in early days no longer exist, the result is social homogeneity within the school and social diversity between schools. In this situation, there are two obvious policy alternatives, and a third that is not so obvious:

1. Withdrawing individual rights, vesting them in a central authority which can assign children from different backgrounds in equal measures to all schools. This option attaches total value to equality, and is indifferent to any loss of liberty that may result.

2. Retaining the individual rights of families and children to the choice of school by choice of residence. This option attaches total value to individual liberty, and is indifferent to whatever inequality may result.

3. Rather than withdrawing rights from those who have the (economic) power to exercise them effectively, enlarging the rights of others. This is a

less obvious alternative to both positions that provides a set of "countervailing rights" which when exercised will increase equality rather than inequality. In the case of busing, this alternative would be to provide any child in a metropolitan area the right to transfer to a school of his choice, so long as the receiving school has a smaller proportion of his race than the school he leaves. The school would be required to accept children from outside its attendance zone, up to its capacity (which would be arbitrarily defined as a fixed percentage of the student body). Thus the right to choose school by residence remains; but in addition, the right is added to choose a school even if a family is otherwise effectively excluded, by economics or by race, from the residential area of that school—a right that when exercised reduces inequality. By this alternative full equality is not realized, nor is the full liberty of the economically advantaged to maintain homogeneous schools realized. But neither is equality fully sacrificed for that liberty, nor is liberty fully sacrficed for equality. And in addition, a new liberty or right is provided for those previously without it (I should mention that I am not the first to suggest this alternative. Congressman Richardson Preyer has introduced in Congress a "National Educational Opportunities Act" affirming this principle.)

If the addition of this right did not create desegregation to the degree desired by the community (that is, if the community regards a greater degree of desegregation as a public good), then the proper solution according to this alternative would not be to remove liberty by coercive reassignment of children to achieve racial balance. The costs of this public good should be borne, instead, by the same group that demanded the greater degree of desegregation—that is, the community as a while. Schools that are less integrated than desired could only use inducements to obtain a more heterogeneous student body. The most obvious inducement would be a direct payment from public funds to the family of any child whose enrollment would make the school more heterogeneous. Thus the liberty to attend the school of one's choice remains, and a degree of equality is realized at the expense of a tax on the community as a whole.

The second area of impasse between the two movements—toward social homogeneity of schools, and away from local finance and control—is equity in school finance. So long as schooling was locally financed from the relatively self-contained economies of independent towns and cities, few problems of equity arose among school districts. As with Nozick's position concerning individual liberty, each school district was regarded as entitled to its own resources, locally generated and locally held, whatever inequalities may have resulted. But the situation has changed, in part, to resemble that presupposed by the Rawlsian imagery: Half the school resources are now collected by a central authority (the state or federal government) and redistributed to local levels. In such a circumstance, the presuppositions behind the notion of equality in financing are met—for at least half the finances—and Berlin's or Rawls's arguments for equality become persuasive. In this case, the issue of liberty versus equality is a little different: It is the liberty not of the individual, but of the local school district, to use freely its own resources for its own schools. And it is the equality, or equity, not among individuals but among districts, which opposes this district-level liberty.

This issue has arisen in several court cases in which the plaintiffs demanded equal financing by the state, or at least financing in which the level of expenditure is made independent of the wealth of the district. The plaintiffs lost in the Supreme Court, but the issue remains alive, in state courts and legislatures.

The principle in this case seems less in dispute than in the case of school segregation: Individual rights to keep one's own resources for the schooling of one's own children have been voluntarily surrendered long ago by votes to impose taxes for public schooling. So school resources are now, and have been, collected and redistributed from a central authority. The only point at issue is the *size* of the unit within which equal expenditures are to occur: Is it the local school district, the state, or even the nation as a whole? Equal expenditures at the last of these levels, the national level, are not currently an issue, probably because of the small fraction of total school expenditures that are federally financed. It is between the other two levels that the issue lies.

As in the issue of school segregation, there exist two obvious alternatives, and a third that is not so obvious:

1. Expanding the equality position, providing full state funding. This forecloses the liberty of individual districts to spend more on education by taxing themselves more heavily, and it does so to insure full equality of financing for all children in the state. (The issue is made more complex by the different costs of education in different localities of a state, but I will ignore these complexities here.)

2. Maintaining the position of liberty for local communities by maintaining local taxation and local decision-making about the level of expenditure. State supplementation occurs as at present, but with no attempt to constrain expenditures of local districts in the name of equality. This position ignores the principle of equality throughout the state, except in a secondary way through state supplementation, in order to preserve the liberty of individual districts to use their taxes as they see fit for education.

3. Neither maintaining the full liberty of local control nor wholly discarding it in favor of equity. This alternative to both positions would be to permit each district to determine its own *rate* of taxation, based on the desired level of expenditure for education; but the taxable wealth is in effect equalized throughout the state; so that two districts which vote the same tax *rate* will raise the same educational *revenues* per pupil, though one district may contain little taxable property and the other much. This proposal has been made by others, and I merely restate it here (John Coons, William Clune, and Stephen Sugarman, *Private Wealth and Public Education*, Cambridge, Belknap Press, 1970). This alternative, like the third alternative in the issue of school segregation, does not achieve full equality, nor does it sacrifice full liberty. It gives each district in effect the same wealth, and then allows the district the liberty of determining its tax rate for education.

*   *   *

It is not often that theoretical statements in disciplines as arcane as academic moral philosophy are directly relevant to issues of social policy, or are in such sharp opposition on these issues. But the recent theoretical statements by John Rawls and Robert Nozick are both relevant and im-compatible concerning the two central issues of current educational policy, and they illumnate the moral or philosophical bases on which the opposing policy positions are grounded. The benefit of drawing out the policy implications of these philosophical theories lies not in any greater persua-siveness lent to the respective policies; on neither issue does the policy position that I personally favor (the third alternative on both issues) follow from either Rawls's or Nozick's theory. Rather, the benefit lies in showing the inherent conflicts in educational policy between equality (which Rawls elevates to supremacy) and liberty (which is supreme for Nozick). And the connection in moral theory between the conception of centrally held resources and a principle of equality (evident in the work of both Berlin and Rawls) suggests the social conditions under which the principle of equality will gain greater or lesser ascendancy. In addition, the fact that for certain policies (such as school desegregation) children themselves are regarded as resources implies that however centralized the financial resources of the schools are, these human resources—not centrally held, but rather products of individual families—will offset the centrally held resources, thus providing the context in which natural rights theories (like that of Nozick) are persuasive.

Notes

1. There are passages in Rawls's book which indicate that he does not envision such a radical transformation of the child's environment. Nevertheless, such a transformation does follow quite directly from his position concerning permissible inequalities.

5

What Is Meant by 'an Equal Educational Opportunity'?

The term 'equality of educational opportunity' has occasioned in recent years enormous confusion. The confusion centers around one issue: the question of whether such equality implies equality of input school resources or equality of results of schooling. The reason that the issue cannot be laid to rest by fixing on one of these definitions is that neither definition, neither inputs nor outputs, is viable when taken at the extreme.

If equality outputs is taken as the definition, then it appears incapable of being achieved, because of the massive unequal influences in the environments of different children—particularly families which differ sharply in what they are able to give to their children, educationally. Perhaps the most pervasive research result of recent research in educational achievement, from that of *Equality of Educational Opportunity* (1966) onwards (including Mosteller & Moynihan, *On Equality of Educational Opportunity*, 1972), the *Harvard Educational Review* special publication, *Perspectives on Inequality* (1973) and Jencks, *Inequality* (1973), is the strength of effect of family differences in creating achievement differences among children, compared to the relative weakness of effect of school differences. Thus no one except an advocate of state omnipotence with full power to extract a child from its unequalizing family environment could consistently maintain a definition of equality of educational opportunity in terms of results.

If equality of input school resources is taken as the definition, then two serious objections arise: one is that such equality would be upheld even if the total school resources provided to each child were minimal, and in the extreme, absent altogether. Thus interpreted in this way, 'equality of educational opportunity' is quite compatible with little or no schooling. The second objection is that some children (say handicapped children or children whose native language is not English) may require more input school resources if any kind of reasonable results are to be achieved. Consequently, no one, on humanitarian grounds, would want to restrict those children to

Reprinted with permission from *Oxford Review of Education*, vol. 1, no. 1 (1975): 27–29.

exactly the same, or equivalent, input school resources as other children receive.

But if equality of educational opportunity means neither equality of output nor equality of input resources, then what does it mean? The answer, I have concluded after examining the issue for a long time, is that it is not a meaningful term. If conceived in terms of results of schooling, it is unachievable, and if conceived in terms of input school resources it is a weak term that offers little constitutional protection. Thus I think we must resort to atempting to understand what is intended by a court or a legislative body in use of the term 'equal educational opportunity'. In the case of the legislative body representing diverse interests, there may be many different conceptions obscured by the single term. In planning the research for *Equality of Educational Opportunity,* I and my staff undertook to assess the possible definitions of equality of educational opportunity held by the Congress, and arrived at five different conceptions, embracing both input-oriented and output-oriented conceptions.

When we turn to the Surpreme Court in its statement, the surrounding language indicates that they had in mind something attentive to output, without going so far as the kind of actions that a full equality measure in terms of output would imply. Something of this sort is what does, in fact, appear most reasonable. Equality of educational results is wholly unachievable (at least without state intervention in the family to the extent of taking the child completely out of it); yet equality defined according to inputs is inattentive to the effects of education which is the whole purpose of public schooling. What appears to be at the base of the idea of equality of educational opportunity as used by the Court is a public educational system that is sufficiently effective to prevent, for normally intelligent children, the disadvantages that result from their family circumstances from handicapping them severely in adult life, in occupation and otherwise. The word 'equality' seems misplaced in the term: in its usage by the Court (which is, I believe, its most common and most reasonable usage), the idea seems to be more nearly one of education leading to equality of adult opportunity than of equal educational opportunity. Thus education is a means to an end, not an end in itself, and equal opportunity refers to later life rather than the educational process itself. Even here, however, the word 'equality' is either too strong or the word 'opportunity' must be regarded as purely formal, not substantive opportunity. For equality of effective opportunity in competition as an adult is again unachievable through schooling, even an unequalized schooling that would attempt to compensate for initial handicaps.

What does appear achievable and attentive to results is the idea of effective public schooling that leads *in the direction of* equal adult opportunities. Such a formulation implies that public schooling is to reduce handicaps that children face as a function of their early environments, without committing the educational system to an unachievable end.

These matters cannot be properly understood without an understanding of the relative responsibility of the school and of the student for his achievement, and how that responsibility has shifted over time. In the early days of public schools in the United States, the community's responsibility was seen to lie only in providing free and available facilities of reasonably high quality, including teachers, and all else was the child's and parent's responsibility. That division of responsibility has shifted over time until it is now regarded as largely the community's responsiblity to insure that the child takes advantage of the facilities. That is, there has been a shift somewhat similar to the disappearance of the concept of 'caveat emptor' from the buyer-seller relationship in private goods markets. The seller now has legal responsibility for a variety of matters relating to the quality, safety, and efficacy of the product he sells. Similarly with schools: it is now commonly regarded as the schools' responsibility to motivate the child to learn, to teach him reading and not merely to provide free facilities for learning to read. How far does this responsibility go? Certainly it cannot encompass everything, absolving the child completely from any responsibility concerning his learning. The school can never go beyond joint responsibility with the child and his family for his learning. It can accept that partial responsibility, and current norms imply that it must. But it can do so only subject to the state of the art, subject to the realm of authority it has over the child's activities, and subject to the amount of resources the community is willing to commit to public education.

Although then, I believe that the concept of 'equality of educational opportunity' is a mistaken and misleading concept. It is mistaken because it locates the 'equality of opportunity' within the educational institutions, and thus focuses attention on eduction as an end in itself rather than as properly it is, a means to ends achieved in adulthood. It is misleading because it suggests that equal educational opportunity, defined in something other than a purely formal (input) way, is achievable, while it is not. A proper formulation would use the term 'reduction in inequality . . .' rather than 'equality. . .' . Such a formulation would properly connote the fact that the initial state in which schools find children, and the continuing environments outside the school that compete for the child's time, are unequal, and that the school's task is—besides increasing opportunity for all, through what it imparts—to reduce the unequalizing impact on adult life of these differential environments.

PART TWO

Equality of Educational Opportunity

Equality of Educational Opportunity examines two major questions: What is the existing degree of inequality of educational opportunity by race? What are the principal aspects of the school system that lead to this inequality?

As the chapters of Part 1 made evident, the first of these questions raises the complications of exactly what constitutes inequality of educational opportunity. Stated most simply, this is the principal question: Can inequality of opportunity be measured solely through examination of inputs to the educational process, or does it require measuring outputs as well? Chapter 2 in Part 1 makes clear the position that guided the *Equality of Educational Opportunity* survey and report: Although the measurement of inputs would accord with the definitions of inequality of opportunity that some interested parties and many in the educational establishment hold, it is not sufficient to assess effective inequality of opportunity. In order to go beyond a merely formal definition of the degree of inequality, the measurement of outputs of education, and the correspondence between variations in outputs and variations in inputs is necessary.

It is this perspective that occasioned most of the controversy surrounding the report, and it is this perspective that led to the principal policy implications of the report. Part 2 gives a brief summary of the report (Chapter 6), then extracts (in Chapter 7) from that section of the report responsible for most of the controversy and most of the policy uses. The controversy surrounded both the methods of analysis used in this section and the policy implications; two of the chapters (Chapters 10 and 11) address the methods issues, and two (Chapters 8 and 9) address the policy issues. As these chapters make clear, policy issues in such an arena cannot be separated from questions of definition and of method.

One element clearly illustrates this last point. This element concerns the *intensity* of school influences. One of the results of the analysis carried out in the *Equality of Educational Opportunity* report is that a major source of inequality of opportunity lies not in the distribution of either material or social school resources by race, but in the lack of intensity of the schooling experience. Because out-of-school resources and environment are highly unequal, while school resources are much more alike (as found by the report), it follows that opportunity will come to be more equal as the intensity of school experience increases relative to out-of-school experience.

This result has implications both for method and policy. Chapter 11, which focuses on the design of future research on equality of educational opportunity, examines some of the implications for method. Chapter 8 discusses implications for policy. But as Chapter 11 makes clear, the implications for policy cannot become apparent if the methods used in the research allow the researcher or the policy analyst to overlook the intensity of the schooling experience.

The discussion of intensity and its importance for equalization of opportunity also leads back to the issues of moral philosophy examined in Part 1. My claim there is that a major error of Rawls's conception of the just society was his assumption that inequalities arose primarily from governmental or economic institutions beyond the family. The implications of this conception are that mere equality of treatment by these institutions will create a just society. However, the research results argue that a more active stance is implied. Children bring extensive inequalities with them from their family environments. Equality of opportunity requires not simply the equalization of resources from institutions outside the family; it requires recognition that most of the inequalities are generated from within the family and that equalization of opportunities depends as much on the strength of the schooling resources as it does on the equality of resource distribution.

6

A Brief Summary
of the Coleman Report

The *Equality of Educational Opportunity* Report contains seven sections dealing with different aspects of educational opportunity (sections 2–8), a summary of the Report (section 1), and technical appendices (section 9) which are separately bound.

Of the seven sections dealing with equal educational opportunity, sections 2 and 3 have been seen as the most relevant to questions of school policy, and it is almost exclusively the conclusions represented in these sections that have been the subject of the discussion and controversy surrounding the Report. These sections describe the results of a national survey which covered approximately 4000 elementary and secondary schools. This large survey study was designed to identify the extent and sources of inequality of educational opportunity among six racial and ethnic groups (blacks, Puerto Ricans, American Indians, Mexican Americans, Oriental Americans, and whites).

In this summary, I will first review briefly the range of topics that were investigated in the less well-known sections of the report and then summarize the major findings of sections 2 and 3 which have been the focus of controversy.

Section 4 describes the results of a survey of colleges and universities in which black and white teachers are trained. Since nearly all white students are taught by white teachers, and most black students (nearly all in the South, fewer than half in the North) are taught by black teachers, the results of this survey show the level of skill to which the teachers of the next generation of black and white students have been brought, giving some indication of the degree to which inequalities of opportunity may be self-perpetuating through racial matching of teachers and students.

Section 5 shows the distribution of blacks and other non-whites in colleges with various characteristics. The basic data on characteristics of colleges

Reprinted with permission from James S. Coleman, *Equal Educational Opportunity* (Cambridge, Mass.: Harvard University Press, 1969), pp. 253–259.

were taken from existing records, principally those from the regular surveys of the Higher Education Branch of the U.S. Office of Education. No new data were collected for section 5. However, since the Office of Education did not begin collecting data on the racial composition of student bodies before 1965, this section contains the first tabulation of the distribution of blacks and of other nonwhites in colleges with various characteristics. The characteristics include a number ordinarily used to assess the quality of a college: student-faculty ratio, percentage of the faculty with doctoral degrees, average faculty salary, expenditure per student, the presence of Phi Beta Kappa and AAUP chapters, and library resources.

Section 6 addresses an aspect of educational opportunity that could not be studied in the main survey of public schools: nonenrollment, or school dropout. Since the main survey was based on a sample of schools, the rate of nonenrollment at given age levels could not be determined. Consequently, data on nonenrollment for whites are reported from two sources: the 1960 decennial census, and a special addition to the October 1965 Current Population Survey of the Census Bureau. These tabulations show nonenrollment for whites and nonwhites aged 16 and 17 years old grouped by various other social characteristics: region, sex, metropolitan-nonmetropolitan, religion, and white-collar vs. non-white-collar father's occupation.

Section 7 consists of excerpts from a number of qualitative community studies carried out as part of the over-all study. These community studies examined the social and political forces involved in achievement of, or resistance to, racial integration in the schools. The studies were carried out in metropolitan areas and smaller communities, in the North and the South, and thus examined attempts to overcome both *de facto* segregation and *de jure* segregation.

Section 8 reports on four special analyses that were carried out from the data of the large national survey. One is an analysis of the performance of children who had participated in Project Headstart. The second is an examination of the effect of a foreign language spoken in the home upon verbal skills. The third and fourth are analyses of differences in the availability to black and white students of guidance counselors and vocational education. These last two analyses are extensions of the analysis of section 2, carried out for these two school resources.

This elaboration of the outline shows the variety and range of topics covered in the report. I will make no attempt here to summarize the results from all these sections. Although these sections give comprehensiveness and in some cases can provide statistics for reference purposes, there are only two sections of relevance to the central policy questions that have arisen from the report, sections 2 and 3. It is only the results from these sections that I will discuss.

Section 2 constitutes an examination of the inequality of educational opportunity through a comparison of objective characteristics, most of which can be regarded as "resources" of the school or measures of its quality, in schools attended by each of the groups under study. These groups were

American Indians, Puerto Ricans (living in the United States proper), Mexican Americans, Oriental Americans, other whites, and blacks. The latter two groups were compared both nationally and in eight kinds of locations: the metropolitan Northeast, Midwest, South, Southwest, and West, and the nonmetropolitan North, West, South, and Southwest. Therefore, it is a straightforward statistical description of the intput resources of the schools in the survey, which were obtained from the superintendent's questionnaire, the principal's questionnaire, the teacher's questionnaire, and data from the students themselves.

The aim of section 2 is to give some indicators of inequality of opportunity by measuring qualities of inputs to schools, the most traditional conception of what constitutes school quality. It used the characteristics of schools that principals, superintendents, and school boards traditionally employ in comparing the "quality of education" their schools provide. These are items such as teachers' salary, the number of books in the library (and books per student), the age of buildings and of textbooks, the degrees of teachers and principals, specialized facilities and curricula, free kindergarten, and nearly all the objective measures of schools that exist in principals' records or that can be obtained from averaging responses of teachers to questionnaires. In addition, some less traditional measures of schools were used in comparing schools attended by each of the groups in question: the attitudes of the principals and teachers about their school, about their students, about the kinds of students they would most prefer to teach, and attitudes about school policy related to integration (for example, busing). In addition, teachers took a short vocabulary test. Finally, the chapter contains measures of another input to schools that obviously affects the opportunity of each student in the school: the characteristics of other students in the school. Their socioeconomic background and characteristics of their home environment, their race, their attitudes, and their aspirations were included in these tabulations.

The results of all these statistical comparisons can be summarized in only the most superficial way. They show differences between schools attended by each of the minorities and whites, and in particular between schools attended by blacks and whites in the same geographic region.[1] In general, the differences show whites attending schools with greater resources, although this is not uniformly true, and perhaps the most striking point is the small size of the differences. The differences between locales (in particular, North-South differences, and to a lesser extent, metropolitan-nonmetropolitan differences) are for most resources strikingly greater than within-locale or national differences between schools attended by minority students and those attended by whites.

This finding has been one of the conclusions in the Report most subject to attacks by its critics, who argue that differences in the resources of schools attended by blacks and whites are masked in one way or another. It is true that the reported differences do not show everything—for example, the fact that it probably costs more to run a school at the same level in the ghetto than in a suburb. To compete successfully for the same teachers, urban systems must pay higher salaries; among other things, depreciation on textbooks and buildings is greater, and the tabulation of numbers of books in the library does not show the quality of the books. Nevertheless, the criticism probably stems largely from the preconceptions that influence perception: many persons, white and black, when they see a school attended largely by black students, unconsciously depreciate it, seeing it as inferior, and then search for physical reasons to justify this perception.

The differences that do show up strongly in the mass of statistics in section 2 are largely differences in the student bodies. The fact that school boards do not control this input into the schools does not make it less important to a child who enters. Thus, although these differences emanate from the aggregate of students in the school, they are no less real for each student there.

The most striking of these differences is the racial difference in student bodies of schools attended by the average black and the average white. This segregation is greatest in the South and greatest in elementary grades, so that the segregation is greatest at elementary grades in the South, next in secondary grades in the South, next in elementary grades in the North, and least in secondary grades in the North.

Stemming fundamentally from this racial segregation, and from the lower economic and educational backgrounds of black students, the social and academic characteristics of the student environment experienced by the average black and the average white are very great—greater in fact than differences in any other characteristics of their respective schools.

Next to differences in student environment are the differences among teacher characteristics for black and white students, differences that are least in length of training, salary, and other external characteristics, and greatest in attitudes and scores on the vocabulary test. These differences too stem largely from the racial matching of students and teachers, a matching that is greatest in the South, but existent in the North as well. Thus one might summarize these differences in school characteristics by saying that the major differences stem from the racial segregation of student bodies, and the racial matching of teachers and students. There are some differences in other inputs to schools, but these are not as large as had been generally believed.

Section 3 focuses on the outputs of schools, using achievement of various sorts as measures of output. The aim of the report was to use achievement output as the criterion by which various input differences might be evaluated: by assessing what inputs to the schools were most important for achievement, the relative importance of the intput differences found in section 2 could be determined, and in fact, by applying weights to these differences in terms of their relevance to achievement, a measure of the over-all inequality of opportunity for achievement could be constructed. The report was only partially successful in this, never reaching the final stage of providing such a measure. Nevertheless, the success was sufficient to be relevant to broad policy questions (in contrast to specific policy questions, such as the relative importance of providing bigger libraries or newer textbooks, or integrating schools by busing or by creating larger school district boundaries).

In the measurement of achievement itself, in section 3.1, a number of results were evident. In all areas of achievement tested (verbal skills, mathematical skills, and in higher grades, tests in practical knowledge, natural sciences, social sciences, and humanities), results were similar. The whites and oriental Americans achieved at comparable levels in all grades tested (1, 3, 8, 9, and 12), and the other minorities achieved at a level sharply lower, with blacks and Puerto Ricans achieving lowest of all. Over the span of grades from 1 to 12, the relative achievement of low-achieving groups declined. For blacks, this decline occurred in all areas except the metropolitan North. The decline was greatest in the South, and greatest of all in the nonmetropolitan South. Thus in the nonmetropolitan South, black students at grade 12 were about one and a half times as far below whites in that region as at grade 1 (about 1.5 standard deviations compared to about 1.0 at grade 1).

When the relative importance of school factors for achievement was assessed, achievement for each racial group separately was regressed upon various school factors, after family background characteristics were controlled. This control was carried out so that those school factors most highly correlated with family background would not spuriously show a high relation to achievement. In carrying out this control, however, the analysis showed what had already been well-known: the powerful relation of the child's own family background characteristics to his achievement, a relation stronger than that of any school factors.

In assessing the importance of various school factors for achievement, the school factors were grouped into three large clusters, and the additional variance in achievement accounted for by each cluster—after controlling on the student's own family background, and in some analyses, after controlling on other school factors as well—was examined. The clusters were teachers' characteristics, all school-facility and curriculum characteristics excluding teachers, and characteristics of the student environment, obtained by aggregating student characteristics in his grade in school.

The general result was that the factors that, under all conditions, accounted for more variance than any others were the characteristics of the student's peers; those that accounted for the next highest amount of variance were teachers' characteristics; and finally, other school characteristics, including per pupil expenditure on instruction in the system, accounted for very little variance at all. The total variance accounted for by these three sets of school factors was not large—in fact, an analysis of variance showed that only about 10 percent of the variance in achievement lay between schools (for each racial group separately), most of it residing within schools.

Another result was that the variance in achievement accounted for by school characteristics was least for whites, and most for southern blacks outside metropolitan areas. The inference was drawn that it is in general for the students from poorest family backgrounds that school characteristics were most important for achievement, but the analysis did not directly test this.

These results of the analysis of the relation of school characteristics to achievement have produced the largest portion of controversy surrounding the Report—a result which is to be expected, since they constituted the major causal inferences in the Report, and causal inferences from statistical analysis are always subject to debate, whether the issue be smoking and lung cancer or school factors and achievement.

The results clearly suggest that school integration across socioeconomic lines (and hence across racial lines) will increase black achievement, and they throw serious doubt upon the effectiveness of policies designed to increase non-personal resources in the school. A simple general statement of the major result is that the closest portions of the child's social environment—his family and his fellow-students—affect his achievement most, the more distant portion of his social environment—his teachers—affect it next most, and the non-social aspects of his school environment affect it very little. This of course is an oversimplification because of the interactions of some of these factors; but the results remain, with clear implications for school policies designed to increase the achievement of minority groups and lower-class white students.

Notes

1. An additional analysis compares the schools attended by the average minority group student and average white within the same county or metropolitan area.

7

Equality of
Educational Opportunity

JAMES S. COLEMAN, ERNEST Q. CAMPBELL,
CAROL J. HOBSON, JAMES McPARTLAND,
ALEXANDER M. MOOD, FREDERIC D. WEINFELD,
AND ROBERT L. YORK

3.22 School-to-School Variations in Achievement

The question of first and most immediate importance to this survey in the study of school effects is how much variation exists between the achievement of students in one school and those of students in another. For if there were no variation between schools in pupils' achievement, it would be fruitless to search for effects of different kinds of schools upon achievement.

Thus the variation in achievement that exists between schools represents an upper limit to the effect of factors that distinguish one school from another in its ability to produce achievement. But other factors as well may be responsible for these variations in achievement from school to school. It may be useful to list possible factors that could be involved in school-to-school achievement differences.

Possible sources of school-to-school variation in achievement are—

1. Differences from one school to another in school factors affecting achievement.
2. Differences from one community to another in family backgrounds of individual students, including abilities of students.
3. Differences from one community to another in influences outside school, apart from the student's own family.

Reprinted from James S. Coleman, Ernest Q. Campbell, Carol J. Hobson, James McPartland, Alexander M. Mood, Frederic D. Weinfeld, and Robert L. York, *Equality of Educational Opportunity* (Washington, D.C.: U.S. Government Printing Office, 1966), pp. 295–325 (excerpts).

Possible sources of within-school variation in achievement—

1. Differences in pupils' abilities in the same school.
2. Differences in family backgrounds of the pupils in the same school.
3. Differences in school experience among students within the same school (i.e., different teachers, different courses, etc.).
4. Different influences within the community on different students toward achievement (such as community attitudes which may discourage high achievement among lower status children, and encourage it among higher status children).

These two lists indicate that the finding of school-to-school variation in achievement is neither a necessary nor a sufficient basis for inferring the effect of school factors; other factors can cause variations among schools, and school factors can cause variations within a school. Nevertheless, when we find school-to-school variations in achievement, we can proceed with the use of the appropriate techniques, one step toward the identification of school factors producing different levels of achievement in different schools.

The effect of school factors in producing variations within a school cannot be assessed in this study, because data were not gathered on the differential experiences within school, such as the particular set of teachers in a school who had taught each student (except for those experiences that are highly dependent on a student's achievement itself; for example, the number of mathematics courses he has taken).

Thus the effects of school factors studied in this survey must manifest themselves in school-to-school variation in achievement. The task becomes one of separating the three possible sources of such variation, so that some idea can be gained of the magnitude of school effects.

Ordinarily, when one finds that the level of achievement in one school is much higher than the achievement in another, there comes to his mind these sources of difference: The different students with which the school begins, the different community settings, or student body climates which encourage or fail to encourage high achievement, and the differences in the school itself. When we find school-to-school variation in achievement, we shall keep these same sources of variation in mind. Part of the subsequent analysis will be an attempt to separate them out, so that some assessment of the effect of each can be made.

For each racial and ethnic group there is a total variation of test scores that can be divided into two parts: (1) a part consisting of the variations of individual scores of pupils in a school about the average score of his ethnic group in the school—this is the within-school variance; (2) a part consisting of the variations of the school averages about the average score of the Nation or region—this is the school-to-school or the between-school variance. Table 3.22.1 exhibits the percentage that the between-school variance is of the total variance. Examination of the figures shows that the

TABLE 3.22.1
Percent of Total Variance in Individual Verbal Achievement Scores that
Lies Between Schools*

	Grades				
	12	9	6	3	1
Mexican-Americans__	20. 20	15. 87	28. 18	24. 35	23. 22
Puerto Rican_____	22. 35	21. 00	31. 30	26. 65	16. 74
Indian Americans___	30. 97	24. 44	30. 29	37. 92	19. 29
Oriental Americans__	5. 07	5. 64	22. 47	16. 25	9. 54
Black South_____	22. 54	20. 17	22. 64	34. 68	23. 21
Black North_____	10. 92	12. 67	13. 89	19. 47	10. 63
White South_____	10. 11	9. 13	11. 05	17. 73	18. 64
White North_____	7. 84	8. 69	10. 32	11. 42	11. 07

*Corrected for degrees of freedom. See p. 327.

between-school part of the variance is about 5 percent to 35 percent of the total variance.

This table leads to the first important result in the assessment of school factors associated with achievement: School to school variations in achievement, from whatever source (community differences, variations in the average home background of the student body, or variations in school factors), are much smaller than individual variations within the school, at all grade levels, for all racial and ethnic groups. This means that most of the variation in achievement could not possibly be accounted for by school differences, since most of it lies within the school. The table presents only the results for verbal achievement, but as section 3.21 indicated, the results hold equally or even more strongly for other test scores. This result indicates that despite the wide range of diversity of school facilities, curriculum, and teachers, and despite the wide diversity among student bodies in different schools, over 70 percent of the variation in achievement for each group is variation within the same student body. The school-to-school difference is even less than overall figures for all groups indicate, because the school-to-school differences are generally least for blacks and whites, and it is these groups which are numerically greatest. Consequently, only about 10 to 20 percent of the total variation in achievement for the groups that are numerically most important lies between different schools.

A further examination of table 3.22.1 gives some indication of the possible sources of the school-to-school differences. The existence of variations among schools gives no indication of whether these differences are related to school factors, community differences in support of school achievement, or background differences. However, if these variations were largely a result of either school factors or community differences in support of school achievement, then the school-to-school differences would increase over the grades in school. (Because of different school sizes in elementary and secondary schools, direct comparison can be made only up through grade 6.) However, this is not the case; there is no consistent increase for all groups in grades 1–6, and only a slight increase when an average of all groups is taken. Grade 1 is the crucial case here, because the tests were given shortly after the beginning of school, and thus school factors could have had little effect— nor could community factors outside the family have had much effect (except insofar as they acted through the family). Thus, the school-to-school component of test score variance at grade 1 is almost wholly a measure of the skills with which children in different schools begin school. And as table 3.22.1 indicates, this school-to-school component is already large at grade 1, for whites as large as that at grade 3. Thus the larger part of school-to-school variation in achievement appears to be not a consequence of effects of school variations at all, but of variations in family backgrounds of the entering student bodies.

A reasonable conclusion is, then, that our schools have great uniformity insofar as their effect on the learning of pupils is concerned. The data suggest that variations in school quality are not highly related to variations in achievement of pupils. Section 3.1 showed this indirectly, in that achievement of those minority groups with poorest family backgrounds not only began lowest but remained so. Here, the comparison is wholly within each group, and indicates that the relative lack of effect of the school which is suggested by comparison among ethnic groups is true for variations in achievement within each group as well. The present data suggest why the minorities that begin with an educational disadvantage continue to exhibit this disadvantage throughout the twelve grades of school: The school appears unable to exert independent influences to make achievement levels less dependent on the child's background—and this is true within each ethnic group, just as it is between groups.

There are differences among the different ethnic groups in school-to-school variation in achievement. First, comparison of blacks and whites shows important differences. The school-to-school variations in achievement are larger in the South than in the North for both blacks and whites. However, it is among the blacks that these school-to-school variations are especially high in the South. This result, coupled with the fact that for the blacks and the other minority groups, the school-to-school component of variance increases from grade 1 to grade 3, while it does not for whites, leads to a third important result of the section. Indirect evidence suggests that school factors make more difference in achievement for minority group members than for whites; for blacks, this is especially true in the South. This result suggests that insofar as variations in school factors are related to variations in achievement, they make most difference for children of minority groups. The evidence is only indirect here, and the point requires further examination when school factors are explicitly studied in a later section: But at this point the indirect evidence suggests that it is those children who come least prepared to school, and whose achievement in school is generally low, for whom the characteristics of a school make the most difference.

These results suggest (and subsequent sections will reinforce this suggestion) that these children may be thought of as differing in sensitivity to variations in school quality. The data indicate that the least sensitive are in general those children from groups where achievement is highest at the beginning of school (and remains so), and the most sensitive are those with lowest initial levels of achievement. A rough order of the sensitivity to school effects can be obtained by inspection of table 3.22.1, giving perhaps the following order from high to low sensitivity:

> Puerto Rican
> Indian American
> Mexican-American
> Black, South
> Black, North
> Oriental American
> White, South
> White, North

Since it is important to assess whether in fact there is this general difference in sensitivity to school effects, the data in succeeding tables will be presented in the order indicated above. Thus if there is a general difference in sensitivity to school effects, the size of the relationship to school factors shown in subsequent tables should tend to become progressively less, moving down the table.

The overall results of this examination of school-to-school variations in achievement can be summed up in three statements:

1. For each group, by far the largest part of the variation in student achievement lies within the same school, and not between schools.
2. Comparison of school-to-school variations in achievement at the beginning of grade 1 with later years indicates that only a small part of it is the result of school factors, in contrast to family background differences between communities.
3. There is indirect evidence that school factors are more important in affecting the achievement of minority group students; among blacks, this appears especially so in the South. This leads to the notion of differential sensitivity to school variations, with the lowest achieving minority groups showing highest sensitivity.

In examining the ability of school variations to account for variance in individual achievement, these school-to-school variations in table 3.22.1 will constitute a kind of upper limit. Thus, in some cases, it will be useful to study the variance accounted for by a given factor relative to this upper limit, as well as to the overall variation in achievement. Two different questions are being answered: When the total variation in individual achievement is the standard, the question is what part of individual achievement can this variable account for? When the school-to-school variation from table 3.22.1 is the standard, the question is what part of the school-to-school variation in achievement does the variable account for?

To continue the focus on the overall effectiveness of particular factors, the subsequent tables will report percent of individual variance accounted for. Obviously, the amount accounted for will be quite low, since the upper limit is itself low. To determine the proportion of school-to-school variance accounted for, the numbers in table 3.22.1 may be taken as upper limits.

3.221 The Influence of Student Background Factors on Achievement

Before examining the relation of school characteristics to student achievement, it is useful to examine the influence of student background characteristics. Because these background differences are prior to school influence, and shape the child before he reaches school, they will, to the extent we have succeeded in measuring them, be controlled when examining the effect of school factors. This means that the achievement differences among schools which are due only to differences in student input can be in part controlled, to allow for more accurate examination of the apparent effects of differences in school or teacher factors themselves.

It is useful, then, at the outset, to examine the relation of these background factors to achievement, to get a view of some of the family factors that predispose children to learn well or poorly in school. The survey cannot investigate the effects of background factors in detail, but it is critically important to control as much of their effect as possible before examining school factors.

A preliminary analysis of the relation of particular background factors to achievement showed that family background differences measured in this survey could be clustered into eight variables. The relation of these variables to achievement will be examined only at grades 12, 9, and 6, since several of the questions were not (and most could not have successfully been) asked of the children at grades 3 and 1. (Except where indicated below, the question numbers refer to the 12th and 9th grade questionnaires. If the question content differs for the sixth grade, indication will be made.)

A (1) (Grades 9 and 12) Urbanism of background (based on Q6 and Q21 about community in which self and mother grew up); (2) (Grade 6) Migration (based on Q3 and Q13 about own and mother's birthplace).

B Parents' education (based on Q19 and Q20 about mother's and father's education).

C Structural integrity of the home (based on Q18 and Q17 about mother and father in the home).

D Smallness of family (number of brothers and sisters, in a negative direction (based on Q10).

E Items in home (based on Q31, Q32, Q33, Q34, Q37, and Q38: TV, telephone, record player, refrigerator, automobile, vacuum cleaner).

F Reading material in home (based on Q35, Q36, Q39, Q41, and Q42: Dictionary, encyclopedia, daily newspaper, magazines, books. Last two items missing in 6th grade).

G Parents' interest (based on Q26 and Q30: Talk with parents about school; anyone read to you when small).

H Parents' educational desires (based on Q24, Q25, Q27, Q28, and Q29: How good a student do mother and father want child to be; how far in school do mother and father want child to go; attendance at PTA. Last three items missing in 6th grade).

These clusters of variables range from factors in the parents' background (father's and mother's education, urbanism of background) to factors which describe the present interest in his school work that his parents show. In all cases, the data are based on the child's report, which may include distortions or misperceptions or absence of information, especially at grade 6.

One way of examining the influence of background factors on achievement is to examine the percent of within-school variance and the percent of school-to-school variance accounted for by these family factors. First, taking the school-to-school variations as given, and examining the added variance accounted for by family background characteristics shows what portion of the within-school variance may be accounted for by these factors. This is a severe restriction, because from table 3.221.2 it appears that much of the school-to-school variance is itself a result of family background differences. Table 3.221.1 shows at grades 12, 9, and 6, the variation accounted for at each of these stages, first by the objective conditions in the home, as reported by the child, then by these plus "subjective" background factors, and finally, in addition, by his own attitudes. The table shows that at each grade level, the amount of within-school variance accounted for by these factors taken together is of the same order of magnitude as the variance associated with school-to-school factors. For whites and for Oriental Americans especially, the percent of within-school variance accounted for by objective family conditions (b, and those plus subjective family conditions (c) is very great. For all groups, the total variance accounted for, including the school-to-school variation (column a) and the within-school variation explained by background and attitudes, is between 30 percent and 50 percent of the total variance in achievement.

Second, we may ask about the proportion of school-to-school variance accounted for by background factors. Taking the variance in column (2) of table 3.221.1 as the total variance to be explained, the question becomes what percent of this school-to-school variance is accounted for by these same background factors? Table 3.221.2 shows the percent of school-to-school variance (of which the total as a percent of individual variance is given in column (a) of table 3.221.1) is accounted for by the same background factors as in the third column of table 3.221.1. Much of the effect of these

TABLE 3.221.1

Percent of Variance Accounted for in Verbal Achievement at Grades 6, 9, and 12, by Successively Adding Additional Factors [A Variance associated with school-to-school differences (measured and unmeasured),[1] B objective background factors (as reported by student) added (A through F); C subjective background factors added (G and H); D child's attitudes added (1) interest in school, (2) self-concept, (3) control of environment]

	A	A+B	A+B+C	A+B+C+D
Grade 12:				
Puerto Ricans	23.40	24.69	26.75	31.54
Indian Americans	24.13	30.73	34.81	43.61
Mexican Americans	20.07	22.60	26.09	34.33
Black, South	22.15	26.17	28.18	38.97
Black, North	11.19	15.34	18.85	31.04
Oriental Americans	2.33	13.65	21.99	32.04
White, South	10.39	18.14	24.06	39.07
White, North	8.25	17.24	27.12	40.09
Blacks, total	20.90	24.73	27.31	38.18
Whites, total	9.49	17.93	26.42	39.80
Grade 9:				
Puerto Ricans	16.77	19.11	21.88	30.41
Indian Americans	19.75	25.89	29.31	36.64
Mexican Americans	20.28	25.26	27.79	34.10
Black, South	18.55	22.84	26.93	38.88
Black, North	8.96	13.84	17.73	30.48
Oriental Americans	7.36	17.58	27.66	34.93
White, South	10.50	21.54	26.63	42.09
White, North	8.31	19.32	25.55	39.56
Blacks, total	17.43	21.68	25.47	37.21
Whites, total	10.00	20.78	26.57	40.90
Grade 6:				
Puerto Ricans	22.49	34.25	36.40	40.35
Indian Americans	26.67	33.93	35.05	41.20
Mexican Americans	37.60	35.79	37.74	45.04
Black, South	22.25	27.95	28.89	37.69
Black, North	11.86	16.97	17.93	26.39
Oriental Americans	24.31	41.20	42.25	51.76
White, South	12.33	21.58	23.52	34.61
White, North	12.77	19.95	21.70	35.77
Blacks, total	19.77	24.83	25.77	34.12
Whites, total	13.71	21.25	23.06	35.95

[1] The first column is only an estimate of the school-to-school variations in achievement for each group, obtained by regressing individual achievement on overall school mean achievement (for all groups together) and proportion white. These two measures together (except for the presence of third groups in the school) provide an estimate of the group's mean score in the school under the assumption that differences between the white mean and the group mean are constant over all schools.

TABLE 3.221.2
Percent of School-to-School Variance in Verbal Achievement (approximated by mean school achievement, controlling on proportion white in school) Accounted for by Eight Background Factors (see (B) and (C) in Table 3.221.1). Variance explained is a percent of that shown in column (A) of Table 3.221.1.

	Grade 12	Grade 9	Grade 6
Puerto Ricans_____	3. 05	4. 74	7. 54
Indian Americans_____	2. 96	3. 41	7. 28
Mexican Americans_____	11. 56	10. 49	6. 55
Black, South_____	32. 69	23. 47	12. 37
Black, North_____	12. 25	7. 37	6. 75
Oriental Americans_____	5. 67	7. 24	28. 36
White, South_____	28. 86	23. 82	19. 96
White, North _____	15. 99	14. 42	10. 99
Blacks, total _____	29. 05	21. 82	12. 80
Whites, total_____	21. 89	21. 28	17. 09

individual background factors is within schools, as shown by table 3.221.1, but table 3.221.2 shows that an additional amount is associated with school-to-school differences in achievement. This table, together with the following one, shows the strength of background factors in accounting for the variation in achievement, both within and among schools.

The overall variance in verbal achievement including both within- and between-school related to these background factors is shown in table 3.221.3. Three columns are shown in the table for each grade, the first consisting of the variance accounted for by the first six background factors alone, excluding the parents' interest and aspirations (as reported by the child). The second column shows the variance accounted for by all eight, and the third column is the difference between the first two, showing the added variance accounted for by parents' interest and aspirations for the child.

The table shows that overall, the background factors measured by these six or eight variables account for about 10 percent to 25 percent of variance in individual achievement. There are, of course, many other aspects of the child's background that are not measured here; thus the variance accounted for by these variables can be interpreted as a kind of lower limit to the actual effects of background differences. (This is the opposite situation to that for school-to-school variation, where the variation between schools constituted an upper limit to the amount that could be related to school differences.)

The data show a number of variations among grade levels and among different groups. First, the six measures of objective conditions in the home account for more of the variance in achievement at earlier grades than at

TABLE 3.221.3
Percent of Variance in Verbal Achievement Accounted for at Grades 12, 9, and 6, by Six and by Eight Background Factors

	Grade 12			Grade 9			Grade 6		
	Six	Eight	Eight-Six	Six	Eight	Eight-Six	Six	Eight	Eight-Six
Puerto Ricans	3.64	4.69	1.05	3.89	6.18	2.29	23.71	25.51	1.80
Indian Americans	18.89	22.07	3.18	13.92	16.30	2.38	18.40	19.65	1.25
Mexican Americans	7.92	10.23	2.31	12.79	14.25	1.46	21.82	23.07	1.25
Black, South	14.41	15.79	1.38	12.27	15.69	3.42	14.66	15.44	.78
Black, North	7.53	10.96	3.43	7.68	11.41	3.73	9.51	10.25	.74
Oriental Americans	11.81	19.45	7.64	12.75	22.81	10.06	34.77	36.16	1.39
White, South	14.75	20.13	5.38	18.40	23.12	4.72	18.14	19.91	1.77
White, North	14.28	24.56	10.28	16.49	22.78	6.29	14.10	15.57	1.47
Blacks, total	13.48	15.14	1.66	12.15	14.99	2.84	14.01	14.62	.61
Whites, total	14.71	23.03	8.32	17.81	23.28	5.47	16.20	17.64	1.44

later ones. The decline from grade 6 to 12 is very slight for blacks and whites, and larger for some of the other groups.

This decline is especially noteworthy because of the lesser reliability of reporting of family background at earlier grades, which would reduce the observed relationship. Thus, the true decline in the relationship between objective conditions in the home and achievement is probably greater than the slight observed decline.

Two rather simple models of the impact of family background on achievement are *a priori* reasonable: (1) The family's impact on the child has its greatest effect in earliest years, so that family-to-family differences in achievement should decline after the beginning of school; and (2) the family's impact on the child affects his receptivity to later experience, so that family-to-family differences in achievement should increase over the years of school. The data from objective conditions of the home appear to support the first of these models, because of the decline (probably underestimated) in the relation of these conditions to achievement from grade 6 to 12.[1]

A second point to be observed in the table is that the measures of the subjective home conditions show the opposite trend over grades: Their relation to achievement increases over the grades 6 to 12. The third column at each grade level shows the amount added to the accounted-for-variance by the two measures of parents' interest. This column shows an increase from grades 6 to 12. The increase indicates either that the older students perceive their parents' interest more accurately than the younger ones, or that their parents' interest has more impact on their achievement in the later years of school.

A third point from this table is of more direct relevance to this study. This is the difference in the relation of subjective home conditions to achievement for the different groups. For whites and Oriental Americans, parents' interest accounts for much more variation than it does for any of the other groups. This result may be due to either of two conditions: Either a given amount of parents' interest has the same effect for all groups, but there is more variation in parents' interest for these two groups, or it in fact does have a greater effect for these two groups. To decide between these two interpretations, the unique contribution of these two measures (from the third column at each grade level in table 3.221.3), was divided by the variance of the one variable H in the list above) that accounts for nearly all the added variance in all groups. The data show . . . that almost none of the variation in achievement accounted for is related to the different variances in each group, and nearly all of it is related to different strength of the effect of parents' interest. This leads to an important result:

Either (*a*) black, Mexican American, Puerto Rican, and Indian American children fail to perceive their parents' interest or lack of interest in their schooling as fully as do whites and Oriental Americans; or (*b*) the parents of these minority group children are less able to translate their interest into effective support for the child's learning than are white or Oriental American parents.

There is some evidence to support both of these possibilities. Earlier in section 3.1, the greater unreality of black children's aspirations was evident; this suggests that the same lack of realism may inflate his report of his parents' interest. At the same time, black parents do show a greater interest in their child's education and greater aspirations for his success in education than do white parents of the same economic level. Thus, the children may be reporting reliably. If so, the data in table 3.221.3 suggest that black and other minority parents are not able effectively to translate their interest into practices that support the child's achievement. . . .

3.23 Student Body Characteristics

In examining the relation of school characteristics to achievement of children in each group, the first caution is provided by the results of section 3.22. The pattern of school-to-school differences in achievement at the different grade levels indicated small relation to school factors. Yet some idea of the possible effects of school factors can be gained by a few simple examinations. It is convenient to separate school characteristics into three groups, as was done in part 2: First, facilities, curriculum, and other characteristics of the school itself. Second, characteristics of the teaching staff; and third, those of the student body.[2]

Subsequent sections will examine variables within each of these broad classifications, to study their relation to achievement. However, if that were done without an initial view of all three together, the relative strength of the three, and thus an important result, would be overlooked. The principal result, based on a variety of analyses, is as follows:

Attributes of other students account for far more variation in the achievement of minority group children than do any attributes of school facilities and slightly more than do attributes of staff.

In general, as the educational aspirations and backgrounds of fellow students increase, the achievement of minority group children increases. Such a result must be subject to special scrutiny, because it may be confounded by the student's own educational background and aspirations, which will generally be similar to those of his fellow students. For this reason, throughout the analysis except where indicated, his own background characteristics are controlled to reduce such an effect.

It is useful to examine two tables which provide some of the evidence on which this result is based. One (table 3.23.1) presents the results of regression analyses using eight variables. The eight variables consist of three to represent student backgrounds and attitudes; two to represent school factors; two to represent teacher factors, and one to represent student body qualities. The three background variables are control variables and their effect is not shown. The unique parts of variance accounted for by the other five are shown individually in the table. The unique part associated with a single variable is calculated by obtaining the variance accounted for by all eight variables and then independently obtaining the variance accounted for by seven variables (omitting the single variable); the difference between the two variances thus obtained is the unique contribution (to the accounting for of variance) of the single variable.

The first column shows the part of the variance (over and above the part accounted for by the three background control variables) for which the whole set of five variables accounts together. The second column is the "common" part of the five; it is calculated by subtracting the sum of the unique percents of variance from the joint percent. (Grades 1 and 3 are not shown here because extremely small proportions of the variance are accounted for by any of the five school characteristics.)

The table shows vanishingly small unique contributions of school and teacher characteristics, but very large unique contributions of student body characteristics. In addition, the second column of the table shows the variance that is explained in common; that is, variance that could alternatively be explained by more than one of the five variables. Some of this variance is of course attributable to school or teacher variables, and we shall see later that most of it is to be attributed to teacher variables. In any case, an impressive percent of variance is accounted for by student body characteristics.

A different way of viewing the relative importance of school and fellow-student variables for achievement is to give a special advantage to school variables, by letting them account for as much variance as possible, and then introducing characteristics of fellow students to account for whatever additional variance they will. This was done in another analysis, in which the student's own background was statistically controlled. The result is shown in table 3.23.2 for each grade level. At grades 3 and 1, little variance is accounted for either by school characteristics or student body characteristics. This result, in which no variables account for much of the variance in achievement, is true throughout the analysis for grades 3 and 1, despite the large school-to-school variations shown in table 3.22.1. . . .

However, in grades 12, 9, and 6, the greater importance of student body characteristics becomes evident. Even when they are added after school characteristics, they more than double the explained variance for many groups, and sharply increase it for all groups.

These demonstrations could be supplemented by many others; in the many analyses that have been carried out, nearly any student body characteristic is more effective in accounting for variations in individual achievement than is any characteristic of the school itself.

A second general result indicated by tables 3.23.1 and 3.23.2 is that the highest achieving groups, whites and Oriental Americans, show generally least dependence of achievement on characteristics of fellow students. This statement assumes that the differences shown in table 3.23.1 and table 3.23.2 are not due to lesser variation in characteristics of fellow students for Oriental Americans and whites. The variances for student body characteristics (as used in table 3.23.1) and for encyclopedia and students' college plans (the two variables that account for most of the variance at grades 9 and 12 in table 3.23.2) are slightly smaller for these groups. However, when these

TABLE 3.23.1

Percent of Variance in Verbal Achievement Uniquely Accounted for by One Variable Representing Each of: School Facilities (A), Curriculum (B), Teacher Quality (C), Teacher Attitudes (D), Student Body Quality (E), at Grades 12 and 9, 12, 9 and 6

	Joint ABCDE	Common	Unique				
			A	B	C	D	E
GRADE 12							
Puerto Ricans	21.83	11.93	1.00	0.01	0.44	0.89	8.55
Indian Americans	10.60	3.56	.31	.52	0	2.77	3.44
Mexican Americans	15.70	7.45	.22	.20	.27	.42	7.14
Black, South	11.06	2.80	0	0	.01	.18	8.07
Black, North	7.59	3.58	.13	.04	0	.17	3.67
Oriental Americans	1.18	.44	.03	.03	.18	.09	.41
White, South	3.02	.25	.02	0	0	.24	2.34
White, North	1.58	.25	.02	0	0	0	1.31
Black, total	12.43	5.58	.02	1.01	.02	.03	6.77
White, total	2.52	.50	.01	0	0	0	2.01

GRADE 9

Puerto Ricans	14.46	2.95	.13	.23	.05	.31	10.79
Indian Americans	8.69	2.39	.89	.16	.19	.30	4.76
Mexican Americans	9.22	3.88	.05	.19	.28	1.18	3.64
Black, South	8.84	3.40	0	0	.07	.02	5.35
Black, North	3.37	1.38	.07	.01	.01	.24	1.66
Oriental Americans	3.79	-.34	.05	.20	.27	.13	3.48
White, South	2.05	.15	.03	.03	.01	.05	1.78
White, North	1.23	.01	.01	.12	.08	.01	1.10
Black, total	8.21	3.99	.01	0	.08	.08	4.05
White, total	1.88	-.06	.02	.08	.06	.09	1.69

GRADE 6

Puerto Ricans	12.01	4.07	.01	.02	.03	.02	7.86
Indian Americans	9.14	2.28	.54	.09	.40	.34	5.49
Mexican Americans	12.91	4.91	0	.01	.10	.22	7.67
Black, South	9.48	3.22	.05	.03	.06	.04	6.12
Black, North	4.81	.87	0	.05	.19	.01	3.69
Oriental Americans	4.99	1.39	.15	.42	.08	.04	2.91
White, South	2.13	-.02	.03	0	0	.01	2.11
White, North	4.56	.02	.15	0	.08	0	4.31
Black, total	9.38	2.85	0	.03	0	.01	6.49
White, total	4.37	-.06	.03	0	.05	.09	4.26

TABLE 3.23.2

Percent of Variance in Verbal Achievement Accounted for by School Characteristics (A) and by School Characteristics Plus Student Body Characteristics (A+B).
Background characteristics controlled are the first six appearing in Table 3.221.5.

	Grade 12			Grade 9			Grade 6			Grade 3			Grade 1		
	A [1]	A+B [2]	Gain	A [1]	A+B [2]	Gain	A [1]	A+B [2]	Gain	A [1]	A+B [1]	Gain	A [1]	A+B [2]	Gain
Puerto Ricans	6.67	22.59	15.92	4.07	15.70	11.63	3.21	11.83	8.62	2.27	8.18	5.91	4.52	6.26	1.74
Indian Americans	11.48	22.78	11.30	2.59	9.98	7.39	5.64	9.25	3.61	4.04	5.35	1.31	3.62	5.75	2.13
Mexican Americans	6.59	15.90	9.31	2.82	10.68	7.86	1.47	11.92	10.45	3.50	6.76	3.26	5.64	6.10	.46
Black, South	8.64	12.69	4.05	7.52	12.66	5.14	4.90	7.77	2.87	.80	1.40	.60	2.14	2.93	.79
Black, North	3.14	7.73	4.59	1.45	4.62	3.17	.77	2.73	1.96	2.96	5.13	2.17	2.38	3.28	.90
Oriental Americans	3.83	4.40	.57	5.66	11.12	5.46	9.06	12.10	3.04	2.62	7.28	4.66	3.88	6.45	2.57
White, South	3.16	4.61	1.45	1.60	2.82	1.22	.57	1.92	1.35	.83	1.91	1.08	.96	1.53	.57
White, North	1.87	2.94	1.07	.73	2.34	1.61	.32	3.63	3.31	.33	1.46	1.13	.83	2.35	1.52
Blacks, total	6.96	12.82	5.86	5.19	10.59	5.40	2.77	5.48	2.71	2.26	2.96	.70	.72	1.76	1.04
Whites, total	2.53	3.69	1.16	1.15	2.44	1.29	.47	3.13	2.66	.33	1.28	.95	.32	1.33	1.01

[1] School characteristics are:
Per pupil expenditure on staff
Volumes per student in library
Science lab facilities (9 and 12 only)
Extracurricular activities (9 and 12 only)
Presence of accelerated curriculum (9 and 12 only)
Comprehensiveness of curriculum (9 and 12 only)
Use of tracking (9 and 12 only)
Movement between tracks (9 and 12 only)
Size
Guidance counselors (9 and 12 only)
School location (city suburb, town, country)

[2] Student body characteristics are:
Proportion whose families own encyclopedias
Number of student transfers
Attendance
Proportion planning to attend college (9 and 12 only)
Teachers' perception of student-body quality (1, 3, 6 only)
Average hours of homework (9 and 12 only)

variances are divided into the numbers in tables 3.23.1 and 3.23.2 the difference still holds with nearly the same strength. This means that a given difference in characteristics of fellow students makes less difference in achievement of these two groups. This indicates, as in previous data, a lesser sensitivity to school environments for children in these groups. It suggests also, as in previous data, that family background which encourages achievement reduces sensitivity to variations in schools. The school, including the student body, apparently has less differential effect upon achievement of children from such backgrounds.

The results suggest, then, that the environment provided by the student body is asymmetric in its effects, that it has its greatest effect on those from educationally deficient backgrounds. The matter is of course more complex than this simple relation, doubtless depending on the relative number of high and low achieving students in the school, and on other factors.

Another result from the data of tables 3.23.1 and 3.23.2, which is consistent with the general difference in sensitivity shown earlier, concerns differences among blacks. It is those blacks who are in the South whose achievement appears to vary most greatly with variations in the characteristics of their fellow students. Here, where the most educationally disadvantaged backgrounds are found, and where achievement is lowest, is where student body characteristics make most differences for black achievement. It is in these more stable, less urban areas where exposure to children of different educational backgrounds and aspirations has in the past been least possible for black children. . . .

There is one special characteristic of the student body for which the regression analysis provides some additional evidence. This is the racial composition of the student body. The problem of assessing its effect is vastly complicated by the fact that students of both races in racially heterogeneous schools are not representative of all students of their race, but are often highly unrepresentative. Nevertheless, with this caution it is useful to examine the achievement of students of each race in schools of varying different racial composition.

The question of performance of children in schools of different racial composition is often confused by not separating several different components:

i. Effects due to different facilities and curriculum in the school itself.
ii. Effects due to differences in educational deficiency or proficiency of fellow students that are correlated with race, though not universally so.
iii. Effects due to racial composition of the student body apart from its level of educational proficiency.

Some insight into these effects may be gained by examining what the racial composition of the student body can tell us about the achievement of students of each race under different levels of prior information, as follows (under all conditions, his own family background characteristics are controlled):

(A) In the first instance, if we know nothing about the school except its per-pupil instructional expenditure;
(B) In the second case, if we know also a variety of school facility and curriculum characteristics;
(C) In the third case, if we know also several characteristics of the student body, such as those examined in the preceding section.

In all these cases, we ask what does the racial composition of the student body (measured as proportion of students that are white and not Puerto Rican or Mexican American) tell us in addition about the achievement of a student of a given racial or ethnic group. These various conditions are presented in table 3.23.4 for grades 3, 6, 9, and 12. It is worth remarking that the added variance accounted for under some of the conditions is large indeed, relative to the variance explained by most school factors. There are a few other student body variables that add more to the explained variance, but not much more. These numbers must also be viewed relative to the total between-school variance, which is less than 20 percent for blacks and less than 10 percent for whites. (See table 3.22.1.)

The first quite general result in this table is that as the proportion white in a school increases, the achievement of students in each racial group increases. This does not yet separate out the effects i, ii, and iii. We shall raise the question shortly about which of these effects appear to be most important.

The second general result is that this relationship increases as grade in school increases. The relationship is absent at grade 3, and strongest at grade 9, and 12. This gives some assurance that the relation is not due to associated factors, which should produce an apparent effect at all grades alike.

A third point to note is that the additional knowledge of school characteristics (condition A+B compared to A) reduces only slightly the added influence of racial composition. This leads to the third important result: The higher achievement of all racial and ethnic groups in schools with greater proportions of white students is not accounted for by better facilities and curriculum in these schools (to the extent these were measured by our questionnaires). But a comparison of this condition with the next (A+B+C) which includes information about the student body's educational background and aspirations shows that the latter characteristics do sharply reduce the added variance explained by racial composition. (As explained in section 3.2A, an appearance of sharp reduction in apparent effect is likely to mean in reality complete absence of effect.) This leads to still another important result: The higher achievement of all racial and ethnic groups in schools with greater proportions of white students is largely, perhaps wholly, related to effects associated with the student body's educational background and aspirations. This means that the apparent beneficial effect of a student body with a high proportion of white students comes not from racial composition per se, but from the better educational background and higher educational aspirations that are, on the average found among white students. The effects of the student body environment upon a student's achievement appear to lie in the educational proficiency possessed by that student body, whatever its racial or ethnic composition.[3]

This result does, however, give some insight into the way in which achievement levels of two groups can remain quite different over a long period of time. If a large part of the effect of a school on a student is accounted for by the achievement level of other students in the school, then in a segregated system, if one group begins at an educationally impoverished level, it will tend to remain at that level.

Ordinarily, one has a conception of school's effect as consisting of a strong stimulus from the outside, independent of the immediate school context of the students. In view of the results of this section, it appears that a more appropriate conception may be that of a self-reproducing system, in which most of the effects are not independent of the social context, but are, rather, internal ones.

3.231 Two Comments on the Analysis

The results of the preceding sections are enough at variance with common beliefs that a number of questions are likely to be raised about the analysis.

One such question is this: Why are the racial and ethnic groups separated in the analysis? Let us suppose that all blacks go to equally bad schools and all whites go to equally good schools, or vice versa. Then the analysis which keeps the groups separate will show no effectiveness of school characteristics, because for each racial or ethnic group, the schools are uniformly bad or good.

First, it is important to make clear why the racial groups were kept separate in the analysis. When achievement differs as much as it does between these groups, then to analyze the groups together, without controlling for race or ethnicity of the student, would cause any school characteristics highly associated with race or ethnicity to show a spurious relation to achievement. For example, race of teacher, which is highly correlated with the student's own race, would show a high relation to achievement if the student's race were not controlled. In short, it would not be good methodology to fail to control on a variable—race or ethnicity in this case—which is known to have a high and stable relation to the dependent variable, independently of characteristics of the school attended by the student.

An examination was carried out, without controlling for race, of whether school factors might appear to account for large portions of the variance.[4] It used the five school average variables shown in table 3.23.1, together with the same three individual student variables used in that analysis: Family economic background, family educational background and interest, the student's attitude. The five variables characterizing the school were

TABLE 3.23.4

Additional Percent of Variance in Achievement Explained by Proportion White in School Under Different Prior States of Information: (6 variables in student's own background controlled), Per Pupil Expenditures on Staff in the School (A); Additional Facilities and Curriculum Characteristics of School (B); Characteristics of Student Body (C); effect is toward higher achievement except where (—) precedes number

	Grade 12			Grade 9		
	A	A+B	A+B+C	A	A+B	A+B+C
Puerto Ricans	17.06	13.53	3.98	7.76	8.45	0.81
Indian Americans	12.61	6.93	.15	8.50	11.21	5.19
Mexican American	12.51	9.45	1.87	11.50	11.52	4.20
Black, South	1.52	1.67	.39	2.35	1.62	.34
Black, North	2.90	1.83	.41	2.41	1.36	.82
Oriental Americans	.77	1.70	(*)	.89	.30	(*)
White, South	.00	.01	(—).01	.00	.04	.00
White, North	.56	.81	.21	1.40	1.40	.41
Black total	3.29	3.54	.68	3.01	1.54	.67
White total	.29	.29	.13	.69	.91	.25

	Grade 6			Grade 3		
	A	A+B	A+B+C	A	A+B	A+B+C
Puerto Ricans	6.34	6.66	0.78	5.24	5.02	1.51
Indian Americans	2.83	4.59	2.02	2.60	1.91	.96
Mexican American	9.70	9.06	1.67	3.08	3.52	1.00
Black, South	1.31	1.62	.56	(−).23	(−).18	(−).28
Black, North	1.46	1.36	.37	.09	.14	(−).07
Oriental Americans	.06	.09	.04	3.52	2.25	.52
White, South	.34	.39	.15	.19	.16	.04
White, North	1.50	1.38	.34	.01	.04	(−).05
Black total	1.12	1.54	.40	(−).01	.00	(−).07
White total	1.06	1.04	.23	.04	.06	(−).01

*The regression had insufficient data for estimation.

TABLE 3.231.1
Unique Percent of Variance in Verbal Achievement Accounted for by
Characteristics of Schoolteachers, and Student Body, in Regression with
2 Family Background Factors and 1 Individual Attitude

	Grades			
	12	9	6	3
Unique contribution to variance accounted for by—				
School facilities_____	0	0	0	0
School curriculum _____	0	. 2	0	0
Teacher qualities_____	0	0	0	. 1
Teacher attitudes_____	. 8	. 9	. 4	. 3
Student body characteristics_____	4. 7	4. 9	8. 2	1. 4
Unique of all 5 jointly____	9. 6	8. 1	10. 9	2. 5
Total by all 8_____	35. 4	38. 1	37. 7	12. 9

school facilities, school curriculum, teacher qualities, teacher attitudes, and
student body characteristics. Table 3.231.1 shows the unique contribution
of each of these five, in a regression containing all eight variables, as well
as the unique contribution of all five together, at grades 3, 6, 9, and 12.
The table shows that the school and staff factors make very small unique
contributions to the variance, just as in the case when the racial and ethnic
groups were treated separately (table 3.23.1). The one variable at the level
of the school that does make a strong unique contribution is the educational
backgrounds and aspirations of fellow-students—the student body variable.
It may be noted parenthetically that even the meager contribution of teacher
attitudes may be largely a result of the correlation of these attitudes with
the race or ethnicity of the student in the school.

Also it must be emphasized that with respect to teacher quality we deal
only with school averages. The variance of pupil achievement accounted
for differences between teachers in the same school cannot be explored by
means of the data of the survey.

A second question will likely be raised for which the data of the survey
provide less direct evidence. The question can be posed in this way: School
effects were not evident because no measurement of educational growth
was carried out. Had it been, then some schools might have shown much
greater growth rates of students than would others and these rates might
have been highly correlated with school characteristics.

If this were the case, then one of the strongest implications would be
that the correlation between family background and achievement should
show a decrease over the years of school roughly proportioned to the school

effect, and correspondingly, school factors should show an increase in correlation with achievement. Only if family background were homogeneous within schools, and if the school's effect were highly correlated with family background, would a school effect maintain a high correlation of achievement to family background. But it has already been shown that schools appear to have an effect that is dependent upon the average family background in the school—an effect through the student body not through the characteristics of the school itself. Thus, the question posed above can only be meaningful if it refers to an effect independent of the student body composition. And such an effect, as indicated above, would reduce the correlation between family background factors and achievement, and increase the relation of school factors with achievement. Yet there is little increase in the variance in achievement explained by school characteristics, though there is some increase in variance explained by teacher characteristics (as section 3.25 will show), and more increase in variance explained by student body charac- teristics. Also, table 3.221.3 showed that considering both subjective and objective background, the multiple correlation between background factors and achievement remains constant or increases over grades 6 to 12 for blacks, and whites. (Grades 1 and 3 could not be included in the comparison because several family background measures were not obtained at the grades 1 and 3.) It is likely that measurement was not as good at grade 6, which makes precise comparison not possible; but it is clear that no strong outside stimulus is making its impact felt in such a way as to interfere with the general relation of background to achievement; that is, it is clear that schools are not acting as a strong stimulus independent of the child's background, or the level of the student body. For if they were, there would be a decline in this correlation, proportional to the strength of such stimulus. This is not to say, of course, that schools have no effect, but rather that what effects they do have are highly correlated with the individual student's background, and with the educational background of the student body in the school; that is, the effects appear to arise not principally from factors that the school system controls, but from factors outside the school proper. The stimulus arising from variables independent of the student background factors appears to be a relatively weak one.

3.24 School Facilities and Curriculum

The study of characteristics of school facilities and curriculum must take as its starting point the surprisingly small amount of variation in student achievement accounted for by variations in these characteristics. Nevertheless, something can be learned about achievement in schools with differing characteristics by proceeding somewhat arbitrarily to introduce successively selected school characteristics to examine what aid they give in accounting for variance in achievement. In carrying out this examination of particular school factors, the comparatively small samples of groups other than black and white make results from these groups quite variable, and of little value

TABLE 3.24.1

Variance Accounted for by per Pupil Instructional Expenditure Grades 12, 9, 6, After 6 Background Variables Are Controlled

	12	9	6
Black, South_____	2.98	2.89	3.49
Black, North_____	.09	.02	.14
White, South_____	.06	.21	.15
White, North_____	.29	.14	.05
Blacks, total _____	2.62	2.55	2.17
Whites, total_____	.80	.64	.36

in learning the achievement associated with given school characteristics. Thus, only blacks and whites, for the country as a whole and for North and South separately, will be examined. The overall per pupil expenditure on staff is introduced first, as an overall measure of the community's input of resources into the school. Even at this initial point, however, student background differences are controlled so that the results will not be masked by the community's input of students into the school. Hence, the residual relationship shows the higher achievement of children who report similar backgrounds in schools with high per pupil expenditure. The data from this examination are presented in table 3.24.1, and they lead to the first result of this section: For schools attended by blacks in the South, but among no other groups, high per pupil expenditure is associated with higher achievement, at grades 6, 9, and 12, after background differences of students are controlled. This result means that for blacks in the South, achievement is appreciably lower in schools with low per pupil expenditure than in schools with high expenditure. Another comparison makes the differences between this group and others even sharper: the variance in per pupil expenditure among blacks and whites in the South is only a tenth to a third as great as that for other groups. Consequently, the contrast between this relationship for Southern blacks and its relative absence elsewhere is even more marked.

This is not to say by any means that expenditure differences in themselves create such differences in achievement for Southern blacks. This measure very likely represents other differences in the community. As section 3.23 showed, when student body characteristics are taken into account, the variance accounted for by a facilities measure (which includes per pupil expenditure) is very small indeed. In fact, if adjustments had been made to remove student body factors in the present analysis, together with facilities and curriculum measures, the unique contribution of per pupil expenditure for Southern blacks would have nearly vanished.

The next step in the examination is to introduce certain selected facilities and curriculum measures which gave evidence in early analyses of showing most relation to achievement or appear to be intrinsically important in school policy (such as grouping or tracking). Some facilities measures, such as the pupil/teacher ratio in instruction, are not included because they showed a consistent lack of relation to achievement among all groups under all conditions.

The facilities and curriculum measures are—

volumes per student in school library
science laboratory facilities (9 and 12 only)
number of extracurricular activities (9 and 12 only)
presence of an accelerated curriculum
comprehensiveness of the curriculum (9 and 12 only)
strictness in promotion of slow learners (6 only)
use of grouping or tracking (9 and 12 only)
movement between tracks (9 and 12 only)
school size
number of guidance counselors (9 and 12 only)
urbanism of school's location.

For all blacks and all whites, . . . the analysis allows us to examine the added variance that any one of these measures would account for under two different conditions—when only knowledge of student background and per pupil instructional expenditure of the school is given, and when in addition knowledge of all the other facilities and curriculum measures is given. That is, under the first condition, only the measures of student input and financial input into the school are controlled; under the second condition, a variety of other facilities and curriculum measures are also controlled. The data are given in table 3.24.2.

Variations among grades.—The general comparison between grades shows that the facilities and curriculum measures account for an increasingly larger amount of variance in achievement from the 6th to the 12th grades. Very little of the variance is accounted for at the 6th grade by most measures, somewhat more at the 9th, and still more at the 12th. The absence of relation for most items at grade 6 is a result of the low variation among schools with respect to these facilities in elementary schools.

Variations between blacks and whites.—The generally lesser variance accounted for by school-to-school differences for whites is evident here. For whites, less variance is accounted for by all characteristics, and little or none is accounted for by many. . . .

Particular facilities and curriculum measures.—One variable that explains a relatively large amount of variance at grades 9 and 12 under the first condition (A) is school size. (The lack of relation at grade 6 may be a result of the lesser variation in size of elementary schools.) . . . However, most of its apparent effect vanishes if various facilities and curricular differences are controlled. That is, the higher achievement in larger schools is largely accounted for by the additional facilities they include. . . .

TABLE 3.24.2
Unique Percentage Contributions to Variance in Verbal Achievement by Individual Facilities and Curricular Measures, Given Knowledge of Student Background (6 background variables controlled) and per Pupil Expenditure (A), and Given Knowledge of A Plus 10 Facilities and Curriculum Measures (B)

	Grade 12		Grade 9		Grade 6	
	A	A+B	A	A+B	A	A+B
Black total:						
Total variance accounted for [1]	(2.62)	((6.96))	(2.55)	((5.19))	(2.17)	((2.77))
Expenditure		.54		.87		1.62
Volumes	.04	.05	(−).04	0	(−).01	.02
Laboratories	1.61	.42	.04	.07		
Extracurricular	1.64	.10	.12	.01		
Accelerated	.59	.11	.11	.04	.08	.07
Comprehensiveness (12, 9)	.61	0	.08	(−).01		
Promotion strictness (6)					.25	.22
Grouping or tracking	(−).01	.10	(−).14	(−).01		
Movement between tracks	(−).40	(−).19	(−)1.14	(−).88		
Size	2.55	.16	1.32	.09	0	.04
Guidance	2.61	.06	1.25	.06		
Urbanism	2.12	.11	.88	.15	.23	.28

White total:

Total variance accounted for[1]	(0.80)	((2.53))	(0.64)	((1.15))	(0.36)	((0.47))
Expenditure	(−).11	.54	.06	.87		1.62
Volumes	.62	(−).12	0	.03	.01	.01
Laboratories	.04	.20	.07	(−).05		
Extracurricular	.67	.93	.01	.02	.02	.02
Accelerated		.33		0		
Comprehensiveness (12, 9)	0	(−).02	(−).14	(−).13	.05	.05
Promotion strictness (6)						
Grouping or tracking	(−).02	0	(−).01	0		
Movement between tracks	.02	0	(−).02	0	0	0
Size	(−).22	(−).19	.04	.04		
Guidance	.16	.81	.22	.17		0
Urbanism	.04	.28	.08	0	(−).03	.03

[1] Total variance accounted for under condition A ( ) does not include in the regression the listed facilities. Under condition A+B (( )), it does include these facilities.

Several of the measures in table 3.24.2 can be dismissed rather quickly. Tracking shows no relation to achievement, and thus the apparent relation of movement between tracks to achievement cannot be meaningfully interpreted.

Comprehensiveness of the curriculum shows small and inconsistent relations to achievement. The existence of an accelerated program in the curriculum does, however, show a consistent relation to achievement at grade 12, . . . both before and after other curriculum and facilities measures have been controlled. It is not possible to tell conclusively, however, whether the accelerated program is truly effective in providing additional opportunity, or merely an additional indicator of a student body with high achievement or of a community with high educational interest.

The number of volumes per student in the school library shows small and inconsistent relations to achievement. However, both the number of science laboratories and the number of extracurricular activities have a consistent relation of moderate size to achievement. The number of extracurricular activities accounts for more variation in achievement before other school factors are controlled, but it accounts for less than laboratories after they are controlled. This indicates that extracurricular activities are more highly associated with other attributes found in schools with high achievement, but that the existence of laboratories has a more intrinsic relation to high achievement.

The general picture that all these results give of schools that come closest to taking full advantage of their student input is one with generally greater resources. The relations are not large, but they are all in the direction of somewhat higher achievement: higher per pupil instructional expenditure, a curriculum that offers greater challenges, more laboratories and more activities. However, probably the most important result is the one stated in the preceding section: that characteristics of facilities and curriculum are much less highly related to achievement than are the attributes of a child's fellow students in school.

It is clear that the other variations among the schools in this survey have almost overwhelmed any effects of variations in the curriculum. A more intensive study, more fully focussed on these curricular variables alone, would be necessary to discover their effects. But this fact alone is important: Differences in school facilities and curriculum, which are the major variables by which attempts are made to improve schools, are so little related to differences in achievement levels of students that, with few exceptions, their effects fail to appear even in a survey of this magnitude.

3.25 Teachers' Characteristics

Teachers of these students differed in a number of ways. Most blacks are taught by black teachers, whites are almost always taught by whites; teachers of blacks tend to have more positive attitudes toward school integration, and less often express a preference for teaching middle class, white-collar workers' children. Teachers of blacks scored lower on the vocabulary test taken by teachers; and there were other differences as well— all as indicated in part 2.

In assessing the effect of teachers' characteristics upon achievement, teachers in a school were aggregated to obtain averages for the teaching staff in that school. For grades 1, 3, and 6, aggregation was done only over teachers who taught grades 1–6; for grade 9, aggregation was done only over teachers who taught grades 7–12; and for grade 12, aggregation was done only over teachers who taught grades 9–12.

Altogether, variation in school averages of teachers' characteristics accounted for higher proportion of variation in student achievement than did all other aspects of the school combined, excluding the student body characteristics. Several teachers' characteristics were selected for special examination, after eliminating a number of characteristics that appeared, in early regressions, to have little effect. Other variables were eliminated because they were highly correlated with one or more of those remaining, and thus their effects could not easily be distinguished. The variables which remain must be regarded in part as surrogates for other variables that are related to them. Thus, as with any investigation into a complex set of relations, the results must be interpreted with caution because of the many factors that could not be simultaneously held constant.

The teacher variables selected for special examination were—

1. The average educational level of the teachers' families (mother's education was used).
2. Average years of experience in teaching.
3. The localism of the teachers in the school: whether they had attended high school and college in the area, and had lived there most of their lives.
4. The average level of education of the teachers themselves.
5. The average score on vocabulary test self-administered by the teachers.
6. The teachers' preference for teaching middle-class, white-collar students.
7. The proportion of teachers in the school who were white.

The first important result from this examination is that the effect of teachers' characteristics shows a sharp increase over the years of school. The variance in achievement explained by variation in average teacher characteristics by variation in average teacher characteristics is very small at lower grades and increases for higher grades. This effect is shown in table 3.25.1. In this table, attention should be focused particularly on shifts from grades 6 to 12, since analyses in earlier sections have shown the generally lesser relation of any variables to achievement at grades 1 and 3. When grades 6, 9, and 12 are considered, there is a general increase for whites and blacks in both regions. The other minority groups show less consistency; however, the relation is greatest at grade 12 for nearly all groups.

TABLE 3.25.1

Percent of Variance in Verbal Achievement Accounted for by 7 Selected Teacher Variables at Grades 12, 9, 6, 3, and 1, with Background Factors Controlled[1]

	Grade 12	Grade 9	Grade 6	Grade 3	Grade 1
Puerto Ricans	18.38	9.70	8.11	2.60	4.70
Indian Americans	15.75	7.25	17.95	3.71	10.97
Mexican-Americans	14.63	11.71	12.59	2.31	2.18
Blacks, South	9.97	7.72	5.29	1.73	.91
Blacks, North	4.35	1.58	2.19	2.38	1.38
Oriental Americans	1.77	3.18	4.19	3.92	6.04
Whites, South	2.07	2.49	1.12	1.08	.46
Whites, North	1.89	1.02	1.67	.85	.87
Blacks, total	9.53	6.77	3.52	2.83	.52
Whites, total	1.82	1.03	1.23	.59	.37

[1] Only the 4 background variables 1, 2, 5, and 6 from table 3.221.1, measured in all 5 grades, were controlled in grades 1 and 3; for comparability with secs. 3.23 and 3.24, 6 background variables were controlled in grades 6, 9, 12.

The table shows a second important result. The apparent effect of average teacher characteristics for children in a given group is directly related to the "sensitivity" of the group to the school environment. In particular, Southern blacks appear to be more affected than Northern blacks, and whites appear least affected of all groups.[5]

This result is an extremely important one, for it suggests that good teachers matter more for children from minority groups which have educationally deficient backgrounds. It suggests as well that for any groups whether minority or not, the effect of good teachers is greatest upon the children who suffer most educational disadvantage in their background, and that a given investment in upgrading teacher quality will have most effect on achievement in underprivileged areas.

The specific teacher variables selected for examination show the contribution of each of these variables to explanation of the overall variance. These effects are shown for blacks and whites at each grade level in table 3.25.2. The table shows the cumulative amount of variance explained as each of these variables is added, in the order indicated above.

These data show again the strikingly stronger effect of teacher variables for blacks than for whites. For whites, none of these characteristics of teachers show much effect at any grade level. For blacks, the variables which do show an effect do so increasingly with higher grade levels.

The variables that show most effect are the teachers' family education level (a positive effect), the teachers' own education (positive effect), and the score on the vocabulary test (positive effect). Teachers' attitudes show a slight effect in some grades (negative effect of preference for middle-class students); as does experience (positive effect), while localism and proportion white show little or no effect. For other minority groups, similar results hold, except that teachers' experience shows inconsistent directions of effect, suggesting that it has no effect of its own, teachers' preference for middle-class students has a stronger and consistently negative effect for Mexican Americans, Puerto Ricans, and Indians, and proportion white teachers has a consistently positive effect for these three groups.

The strongest result to derive from these tabulations (beyond the greater effect for groups of high sensitivity to school environments and the greater effect with increasing grade level) is that the teachers' verbal skills have a strong effect, first showing at the sixth grade, indicating that between grades 3 and 6, the verbal skills of the teacher are especially important. This result is shown in the table for blacks, and it holds as well for each of the other minority groups. For each of those groups the jump from grade 3 to grade 6 in added variance explained by teachers' verbal skills is even greater than that for blacks.

The second, and less strong effect for blacks, is that the teachers' educational level (both family education and teachers' own education) or some variable for which this is a surrogate, begins to make a difference at grades 9 and 12. (The same general result holds for the other minority groups, except that the teachers' own education shows more variable effects from these groups.)

TABLE 3.25.2

Cumulative Variance in Achievement Explained for Blacks and Whites at Each Grade Level by Adding School Average of Specified Teacher Variables in Order Listed [4 background variables controlled]

Variable added	Grade 12		Grade 9		Grade 6		Grade 3		Grade 1	
	N	W	N	W	N	W	N	W	N	W
Teachers' family educational level	2.26	0.10	1.42	0.14	0.58	0.21	0.03	0.01	0.03	0.00
Years experience	3.37	.12	1.53	.22	.61	.21	1.50	.05	.14	.15
Localism	3.38	.47	1.54	.47	.93	.49	2.34	.21	.26	.19
Teachers' educational level	4.87	1.08	3.20	.60	.93	.51·	2.40	.23	.26	.21
Score on vocabulary test	7.05	1.21	5.05	.62	2.82	.67	2.74	.27	.34	.27
Preference for middle class	8.09	2.07	5.42	.69	3.03	.82	2.76	.56	.35	.33
Proportion white	8.23	2.10	5.55	1.04	3.33	1.20	2.83	.59	.52	.37

An overall examination of school, teacher, and student environment variable together is possible, now that all three have been examined individually. This examination is carried out in table 3.25.3, which shows the variance accounted for by teacher variables, by teacher variables plus the school characteristics examined in section 3.24, and by these two sets of variables plus the student environment variable examined in section 3.23. The third column of this table shows that, altogether, these variables account for nearly all of the school-to-school variation for the groups other than blacks and whites at grade 12, but considerably less than that for blacks and whites, and less for all groups at grades 9 and 6. The relative strength of these three acts of variables can be examined by comparing the first column (teacher variables alone) with the first line in the second column of table 3.24.2 (school characteristics alone) and the second column (teacher plus school characteristics) with the second column of table 3.23.2 (student environment plus school characteristics). This comparison shows that the school characteristics are the weakest of the three, and that teachers' characteristics are comparable to but slightly weaker than characteristics of the student environment.

Thus the effects of teacher variables upon student achievement show several important results. Restating these results, they are—

1. Teacher differences show a cumulative effect over the years in school.

2. Teacher differences show more relation to difference in achievement of educationally disadvantaged minority groups than to achievement of the white majority. The relation corresponds roughly to the general sensitivity of the minority group to variations in school environments. In addition, teacher differences are over twice as strongly related to achievement of Southern blacks as to achievement of Northern blacks.

3. Teachers' verbal skills have an effect first showing strongly at grade 6 for all minority groups.

4. Teachers' educational background (own and family's) shows an effect first showing strongly at grade 9, for all minority groups.

3.26 Attitudes of Students

Three expressions of student attitude and motivation were examined in relation to achievement. One was the student's interest in school and his reported pursuit of reading outside school; another was his self-concept, specifically with regard to learning, and success in school; and a third was what we have called his sense of control of the environment.

As indicated in an earlier section, both black and white children expressed a high self-concept, as well as high interest in school and learning, compared to the other groups. Blacks, however, were like the other minority groups in expressing a much lower sense of control of the environment than whites.

These attitudes were not measured at all grade levels; the table below shows the questions on which each was based at each grade level. (At grade 3, only one question could be used for each of the first two attitudes,

108

TABLE 3.25.3

Percent of Variance in Verbal Achievement Accounted for by Teacher Variable (T), These Plus School Variables (S), and These Plus Student Environment Variables (E), Grades 12, 9, and 6 [6 background variables controlled]

	Grade 12			Grade 9			Grade 6		
	T	T+S	T+S+E	T	T+S	T+S+E	T	T+S	T+S+E
Puerto Rican	18.38	20.00	26.39	9.70	11.37	16.26	8.11	10.81	13.97
Indian Americans	15.75	19.56	26.33	7.25	10.17	14.04	17.95	19.41	20.95
Mexican-Americans	14.63	16.94	19.16	11.71	14.12	15.04	12.59	13.57	16.52
Black, South	9.97	11.68	13.90	7.72	11.24	13.33	5.29	7.76	9.02
Black, North	4.35	6.68	8.97	1.58	3.32	5.36	2.19	2.66	4.93
Oriental Americans	1.77	6.63	(1)	3.18	(1)	(1)	4.19	11.99	14.54
White, South	2.07	3.60	4.80	2.49	3.36	3.83	1.12	1.56	2.94
White, North	1.89	3.16	3.82	1.02	2.06	3.07	1.67	2.02	4.84
Black total	9.53	10.70	13.78	6.67	8.70	11.22	3.52	4.42	6.52
White total	1.82	3.42	4.18	1.03	2.41	3.18	1.23	1.77	4.13

1 The regression had insufficient data for estimation.

and there were no items for the third. At grade 1, no attitudinal questions were asked. Thus the comparisons are all for grades 6, 9, and 12.)

Grade	Interest in learning and reading	Self-concept	Control of environment
12_____	q 57, 59, 60, 63	q 91, 108, 109	q 102, 103, 110
9_____	q 54, 56, 57, 60	q 88, 99, 100	q 93, 94, 103
6_____	q 36, 51, 28	q 37, 40	q 38

Because questions were not identical between grade 6 and grades 9 and 12, the measures are not exactly the same. Despite this variation between grade 6 and grades 9 and 12, however, one point stands out clearly in the analysis.

Of all the variables measured in the survey, including all measures of family background and all school variables, these attitudes showed the strongest relation to achievement, at all three grade levels. The zero-order correlations of these attitudes with achievement were higher than those of any other variables, in some cases as high as the correlation of some test scores with others (between .4 and .5). Taken alone, these attitudinal variables account for more of the variation in achievement than any other set of variables (all family background variables together, or all school variables together). When added to any other set of variables, they increase the accounted-for variation more than does any other set of variables. Tables 3.26.1 and 3.26.2 give a comparison between these attitudes and the eight strongest background variables. Table 3.26.1 shows the amount of variance accounted for by these three attitudes and by the eight background factors used throughout this analysis. In the 9th and 12th grades, with only two exceptions (Oriental Americans in grade 9, and Indian Americans in grade 12), the attitudes account for more of the variance. In grade 6, the attitudes account for most variance for whites and for blacks, when North and South are considered separately; background factors account for more variance in the other groups. Table 3.26.2 compares them in several ways to background factors, showing the amount they add to accounted-for variance, when included as independent variables; and the unique contribution of each to the explained variance, which shows the reduction in accounted-for variance that would occur if the variable was removed from the equation. Included in the table are comparable quantities for the background variable that is most strongly associated with achievement.

These tables show that, whatever measure is chosen, the attitudinal variables have the strongest relation to achievement. It is, of course, reasonable that self-concept should be so closely related to achievement, since it represents the individual's own estimate of his ability. (See again the items on which this variable is based, section 3.1.) The relation of self-concept to achievement is, from one perspective, merely the accuracy of his estimate

110

TABLE 3.26.1
Total Variance in Verbal Skills as a Percent by Three Attitudes, and by Eight Background Variables, at Grades 12, 9, and 6

	Attitudes			Background		
	Grade 12	Grade 9	Grade 6	Grade 12	Grade 9	Grade 6
Puerto Ricans	9.09	13.99	8.97	4.69	6.18	25.51
Indian Americans	21.62	18.81	14.23	22.07	16.30	19.65
Mexican-Americans	14.04	16.32	13.38	10.23	14.25	23.07
Black, South	17.18	20.84	15.55	15.79	15.69	15.44
Black, North	17.54	20.77	13.27	10.96	11.41	10.25
Oriental Americans	19.58	21.69	25.78	19.45	22.81	36.16
White, South	26.52	31.53	23.69	20.13	23.18	19.91
White, North	29.14	31.10	24.20	24.56	22.38	15.57
Blacks, total	15.89	20.12	14.16	15.14	14.99	14.62
Whites, total	27.68	31.10	24.26	23.03	23.28	17.64

TABLE 3.26.2
Unique Contribution to Accounted-for Variance of Verbal Skills for Three
Attitudes and Single Strongest Background Variable, in Regression Equation
with Eight Background Variables, Grades 12, 9, and 6

	Unique contribution		
	Grade 12	Grade 9	Grade 6
Puerto Ricans:			
Interest in learning	(−)4. 33	(−)0. 37	1. 01
Self-concept	2. 09	. 86	. 09
Control of environment	2. 18	7. 89	2. 67
Strongest background item	. 90	1. 05	5. 35
Background item	(¹)	(¹)	(²)
Overall including attitude	12. 87	17. 26	29. 68
Overall excluding attitude	4. 69	6. 18	25. 51
Indian Americans:			
Interest in learning	. 01	0	2. 92
Self-concept	2. 91	1. 90	. 70
Control of environment	5. 06	5. 41	3. 08
Strongest background item	1. 34	1. 37	3. 60
Background item	(¹)	(³)	(²)
Overall including attitude	32. 86	26. 34	27. 59
Overall excluding attitude	22. 07	16. 30	19. 65
Mexican Americans:			
Interest in learning	. 00	. 05	. 88
Self-concept	. 70	. 49	1. 21
Control of environment	7. 29	6. 26	3. 60
Strongest background item	2. 15	. 93	3. 35
Background item	(³)	(⁴)	(²)
Overall including attitude	20. 59	22. 96	29. 91
Overall excluding attitude	10. 23	14. 25	23. 07
Black, South:			
Interest in learning	(−). 05	. 07	1. 79
Self-concept	3. 06	. 87	1. 00
Control of environment	5. 76	9. 68	5. 41
Strongest background item	2. 09	1. 26	1. 81
Background item	(¹)	(¹)	(²)
Overall including attitude	27. 94	29. 63	25. 31
Overall excluding attitude	15. 79	15. 69	15. 44
Black, North:			
Interest in learning	(−). 03	. 01	1. 19
Self-concept	3. 72	1. 95	1. 23
Control of environment	5. 07	7. 96	4. 89
Strongest background item	1. 13	1. 44	1. 34
Background item	(¹)	(¹)	(²)

See footnotes at end of table.

Table 3.26.2 *(continued)*

	Unique contribution		
	Grade 12	Grade 9	Grade 6
Black, North—Continued			
Overall, including attitude_____	22. 67	25. 20	19. 22
Overall, excluding attitude_____	10. 96	11. 41	10. 25
Oriental Americans:			
Interest in learning_____	(−). 12	. 27	1. 33
Self-concept_____	5. 20	1. 48	. 83
Control of environment_	1. 59	3. 11	5. 27
Strongest background item_____	3. 88	4. 36	2. 85
Background item_____	(¹)	(¹)	(²)
Overall, including attitude_____	28. 81	30. 48	46. 82
Overall, excluding attitude_____	19. 45	22. 81	36. 16
White, South:			
Interest in learning_____	·1. 60	1. 52	1. 96
Self-concept_____	7. 67	3. 62	3. 17
Control of environment_	. 69	4. 84	2. 92
Strongest background item_____	1. 33	1. 04	1. 94
Background item_____	(³)	(³)	(³)
Overall, including attitude_____	35. 51	39. 60	32. 11
Overall, excluding attitude_____	20. 13	23. 12	19. 91
White, North:			
Interest in learning_____	1. 37	1. 82	1. 79
Self-concept_____	5. 02	3. 36	4. 40
Control of environment_	1. 55	3. 42	3. 52
Strongest background item_____	3. 09	1. 27	1. 45
Background item_____	(¹)	(³)	(³)
Overall, including attitude_____	37. 32	37. 85	30. 80
Overall, excluding attitude_____	24. 56	22. 78	15. 57
Blacks, total:			
Interest in learning_____	(−). 13	0	1. 36
Self-concept_____	2. 91	1. 16	. 98
Control of environment_____	5. 33	8. 89	5. 25
Strongest background item_____	1. 39	1. 03	2. 34
Background item_____	(⁵)	(¹)	(²)
Overall including attitude_____	26. 11	28. 18	23. 74
Overall excluding attitude_____	15. 14	14. 99	14. 62

See footnotes at end of table.

Table 3.26.2 (continued)

	Unique contribution		
	Grade 12	Grade 9	Grade 6
Whites, total:			
Interest in learning_____	1. 31	1. 61	1. 83
Self-concept_____	5. 82	3. 49	3. 95
Control of environ- ment_____	1. 26	3. 88	3. 27
Strongest background item_____	2. 19	1. 24	1. 66
Background item_____	(¹)	(³)	(³)
Overall including attitude_____	36. 30	38. 75	31. 82
Overall excluding attitude_____	23. 03	23. 28	17. 64

¹ Parents' educational desires.
² Items in home.
³ Parents' education.
⁴ Structural integration
⁵ Urbanism.

of his scholastic skills, and is probably more a consequence than a cause of scholastic achievement. His interest in learning, it can be assumed, partly derives from family background, and partly from his success in school. Thus, it is partly a cause of achievement in school. Of the three attitudinal variables, however, it is the weakest, especially among minority groups, where it shows inconsistent relations to achievement at grades 9 and 12. The absence of a consistent relation for blacks, along with the data presented in section 3.1 which showed blacks even more interested in learning than white, gives a picture of students who report high interest in academic achievement, but whose reported interest is not translated through effective action into achievement. Thus the causal sequence which is usually assumed to occur, in which interest leads to effort and thereby to achievement, appears not to occur in this way for blacks and other minority groups.

Clues to the causal sequence that may occur are provided by the relation of the two other attitudes to achievement. One of these clues lies in the second important result of this section: At grade 12, for whites and Oriental Americans, self-concept is more highly related to verbal skills before or after background is controlled than is control of environment; for all the other minority groups, the relative importance is reversed: the child's sense of control of environment is most strongly related to achievement.

Table 3.26.3 shows this comparison. This result is particularly impressive because this attitude has no direct logical relation to achievement in school or to ability. The three questions on which it is based are a statement that "good luck is more important than hard work for success," a statement that "every time I try to get ahead, something or someone stops me," and a statement that "people like me don't have much of a chance to be successful in life." Yet for minority groups which achieve least well, responses to these statements (individually or together) are more strongly related than any

TABLE 3.26.3

Unique Contributions to Accounted-for Variance in Verbal Skills of Self-concept and Control of Environment at 12th Grade, in Conjunction with One Other Attitude, With and Without Eight Background Factors Included [Total variance accounted for in regression at left is given in Table 3.26.1, in regression at right in Table 3.26.2]

Group and region	Without background		With background	
	Self-concept	Control of environment	Self-concept	Control of environment
Puerto Ricans	2.59	3.00	2.09	2.18
Indian Americans	4.94	9.69	2.91	5.06
Mexican-Americans	1.43	8.64	0.70	7.29
Black, South	3.64	8.36	3.06	5.76
Black, North	5.30	6.41	3.72	5.07
Orientals	6.46	3.60	5.20	1.59
White, South	10.97	1.29	7.67	0.69
White, North	8.50	2.55	5.02	1.55
Blacks, total	3.61	7.88	2.91	5.33
Whites, total	9.31	1.99	5.82	1.26

other variable to achievement. It was evident earlier in section 3.1 that children from these groups are much more likely to respond to these statements in terms showing a sense of lack of control of the environment. Now the present data show that children in these minority groups who do exhibit a sense of control of the environment have considerably higher achievement than those who do not. The causal sequence in this relation is not implied by the relationship itself. It may very well be two-directional, with both the attitude and the achievement affecting each other. Yet in the absence of specific evidence about causal direction, it is useful to examine one direction at length—the possible effect of such an attitude; that is, feeling a high or low sense of control of the environment, on achievement.[6]

Table 3.26.4 shows, for each minority group, and separately for blacks and whites in the North and South, the average verbal achievement scores for boys and girls who answer "good luck" and those who answered "hard work" on one of these questions. Those minority group students who give "hard work" or "control" responses score higher on the tests than do whites who give "no control" responses.

The special importance of a sense of control of environment for achievement of minority-group children and perhaps for disadvantaged whites as well suggests a different set of predispositional factors operating to create low or high achievement for children from disadvantaged groups than for children from advantaged groups. For children from advantaged groups, achievement

TABLE 3.26.4

Verbal Achievement Scores of Grade-9 Pupils Who Have Differing Responses to the Question: "Agree or Disagree: Good Luck is More Important Than Hard Work for Success"

Group and region	Agree (good luck)	Disagree (hard work)
Mexican American	38. 6	46. 8
Puerto Rican	38. 5	45. 5
Indian American	39. 9	47. 3
Oriental	44. 0	52. 5
Black, South	36. 6	43. 3
Black, North	40. 0	47. 1
White, South	42. 9	52. 5
White, North	45. 4	54. 8

or lack of it appears closely related to their self-concept: what they believe about themselves. For children from disadvantaged groups, achievement or lack of achievement appears closely related to what they believe about their environment: whether they believe the environment will respond to reasonable efforts, or whether they believe it is instead merely random or immovable. In different words, it appears that children from advantaged groups assume that the environment will respond if they are able enough to affect it; children from disadvantaged groups do not make this assumption, but in many cases assume that nothing they will do can affect the environment— it will give benefits or withhold them but not as a consequence of their own action.

One may speculate that these conceptions reasonably derive from the different experiences that these children have had. A child from an advantaged family most often has had all his needs satisfied, has lived in a responsive environment, and hence can assume that the environment will continue to be responsive if only he acts appropriately. A child from a disadvantaged family has had few of his needs satisfied, has lived in an unresponsive environment, both within the family (where other demands pressed upon his mother) and outside the family, in an outside and often unfriendly world.[7] Thus he cannot assume that the environment will respond to his actions. Such a state of affairs could be expected to lead to passivity, with a general belief in luck, a belief that that world is hostile, and also a belief that nothing he could ever do would change things. He has not yet come to see that he can affect his environment, for it has never been so in his previous experience.

Thus, for many disadvantaged children, a major obstacle to achievement may arise from the very way they confront the environment. Having experienced an unresponsive environment, the virtues of hard work, of diligent and extended effort toward achievement appear to such a child unlikely to be rewarding. As a consequence, he is likely to merely "adjust" to his environment, finding satisfaction in passive pursuits.

It may well be, then, that one of the keys toward success for minorities which have experienced disadvantage and a particularly unresponsive environment—either in the home or the larger society—is a change in this conception.

There is a further result in these data which could provide some clues about the differential dynamics of these attitudes among children from disadvantaged and advantaged groups, or from different kinds of families. When all three attitudes are examined together as predictors of verbal achievement, then the following shifts from grade 6 to 9 and 12 occur: (*a*) At grade 6, professed interest in school is related to achievement for all groups; but this relation vanishes at grades 9 and 12 except for Oriental Americans and whites; (*b*) control of environment is strongly related to achievement for all groups at grade 6; but this relation declines for Oriental Americans and whites in grades 9 and 12, while it increases for the other minority groups. These relationships can be seen in table 3.26.5, which shows the unique contributions to variance of the three attitudes at the three grade levels.[8]

These data indicating changes in the relationships must be viewed with caution, since some differences existed between grade 6 and grades 9 and 12 in the measures themselves. However, the data suggest that the child's sense of control of his environment (which, as section 3.1 showed, is lower at grade 6, and increases with age) is important in the early achievement of children from all groups, but that it is these children from disadvantaged groups whose sense of control of environment continues to be associated with an important difference in later achievement. These results of course are only suggestive, and indicate the need for further investigations of the dynamics of attitudes and achievement among disadvantaged groups in society. Because of the likely mutual dependence of these attitudes and achievement, such investigations will require special care on determining the extent to which each influences the other.

It is useful to inquire about the factors in the school and the home which affect children's self-concept and sense of control of the environment. First, this study provides little evidence concerning the effect of school factors on these attitudes. If family background characteristics are controlled, almost none of the remaining variance in self-concept and control of environment is accounted for by the school factors measured in this survey. One variable, however, is consistently related to control of environment and self-concept. For each group, as the proportion white in the school increases, the child's sense of control of environment increases, and his self-concept decreases. This suggests the possibility that school integration has conflicting effects on attitudes of minority group children: it increases their sense of control of the environment or their sense of opportunity, but decreases their self-concept. This relationship may well be an artifact, since the achievement level of the student body increases with percent white, and may be the

TABLE 3.26.5
Unique Contributions to Accounted for Variance of Verbal Achievement at Grades 12, 9, and 6* [Total variance given in Table 3.3.1]

Group and region	Grade 12			Grade 9			Grade 6		
	Interest	Self-concept	Control	Interest	Self-concept	Control	Interest	Self-concept	Control
Puerto Ricans	(−)6.25	2.59	3.00	(−)0.15	1.54	8.59	5.10	0.42	2.30
Indian Americans	.05	4.94	9.69	.31	2.45	9.20	5.81	1.40	4.35
Mexican-Americans	(−).11	1.43	8.64	.64	.64	9.26	3.30	2.11	4.77
Black, South	(−).07	3.64	8.36	.51	1.26	13.09	4.11	1.60	6.32
Black, North	0	5.30	6.41	.19	2.84	10.03	1.91	1.94	6.37
Oriental Americans	1.09	6.46	3.60	3.62	2.38	5.39	6.15	2.53	7.33
White, South	2.24	10.97	1.29	2.78	5.93	7.08	3.83	5.06	5.18
White, North	3.97	8.50	2.25	3.86	5.31	4.87	2.67	6.96	5.33
Black total	.25	3.61	7.88	.08	1.70	12.30	2.60	1.55	6.93
White total	3.02	9.31	1.99	3.13	5.71	5.74	3.05	6.30	5.38

*(−) preceding the number indicates that the partial relationship of the attitude to achievement is negative.

proximate cause of these opposite relationships. If so, these effects are merely effects or achievements and motivations of fellow students, rather than direct effects of integration. Whatever the time structure of causation, the relations, though consistent, are in all cases small.

It appears reasonable that these attitudes depend more on the home than the school. Reference was made earlier to a study which suggests that a mother's sense of control of the environment affects her young child's cognitive skills. It appears likely that her child's sense of control of environment depends similarly on her own. Such inquiry into the source of these attitudes can best be carried out by such intensive studies on a smaller scale than the present survey. However, some results from the present survey may be stated as clues to the sources of these attitudes.

At grades 6, 9, and 12, the simultaneous relation of eight family background factors to the two attitudes was studied. These background factors are:

Structural integrity of the home (father's presence, primarily).
Number of brothers and sisters.
Length of residence in an urban area.
Parents' education.
Economic level of home environment.
Reading material in home.
Parents' interest in child's schooling.
Parents' desires for child's further education.

The pattern of relationships between these factors and the two attitudes is similar for all groups in the survey with minor exceptions noted below. First, only a small fraction of the variance in these attitudes, averaging less than 10 percent, is accounted for by all these background factors, combined. For minority groups other than blacks, control of environment is better accounted for by these background factors than is self-concept. For blacks, both are about the same; and for whites self-concept is better accounted for than control of environment.

For both attitudes and for all groups, the parents' desires for the child's further education have the largest unique contribution to positive self-concept and a sense of control of environment. For self-concept, the only other variables which show a consistent relation (positive) are parents' education and the amount of reading material in the home. For the child's sense of control of the environment, there is in addition a consistent relation to the economic level of the home and the structural integrity of the home. That is, children from homes with a higher economic level, and children from homes where the father is present, show a higher sense of control of the environment than do children from homes with lower economic level or children from homes where the father is absent.

These results can be seen only as minor indications of the source of these attitudes in children's backgrounds. The major result of this section, which appears of considerable importance and warrants further investigation, is the different role these two attitudes appear to play for children from advantaged and disadvantaged backgrounds.

Implications of the results of section 3.2 for equality of educational opportunity.—Of the many implications of this study of school effects on achievement, one appears to be of overriding importance. This is the implication that stems from the following results taken together:

1. The great importance of family background for achievement;
2. The fact that the relation of family background to achievement does not diminish over the years of school;
3. The relatively small amount of school-to-school variation that is not accounted for by differences in family background, indicating the small independent effect of variations in school facilities, curriculum, and staff upon achievement;
4. The small amount of variance in achievement explicitly accounted for by variations in facilities and curriculum;
5. Given the fact that no school factors account for much variation in achievement, teachers' characteristics account for more than any other— taken together with the results from section 2.3, which show that teachers tend to be socially and racially similar to the students they teach;
6. The fact that the social composition of the student body is more highly related to achievement, independently of the student's own social background, than is any school factor;
7. The fact that attitudes such as a sense of control of the environment, or a belief in the responsiveness of the environment, are extremely highly related to achievement, but appear to be little influenced by variations in school characteristics.

Taking all these results together, one implication stands out above all: That schools bring little influence to bear on a child's achievement that is independent of his background and general social context; and that this very lack of an independent effect means that the inequalities imposed on children by their home, neighborhood, and peer environment are carried along to become the inequalities with which they confront adult life at the end of school. For equality of educational opportunity through the schools must imply a strong effect of schools that is independent of the child's immediate social environment, and that strong independent effect is not present in American schools.

Notes

1. It should be noted, however, that in grades 1 and 3 these conditions (incompletely measured) show a lower relation to achievement than in any of the three grades examined here. This is true for the relation of all variables to achievement at these two grades. While this may result from incompleteness and unreliability of response at these grade levels, it may indicate that the relation does in fact increase over time.

[2.] The general finding of the importance of student body characteristics for educational outcomes has been shown by several investigators. One of the first systematic investigations is reported in Alan B. Wilson, "Residential Segregation of Social Classes and Aspirations of High School Boys." *American Sociological Review,* v. 24, 1959, pp. 836–845.

[3.] The data show a lesser residual relationship (column A+B+C) for whites than blacks and for Southern whites than for Northern ones. However, this is largely due to the lesser variation in racial composition of student body for whites than for blacks, and for Southern whites than for Northern ones.

[4.] If any school factors were highly associated with race, they would certainly account spuriously for a large fraction of the variance in achievement. Thus, an apparent school effect would not necessarily represent a true school effect.

[5.] To determine whether this differential relation is merely a result of greater variation in teachers' characteristics for Southern blacks compared to Northern ones, or in fact a greater effect of a given amount of variation, the variances of the three most important variables, teachers' verbal ability, family educational background, and own education, were examined. These variances are approximately the same for Northern and Southern blacks, indicating that it is not a difference in variability of teachers, but a difference in the effect of a given degree of variability that is responsible for the different relation.

[6.] In this regard, a recent social-psychological experiment is relevant. Black and white adults were offered an alternative between a risky situation in which the outcome depended on chance, and one in which the outcome, though no more favorable altogether, was contingent on their own response. Black adults less often chose the alternative contingent on their own behavior, more often chose the chance alternative, as compared to whites. Herbert M. Lefcourt, "Risk-Taking in Negro and White Adults," *Journal of Personality and Social Psychology* 2, 1965, pp. 765–770.

[7.] Recent research on black mothers and their 4-year-old children has shown that those mothers with a sense of futility relative to the environment have children with lower scores on Stanford-Binet IQ tests, after other aspects of the mother's behavior, including her own IQ score, are statistically controlled. See Roberta M. Bear, Robert D. Hess, and Virginia C. Shipman, "Social class difference in maternal attitudes toward school and the consequences for cognitive development in the young child," mimeographed, 1966, Urban Child Center, University of Chicago.

[8.] An investigation of the relative sizes of the variances of these attitudes for the different groups shows that it is not the different amount of variation in the attitudes that is responsible for the different relations to achievement among the different groups, for the attitude variances do not differ widely. It is instead the different relation that a given amount of attitude difference has to achievement in these groups.

8

Equal Schools
or Equal Students?

The Civil Rights Act of 1964 contains a section numbered 402, which went largely unnoticed at the time. This section instructs the Commissioner of Education to carry out a survey of "concerning the lack of availability of equal educational opportunities" by reason of race, religion or national origin, and to report to Congress and the President within two years. The Congressional intent in this section is somewhat unclear. But if, as is probable, the survey was initially intended as a means of finding areas of continued intentional discrimination, the intent later became less punitive-oriented and more future-oriented: *i.e.*, to provide a basis for public policy, at the local, state, and national levels, which might overcome inequalities of educational opportunity.

In the two years that have intervened (but mostly in the second), a remarkably vast and comprehensive survey was conducted, focusing principally on the inequalities of educational opportunity experienced by five racial and ethnic minorities: blacks, Puerto Ricans, Mexican Americans, American Indians, and Oriental Americans. In the central and largest portion of the survey, nearly 600,000 children at grades, 1, 3, 6, 9, and 12, in 4000 schools in all 50 states and the District of Columbia, were tested and questioned; 60,000 teachers in these schools were questioned and self-tested; and principals of these schools were also questioned about their schools. The tests and questionnaires (administered in the fall of 1965 by Educational Testing Service) raised a considerable controversy in public school circles and among some parents, with concern ranging from Federal encroachment on the local education system to the spectre of invasion of privacy. Nevertheless, with a participation rate of about 70% of all the schools sampled, the survey was conducted; and on July 1, 1966, Commissioner Howe presented a summary report of this survey. On July 31, the total report, *Equality of*

Reprinted with permission from *The Public Interest*, no. 4 (Summer 1966): 70–75. Copyright © 1966 by National Affairs, Inc.

Educational Opportunity, 737 pages, was made available (Government Printing Office, $4.25).

The summary of the report has appeared to many who have read it to be curiously "flat," lacking in emphases and policy implications. Much of the same flatness can be found in the larger report. The seeming flatness probably derives from three sources: the research analyst's uneasiness in moving from description to implications; the government agency's uneasiness with survey findings that may have political repercussions; and, perhaps more important than either of these, the fact that the survey results do not lend themselves to the provision of simple answers. Nevertheless, the report is not so uncontroversial as it appears. And some of its findings, though cautiously presented, have sharp implications.

Perhaps the greatest virtue of this survey—though it has many faults—is that it did not take a simple or politically expedient view of educational opportunity. To have done so would have meant to measure (a) the objective characteristics of schools—number of books in the library, age of buildings, educational level of teachers, accreditation of the schools, and so on; and (b) the actual extent of racial segregation in the schools. The survey did look into these matters (and found less inequity in school facilities and resources, more in the extent of segregation, than is commonly supposed); but its principal focus of attention was not on what resources go into education, but on what product comes out. It did this in a relatively uncomplicated way, which is probably adequate for the task at hand: by tests which measured those areas of achievement most necessary for further progress in school, in higher education, and in successful competition in the labor market—that is, verbal and reading skills, and analytical and mathematical skills. Such a criterion does not allow statements about absolute levels of inequality or equality of education provided by the schools, because obviously there are more influences than the school's on a child's level of achievement in school, and there are more effects of schools than in these areas of achievement. What it does do is to broaden the question beyond the school to all those educational influences that have their results in the level of verbal and mathematical skill a young person is equipped with when he or she enters the adult world. In effect, it takes the perspective of this young adult, and says that what matters to him is, not how "equal" his school is, but rather whether he is equipped at the end of school to compete on an equal basis with others, whatever his social origins. From the perspective of society, it assumes that what is important is not to "equalize the schools" in some formal sense, but to insure that children from all groups come into adult society so equipped as to insure their full participation in this society.

Another way of putting this is to say that the schools are successful only insofar as they reduce the dependence of a child's opportunities upon his social origins. We can think of a set of conditional probabilities: the probability of being prepared for a given occupation or for a given college at the end of high school, conditional upon the child's social origins. The effectiveness of the schools consists, in part, of making the conditional probabilities less conditional—that is, less dependent upon social origins. Thus, equality of educational opportunity implies, not merely "equal" schools, but equally effective schools, whose influences will overcome the differences in starting point of children from different social groups.

The Widening Educational Gap

This approach to educational opportunity, using as it does achievement on standardized tests, treads on sensitive ground. Differences in average achievement between racial groups can lend themselves to racist arguments of genetic differences in intelligence; even apart from this, they can lead to invidious comparisons between groups which show different average levels of achievement. But it is precisely the avoidance of such sensitive areas that can perpetuate the educational deficiencies with which some minorities are equipped at the end of schooling.

What, then, does the survey find with regard to effects of schooling on test achievement? Children were tested at the beginning of grades 1, 3, 6, 9, and 12. Achievement of the average American Indian, Mexican American, Puerto Rican, and black (in this descending order) was much lower than the average white or Oriental American, at all grade levels. The amount of difference ranges from about half a standard deviation to one standard deviation at early grade levels. At the 12th grade, it increases to beyond one standard deviation. (One standard deviation difference means that about 85% of the minority group children score below the average of the whites, while if the groups were equal only about 50% would score below this average.) The grade levels of difference range up to 5 years of deficiency (in math achievement) or 4 years (in reading skills) at the 12th grade. In short, the differences are large to begin with, and they are even larger at higher grades.

Two points, then, are clear: (1) *these minority children have a serious educational deficiency at the start of school, which is obviously not a result of school;* and (2) *they have an even more serious deficiency at the end of school, which is obviously in part a result of school.*

Thus, by the criterion stated earlier—that the effectiveness of schools in creating equality of educational opportunity lies in making the conditional probabilities of success less conditional—the schools appear to fail. At the end of school, the conditional probabilities of high achievement are even *more* conditional upon racial or ethnic background than they are at the beginning of school.

There are a number of results from the survey which give further evidence on this matter. First, within each racial group, the strong relation of family economic and educational background to achievement does not diminish over the period of school, and may even increase over the elementary years. Second, most of the variation in student achievement lies within the same school, very little of it is between schools. The implication of these last two results is clear: family background differences account for much more variation in achievement than do school differences.

Even the school-to-school variation in achievement, though relatively small, is itself almost wholly due to the *social* environment provided by the school: the educational backgrounds and aspirations of other students in the school, and the educational backgrounds and attainments of the teachers in the school. *Per pupil expenditure, books in the library, and a host of other facilities and curricular measures show virtually no relation to achievement if the "social" environment of the school—the educational backgrounds of other students and teachers—is held constant.*

The importance of this last result lies, of course, in the fact that schools, as currently organized, are quite culturally homogeneous as well as quite racially segregated: teachers tend to come from the same cultural groups (and especially from the same race) as their students, and the student bodies are themselves relatively homogeneous. Given this homogeneity, the principal agents of effectiveness in the schools—teachers and other students—act to maintain or reinforce the initial differences imposed by social origins.

One element illustrates well the way in which the current organization of schools maintains the differences over generations: a black prospective teacher leaves a black teacher's college with a much lower level of academic competence (as measured by the National Teacher's Examination) than does his white counterpart leaving his largely white college; then he teaches black children (in school with other black children, ordinarily from educationally deficient backgrounds), who learn at a lower level, in part because of his lesser competence; some of these students, in turn, go into teacher training institutions to become poorly-trained teachers of the next generation.

Altogether, *the sources of inequality of educational opportunity appear to lie first in the home itself and the cultural influences immediately surrounding the home; then they lie in the schools' ineffectiveness to free achievement from the impact of the home, and in the schools' cultural homogeneity which perpetuates the social influences of the home and its environs.*

A Modest, Yet Radical, Proposal

Given these results, what do they suggest as to avenues to equality of educational opportunity? Several elements seem clear:

a) For those children whose family and neighborhood are educationally disadvantaged, it is important to replace this family environment as much as possible with an educational environment—by starting school at an earlier age, and by having a school which begins very early in the day and ends very late.

b) It is important to reduce the social and racial homogeneity of the school environment, so that those agents of education that do show some effectiveness—teachers and other students—are not mere replicas of the student himself. In the present organization of schools, it is the neighborhood school that most insures such homogeneity.

c) The educational program of the school should be made more effective than it is at present. The weakness of this program is apparent in its inability to overcome initial differences. It is hard to believe that we are so inept in educating our young that we can do no more than leave young adults in the same relative competitive positions we found them in as children.

Several points are obvious: It is not a solution simply to pour money into improvement of the physical plants, books, teaching aids, of schools attended by educationally disadvantaged children. For other reasons, it will not suffice merely to bus children or otherwise achieve pro forma integration. (One incidental effect of this would be to increase the segregation within schools, through an increase in tracking.)

The only kinds of policies that appear in any way viable are those which do not seek to improve the education of blacks and other educationally disadvantaged at the expense of those who are educationally advantaged. This implies new kinds of educational institutions, with a vast increase in expenditures for education—not merely for the disadvantaged, but for all children. The solutions might be in the form of educational parks, or in the form of private schools paid by tuition grants (with Federal regulations to insure racial heterogeneity), public (or publicly-subsidized) boarding schools (like the North Carolina Advancement School), or still other innovations. This approach also implies reorganization of the curriculum within schools. One of the major reasons for "tracking" is the narrowness of our teaching methods—they can tolerate only a narrow range of skill in the same classroom. Methods which greatly widen the range are necessary to make possible racial and cultural integration within a school—and thus to make possible the informal learning that other students of higher educational levels can provide. Such curricular innovations are possible—but, again, only through the investment of vastly greater sums in education than currently occurs.

It should be recognized, of course, that the goal described here—of equality of educational opportunity through the schools—is far more ambitious than has ever been posed in our society before. The schools were once seen as a supplement to the family in bringing a child into his place in adult society, and they still function largely as such a supplement, merely perpetuating the inequalities of birth. Yet the conditions imposed by technological change, and by our post-industrial society, quite apart from any ideals of equal opportunity, require a far more primary role for the school, if society's children are to be equipped for adulthood.

Self-confidence and Performance

One final result of the survey gives an indication of still another—and perhaps the most important—element necessary for equality of educational opportunity for blacks. One attitude of students was measured at grades 9 and 12—an attitude which indicated the degree to which the student felt in control of his own fate. For example, one question was: "Agree or disagree: good luck is more important than hard work for success." Another was:

"Agree or disagree: every time I try to get ahead someone or something stops me." Blacks much less often than whites had such a sense of control of their fate—a difference which corresponds directly to reality, and which corresponds even more markedly to the black's historical position in American society. However, despite the very large achievement differences between whites and blacks at the 9th and 12th grades, *those blacks who gave responses indicating a sense of control of their own fate achieved higher on the tests than those whites who gave the opposite responses. This attitude was more highly related to achievement than any other factor in the student's background or school.*

This result suggests that internal changes in the black, changes in his conception of himself in relation to his environment, may have more effect on black achievement than any other single factor. The determination to overcome relevant obstacles, and the belief that he will overcome them—attitudes that have appeared in an organized way among blacks only in recent years in some civil rights groups—may be the most crucial elements in achieving equality of opportunity—not because of changes they will create in the white community, but principally because of the changes they create in the black himself.

9

Toward Open Schools

Since the publication, in July, 1966, of the Office of Education's report to Congress and the President on "Equality of Educational Opportunity," there has been much speculation and discussion concerning the policy implications of the report. The report itself, which focused principally on inequalities experienced by blacks and other racial and ethnic minorities, contained only research results, not policy recommendations. Indeed, if recommendations had been requested, they could hardly have been given—for the facts themselves point to no obvious solution.

In some part, the difficulties and complexity of any solution derive from the premise that our society is committed to overcoming, not merely inequalities in the distribution of educational *resources* (classrooms, teachers, libraries, etc.), but inequalities in the opportunity for educational *achievement*. This is a task far more ambitious than has even been attempted by any society:—not just to offer, in a passive way, equal access to educational resources, but to provide an educational environment that will free a child's potentialities for learning from the inequalities imposed upon him by the accident of birth into one or another home and social environment.

The difficulty that attends this task can be seen by confronting some of the results published in the report with one another. First, the inequality in results of elementary and secondary schooling for different ethnic groups, as measured by standardized tests, is very large for blacks, Puerto Ricans, American Indians, and Mexican Americans. At the beginning of the twelfth grade, these groups were, on the average, three, four, or five grade levels behind whites in reading comprehension, and four, five, or six grade levels behind in mathematics achievement. Second, the evidence revealed that within broad geographic regions, and for each racial or ethnic group, the physical and economic resources going into a school had very little relation to the achievement coming out of it. This was perhaps the most surprising result to some persons: that variations in teacher salaries, library facilities, laboratories, school size, guidance facilities had little relation to student achievement—when the family backgrounds of the students were roughly

Reprinted with permission from *The Public Interest*, no. 9 (Fall 1967): 20–27. Copyright © 1967 by National Affairs, Inc.

equated. Such equating of background is necessary because, within each racial or ethnic group, the factor that showed the clearest relation to a child's achievement was his home background—the educational and economic resources provided within his home.

This pair of results taken together—the serious differences in educational output and their lack of relation to differences in the input of conventional educational facilities—create the complexity of the problem. For if it were otherwise, we could give simple prescriptions: increase teachers' salaries, lower classroom size, enlarge libraries, and so on. But the evidence does not allow such simple answers.

Heterogeneity and Achievement

Another finding of the survey does give some indication of how different schools have different effects. The finding is that students do better when they are in schools where there fellow students come from backgrounds strong in educational motivation and resources. The results might be paraphrased by the statement that the educational resources provided by a child's fellow students are more important for his achievement than are the resources provided by the school board. This effect appers to be particularly great for students who themselves come from educationally-deprived backgrounds. For example, it is about twice as great for blacks as for whites.

There are relatively small differences in the physical and economic resources of schools attended by black children and schools attended by white children (another surprising finding); but there are very large differences in the educational resources provided by their classmates. Classmates and schoolmates are usually rather homogeneous in economic and educational backgrounds, especially in large urban areas, and this homogeneity works to the disadvantage of those children whose family's educational resources are meagre. The disadvantage is particularly pronounced for blacks, where historical patterns of school segregation and residential segregation, combined with the lower educational backgrounds of black families, place most black children in schools where the sum of educational resources brought to school by members of the student body is very small.

These results do offer a direct course of action in many communties where racial segregation of schools can be overcome by various means. For the results indicate that heterogeneity of race and heterogeneity of family educational background can increase the achievement of children from weak educational backgrounds with no adverse effect on children from strong educational backgrounds. Such integration cannot be expected to bring about full equality of opportunity for achievement; but the evidence does indicate effects that are far from negligible. In the large cities, however, where lower-class blacks are both concentrated and numerous, this approach quickly exhausts its possibilities. There are simply not enough middle class children to go around.

Some observers have inferred from the Report that through racial integration of schools, and *only* through racial integration, will blacks' educational achievement begin to match that of whites. The Civil Rights Commission has proposed that Congress pass a law requiring that all schools contain fewer than 50 per cent blacks—a recommendation based partly on evidence in our report about black achievement in schools of differing racial and class composition. I believe such inferences are mistaken, and that the recommendations following from them are self-defeating. Racial integration of the schools is an important goal in its own right, affecting the very ability of our society to become truly multiracial. It is important to know, as the Report shows, that this goal does not conflict with, and to some degree aids, the goal of increasing the educational achievement of lower-class children. But these two goals are not identical. The task of increasing achievement of lower-class children cannot be fully implemented by school integration, even if integration were wholly achieved—and the magnitude of racial and class concentrations in large cities indicates that it is not likely to be achieved soon.

Reconstructing the Environment

I suggest that the matter may be better dealt with by inquiring more fully into the question of *how* a child's achievement is affected by the educational resources brought to school by other children. The evidence on this matter is not strong, but it is suggestive.

It is, for instance, a simple fact that the teacher cannot teach beyond the level of the most advanced students in the class, and cannot easily demand performance beyond that level. Thus, a comparison of black students (having similar family backgrounds) in lower class and largely segregated schools with those in middle class and often integrated schools shows that the former get higher grades than the latter, but their performance on standardized tests is lower. The student in a lower class school is being rewarded more highly for lower performance—not as much can be demanded of him.

It is also clear that going to school with other children whose vocabulary is larger than one's own demands and creates a larger vocabulary. Sitting next to a child who is performing at a high level provides a challenge to better performance. The psychological environment may be less comfortable for a lower class child (and there is some evidence that it is), but he learns more.

In short, there is some indication that these middle class schools have their effects through providing a social environment that is more demanding and more stimulating. And once we consider this, we realize that integration is not the only means, nor even necessarily the most efficient means, for increasing lower-class achievement. There may be other and better ways of creating such an environment.

For whatever the benefits of integration, it is also true that even in socially or racially integrated schools a child's family background shows a very high relation to his performance. The findings of the Report are quite unambiguous on this score. Even if the school is integrated, the heterogeneity of backgrounds with which children enter school is largely preserved in the heterogeneity of their performance when they finish. As the Report indicates, integration provides benefits to the underprivileged. But it takes only a small step toward equality of educational opportunity.

Thus a more intense reconstruction of the child's social environment than that provided by school integration is necessary to remove the handicap of a poor family background. It is such reconstruction that is important—whether it be provided through other children, through tutorial programs, through artificial environments created by computer consoles, or by some other means. The goal of increasing lower-class black achievement may be affected through a wide variety of means, which reconstruct a child's social and intellectual environment in any of several ways.

But if we recognize that racial and class integration does not in itself provide a full enough reconstruction of the environment, what happens then to the goal of racial integration in the schools? If more efficient methods for increasing achievement are found, as is likely to be the case, does this imply abandonment of attempts to overcome de facto segregation?

To answer this question requires a full recognition that there are two separable goals involved in current discussions for reorganizing schools. *The aim of racial integration of our schools should be recognized as distinct from the aim of providing equal opportunity for educational performance.* To confound these two aims impedes the achievement of either. It is important to know, as the Office of Education survey shows, that integration aids equality of educational opportunity; that white children perform no less well in a school with a large minority of blacks than in an all-white middle class school; that black students perform somewhat better in such a school than in a predominantly black lower class school. Conversely, of course, greater equality of performance facilitates integration, making "grouping" or "tracking" within schools unnecessary. But integration is important to both white and black children principally for other reasons. We are committed to becoming a truly multiracial society. Yet most white children grow up having no conception of blacks as individuals, and thus develop wholly unnatural and ambivalent reactions to blacks as a group; most black children are in a similar circumstance. All educational policies must recognize the legitimacy and importance of the aim of racial integration. But we should not confound it with the aim of increasing equality of educational performance. Thus the proposals I shall make, though they stem from a single overall principle for reorganizing our schools, are directed to these two goals as *separable* goals.

From Closed to Open Schools

The general principle underlying the proposals may be described as the transformation of schools from closed institutions to open ones—the creation of "open schools."

The general idea is to conceive of the school very differently from the way we have done in the past—not as a building into which a child vanishes in the morning and from which he emerges in the afternoon, but as a "home base" that carries out some teaching functions but which serves principally to coordinate his activities and to perform guidance and testing functions. The specific ways of "opening up" the schools are indicated below.

The essential aims of the elementary school, if the opportunity for further learning is not to be blocked, are the learning of only two things: reading and arithmetic. It is in teaching these basic skills that present schools most often fail for lower class children, and thus handicap them for further learning. Many new methods for teaching these subjects have been developed in recent years; and there is much interest of persons outside the schools in helping to solve the problem; yet the school is trapped by its own organizational weight—innovations cannot be lightly adopted by a massive educational system, and local arrangements that use community resources outside the school cannot easily be fitted into the schools' organization.

In an open school, the teaching of elementary-level reading and arithmetic would be opened up to entrepreneurs outside the school, under contract with the school system to teach only reading or only arithmetic, and paid on the basis of increased performance by the child on standardized tests. The methods used by such contractors may only be surmised; the successful ones would presumably involve massive restructuring of the verbal or mathematical environment. The methods might range from new phonetic systems for teaching reading or new methods for teaching numerical problem-solving to locally sponsored tutorial programs or the use of new technological aids such as talking typewriters and computer consoles. The payment-by-results would quickly eliminate the unsuccessful contractors, and the contractors would provide testing grounds for innovations that could subsequently be used by the school.

One important element that this would introduce into schools is the possibility of parental choice. Each parent would have the choice of sending his child to any of the reading or arithmetic programs outside the school, on released time, or leaving him wholly within the school to learn his reading and arithmetic there. The school would find it necessary to compete with the system's external contractors to provide better education, and the parent could, for the first time in education, have the full privileges of consumer's choice.

One simple control would be necessary to insure that this did not lead to resegregation of the school along racial or class lines: no contractor could accept from any one school a higher proportion of whites than existed in that school, nor a higher proportion of students whose parents were above a certain educational level than existed in the school.

This means of opening up the school, through released time, private contractors, payment by results, and free choice for the consumer, could be easily extended to specific core subjects in high school. It should be a potentially profitable activity to the contractor, but with the profitability wholly contingent upon results, so that the incentives of these teachers and educational entrepreneurs are tied wholly to improving a child's achievement beyond the level that would otherwise be expected of him.

The use of released time and private contracts would be diversified in later years of school, so that a potential contractor could apply for a contract in any of a wide range of subjects, some taught within the school, but others not. The many post-high school business and technical schools that now exist would be potential contractors, but always with the public school establishing the criteria for achievement, and testing the results.

It would still remain the case that the child would stay within the school for much of his time; and in those schools that stood up well to the competition, most children would choose to take all their work in the school. At the same time, some schools might lose most of their teaching functions— if they did not deserve to keep them.

A second major means of opening up the school is directed wholly at the problem of racial and class integration, just as the first is directed wholly at the problem of achievement. The school would be opened up through intensifying the interactions between students who have different home-base schools. To create integrated schools in large urban centers becomes almost impossible; but to bring about social integration through schools is not. Again, the point is to discard the idea of the school as a closed institution, and think of it as a base of operations. Thus, rather than having classes scheduled in the school throughout the year, some classes would be scheduled with children from other schools, sometimes in their own school, sometimes in the other—but deliberately designed to establish continuing relationships between children across racial and social class lines. Certain extra-curricular activities can be organized on a cross-school basis, arranged to fit with the cross-school class schedules. Thus children from different home base schools would not be competing *against* each other, but would be members of the *same* team or club. An intensified program of interscholastic activities, including debates and academic competitions as well as sports events, could achieve the aims of social integration—possibly not as fully as in the best integrated schools, but also possibly even more so—and certainly more so than in many integrated schools.

This second means of opening up the school could in part be accomplished through outside organizations acting as contractors, in somewhat the same way as the reading and mathematics contractors described earlier. Community organizations could design specific cultural enrichment programs or community action programs involving students from several schools of different racial or class composition, with students engaging in such programs by their own or parent's choice. Thus, resources that exist outside the school could come to play an increasing part in education, through contracts with the schools. Some such programs might be community improvement activities, in which white and black high school students learn simultaneously to work together and to aid the community. But the essential element in such programs is that they should not be carried out by the school, in which case they would quickly die after the first enthusiasm had gone, but be undertaken by outside groups under contract to the school, and with the free choice of parent or child.

A Widening of Horizons

The idea of opening up the school, of conceiving of the home school as a center of operations, while it can aid the two goals of performance and integration described above, is much more than an ad hoc device for accomplishing these goals. It allows the parent what he has never had within the public school system: a freedom of choice as a consumer, as well as the opportunity to help establish special purpose programs, clinics and centers to beat the school at its own game. It allows educational innovations the opportunity to prove themselves, insofar as they can attract and hold students. The contract centers provide the school with a source of innovation as well as a source of competition to measure its own efforts, neither of which it has had in the past. The interschool scheduling and interscholastic academic events widen horizons of both teachers and children, and provide a means of diffusing both the techniques and content of education, a means which is not possible so long as a school is a closed institution.

A still further problem that has always confronted public education, and has become intense in New York recently, is the issue of parental control versus control by the educational bureaucracy. This issue is ordinarily seen as one of legitimacy: how far is it legitimate for parents to exert organized influence over school policies? But the issue need not be seen this way. The public educational system is a monopoly, and such issues of control always arise in monopolies, where consumers lack a free choice. As consumers, they have a legitimate interest in what that monopoly offers them, and can only exercise this interest through organized power. But such issues do not arise where the consumer can implement his interest through the exercise of free choice between competing offerings. Until now, this exercise of choice has only been available for those who could afford to buy education outside the public schools.

It is especially appropriate and necessary that such an opening up of schools occur in a period when the interest of all society has become focused on the schools. The time is past when society as a whole, parents as individuals, and interested groups outside the school were willing to leave the task of education wholly to the public education system, to watch children vanish into the school in the morning and emerge from it in the afternoon, without being able to affect what goes on behind the school doors.

10

The Evaluation of
Equality of Educational
Opportunity

In July of 1966, the U.S. Office of Education issued a report titled "Equality of Educational Opportunity," to fulfill a provision of the Civil Rights Act of 1964 which read as follows:

> The Commissioner shall conduct a survey and make a report to the President and the Congress, within two years of the enactment of this title, concerning the lack of availability of equal educational opportunities for individuals by reason of race, color, religion, or national origin in public educational institutions at all levels in the United States, its territories and possessions, and the District of Columbia.

This request was one of the first specific requests made by Congress for social research that might provide a basis for policy. It is a kind of governmental interest in information about the functioning of society that compares to its interest that began some years ago in information about the functioning of the economy. As such, it is likely to increase as national policy becomes increasingly concerned with social institutions, an increase that is already foreshadowed by such developments as the publication of *Toward a social report* in 1970 by the Department of Health, Education, and Welfare.

As a consequence, it becomes important to examine retrospectively this attempt to address social research to social policy, as a way of learning, the problems and pitfalls of such activity, and of learning how best to carry it out. Such activity has not been the central focus of applied social research, and, as a consequence, it raises new problems of design and analysis.

Reprinted from Frederick Mosteller and Daniel P. Moynihan, eds., *On Equality of Educational Opportunity* (New York: Random House, 1972), pp. 146–167. Used by permission of McGraw-Hill Book Company, Inc.

I propose, then, to make such a retrospective examination. To do so as one of the authors of the report carries both advantages and disadvantages. The principal advantages are knowledge of the variety of problems that arose in the study that are not apparent in the final report, and the necessity of having given thought to various alternative designs that were not in fact used. The principal disadvantage lies in the necessity of an author to justify the work as it finally appeared. The disadvantage in this case may be reduced by the fact that I will use as a context for my examination a critical paper reviewing the report, "On the Value of *Equality of Educational Opportunity* as a Guide to Public Policy," by John F. Kain of Harvard University and Eric A. Hanushek of the Air Force Academy. This is one of three papers written by economists critical of the Report, and includes many of the criticisms made by the others.[1] The paper by Kain and Hanushek, both economists, provides not only a check to the self-justification of an author but also the different perspective provided by a discipline that has been traditionally more closely linked to policy than has sociology, and one that has special perspectives of its own.

Defining the Problem

The first question that arises in such a study as that requested by the Civil Rights Act in Section 402 is to determine precisely what the request means, and how it can be best fulfilled. In this case, the difficulty was especially great because the very concept of "equality of educational opportunity" is one that is presently undergoing change, and various members of government and of society have different conceptions of what such equality consists of. There are many such conceptions and I will not go into them here, except to say that this was regarded, as it should have been, as the major problem in the design of the survey, and a great deal of attention was paid to it. A portion of an internal memorandum discussing the varieties of concepts of "equality of educational opportunity" has recently been published elsewhere, and I will not repeat them here.[2] It is sufficient to say that five were discussed: first, inequality defined by degree of racial segregation; second, inequality of resource inputs from the school system; third, inequality in "intangible" resources such as teacher morale; fourth, inequality of inputs as weighted according to their effectiveness for achievement; and fifth, inequality of output as prima facie evidence of inequality of opportunity.

The study as designed and executed gave evidence relevant to all five of these definitions of educational opportunity. Kain and Hanushek argue that the most serious mistake of the study was here, and that the study should have carried out a careful study of inputs, as the necessary minimum, before it could consider questions more difficult to supply definitive answers to, such as the effect of school inputs on achievement. Their charge is worth some discussion because, if indeed a mistake was made at this point, it was the most serious of the study. But I believe that to have taken the approach proposed by Kain and Hanushek would have constituted exactly this magnitude of error.

As the survey was defined and carried out, it was intended to serve three purposes: to provide an accurate description of resource inputs for six different racial and ethnic groups at elementary and secondary school; to provide an accurate description of levels of achievement of each of these groups at three points in elementary school, grades 1, 3, and 6, and two in secondary school, grades 9 and 12; and to provide the basis for an analysis of the effects of various inputs on achievement. In terms of the five definitions of educational opportunity described above, such measures of effects were necessary for the fourth, to provide weights for various inputs, so that the "effective" inequality of opportunity could be assessed, and attention could be focused on those input resources that are effective in bringing about educational opportunity, or by their unequal distribution, effective in maintaining inequality of opportunity.

As Kain and Hanushek point out, the sample design requirements and the kinds of measurement are different for each of these three purposes. In the first, the samplilng variability is at the level of the *school*, even if reporting is ultimately to be done in terms of exposure of the average student to school resources, as the report did. The second and third aims, on the other hand, require measurements on students, in effect reducing the number of schools that can be included within the scope of such a study.[3] The third, analysis of the relation between input and output, imposes different design requirements than the second, in the way that analysis of relationships generally imposes a different sample design than does description of population characteristics, with less attention to sampling error, and more attention to the range of variability in the independent variables. Kain and Hanushek argue that the survey attempted too much; by attempting all three of these things, it failed to do well the first, minimum requirement.

This charge is a telling blow, for much of it is true. The final design *is* a compromise between three objectives, less good for any one of them than if the others had been absent. Its size is a compromise between measurement of school characteristics and of student characteristics, and its design a compromise between descriptive demands of the first two objectives and the analytical objectives of the third (for example, schools with intermediate proportions of blacks and whites had especially high probabilities of being drawn). At one time in the survey design, in fact, a design involving two samples was seriously considered: a large sample of schools to measure school characteristics, and a smaller one for measuring student characteristics, including achievement, and for analyzing the relationship of achievement to school characteristics. This design was rejected because the great effort necessary to secure cooperation of each school in releasing sensitive information would have made a much larger sample of schools difficult to achieve without sacrificing the other objectives.

The alternative, as proposed by Kain and Hanushek, was to do well the minimum necessary task: to measure carefully the input resources to school attended by blacks and those attended by whites, to show what is in fact the kind and degree of discrimination in schooling experienced by blacks. They point to a number of specific weaknesses in such measurement, attributable to the more ambitious objectives.[4]

The defect of the apparently simple and straightforward approach they suggest is the most serious possible: by selective attention to one of the definitions of equality of educational opportunity, that is, equality of inputs, it implicitly accepts and reinforces that definition. In effect, I suggest, it fails to see the forest because of too close attention to the trees. In contrast, the major virtue of the study as conceived and executed lay in the fact that it did *not* accept that definition, and by refusing to do so, has had its major impact in *shifting* policy attention from its traditional focus on comparison of inputs (the traditional measures of school quality used by school administrators: per-pupil expenditure, class size, teacher salaries, age of building and equipment, and so on) to a focus on output, and the effectiveness of inputs for bringing about changes in output.

This effect of the study in shifting the focus of attention did not come about because the study gave selective emphasis to that definition of educational opportunity that entailed examination of effects; only one section of one chapter of the report was devoted to it. The study presented evidence relevant to all five of the definitions that had been initially laid out. It was the audience who, with evidence on all of these before it rather than only the comparisons of inputs that have traditionally served as the basis for comparisons of school "quality," focused its attention on the more relevant questions of output, and effect of inputs upon output. As I indicated above, I regard this shift of attention as the most important impact on policy of the study. It raised questions where none had been before: what is the value of the new large programs of federal aid to education? (The report results indicate very little, except through improving teacher quality, which the programs are not usually designed to do.) Do smaller class sizes bring increased achievement? (The report results say no.) These and numerous other questions had been prematurely answered in the absence of facts, and if the study had taken the apparently straightforward careful approach that Kain and Hanushek propose, they would have continued to be answered prematurely, in the absence of facts. The study would have been celebrated for its careful accuracy, its measurement of inequality, and its irrelevance would have gone unnoticed, as policy-makers busily worked to eradicate those irrelevant inequalities.

I have spent so much attention upon this question of overall design because it is so important, and because one can be so easily misled. It appears most reasonable, from the standpoint of careful scientific inquiry, to limit policy-related research to that narrow definition of the problem that can give the most scientifically defensible results within the limits of time and resources available. But to do so may serve to define, and define incorrectly, the very policy questions that are addressed as a result of the research.

Inputs as Disbursed and as Received

Before turning to other questions concerning the validity of the survey's results in its description of inputs and achievement outputs, and in its analysis of the relation between them, it is necessary to discuss briefly a special problem that arises in the measurement of inputs of public resources to various groups in the population. This is a problem that will arise in other studies of such resource distribution, and it is well that it be discussed in some detail.

The problem arises from the fact that inputs can be viewed in two entirely different ways: inputs as disbursed by the school system, and inputs as received by the child. The difference can be shown by numerous examples: a school board can spend identical amounts on textbooks in two different schools (or two school boards can spend identical amounts in two different systems), so that the inputs as disbursed by school boards are identical. But if texts depreciate more rapidly, through loss and lack of care, in one school or one system than the other, then the text as received by a given child (say the second year after a new text is issued) constitutes a *lesser* input of educational resources to him than if he were in the other school or the other system. The examples could be multiplied endlessly: if teacher salaries in a city and the surrounding suburban area are equal (and, as the Report shows [Table 2.34.2], they are equal for schools attended by blacks [largely in the central cities] and schools attended by whites in the same metropolitan areas [largely in the suburbs]), then the city is not competitive in salary, and loses the best teachers to the suburbs. Again, the inputs as disbursed by the school boards are equal, but the inputs as received by the children are not. As another example, if the expenditures on window glass in a city school in a lower-class neighborhood and a suburban school were equal, the child in the city school would spend much of his time in classrooms with broken windows, while the child in the suburban school would not. Furthermore, nearly all the examples in which this "loss of input" occurs between disbursement and reception go in the same direction, that is, to reduce the resources received by the average black child.

The general principle can be described by an economic concept: the black child experiences external diseconomies through living in a lower-class black neighborhood. (Sociologists often describe these as "contextual effects," but the fact that they represent real reduction of resources is better expressed through the term "diseconomies.") The fact that he himself may create external diseconomies for other black children is beside the point: those he experiences as a result of living where he does sharply reduce the resources he receives below those disbursed by the school system.

Such a difference between inputs as disbursed and inputs as received creates enormous difficulties for any research designed to measure the "amount of resource input" from a governmental unit to any group in society. The fact that different external diseconomies are ordinarily highly correlated (e.g., the school that has frequently broken windows will be the same school that cannot hire the teachers it wants without special salary or other inducements) means that if inputs are measured as disbursed, this imparts a systematic bias to the measure if viewed as inputs received. Yet certainly from one point of view—though not from all—one is interested in input resources as received by the child.

It would be possible, of course, to make a virtue out of a fault—to measure input resources as disbursed *and* received, so that one would obtain not only measures from both points of view but also, by their difference, a measure of the amount of external diseconomy in each resource (for example, in teacher quality, in teaching materials, etc.) imposed on a child as a result of his living in a given kind of neighborhood with a given group of schoolmates.

Yet to do this on a national basis would be an enormous undertaking, because of the difficulty of measuring resources as received, and would require a mixture of depth and comprehensiveness very difficult to achieve. For example, one resource never measured as an input resource is order and quiet in the classroom, presumably because it is a "free" resource. Yet one of the principal diseconomies some lower-class children impose on their classmates is the loss of this resource, the loss of order in the classroom. To measure the level of disorder carefully would be a difficult task. Another serious external diseconomy that lower-class black children impose on others in their classrooms is to depress the level of teaching that a teacher can carry out in the classroom. Thus the teaching received by a child from a teacher in a lower-class black classroom will be at a much lower level than that received from the *same teacher* in a classroom of middle-class students performing at higher levels of achievement. Such a difference in inputs as received would be very difficult to measure. Or to measure the textbook resources as experienced by a child would require an intensive examination difficult to achieve on a national basis. Clearly it is important to measure the amount of diseconomy experienced by a child as a function of the kind of classmates and neighborhood, but it is an intensive analytical study that could hardly be carried out as part of a "simple and straightforward" study of equality of input resources on a national basis.

Thus even the apparently simple study of input resources becomes a rather complex one if it is viewed as it should be—neither solely from the viewpoint of the administrator as distributor of resources, nor solely from the viewpoint of the child as recipient, but from the viewpoints of both.

It should be pointed out that this discrepancy between resources as disbursed and resources as received is and has been the cause of many disputes in the distribution of public resources generally. It can be obvious to a visitor to a ghetto school and a suburban school that the educational resources provided in the two are sharply different, ranging all the way from freshness of paint to the level of instruction in the classroom. But school administrators can then show that the same or greater resources are expended in the ghetto school than in the suburban one. The confused liberal (which many persons are on this question) often explains this as due to administrative juggling of figures to mask differences, and the administrator remains convinced *he* is right. He is right, but so is the observer who sees these sharp differences where the administrator says there are none.

This discrepancy between input resources as disbursed and as received is also very likely responsible for a large part of the confusion and disbelief attending the survey's finding of small differences or none between blacks and whites for many input resources.[5] Many observers "know" those inputs are different, but they know this by observations of the different schools, that is, inputs as received or experienced, not by examining the expenditures. The survey generally measured input resources as disbursed (that is, as reported by principal or superintendent) rather than as received, except in a few areas not ordinarily regarded as resources because they are not provided by the superintendent's office, such as the number of discipline problems reported by the teacher, the attitudes of teachers, and the educational backgrounds of a child's fellow students. These resources, incidentally, showed great differences between schools attended by the average black and those attended by the average white, suggesting the magnitude of the external diseconomy a black child experiences because of his neighborhood and classmates.

The Analysis of School Effects

Much of the paper by Kain and Hanushek is devoted to Section 3.2 of the report, which carries out an analysis of effects of school resources upon verbal achievement. It is this section of the report that has occasioned much of the discussion surrounding it from persons concerned with school policy. This is as it should be, because as I have argued in the preceding pages, the question of effectiveness of school input resources is logically prior to the question of equality of particular inputs. To order things the other way around is reminiscent of the busy activity of southern school systems in constructing new buildings for black schools, increasing salaries of black schoolteachers, and buying new textbooks for black students in the period preceding the Supreme Court decision of 1954, to obtain an apparent equality of educational opportunity while leaving unexamined the question of whether these inputs were the important ones. As an aside, it seems to me likely that the ready acceptance by many whites of the policy of increasing the "quality" of all-black ghetto schools, whether advocated by white conservatives or by black militants, is similarly motivated: that this will solve the problem of black education without threatening the schools of the white suburbs. One might go so far as to say that the earliest cases of compensatory education for blacks were the showcase black schools in the South of the early 1950's.

Thus the examination of effects of school factors was designed as a prior step to the description of "effective" inequalities of educational opportunity. I should go into the general design in a little detail, for it did not appear in the report as published, due to developments I will mention. The original intent was to carry out a regression analysis covering four general clusters of factors that might affect achievement: attributes of the child's own family background, characteristics of teachers, school resource inputs other than teachers, and social characteristics of the student body in his grade in school. The last of these is described in the report as a cluster of student-body factors, and they have been referred to elsewhere as peer factors. In effect, they are measures of some of the attributes of students in school that can exercise external economies or diseconomies upon the learning of a child in the school, through the addition or subtraction of "free" resources, and through the modification of input resources disbursed by the school administrators. The result of these regressions would then be two. The first result is the regression coefficients themselves, showing the relation of each of the teacher, school, and student-body characteristics to achievement when all the other characteristics and family background were controlled. In unstandardized form, these regression coefficients would provide an estimate of the effect of one unit of the input resource on achievement, and in standardized form (e.g., as path coefficients) they would be measures of the relative importance of different factors in affecting achievement.[6]

The second result of the regression analysis was to be the principal one: these regression coefficients were to be used as weights for the various inputs, so that by replacing in the regression equation the levels of input resources for the average black in the region with those of the white in the same region, the predicted level of achievement would be changed. This would produce two results: first, a measure of effective inequality of opportunity would result as the increment in achievement that would be expected for the average black if all the input resources of schools and student bodies were at the level of those for the average white in the region; second, by selectively changing in the equation some of the input resource levels to those held by whites, while keeping others at the levels held by blacks, one could see which input inequalities were the effective ones, thus indicating which input resources would be expected to produce the largest effect if the input inequality for that resource were eliminated. The final form of this analysis was to be much like that of Section 2 of the report, which showed differences in the levels of particular school input resources for the average black in a region, the average white living in the same county or metropolitan area, and the average white in the region and in the nation. The distinction of these tables would be that the inequalities of resources, rather than being expressed by a difference in units of input resources (e.g., hundreds of dollars difference in teachers' salaries), would be expressed by the difference in existing average black achievement and predicted achievement if that input resource were at the level of whites in the same county or whites in that region or in the nation.

However, this plan was never carried through to final completion, but stopped short of the final step. The reason was collinearity among the various input factors, which I will discuss in more detail.

In doing this, I want to discuss several quite general problems that arose in this research and will arise in other research that attempts to assess effects of various input factors on some performance criterion. Some of these problems are directly related to the use that has been made of the report, and to criticisms that have been made of this use, or of the report itself, including that of Kain and Hanushek.

The first problem, well illustrated by this report and its interpretations, is the problem of determining exactly what is the policy question of interest, and then developing an appropriate statistical technique to give evidence regarding it. In this case, there has been widespread confusion about exactly this question, a confusion to which the report itself contributed. The analysis was designed to answer a single question: what is the relative importance for achievement of various resource inputs into schools, including the resources provided by other students (resources which I have earlier described as external economies or, if negative, diseconomies, imposed by other students). In the conceptual model we held of the student's performance, these school inputs, together with the child's own family background and his native ability which we regarded as unmeasurable, particularly in the absence of longitudinal data, constituted the principal determinants of motivation for and attitudes toward achievement, and then, together with such motivation and attitudes, constituted the principal determinants of achievement itself. Now given this model, and given the policy interest in achievement, the overall relative effects of school factors on achievement (though not the mechanisms through which these effects occur) can be assessed by neglecting the intervening variable of motivation and attitudes. But given the differential degree of correlation of various school factors with the student's own background, and given the importance of these background factors for achievement, it is necessary to examine the relation of these school inputs to achievement when the student's own background is controlled. Otherwise, those school factors most highly correlated with the child's family background would show the strongest relation to achievement. The clearest case in which misleadingly high measures of effect would occur is for student-body factors, because the backgrounds of other students are highly correlated with the student's own. Furthermore, these misleadingly high effects of school factors associated with the child's own background would *not* be sufficiently controlled by comparing sizes of standardized regression coefficients in a regression equation that includes family background factors. The mathematics of regression analysis is such that when two variables are highly correlated and related to the dependent variable, then the multiple regression coefficients of both will include variance that is explainable by the other. However, another measure, $b^2 (1 - c^2)$, where b is the standardized multiple regression coefficient of variable x_1 and c^2 is the correlation between the two independent variables, shows only the unique variance attributable to variable x_1.[7] Under such conditions, the following research procedure appeared most reasonable then, as it does now: to assess the relative importance of different school factors (given their differential correlation with the child's family background), the most accurate measure of relative importance is the additional variance in achievement that can be explained by the school factor, *after* family background factors have accounted for as much variance as they are able to, that is, measures of the form of $b^2 (1 - c^2)$ rather than measures of the form of b. This gives an underestimate of the absolute effects of these school factors, insofar as they are responsible for some of the variance in achievement already explained by family background, but a better estimate of the relative effects than does the standardized regression coefficient.[8]

It is at this point that a confusion about the goals of the analysis arose. The way the results were reported contributed to this confusion, but was in no way misleading with regard to the policy conclusions that have been drawn from the report. Many persons, including Kain and Hanushek, have responded as if the goals of the analysis were to measure the relative effects of family background factors and school factors. But as I have indicated above, this was not the case at all, since policy alternatives concerned changes in various school factors (including student bodies, by distributing the external diseconomies imposed by lower-class students among all students, through school integration), but not changes in the child's own family background.

As is evident in the discussion above of the technique used to assess relative effects, the technique would in fact have given misleading results if the goal had been different, for the relative effects of family background and school factors that it shows are biased in the direction of family background. Kain and Hanushek, among others, have mistaken the goals of the analysis, and have criticized the study for exactly this bias. But if the analysis had been carried out symmetrically, as had been initially intended, the goal of the analysis, and its relevance to the policy alternatives, would have been impaired. I will show shortly specific examples of how this might have occurred.

The results of the examination of relative importance of different school factors were that the most important cluster of factors was the social backgrounds of other students, the second most important was teachers' characteristics, and the lowest level of importance, explaining very little additional variance in most regions, was school facilities and curriculum characteristics. The policy questions, of course, are which school factors have more importance for achievement, and this ordering is the result of an analysis designed to answer that question. The most crucial policy issue is the issue of school and staff integration vs. improvement of school facilities and curriculum while leaving unchanged the student bodies, and currently, under black-power pressure, leaving or bringing black teachers for black student bodies. It is worth remarking in this context that, of all the teacher characteristics, those most highly and consistently associated with student achievement were two: the verbal skills of the teacher as measured by the score on a vocabulary test, and the racial composition of the teaching staff. These two were highly correlated, white teachers scoring consistently higher than black ones.

This relation of the racial composition of the staff is not apparent in the report, because it was entered in the regression after the verbal skills were entered, and, under such conditions, explained little additional variance due to its correlation with them. Entering it in this order was based on the a priori assumption that if variance could be alternatively explained by teachers' verbal skills or teachers' race, the causal factor was more likely to be verbal skills than race. This was another example of the use of a priori assumptions rather than a wholly symmetric analysis. It was done, as in the case of family background, to prevent misleading inferences; but as in that case, interpretations should be made with knowledge of the asymmetry used in the analysis.

This high correlation between verbal skills and teachers' race, and their relation to student achievement, means that the policy alternative of improving facilities and programs of black schools and increasing the blackness of the teaching staff should, in terms of the report's results, reduce the achievement of black students, the one effect more than counterbalancing the other.

To return to the general point I wanted to make that has relevance for most policy-related research, this example of confusion about results shows clearly the importance of specifying the goal of the analysis in terms of the policy alternatives. The goal in this case affected even very technical points in the statistical analysis, and my conjecture is that it will do so in much policy-related research.

The confusion about the goals and results of the analysis has been increased in this case by several elements: first, the small amounts of additional variance accounted for by school facilities and curriculum led us as authors of the report to unduly focus attention upon the low absolute levels of additional variance explained, rather than solely upon the relative amounts explained by different factors—although we did not make specific comparisons of family and school effects, because of the bias introduced by the asymmetric analysis; second, the interests of many persons in the report's audience other than those concerned with policy alternatives were in the question of the relative effects of family and school; and third, a very elementary confusion among some readers between effects of the child's own background (the size of which was not explicitly compared to effects of school factors), and effects of the social composition of the student body on a child's achievement, *apart* from his own family background, effects that were explicitly compared to school factors.

To show the misinterpretations that can arise due to technical errors when the policy questions are not kept clearly in mind requires examining in greater detail some of the results of the study. In doing this, I will present some further analysis carried out since the publication of the report.

In carrying out the regression analysis in the report, a technical reason in addition to the intellectual decisions discussed in an earlier section prevented the use of symmetric measures such as standardized regression coefficients for comparing the relative effects of different school and student-body factors on achievement. The result was not entirely satisfactory, because it entailed the comparison of added variances accounted for by school, teacher, and student-body factors, entered in the regression equation in

TABLE 1

Standardized Multiple Regression Coefficients (or path coefficients) as Measures of the Importance of Each of Four Clusters of Variables on Verbal Achievement at Grades 12, 9, and 6. Family background (6 variables), school facilities and curriculum (11 variables), teacher characteristics (7 variables), and student-body characteristics (5 variables). Blacks and whites in North and South, grades 12, 9, 6.

Grade 12

	Black North	Black South	White North	White South
Family	.23	.22	.34	.34
Facilities & curriculum	.13	.07	.10	.07
Teacher	.13	.12	.09	.04
Student body	.23	.23	.09	.11
R^2	.15	.23	.16	.17

Grade 9

	Black North	Black South	White North	White South
Family	.26	.22	.40	.38
Facilities & curriculum	.14	.16	.10	.05
Teacher	.12	.09	.11	.09
Student body	.16	.19	.08	.07
R^2	.12	.21	.19	.20

Grade 6

	Black North	Black South	White North	White South
Family	.27	.29	.34	.41
Facilities & curriculum	.04	.14	.05	.06
Teacher	.14	.12	.07	.10
Student body	.14	.12	.12	.07
R^2	.13	.21	.16	.20

various orders. It is useful, then, to show symmetric measures of these factors and family background, all entered in the same multiple regression equation. The technical problem in doing so has since been overcome, and the solution of the technical problems[9] allows illustration of the problems that arise by the direct use of the multiple regression coefficients.

Two tables are presented here, both containing symmetric measures taken from multiple regression equations in which all four clusters of variables are entered. These clusters were each entered as a single variable, an index which used as weights the multiple regression coefficients on the individual variables within the cluster, so that the total variance accounted for is the same as in the original equation, but unlike that equation, a single standardized regression coefficient for the cluster is obtained. Table 1 contains these standardized regression coefficients (which can also be regarded as path coefficients). Table 2, however, contains measures of the sort that were used in the report, except that these measures are presented for all four of the clusters at issue: the student's own background, school curriculum and facilities, teacher characteristics and characteristics of the student body. The measures are measures of the unique contribution to variance in verbal achievement, after all three of the other clusters of variables are entered in

TABLE 2

Unique Contributions to Variance in Verbal Achievement (scaled up to sum to R^2 in each regression) as Measures of the Importance of Each of Four Clusters of Variables: Family Background (6 variables), School Facilities and Curriculum (11 variables), Teacher Characteristics (7 variables), and Student-Body Characteristics (5 variables). Blacks and whites in North and South, grades 12, 9, 6.

Grade 12

	Black North	*Black South*	*White North*	*White South*
Family	.067	.119	.133	.144
Facilities & curriculum	.018	.009	.014	.007
Teacher	.016	.026	.009	.002
Student body	.046	.078	.008	.013
R^2	.146	.232	.165	.166

Grade 9

	Black North	*Black South*	*White North*	*White South*
Family	.065	.098	.160	.183
Facilities & curriculum	.017	.046	.010	.004
Teacher	.012	.014	.010	.010
Student body	.027	.053	.006	.005
R^2	.121	.211	.186	.203

Grade 6

	Black North	*Black South*	*White North*	*White South*
Family	.086	.137	.135	.179
Facilities & curriculum	.002	.033	.004	.003
Teacher	.024	.023	.007	.011
Student body	.021	.021	.017	.006
R^2	.132	.213	.163	.199

TABLE 3

Averages of Standardized Multiple Regression Coefficients (from Table 1) and Unique Contributions to Variance (from Table 2) for Blacks and Whites Separately, Averaged over Grades 12, 9, and 6

	Average of standardized regression coefficients		*Average of rescaled, unique variance contributions*	
	Black	*White*	*Black*	*White*
Family	.25	.37	.095	.156
Facilities & curriculum	.11	.07	.019	.007
Teacher	.12	.08	.021	.008
Student body	.18	.09	.041	.009

the equation. These unique contributions have been scaled up so that their sum equals the total variance explained (the square of the multiple correlation coefficient).

Table 3 summarizes these two tables over grades and regions, for blacks and whites separately, to facilitate comparison.

The major difference between these two measures is that they "control" on the other variables in different senses. When two independent variables are correlated, then the variance that may be explained by either contributes to the regression coefficients of both. In using the variance uniquely explainable by a variable, however, the variance explainable by either is not allocated to either variable. Thus the regression coefficients give a liberal estimate of the effect of each, and the unique contributions to the variance give a conservative measure. The question in using one or the other for purposes such as this, however, is to get a good estimate of the *relative* effects of each cluster of variables (in this study, an estimate of the relative effects of the three school-related clusters).

The problem that can arise by using regression coefficients is well illustrated by the coefficients for family characteristics and student-body characteristics. Among blacks in the South, at every grade level, the regression coefficient for student-body characteristics (which is correlated with the child's own family background) is comparable in size to the coefficient for family background, and in grade 12, it is even higher than that of family background. The unique contributions to variance in Table 2, however, show that in no cases is the unique contribution of student-body characteristics near that of family background. In grade 12, where the multiple regression coefficients are .23 and .22 for student body and the child's own family, the unique contributions are .078 and .119.

It is in cases like this that the use of multiple regression coefficients can be misleading. If such coefficients had been presented for the four sets of variables, then it would have led to the conclusion that, in the South, the characteristics of the student body in the school are as important for a child's achievement as is his own background, a conclusion that appears false on its face and a conclusion that is not drawn from the relative sizes of the unique variance contributions.

It is paradoxical that the objections to the report's use of unique variance contributions rather than regression coefficients have been by the two pairs of economists, Bowles and Levin, and Kain and Hanushek, since both of them objected also that the use of regression coefficients would have shown greater school and teacher effects relative to the student-body effects. But as comparison of these two tables shows, the variable whose apparent effect is most reduced by examining unique contributions rather than multiple regression coefficients is the student-body characteristics.[10]

However, apart from the extreme cases exemplified by the Southern blacks, the regression coefficient and unique contributions do not give radically different results. Table 3 shows that by both measures, family background is clearly the strongest cluster, with student-body characteristics following for blacks, and both school and teacher characteristics following that, while for whites all three of the latter are smaller, and all three are nearly alike. The similarity of these two measures is more apparent if it is recalled that the unique variance is a measure that should be compared to the *square* of the regression coefficients. If the regression coefficients in Table 3 are squared,

TABLE 4
Total Variance Explained (R^2) and the Sum of Unique Contributions to the Variance for Each Grade, Race, and Regional Group

	Black North	Black South	White North	White South
Grade 12				
R^2	.146	.232	.165	.166
Sum of unique contributions	.111	.080	.127	.121
Grade 9				
R^2	.121	.211	.186	.203
Sum of unique contributions	.111	.097	.179	.146
Grade 6				
R^2	.132	.213	.163	.199
Sum of unique contributions	.108	.115	.119	.180

they are much more comparable in relative magnitudes to the unique contributions.

The reason for the rather good comparability between the square of the regression coefficients and the unique contributions for most of the grade-region-race groups in Tables 1 and 2 is shown in Table 4, which gives an indication of just how highly correlated these four clusters of variables are for each grade-region-race group. Table 4 gives the total variance explained and the sum of the unique contributions to this variance. If the four clusters of variables were uncorrelated, the two numbers would be the same, and the squared multiple regression coefficients would equal the unique contributions. If they were all perfectly correlated, the unique contributions would be zero.

As Table 4 shows, it is for blacks in the South where the clusters of variables are most highly correlated.

Multiple Modes of Analysis

Another quite general point I want to make about policy-related research is the importance of using different modes of analysis to examine the same question. If these modes are mutually confirming, the results are considerably strengthened; if not, they are weakened. In this case, the example I want to use is the question of the absolute magnitude of school effects, for in articles subsequent to the report, I have used evidence from the study to draw strong policy conclusions from the absolute level, arguing that the low absolute level of effect means that a more radical modification of a child's environment than that provided by schools is necessary to induce achievement in children whose family environments do not insure learning.

In the present research, it would have been incorrect to base such arguments principally on the results of the regression analysis, because the techniques used there were designed to more accurately assess relative effects of school factors at the risk of underestimating absolute size of effects. For this reason, it is especially important to have several alternative grounds for such inference. And it is useful to have these other sources of evidence based on analyses as different as possible in form, so that the errors of one will not appear in the other. There were three sources of such evidence, supported by the results of the regression analysis:

1. In an analysis of variance, a generally low proportion of variance in achievement lay between schools, for each racial group: between 15 and 20 percent for blacks, and less than 15 percent for whites. This means that the major portion of the variance in achievement could never be accounted for by differences between schools, for it resides within the school itself. If schools had strong and differential impacts on achievement (and the size of the differences in impact can be expected to be proportional to the strength of impact), then children within a given school should be achieving more nearly at the same level than the study showed to be the case.

2. This analysis of variance was carried out for each of the grade levels, grades 1, 3, 6, 9, and 12. If schools have strong and differential impacts, then the proportion of variance between schools should change over the school years. The between-school variance at the beginning of grade 1 is merely due to the differences between differing entering student bodies, due solely to family backgrounds, except for variance due to the test-taking situation in the school. If school effects are strong and positively correlated with family background, as all evidence would suggest, the between-school component of variance should *increase* over the years of school. If they are strong and uncorrelated with family background, the between-school component of variance should *decrease* over the years of school, or perhaps first decrease as student input differences are washed out, and then increase as school differences make student bodies diverge in achievement.

But as it turns out (Table 3.22.1), very little happens to the between-school component of variance. It remains about the same over the years of school. The simplest explanation of this is that the initial differences with which children enter school simply continue over the years of school, unaffected by the impacts of good or poor schools. The kind of school influences that would produce such a result are those that merely carry children along at the same relative levels of performance with which they begin school.[11]

3. The correlation between family background and achievement is approximately constant over grades 6 to 12 for both blacks and whites (Table 3.221.3). (For grades 1 and 3 it is lower than for the later years, but this may be due to poorer measurement of background at these levels.) The absence of a steady decline in this relation over time indicates that schools do not constitute an important enough modification of the child's environment to interrupt the family processes that in the absence of school would be expected to show the same constant correlation with achievement that they now show.[12]

These three modes of analysis, reinforced by the regression analyses, that show low unique variance explained by school factors (with the exception of some teachers' characteristics), provide a rather strong base of evidence for the inference that school factors constitute a relatively minor modification of the child's learning environment—a firm foundation for the argument that much more radical modifications of the environment are necessary in order to greatly increase achievement of presently low-achieving groups.

This result illustrates my more general point about policy-related research—that it should obtain evidence from analyses as technically different as possible, to strengthen the grounds for inference. It is particularly important in this case that two of the results (numbers 2 and 3) were based on comparison over grade levels from grade 1 to grade 12, since the regression analyses were necessarily carried out within the same grade level, and the inferences about small school effects were not based on trends over different grades.

The Inadequacy of General Field Surveys for Answering Specific Policy Questions

The problems of interpretation of results in a massive study like this one illustrate another general point in policy research. This is the inadequacy of analysis of a general sample of institutions or students for answering very specific questions relevant to policy, when the policy-related variables of policy interest are highly correlated, and have relatively small effect on the dependent variable under study. The results of this survey show only the most general outlines of the factors affecting school achievement. For answering specific questions, it is clear that methods are necessary which empirically rather than analytically separate out the variables of policy interest. One way in which this can be done is, of course, through experimental research. This, however, has the defect that the effects occur over time, and experimental research much involve time in which the experimental variables can have their effect.

In the absence of the necessary time, it appears likely that other methods are possible, if one recognizes certain dangers inherent in them. One of the most appealing for a study like this, in which much data beyond that necessary for analysis are obtained, is the use of computer procedures for selecting students within schools for which certain input variables are orthogonal and others are perfectly correlated. Regression analysis on those orthogonal sets of variables will provide estimates of the effects of the sets of perfectly correlated variables. Then further computer selection can be used to identify students for which the variables perfectly correlated in the first analysis are orthogonal, and an analysis of these students used to examine the relative effects of the newly orthogonal variables.

The details of such a procedure, the statistical problems it might introduce, and the methods for reducing these problems, are not clear. It is evident, however, that since the samples are not representative of the population of students of interest, the parameters estimated are specific to the students thus sampled, and may be in considerable error for the population of interest.

Even so, some procedures, in which estimates made on the samples resulting from search were used for prediction in the unbiased sample and inferences about biases made from the errors of prediction, seem possible.

In short, it is quite evident that much work remains to be done in devising techniques that can, within reasonable time constraints imposed by policy problems, give better estimates of the expected effects of policy changes.

One aid to this, suggested by Kain and Hanushek in their critique, is the development of more fully elaborated conceptual models for use in the statistical analysis. For example, as they point out, school effects are, or should be, cumulative over time. As a consequence, the appropriate model and measurement should involve the product of the school resource times the length of time to which the child has been exposed to it. If all children remained in the same schools, were subject to the same home environmental conditions, and were in schools with the same kinds of other students, throughout their school lives, then time would be unnecessary in the model. However, if he has moved and if his peers in school have changed, both of which are true for some students, then resources have been available for different amounts of time, and time should be explicitly incorporated into the analysis.

Still another approach to these policy questions might be to examine students at different grade levels in the same schools, controlling on family backgrounds to "standardize" the student body at one level against that at another. The dependent variable in this case would be the difference in achievement levels of standardized student bodies at two grades, or the inputed "growth rates." These "growth rates" can then be related to the characteristics of the school.

More generally, it appears that the most promising possibility for policy research lies in much more systematic and careful administrative records of social institutions. These records, if they were all maintained and comparable among schools (or for other policy questions, among other institutions), would allow analyses for policy questions to be carried out regularly and at minimal cost, by local school systems, by state systems, or nationally.

Altogether, it is clear that research to examine questions of policy can be done to provide a better base for general directions of policy. I believe *Equality of Educational Opportunity* has done so principally through the way in which the problem was defined, resulting in a redirection of attention from school inputs as prima facie measures of quality to school outputs, and resulting as well in an expansion of the conception of school inputs beyond those intentionally suppliled by the school board. It is equally clear, however, that policy research in social areas is only beginning, and that social scientists have much to learn about how to answer policy-related research questions.

Notes

[1.] [Eric A. Hanushek and John F. Kain, "On the Value of *Equality of Educational Opportunity* as a Guide to Public Policy," in Frederick Mosteller and Daniel P.

Moynihan, eds., *On Equality of Educational Opportunity* (New York: Random House, 1972), pp. 116–45.] The other papers are Samuel Bowles and Henry Levin, "The Determinants of Scholastic Achievement—An Appraisal of Some Recent Evidence," *Journal of Human Resources,* Winter 1968 and Glen G. Cain and Harold W. Watts, "Problems in Making Policy Inferences from the Coleman Report," *American Sociological Review,* V. 35, 1970, pp. 228–42.

[2.] James S. Coleman, "The Concept of Equality of Educational Opportunity," *Harvard Educational Review, 38,* Winter 1968, pp. 7–22.

[3.] About 90 percent of the variance in student achievement lies within schools, so that the clustering effect that would be caused by sampling fewer schools and not sampling within schools (the latter of great administrative convenience) is not serious for measurement of achievement.

[4.] I will not comment on these points in the text, but some comments on specifics are useful to correct misleading impressions some of the points may leave. First Kain and Hanushek point out the levels of nonresponse.

This nonresponse of schools, together with item nonresponse on the questionnaires, is a problem that would have arisen in any of the research designs that might have been chosen, given the sensitivity of the problem. Serious biases may have been introduced, though a sample of nonresponding schools was drawn, and state records checked, showing little systematic differences on comparable items from the responding schools; but here as elsewhere, the question is whether to use data from a sample that may be biased, or to make policy decisions in the absence of data.

On the major points of nonresponse and miscoding mentioned by Kain and Hanushek (for example, nonresponse on principals' attitude questions, miscoding of school size by principal, poor coding of fathers' occupation), the problems were recognized by the staff, and the information not used in the analysis. School size, as used in the analysis, was obtained from the number of student questionnaires, because of the possible coding errors by principals, and the principals' attitude items were used only in the tabulations of school characteristics, where nonresponse was shown in the tabulation. Neither these attitude items nor the occupation of child's father were used in the analysis of effects of school inputs on achievement. Thus the points made by Kain and Hanushek on these items are not relevant to the question of biases in the analysis.

[5.] This unwillingness to accept the small degree of inequality of input resources is exhibited both in the paper by Kain and Hanushek and in the paper by Bowles and Levin. They cite several studies in particular cities; but many of these studies are marked by severe selective biases, since they aim to show how great the inequality of expenditures can be in selected cases, rather than how large it in fact is on the average.

[6.] A note should be added here concerning what is meant by "achievement." Standardized tests, constructed by Educational Testing Service, were given in areas of verbal comprehension, nonverbal classification and analogy, reading comprehension, mathematics achievement, and at grades 9 and 12, five tests of specific subject areas. These test results correlated highly, and the one showing consistently higher correlations (both zero-order and partial) with school characteristics was the verbal comprehension test (taken from the SCAT series, principally a vocabulary test). This test was used throughout in the reported regression analyses. Regressions were carried out also on reading comprehension and mathematics achievement, and these showed similar results to the verbal achievement test, except that smaller proportions of variance were explained. Thus achievement as I will use it in this discussion refers to vocabulary skills, but can stand also as a surrogate for achievement in the other areas mentioned.

[7.] Kain and Hanushek describe this alternatively explainable variance as "interaction," a curious choice of words. Interaction terms in regression analysis are not this at all. An interaction term accounts for variation in the dependent variable that *neither* variable alone could account for. The terms they describe would account for variation in the dependent variable that *either* variable alone could account for. "Overlap" would have been a better choice of words.

[8.] This statement must be qualified, because the latter half is true only under conditions that are not precisely known. I conjecture, however, that these conditions are that over half of the variance that could be alternatively accounted for by a given school factor or by family characteristics is in fact due to family. Results of numerous studies show that this condition is true for the case under consideration, that is, school and family characteristics.

[9.] The technical problem in short was this: it was desired to get a measure of the overall relation of the cluster of teacher characteristics, the cluster of school facilities and curriculum characteristics, the cluster of student-body characteristics, and the cluster of characteristics of the child's own family background. But it is not possible to do this by adding the multiple regression coefficients for all variables within a cluster, because the sum would be too large, containing the same variance included in the regression coefficients for several different correlated variables. The solution is to use the regression coefficients from the total equation including all variables, as weights in forming four new composite variables representing the four clusters mentioned above. Then a regression of achievement on these four composite variables gives a standard regression coefficient for each of the four clusters. In the new regression equation with four independent variables, rather than 29, exactly the same amount of variance in achievement is explained; it merely allows one to obtain a standardized regression coefficient for each of the clusters.

[10.] Kain and Hanushek carry out a regression analysis which purports to cast doubt on our conclusions, but does so by leaving out two of the three most important Student Body variables (School Attendance and Proportion Planning to Attend College) and substituting others in their place. The major difference from our results, which is the small variance attributable to peer effects, stems directly from this omission. The table is presented here with their results and with the results obtained from using those variables that were used in the report. I have not run regressions in every order, but those that have been run are sufficient to show how the omission of these two variables emasculated any effects attributable to peers. The case of blacks in the urban North, incidentally, is hardly representative, since a number of school characteristics are negatively correlated with family characteristics for this group but for no others. This produces the increase in unique contribution shown in comparing the figures in parentheses for the third and fifth columns for family characteristics and the figures outside parentheses for the third and fifth columns on school characteristics.

An extended reanalysis of these data has been carried out in the U.S. Office of Education, showing separately the unique explanation of variance and the overlap in variance explanation, for all clusters of variables. That extensive reanalysis does not lead, as Kain and Hanushek argue from their "representative case," to any substantial revision in inferences drawn from the data. See G. W. Mayeske, *et al.*, "A Study of Our Nation's Schools," Washington, D.C.: U.S. Department of Health, Education, and Welfare, 1969.

Table 1 from Kain and Hanushek, Together with Comparable Figures in Parentheses, using Variables from the Report. Added proportion of variance explained.

Variable Cluster	Order of entry				
	1	2 after S	2 after P	2 after F	3
S (Teacher, facilities, curriculum)	(.0466) .0808	— —	— .0222	(.0363) .0560	(.0185) .0212
P (student body)	(.0788) .0703	(.0487) .0117	— —	— .0420	(.0349) .0072
F (family)	(.0748) .0777	— .0529	(.0487) .0494	— —	(.0505) .0484

[11.] Various persons have argued that this and other results of the study simply show the importance of fixed genetic differences among children. Such genetic differences, within and between schools, could produce the observed constancy of the between-school component of variance, but only if school effects were relatively weak or uniform. If school effects were strong, and different for different schools, they would magnify the between-school component of variance through interaction with the genetic factors.

[12.] For some of the ethnic groups other than blacks and whites, a decline does occur between grades 6 and 12. For technical reasons, however, less confidence should be placed in those regressions than in those for blacks and whites.

11

Equality of Educational Opportunity, Reexamined

The question I want to pose in this paper, together with some steps toward an answer, is how to measure the equality, or perhaps better, the degree of inequality of educational opportunity for specific subgroups in a society—whether it be racial or ethnic groups, social class groups, regional groups, religious groups, or something still different.

I would like to proceed according to several ground rules. The first of these ground rules is that I will not take the survey of Equality of Educational Opportunity either as a target to attack or as a bastion to defend. The uses to which I shall put it, in the first section of this paper, will be two: first, to establish the context which aids the definition of the present problem, and second, to provide information that narrows this problem. For I will argue, first, that the very definition of the problem is itself not straightforward, and requires careful consideration.

The Concept of
Equality of Educational Opportunity

If one reviews the concept of educational opportunity in the history of public education, as I have done recently for the United States and England, he sees one idea that dominates from the outset. This is the general idea that educational opportunity is provided by a community through the provision of facilities with free and open access for all.

The idea of *equality* of opportunity is a relatively new concept in England and Europe, though it existed from the outset in the U.S. and Canada. This idea of equality of opportunity would seem to derive in a straightforward way from the concept of educational opportunity itself: equality of educational

Reprinted with permission from *Socio-Economic Planning Sciences*, vol. 2 (1969): 347–354. Copyright © 1969 by Pergamon Press, Inc.

opportunity exists when the community provides the *same* resources, the same facilities, for all children. So long as residential distributions are such as to allow a single common school for all social classes, as in small towns and rural areas, then this idea of equality of educational opportunity is not difficult to implement. The resources are alike for all children within the locality, since all are exposed to exactly the same resources. However, if residential concentrations are larger than the smallest towns, then there are several schools in a locality, and new questions immediately arise. (I will not deal with the cases in which, even in the most sparsely populated areas, there was intentional inequality of opportunity, on a social class basis in Europe at least until World War II, and on a racial basis in the United States, through the use of parallel school systems for different classes or different races.) Questions about the distribution of resources among different schools arise, questions about the concentration of best teachers in certain schools—and even questions about the educational resources provided by classmates, which might make the experience of a child in a lower-class school quite different from that of a child in a middle-class school—even if all other things about the school were alike.

Thus one general concept of equality of educational opportunity would appear to derive quite directly from the initial idea of educational opportunity itself—the idea that opportunity consisted of free and open access to the same school resources for all children. The question of equality is the question of whether in fact there *is* such equality of resources.

A great deal of attention has been given to this conception of equality in past years: studies of teachers which examine the distribution of teachers between schools with middle-class students and those with lower-class students; studies that compare the allocation of physical plant resources in middle-class neighborhoods and in lower-class neighborhoods, partly through examining both inequities due to school system boundaries and local taxation, and inequities within systems.

Two of the several approaches used in the recent Office of Education survey of Equality of Educational Opportunity were based on this general orientation. The first of these was the most straightforward, and measured equality of opportunity in terms of equality of the distribution of school resources within a county or metropolitan area. Thus inequality of opportunity was measured by the usual measures of school *quality* used by school administrators: expenditure per pupil on teaching, teacher preparation, teacher test performance, pupil-teacher ratio, age of building, size of library, and so on—including as well certain inputs to a child's educational experience not generally recognized as measures of school quality, such as the educational backgrounds of fellow-students. By use of this approach, it is possible to show a vector of differences or inequalities, based on the comparisons of the two resource vectors in schools attended by the average black and the average white in a given county or a given region.

However, it required a second approach to reduce this vector of differences to some meaningful measure of inequality. This second approach was one designed to provide a weight to each of the quantities in the vector—a weight determined by an estimate of the *effect* of this resource upon educational achievement. This involved a radical departure from the idea of school quality ordinarily used—a departure from the definition of school quality by resources that had apparent face validity, to the definition of school quality by the existence of resources *effective* for achievement. This would allow a measure, then, of the degree of inequality of educational opportunity, as the increment in achievement that could be expected to occur if the input resources for schools attended by the average black were brought to the level of those attended by the average white.

Given this second, more sophisticated approach to equality of opportunity, the problem reduced to one of obtaining some estimate of the effect of each of these school resources upon achievement. Because of the time limitation of the survey, this was done through a cross-sectional survey, using multiple regression methods in an attempt to estimate the effects of each of these school resource characteristics. With a greater period of research time, it would have been possible to measure effects by examining changes in the level of achievement—an approach with fewer statistical problems, though with still a great many. However, the important point here is that the analysis of effects of school factors was merely to provide weights to the different school factors, thus allowing a measure of inequality in the *effects* of schooling, rather than merely a set of measures of inequality in input resources.

Now let us return to the initial idea of educational opportunity, which appeared to lead directly in the way indicated to the concept of equality of opportunity described above. Does it in fact lead so directly to this concept? Note that the general principle is that inequality of educational opportunity arises through *differential* resources made available to blacks and whites. But if we examine more carefully the idea of educational opportunity as provided by schools, this conclusion appears less obvious. For suppose we carry out a mental experiment in which blacks and whites were subject to precisely the same school resources, for example, in a single school in a single town, with a single school class at each grade level. One might be prepared to say, on the basis of the idea of equality of educational opportunity described above, that this situation would provide such equality. But suppose, in this mental experiment, that the school met for only one hour each week. Would we still be prepared to assert that it provided equality of educational opportunity? I think not, for the education received by these children would be largely that received outside school. Those children from families with strong educational resources in the home or strong economic resources would supplement these minimal activities of the school, so that children's education would be largely determined by the differential educational resources provided by their families.

From this perspective, equality of educational opportunity depends not merely on the idea of *equality* in the distribution of school resources, but on the *intensity* of the effects of these resources. This concept takes into account the fact that outside school, and before school, children have very unequal educational resources, so that equality of opportunity is provided by making the resources provided by school not only equal, but quite powerful in their effects. In contrast, the previous definition, which focused on equality in distribution of resources, implicitly ignores these outside educational resources, and assumes that opportunity in education derives wholly from a child's experiences within school.

Following the second definition, one may conceive of two sets of educational resources impinging on school children: one set, set A, available to and operative for all children alike, and a second set, set B, available only to a subgroup within the total population. The first definition of equality of educational opportunity focuses on the question of what proportion of school resources is in the set A, and what proportion in set B. The second definition asks a different question: assuming that out-of-school resources are largely in set B, and in-school resources are largely in set A, it asks about the relative size of set A and set B, that is, the intensity of common educational resources relative to the intensity of differential education resources.

If one then combines these two criteria of equality of educational opportunity, there are two distinct dimensions of which the concept is composed: first, equality in the distribution of school resources; and second, intensity of effect of the school resources relative to the intensity of outside educational resources. If a system is high on both these dimensions, it approaches equality of educational opportunity. But inequality of opportunity may be of two quite different sorts. It may occur through the existence of equal resources which have little effect, so that resulting opportunity depends largely on the differences in external educational resources held by these chidren. Or it may occur through the differential distribution of resources, which through their weak or strong effects reinforce the differential resources which exist outside school, prior to and during school years.

Some statistical results from the report Equality of Educational Opportunity give some illustrative information about these different kinds of inequality, by showing the achievement of four different subgroups of students in the United States, divided according to regional and racial criteria, in grades 1, 3, 6, 9, and 12. The educational resources in the home and neighborhood before grade 1 being different, each of these four lines begins, at grade 1, at a different point on the graph. If we assume that the results of these different resources have produced an equilibrium in the difference between the mean achievement of these population subgroups, and that these before-school differences remain the same after age 6, then in the absence of school, the differences at each grade level would be identical to those at grade 1. There would be four parallel horizontal lines showing the relative position of each group from grade 1 through 12. In the presence of school resources that were distributed in exactly the same ratio for the four groups as are out-of-school resources, the four lines would still remain parallel. Although children in each group would be learning more than in the absence of school, the *relative* levels of achievement would remain the same, because the relation between the amounts of resources for each remained the same. In the presence of school resources that were equal for all population groups and intensive in their effects, the lines should converge, because the distribution of effective educational resources *after* grade 1 was nearer equality than before grade 1. Finally, in the presence of school resources that showed even greater inequality than the out-of-school resources, the lines should diverge from grade 1 to grade 12.

The assumptions on which these conclusions are based should be made clear. They are:

(a) The starting-points of achievement at grade 1, averages for each population group, represent an equilibrium position resulting from the environmental resources to which each group is subject, so that the continued application of the same ratio of resources would maintain the same relative positions;

(b) The out-of-school educational resources after grade 1 have the same ratio for these population groups as those before grade 1;

(c) The distribution of potential in each group, apart from environmental resources, is approximately the same.

This third assumption is important, because of the general point that a more intense learning environment might have the effect of creating greater diversity of achievement between children with greater and lesser potential. But so long as potential is distributed equally among the different population groups, this increase in diversity due to intensive and equally distributed learning experiences would not mean a divergence between the population groups, but rather the reverse. Although the overall variance in achievement would increase through time, the population means would converge—simply because achievement which was, at the beginning of school, related to the educational resources available in that population group, would come to be related instead to the child's potential.

If, of course, an intense learning environment that was equal for all did not increase the variance in achievement between children with different potentials, one need not assume that potentials are distributed alike in each of these populations. The difficulty of deciding, in general, whether such intensive and equal learning environments have a converging or diverging effect in a population that has different potentials lies in our inability to determine what is such a learning environment, and our uncertainty about what are differences in potential.

With this general idea of how different kinds and amounts of inequality would manifest themselves in the achievement of subgroups that start grade 1 at different points, it is useful to examine the data referred to above. Figure 1 shows verbal achievement at grade 1, 3, 6, 9, and 12 for whites and blacks in the urban Northeast and the rural Southeast. First comparing the whites and blacks in the urban Northeast, the lines representing group averages remain parallel throughout the period of school. This indicates,

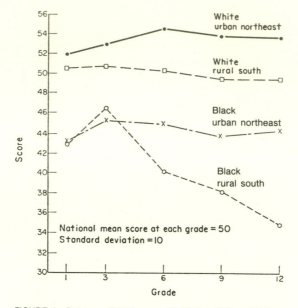

FIGURE 1   Patterns of Achievement in Verbal Skills at Various
Grade Levels by Race and Region

under the assumptions stated earlier, that either (1) the educational resources within schools, though equally distributed for blacks and whites in this region, are ineffective, and the unequal out-of-school resources determine the relative levels of achievement, or (2) the educational resources in school, although effective, are distributed in the same ratio as are the out-of-school resources for these two groups.

Comparing the whites in the two regions shows lines which begin some distance apart, but diverge somewhat over the years of school. This comparison indicates that the educational resources of schools to have some effect, but that they are distributed even less equally between the schools of the urban Northeast whites and the schools of the rural South whites than are the resources in the home. A more striking comparison in this regard is between blacks in these two locations. The starting-points at grade 1 are nearly alike, indicating very similar resources in the two sets of homes; but the lines diverge very sharply, so that by grade 12, the blacks in the rural South are far below the blacks in the urban North. This indicates a great inequality of resources between the schools of the urban Northeast blacks and the rural South blacks. A similar inequality occurs in school resources, greater than the inequality of family educational resources before school, between the schools attended by whites in the rural South, and those attended by blacks in the same region.

There is another statistic from this survey which is relevant to the discussion. This is the proportion of the total variance in achievement, for

TABLE 1

	Grades				
	12	9	6	3	1
Black South	22.5	20.1	22.7	34.9	23.2
Black North	10.9	12.8	13.9	19.5	10.6
White South	10.1	9.1	11.1	17.7	18.6
White North	7.8	8.7	10.3	11.4	11.1

a given population group that lies between schools, at each grade level. At the beginning of school, this between-school variance represents the differences, within that population group, in the starting-points of student bodies in different schools. If the schools' educational resources are (a) more alike between schools than are the out-of-school educational resources; and (b) effective, then this between-school variance should decrease over the years of school. If the school educational resources are either distributed in about the same ratio as the out-of-school educational resources, or are ineffective, the between-school variance should remain about the same. Table 1 shows that the latter is the case; that the proportion of between-school variance remains about the same from grade 1 to 12, with a slight decline.

Initially, the research analysts expected that effectiveness of schools would show up through an increase in the between-school variance over the years of school. The general idea was that differences in school quality would create, over the years of school, increasing divergence between the average achievement in different student bodies. But this was predicated on two assumptions, neither of which held: that the initial between-school variance would be negligible, so that school effects would all show up through an increase in between-school variance; and that if the first assumption did not hold, then the out-of-school resource differences which created the initial between-school variance would be unrelated to the variations in school resources, which would create subsequent between-school variance. If this latter assumption had been true, then the resulting effects should have shown up first as a decrease in between-school variances, as differences in student starting-points were neutralized, and then by an increase in between-school variance, as the different school qualities brought divergence in their student-body achievements.

The results, of course, indicate that even within each population group, either the school resources are distributed about like the out-of-school resources, so as to maintain the between-school variance, or are ineffective, so as to leave the between-school variances like they are at the start of grade 1.

The Measurement of Equality of Opportunity

The discussion above indicates that equality of educational opportunity among different population subgroups depends on two distinct variables, the distribution of effective school resources, and the intensity or effectiveness of these resources, relative to the unequally distributed out-of-school resources. I will describe briefly the method used in the survey to assess the inequalities in distribution of effective school resources, and follow this with a discussion of how it might be better done.

The orientation in the survey required three steps: (1) For each population groups, to measure the list of resources that might be effective for achievement; (2) then, through regression analysis, to estimate the effectiveness of each of these resources for a given group which experienced fewer resources than a given baseline group, such as whites in the same region; and finally (3) using these measures of effectiveness, the regression weights for the different school resources, to obtain a predicted *increment* of achievement if the given group were to have the *same* resources as the baseline group. This predicted increment in achievement thus constitutes a measure of the *effective inequality* in distribution of educational resources for the given group, relative to the baseline group.

In fact, the survey never quite got to the last of these steps, in part because the estimates of effects of school resources showed these effects to be rather small, but in larger part because of a lack of time to carry out this step. Instead, the distribution of input resources, and some crude estimates of effects of various of these resources, the results of steps 1 and 2, were reported.

There has been some discussion and controversy over the methods used in estimating the effects of different school resources. If the study were to be carried out again, however, I would propose that the same method be used. If it were possible to extend the data-collection over a longer period of time, with two points of data-collection, then I would favor carrying out a regression analysis in which the increment of achievement from time of entry into the school is the dependent variable.[1] This method for the estimate of effects of various school resources would be superior to that based on a single cross-sectional analysis—although such a design is not without its statistical pitfalls.

In the process of obtaining the measure of this first dimension, that is the differences in the distribution of effective resources, the essential elements for the measurement of the second, that is, the intensity of effect, have been obtained as well. It is useful to view the matter as follows: to obtain the measure described above, of distribution of effective resources, one examines the differential achievement due to school factors for children from similar family backgrounds. But to find the intensity of effect of school resources, one does the opposite: examine the differential achievement due to family background for children from the same or similar schools. If the intensity of effect of school resources wholly outweighed that of family and other out-of-school factors, then children exposed to the same school factors would all be achieving at the same level. If the intensity of effect of school resources was zero, then children exposed to the same school factors would be achieving no more alike than would be expected by chance. Yet the matter is confounded by the fact that entering student bodies are already somewhat homogeneous in achievement, as Table 1 showed. Because of this selection bias in student bodies, the matter must be examined by comparing cohorts which have been in school different periods of time: first we find, at grade 1, that combination of out-of-school factors (principally family background) which best predict initial performance at the entry to school. Then we examine, for successive grades in school, the relation of these family background factors to achievement, for children subject to the *same* school resources, that is, by controlling on the child's school. The more rapidly this relation between background and achievement declines, for children subject to the same school resources, the more intense the effects of school factors. This does *not* necessarily mean that over the whole population of students, the relation between background and achievement will necessarily decline over the school years, for the differential distribution of these resources over schools could act even to strengthen the relationship. What it does mean, however, if that *if* school resources are distributed independently of student background resources, the relation of achievement to background will decline over the school years.

Thus it seems clear that the appropriate measure for studying equality of educational opportunity lies in both dimensions: in the distribution of school resources, and the intensity of their effect. Only if their distribution was fully equal, and the intensity of their effect was infinitely great relative to the divergent out-of-school factors, would there be complete equality of opportunity. Since the latter cannot be the case, then it can hardly be even appropriate to speak of "equality of educational opportunity", but rather to speak instead of the amount of inequality. In a system with equal resource distribution, but with less than infinite intensity of effects, there remains a degree of inequality—an inequality of opportunity not arising *from* the school system, but arising from outside and *not overcome* by the school system.

All this becomes more fully understandable when we take a somewhat broader perspective, examining the role of an educational system in society. In a society without a formal educational system, the inequalities of position, income, power, and other resources among different households are directly transmitted to the next generation. The increasing importance of the educational system has been in a movement away from hereditary inequalities of opportunity, toward an open system in which each child can enter adult life with resources independent of those in the family into which he was born. Consequently, this movement toward equality of opportunity depends both on the distribution of educational resources and the intensity of effect of these resources. It is only insofar as both the distribution and intensity of the resources act to free a child's opportunity from the accident of birth into a given family that a society can come near to the achievement of equality of opportunity.

Notes

[1.] It might appear that one could merely take the increment in achievement between two years, say grades 5 and 6, as a dependent variable. However, this creates statistical problems. If the school were equally effective in the grades before grade 5 and in grade 5, then *both* the achievement scores at grade 5 and grade 6 would reflect this effectiveness, so the difference in scores should not reflect it. The difference, greater or less than expected given the child's background, would reflect only the differential effectiveness of the school before grade 5 and in grade 5.

PART THREE

Desegregation and Resegregation

The civil rights movement of the 1960s and 1970s accomplished an extraordinary reorganization of American education in a very short period of time, probably more extensive than any other in a comparable period in the history of formal education. This reorganization consisted of the elimination of *de jure* segregation by race in the South and the reduction of *de facto* segregation throughout the country. It took place primarily in the courts, in some cases with the aid of social research, the most important of which was the *Equality of Educational Opportunity* report (see Chapter 7).

Much of the segregation in large cities was associated with segregation of residence, and the court cases, though won on grounds of *de jure* segregation, had as remedy the elimination or reduction of *de facto* segregation of schools produced by segregation of residence. This was carried out principally by large-scale busing, which was necessary if children were to be redistributed from their racially segregated neighborhoods to create racially integrated schools.

The report *Trends in School Segregation 1968–73* (major sections of which appear in Chapter 12) documents the extent of segregation by race in the public schools in 1968 and the extent of school desegregation over the period 1968–1973 (during which most of the change took place). It also shows the impact of desegregation on the racial composition of the school district within which desegregation occurred, an impact that primarily took the form of the loss of white students from the district. This report was among the first to demonstrate that massive school desegregation plans in large cities resulted in the loss of white children from the city's schools. In effect, the school desegregation policies were provoking resegregation actions on the part of individual families. Subsequent to this report, much more detailed and precise information has been obtained about the nature of these resegregation actions: They consisted principally of whites moving to suburban school districts with few black students, though in the South, where there were few such districts, whites more often formed private schools. The conditions under which families take these actions are now better known. For example, white families are much more likely to leave city schools if their child is to be bused out of the neighborhood to a previously black school than if black children are to be bused into the school in their neighborhood. A bit of this more detailed information appears in the latter part of Chapter 13, where the racial composition of individual schools in one city is traced.

The policies of massive and immediate elimination of racial segregation in large cities would appear to be examples of policy gone awry. Policies designed to provide progressive and stable school integration would have the effect of increasing residential integration as well. However, the policies that were used had the reverse effect: They increased residential segregation through the moves of whites beyond the reach of the desegregation order, especially increasing the population instability of those cities with an already high proportion of blacks.

To view these court-ordered plans of school desegregation as policies gone awry, however, may be to miss the point altogether. School desegregation was the spearhead of a social movement to establish and demonstrate once and for all the rights of blacks in American society. The goal of establishing these rights was furthered by policies of massive and immediate desegregation, as a demonstration of the power of blacks to change American society. Policies of progressive desegregation strategically designed to maintain population stability would not have furthered the goal of establishing these rights. Providing incentives for both blacks and whites to maintain integrated schools was not important. What was important was massive and immediate change. From this perspective, the fact that the resulting desegregation policy drove whites out from a city's schools was not a Pyrrhic victory even though it appears so on the surface. For the social movement, it did not lessen the victory; to the contrary, in those cities with already high proportions of black students, it could lead to a further victory: the transfer of the leadership of the school system from white control under a white superintendent to black control under a black superintendent. With the natural increase in the black student population, this would have occurred anyway in many school districts, especially in large cities. But it was brought about more quickly by the increased population movement of whites to the suburbs in response to the massive desegregation programs.

If all this was so, then why was publication of this report in the fall of 1975 (and a presentation of preliminary results at a plenary session of the American Educational Research Association the previous spring) greeted with such attention, with positive interest on the part of many ordinary citizens, especially whites, and outrage on the part of leaders of the social movement and many strong supporters of the existing desegregation plans?

For many who were not sympathetic to the extensive school reorganization that a desegregation plan entailed, the report was seen as a revelation that the emperor had no clothes, as a statistical analysis documenting what ordinary persons had known all along: that busing did not work. Because a person who had been seen to be at the forefront of the social movement—

the person who, as author of the "Coleman Report," was seen by some as the "father of busing"—made the revelation, it was even more powerful.

One can understand the outrage with which many advocates of massive desegregation plans (including the then-president of the American Sociological Association, who proposed to have me censured by the association) greeted the report by recognizing the heterogeneous nature of the coalition on which the social movement depended. Although the principal leaders of the school desegregation movement, black and white, saw this as a movement to establish the rights of blacks in American society, the strength of the support for busing plans depended on their achievement of the announced intention: bringing about effective desegregation. Many of the supporters of desegregation plans supported them for this reason alone, and many others did not oppose the plans because they were seen as the sole means of achieving this goal.

The vehemence with which many of the leaders and most ardent supporters of busing plans greeted the publication of this report stemmed from the report's potential for destroying this heterogeneous coalition by leading those interested only in achieving desegregation to withdraw support: If busing were shown to be ineffective in its announced intention, through its indirect resegregating effects, then the movement would lose a large fraction of the support on which it depended.

This account of the report's reception also accounts for the relative lack of interest in approaches that could achieve progressive and stable school integration. Several of the chapters in this book, Chapters 9, 14, and 15, discuss possible policies that make strategic use of incentives to attract parents and students to schools, independent of their racial composition. Those papers, however, unlike the material contained in Chapter 12, attracted little interest and attention at the time. That work came at the wrong time, when the social movement to demonstrate the power and establish the rights of blacks was the dominant force in school desegregation.

Nevertheless, the task of creating a more integrated society remains. Slowly, living with the consequences of the desegregation policies of the 1960s and 1970s promulgated by the social movement, educators have found means of bringing about partial but more stable integration through positive incentives, for example, via magnet schools in large cities. In this context, some of the proposals of these chapters remain relevant for the long and difficult task of creating an educational system compatible with a racially integrated society. The use of magnet schools is only a starting point; the overall task is to recognize that in the long run both blacks and whites will have choices in education, as they do in the rest of their lives, and to devise schools in such a way that exercise of these choices will reinforce rather than undermine the goal of a racially integrated society.

One of the chapters in Part 3, Chapter 13, represents an unusual episode in the relation between social science and social policy. The chapter is the text of a presentation to the Massachusetts legislature, presented at its invitation, in the wake of the Boston busing plan initiated in 1974. The chapter reviews knowledge about the effects of school desegregation policies, knowledge which, had it not been for the broader social movement spearheaded by desegregation policy, might have had some effect in shaping or reshaping desegregation policy in Boston.[1]

Notes

1. This broader social movement to establish the rights of blacks was especially important in Massachusetts, the seat of the abolitionist movement. Busing in Boston, a relatively small city in a large metropolitan area, was supported by the descendants of those abolitionists now living outside the city of Boston and resisted by the Irish and Italians within Boston to whom the original Bostonians had long ago ceded the city politically. The victory of the abolitionists was possible because the instrument was the court and was not controlled by city politics.

12

Trends in School Segregation, 1968–73

JAMES S. COLEMAN, SARA D. KELLY, AND JOHN A. MOORE

Introduction

School desegregation has been a major issue in the United States in the 1960's and 1970's. In 1954, the Supreme Court decision in the *Brown* case initiated a set of activities which has culminated in the current desegregation efforts in large cities of the North.

"Desegregation" has meant many things during the period since 1954. The term initially referred to elimination of dual school systems, in which one set of attendance zones was used to assign white children to one set of schools, and a second set of attendance zones was used to assign black children to a different set of schools. The classic and plaintive query of the black mother in the South was why should her child be bused to a school far away, past a nearby school, merely because of the color of his skin. The extent of the change is that the same plaintive query is now heard, primarily from white mothers, primarily in large cities, where busing has begun to be used, not to segregate children by race, but to integrate them.

This change is reflected in a change in meaning of the term desegregation. From the initial meaning of eliminating a system of dual assignment, the term desegregation has come to mean reduction of any segregation within a system, and in the strongest meaning of the term, elimination of any racial imbalance among schools in the system. Thus desegregation, which initially meant abolition of a legally-imposed segregation, has come to mean, in many cases, affirmative integration.

Reprinted with permission from James S. Coleman, Sara D. Kelly, and John A. Moore, *Trends in School Segregation, 1968–73*, Urban Institute Paper 722-03-01 (Washington, D.C.: The Urban Institute, August 1975), pp. 1–81 (excerpts). Errata and modified calculations contained in the insert of October 22, 1975, have been incorporated into this version.

However, except for one court case (in Detroit) which was later reversed in the Supreme Court, desegregation has not come to mean elimination of racial imbalance between school districts. Nor, except in a few instances, have two or more school systems combined or cooperated to reduce segregation due to residence in different districts. Thus social policy in school desegregation, although changing over time and different in different districts, has almost wholly been confined to desegregation of schools within a school district.

Given the policies that have been applied, by local school systems, by the Department of Health, Education, and Welfare, and by the courts, we can ask a series of questions concerning the actual state of racial integration in schools, and recent trends in that state. For actions taken by one branch of government and at one level of government interact with actions taken by individuals and by other branches and levels of government. The actual state of school integration is a result of this interaction. It is different than it would be in the absence of the policies designed to bring about integration; but it is more than a simple consequence of the policies. Indeed, there are numerous examples of government policy in which the result of the interaction between policy and response is precisely the opposite of the result intended by those who initiated the policy. It is especially important in the case of school desegregation to examine this interaction, because many of the actions taken by individuals, and some of those taken by their local government bodies, have precisely the opposite effect on school desegregation to that intended by federal government policy. The most obvious such individual action, of course, is a move of residence to flee school integration.

To examine the status and trends in school segregation, the primary (and virtually singular) data source is the set of statistical reports collected by the Department of Health, Education, and Welfare. Beginning in 1968 and continuing to the present, the Office for Civil Rights (OCR) of HEW has obtained from school systems throughout the United States statistics showing the racial composition of each school in the district, the racial composition of teaching staffs, and related information. The data for 1968, 69, 70, 71, 72, and 73 have been processed and are available for analysis. These data allow a detailed statistical analysis of the status and trends in school segregation by race throughout the United States. They are unique in this; and the opportunity they offer is the opportunity to examine what has actually occurred throughout the period 1968–73 during which there have been policies at local, state, and federal levels, in courts, legislatures, executive and administrative branches of government related to school desegregation. Most of these policies have been aimed at bringing about desegregation, though in a few cases, such as anti-busing actions in Congress, they have been aimed at preventing certain kinds of desegregation.

Not all the questions surrounding school desegregation can be answered by these data, as will be evident in subsequent pages, but some can be, in a more complete way than before.

Of the various policy aims that have been the objects of school desegregation policies, these statistical data can give evidence only on a subset of the aims. And from this subset, we will examine a still smaller subset: the aim of eliminating racial segregation among schools within a system, whatever its source, and the aim of eliminating racial segregation between districts. The data gathered by OCR allow also for the examination of teacher assignment, and thus racial segregation among staff and between staff and students. However, we will not pursue that examination here.

The data do not allow, on the other hand, for a study of segregation among classes within a school (often known as "tracking"), because there is no good information on pupil assignment to classes within a school. The Office for Civil Rights attempted, in its 1971 questionnaire, to obtain these data from school systems, but abandoned the effort in 1972. A more detailed and intensive mode of data collection is probably necessary if data of sufficient quality on assignment within school are to be obtained.

No implication is intended by the examination to be carried out below that the policy aim of eliminating segregation among schools with a system, whatever its source, is the "correct" one, and other policies which would either go less far (such as eliminating only that school segregation not due to residence) or further (such as eliminating all segregation among classes within a school) are not correct. The question of what is the correct policy depends not only on the implicitly aimed-for social consequences, but upon the realm of legitimate authority of the governmental units applying the policy. This in turn depends on just which individual rights citizens have vested in their government for collective use, through the Constitution and legislative acts. For example, to accomplish the policy aim of eliminating all segregation among schools, whatever its source, the most effective implementation would be federally-specified pupil assignment to schools to create precise racial balance, disregarding school district and state lines. However, such a policy would be using collectively certain rights that individuals have retained to themselves or vested in a more local level of government. As another example, citizens have vested certain authority in the court, such as constitutional protection, but a wider range of authority in elected legislatures. Thus certain policy aims such as elimination of segregation among schools whatever its source may be appropriate for legislative action if it achieves certain desired consequences, but not appropriate for court action, which must be directed not toward achieving desirable social goals, but insuring constitutional protection for all citizens. It is useful also to point out that data such as these which show the indirect and unintended consequences of school desegregation actions may be relevant for certain desegregation decisions, but not for others. They are relevant for an executive or legislative body which is attempting in its action to achieve a desirable social consequence. They are not relevant for a court decision which is acting to insure equal protection under the 14th Amendment.

Despite the fact that only two aims, student desegregation among schools in a district regardless of the source of segregation, and desegregation between school districts, can be studied, there are a number of important questions that can be answered with these data. In particular, these data show the result of government desegregation actions and individual segregating actions taken together, and allow some assessment of the effects of each. In this way, they suggest the limits of government policy, or at least the limits of policies carried out in the conflict mode that has characterized school desegregation policy.

We will begin by examining the state of racial integration among schools within a district in 1968, and then move to an examination of the changes that occurred over the period 1968–1973. What will be of special interest is the differential changes that occurred over that period of time in different kinds of school settings: in different regions of the country, in school districts of different sizes, and in particular large cities. For different things were happening in different places during this time, giving rise to very different trends in different places. . . .

The Measures of School Integration

A principal consequence of school desegregation that is of major societal interest is the amount of contact between children of different racial groups.[2] Furthermore, most of the attention has been focussed on the amount of contact of "minority" children (principally blacks and Spanish-American children[3]) with "majority whites." Much attention both of courts and legislatures has been directed toward elimination of patterns that result in schools which are overwhelmingly or predominantly minority.

For these reasons, a directly relevant statistical measure on a school system is the proportion of white children in the same school with the average black child [denoted s_{bw} in later analyses]. This gives a measure of the experience of the "average black child" in that school district with whites. A similar measure may be calculated for the proportion of children of each racial group in the school of the average child from each racial group [in later sections, s_{ij} for the proportion of children from group j in the school of the average child of group i]. . . .

This measure is affected not only by the degree of segregation between two groups in different schools in the system, but also by the overall proportion of children in each group. If there are few white children in the system, for example, then whether or not there is the same proportion of whites in each school, the average black child will have a small proportion of white children in his school. Because of this, it is valuable also to have a measure of just how far from an even distribution across the schools the actual distribution is, that is, a measure that is standardized for the number of whites in the system. Such a measure can be constructed [denoted r_{ij} in later analyses], having a value of 0 if there is no segregation between the two groups [i and j] in question, and a value of 1.0 if segregation is complete. . . .

It is important to note, however, that although the standardized measure is a measure of segregation of children in one group from those of another, it is the unstandardized measure which measures directly the presence of

TABLE 1
Proportion of Schoolmates from Each Group for the Average Child of Each Group

For the Average:	American Indian	Black	Oriental American	Spanish Surname	Majority White	Sum
			Proportion of Schoolmates Who Are:			
American Indian	0.31	0.04	0.0+	0.06	0.59	1.00
Black	0.0+	0.74	0.0+	0.03	0.22	0.99
Oriental American	0.0+	0.11	0.11	0.12	0.66	1.00
Spanish Surname	0.0+	0.11	0.01	0.43	0.44	0.99
Majority White	0.0+	0.04	0.0+	0.03	0.93	1.00
Proportion of Each Group	0.0035	0.1530	0.0047	0.0466	0.7922	

children of a group in schools attended by children of another group. Thus the proportion of white schoolmates for the average black child may be low, as in Washington, D.C., where only 3% of the children are white, without the measure of segregation being especially high. . . .

Integration in 1968

In 1968 in the United States, 15% of the children in public schools (grades 1–12) were black, 6% were of another minority, and 79% were majority whites. But the average black child in U.S. schools went to a school which had 74% black children in it, and only 22% white children (and 4% other minorities). Meanwhile, the average majority white child was in a school which was 93% white and only 4% black.

These numbers show that the interracial contact in American schools in 1968 was quite low. Black children had more contact with whites than whites had with blacks, due to the disparity in overall numbers; but the separation was quite marked. Using the standardized measure described earlier, r_{ij}, the segregation between blacks and whites is .72. . . .

Although in the subsequent examination we will focus exclusively on black-white segregation, it is useful to note here the proportion of schoolmates from each of the five racial-ethnic groups for the average child from each group. Table 1 shows this for 1968. . . .

As this table shows, the average white child in the U.S. has far less contact with any minority children than any of the minorities have with children from other groups. Among the minorities, black children have least contact with children from other groups. Construction of standardized measures of segregation from these figures would show that blacks and whites are the most segregated, both from one another and from the other groups. . . .

Regional Variations

The degree of school segregation differed considerably among regions of the country in 1968. Table 2 shows, for the Census geographic regions, the contact of blacks and whites, and the segregation, in each of the regions.[10]

TABLE 2
Black-White Contact and School Segregation in 1968 by Region

	Proportion		Schoolmates		Black-White Segregation	
	1. White	2. Black	3. Whites for Average Black	4. Blacks for Average White	5. Within District	6. Total
U.S.	.79	.15	.22	.04	.63	.72
New England	.93	.05	.49	.03	.35	.48
Middle Atlantic	.81	.14	.31	.05	.43	.61
Border	.79	.21	.26	.07	.48	.68
Southeast	.69	.29	.16	.07	.75	.77
West South Central	.78	.16	.18	.04	.69	.77
East North Central	.87	.12	.29	.04	.58	.67
West North Central	.90	.09	.28	.03	.61	.69
Mountain	.81	.03	.36	.01	.49	.55
Pacific	.78	.08	.26	.02	.56	.68
Outlying	.87	.03	.83	.03	(−).04	.04

Table 2 shows, comparing columns 1 and 3, the disparity between the proportion white in each region and the proportion white among the average black's schoolmates. Although the proportion white ranges from .69 to .93, in no region except the Outlying states does the average black have a majority of white schoolmates. Only in New England does the proportion approach this. Comparing columns 2 and 4 shows a similar disparity for whites: although the proportion black reaches .29 in one region, in no region does the average white have more than 7% black schoolmates.

These disparities are shown in column 6, the measure of total segregation. It is greatest in the two southern regions, though not so much greater than several northern regions as might be expected, given historic differences between North and South in school policy. With this relative similarity between total segregation in North and South in 1968, it is somewhat puzzling that when the goals of desegregation shifted from elimination of dual systems to more ambitious ones, attention continued to be concentrated on the South until the early 1970's. The explanation probably lies in the conflict surrounding desegregation: The desegregation movement was part of a larger movement of the 1960's of liberating the southern black. Only with the success of that movement did attention turn to the North.

In the measure of within-district segregation (column 5), the two southern regions are more distinct from the northern regions. The southeast shows the classic pattern of southern segregation, with nearly all the segregation occurring within districts, while New England, Middle Atlantic, and Border regions show what has emerged as the northern pattern of segregation—

TABLE 6
Black-White Contact and School Segregation in 1968 for 22 Largest Central City School Districts
(Districts ranked by 1972 enrollment)

	Proportion		Schoolmates		
	1. White	2. Black	3. Whites for Average Black	4. Blacks for Average White	5. Segregation Within District
1. New York	.44	.31	.23	.17	.47
2. Los Angeles	.54	.23	.08	.03	.86
3. Chicago	.38	.53	.05	.08	.86
4. Philadelphia	.39	.59	.14	.21	.64
5. Detroit	.39	.59	.13	.20	.66
6. Houston	.53	.33	.06	.04	.89
7. Baltimore	.35	.65	.10	.19	.71
8. Dallas	.61	.31	.06	.03	.91
9. Cleveland	.42	.56	.06	.09	.85
10. Wash., D.C.	.06	.93	.03	.44	.53
11. Memphis	.46	.54	.04	.04	.92
12. Milwaukee	.73	.24	.18	.06	.76
13. San Diego	.76	.12	.26	.04	.66
14. Columbus	.74	.26	.30	.10	.60
15. Tampa	.74	.19	.16	.04	.78
16. St. Louis	.36	.64	.07	.12	.82
17. New Orleans	.31	.67	.09	.19	.72
18. Indianapolis	.66	.34	.22	.11	.67
19. Boston	.68	.27	.27	.11	.60
20. Atlanta	.38	.62	.06	.09	.85
21. Denver	.66	.14	.20	.04	.69
22. San Francisco	.41	.28	.25	.17	.38

segregation due to blacks and whites attending schools in different districts. In those three regions, the ratio of the within-district segregation to the total segregation is lowest, .70 to .73. . . .

Racial Contact and Segregation in the 22 Largest Central-City Districts

. . . Segregation is most pronounced in the largest school districts, which tend to be located in the largest cities. Table 6, in the same format as columns 1–5 of Table 2, shows for the twenty-two largest central-city districts (1972 enrollment) the proportion of schoolmates of the other race in columns 3 and 4, and the measure of segregation in column 5.[13] . . . In only three cities (Columbus, Boston, and San Diego) did the average black child have more than a quarter of his schoolmates white, and in only six cities (Philadelphia, Detroit, Baltimore, New Orleans, New York, and San Francisco, excluding Washington, D.C., which is an aberrant case, almost racially homogeneous) did the average white child have more than 15% of his schoolmates black. This low degree of contact is reflected by the segregation measures, eight of which are .80 or above, and only three of which are below .60. These figures reemphasize . . . that segregation in large cities in 1968 was not concentrated in any region of the country, but appeared to a similar degree in all regions.

Altogether, the picture of racial segregation in U.S. schools in 1968 is one with several components:

1. High segregation in the largest cities of the country, where the proportions of blacks are greatest;
2. Sharply lower segregation in smaller districts everywhere but the South (and slightly lower there), but much smaller proportions of blacks in these smaller districts—except in the South [Results in Table 3, not included here.];
3. A large contribution to total segregation in some northern regions due to blacks and whites living in different districts, so that the difference in total segregation between North and South is considerably less than their difference in segregation within districts;
4. Greater segregation at elementary than at secondary levels, due at least in part to the smaller, more homogeneous areas served by elementary schools [Results in Table 4, not included here.];
5. A seeming paradox: the region with the highest degree of segregation, the Southeast, is also the region in which the average white child had the highest proportion of black schoolmates (.07). The reason, of course, lies in the higher proportion of blacks in the Southeast.

It is clear from these data that by 1968, desegregation of schools was a far from accomplished task in cities and towns of all sizes in the South; but that in the largest cities it was equally high in many places where dual school systems had never existed. But this was the picture in 1968, before the major thrust of desegregation in schools had occurred. The next four years show strong trends toward desegregation. It is these trends to which we now turn.

Trends in Within-System Segregation

Between 1968 and 1972, there was a sharp reduction in black-white segregation in the United States. In 1972, 16% of public school children were black, and 77% white. The average black child in 1972 went to a school that was 61% black (compared to 74% in 1968) and 34% white. And the average majority white child was in a school which was 89% white and 7% black. The comparison below shows the change from 1968 to 1972:

	Proportion		*Schoolmates*		*Black-White Segregation*	
	White	*Black*	*Whites for Average Black*	*Blacks for Average White*	*Within District*	*Total*
1968	.79	.15	.22	.04	.63	.72
1972	.77	.16	.34	.07	.37	.56

The change from 1968 to 1972 is substantial. Indeed, the average within-district segregation in 1972 between blacks and whites may not be greater than that between some pairs of white ethnic groups. But the change from 1968 to 1972 consists of very different changes in different locales. . . . The varying changes can best be seen via a graph. Figure 1 shows the trends in average segregation within school districts (comparable to column 5 of Table 2 and Table 6) in each region over the three points in time, 1968, 1970, and 1972. There is a radical drop in the Southeast, from highest at .75 in 1968 to lowest at .19 in 1972. Among the other regions, there are rather large declines in West South Central, Mountain, and Pacific regions. In New England, Middle Atlantic, and East North Central regions, there has been virtually no change in segregation. These trends show that school desegregation during this period (the period during which most desegregation took place) was almost wholly a southern affair, with the far West being the only exception. This concentration in the South was of course largely the consequence of federal requirements, supported by legal decisions in the courts, aimed at removing segregation where dual school systems had not been eliminated. The graph suggests, however, that the segregation removed was not only that due to dual systems; it was also that due to individual residential location within districts that has led in the North to within-district segregation of .40–.60.

But apart from having occurred primarily in the South and to a lesser extent in the Far West, how did desegregation proceed in districts of different sizes? Figure 2 shows the changes in average within-district segregation in districts of each size over this four-year period. The results are striking: Districts greater than 100,000 in size changed very little; and the amount of change increased steadily as the district size decreased. Among districts 10,000 or below in size, segregation is small indeed, less than .15. The graph shows the very great effectiveness of desegregation policies in the smaller districts (though we have not yet examined the effects on total segregation), and the much lesser effectiveness in the largest districts. . . .

Change in 22 Largest Central-City Districts

A final picture of change in within-district segregation is the change in the 22 largest central-city districts. The left side of Table 10 shows the segregation of each in 1968 and 1973, together with the change, in column 3. The table shows the dramatic reduction in some southern cities, joined by Indianapolis among the northern cities, Denver and San Francisco in the West. It shows, however, an increase in five northern cities and one Border city, showing that even during this period of major desegregation, and even within the city boundaries themselves, there were residential movements increasing the segregation in these cities. There are no more northern cities within which segregation was reduced than there are within which segregation increased.

But this does not tell the whole story, even before examining the question of segregation between districts. There have been substantial population

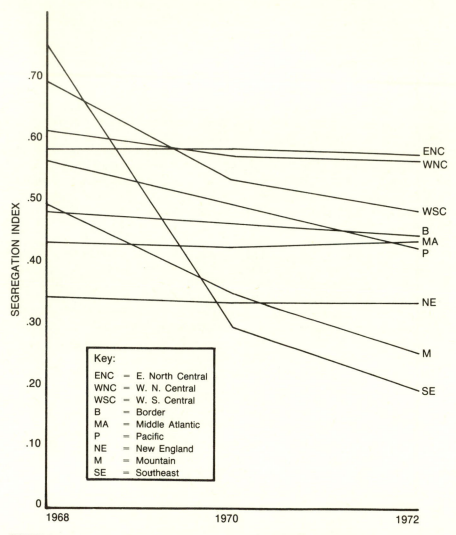

Key:

ENC = E. North Central
WNC = W. N. Central
WSC = W. S. Central
B = Border
MA = Middle Atlantic
P = Pacific
NE = New England
M = Mountain
SE = Southeast

FIGURE 1 Average Within-District Segregation, 1968–1972, by Region (Alaska and Hawaii omitted)

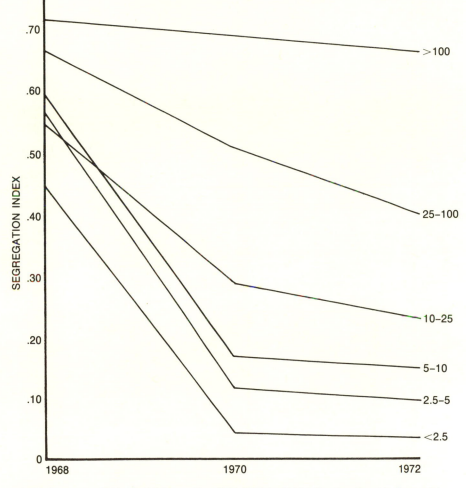

FIGURE 2 Average Within-District Segregation, 1968–1972, by District Size (enrollment in thousands)

TABLE 10

Black-White Segregation and Contact of Blacks with Whites in 22 Largest Central City School
Districts, 1968–1973 (Districts ranked by 1972 enrollment)

	Segregation Measures			Proportion white schoolmates for average black		
	1. 1968	2. 1973	3. Change (1973–1968)	4. 1968	5. 1973	6. Change (1973–1968)
1. New York	.47	.50	+.03	.23	.17	−.06
2. Los Angeles	.86	.79	−.07	.07	.09	+.02
3. Chicago	.86	.88	+.02	.05	.04	−.01
4. Philadelphia	.64	.72	+.08	.14	.10	−.04
5. Detroit	.66	.62	−.04	.13	.11	−.02
6. Houston	.89	.72	−.17	.06	.11	+.05
7. Baltimore	.71	.69	−.02	.10	.09	−.01
8. Dallas	.91	.69	−.22	.06	.15	+.09
9. Cleveland	.85	.87	+.02	.06	.05	−.01
10. Washington, D.C.	.53	.49	−.04	.03	.02	−.01
11. Memphis	.92	.31	−.61	.04	.22	+.18
12. Milwaukee	.75	.73	−.02	.18	.17	−.01
13. San Diego	.66	.53	−.13	.26	.34	+.08
14. Columbus	.60	.56	−.04	.30	.30	0.00
15. Tampa	.78	.04	−.74	.16	.71	+.55
16. St. Louis	.82	.85	+.03	.07	.05	−.02
17. New Orleans	.72	.57	−.15	.09	.09	0.00
18. Indianapolis	.67	.39	−.28	.22	.35	+.13
19. Boston	.60	.63	+.03	.27	.21	−.06
20. Atlanta	.85	.48	−.37	.06	.09	+.03
21. Denver	.69	.31	−.38	.20	.39	+.19
22. San Francisco	.38	.07	−.31	.25	.27	+.02

shifts in some of these cities, and we can ask the question: given these
population shifts, to what extent does the decrease in segregation, where
it occurred, result in an increase in the proportion of white schoolmates
for the average black? The right hand side of Table 10 answers that question
by comparing the proportion of white schoolmates for the average black in
each of these districts in 1968 with the proportion in 1973. The figures
show that although segregation decreased in 16 of the 22 cities, the proportion
of white schoolmates for the average black increased only in ten of those
sixteen. In four it decreased, and it remained unchanged in two. Thus
although segregation was reduced in most of the 22 cities, the contact of
the average black with white schoolmates has increased in less than half
of them. Only in those cities where desegregation was great did the contact
increase substantially—and even in Atlanta, where there was great desegregation, from .85 to .48, the proportion of white schoolmates for the average
black child increased only .03, from .06 to .09—because of the great loss
in numbers of white school children in Atlanta. (In Atlanta, the white school
population in 1973 was only 38% of its size in 1968.)

This last result leads directly to a set of further questions about the larger effects of school desegregation over the 1968–72 or 1968–73 period. The desegregaton policies have been confined wholly to within-district deseg-regation. But as has been evident in earlier examination, there was, especially in the North, substantial segregation due to residence of blacks and whites in different districts—in particular, larger proportions of blacks in large districts and larger proportion of whites in small districts. We can ask, then, what has been the trend, over this period of time, not merely in within-district segregation, as examined so far, but in overall segregation. And we can ask just what has been the change in segregation between districts during this period. Has it increased, as appears likely, and if so, to what extent? Finally, we can ask just what has been the effect of desegregation within districts on the behavior that increases segregation between districts: the movement of whites from districts with high proportions of blacks and low segregation to districts with smaller proportions of blacks.

The importance of these questions for educational policy lies in the fact that the distribution of children by race in schools is a result not merely of policies by the Federal government, nor of court orders, nor of policies by state and local governments. It is also the result of individuals' decisions about where they will live, and about whether they will send their children to public or nonpublic schools. Increasingly, as incomes increase, more families have these options open to them, though residential options are more restricted for black families due to residential discrimination. Thus the resulting distribution of children among schools is the result of the interaction of the collective decisions by governmental units and the individual family decisions. In areas of economic policy, governments have recognized that final outcomes are not merely the direct result of a policy, and are as concerned with the indirect effects of a policy as with the direct ones. In areas of social policy that are not economic, they usually have not, and have proceeded blindly, as if the policies directly controlled the final outcomes.

School segregation can show well these indirect effects, because the indirect effects have their principal impact on the distribution of whites and blacks among districts, and thus upon segregation between districts, while the direct effects of government policy have been on the distribution of whites and blacks among schools within a district.[15] We have examined the direct effects and in the right half of Table 10 taken a glimpse at the indirect effects. We will now turn to examine these indirect effects in more detail.

Changes in Total Segregation and Segregation Between Districts

Figure 5 shows the changes in total segregation in the U.S. as a whole and in each of the regions shown in Figure 1. These changes show roughly the same patterns as the within-district changes in Figure 1, but there are some important differences. First the regions are more tightly bunched in overall segregation in 1968 than in within-district segregation. Secondly,

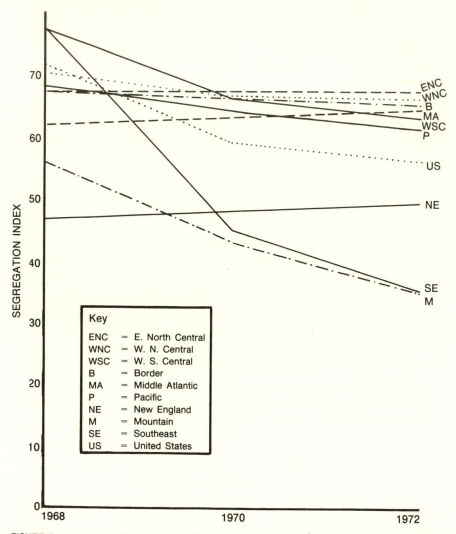

FIGURE 5 Average Total Segregation, 1968–1972, United States, and by Region (Alaska and Hawaii omitted)

TABLE 11
Within-District and Between-District Segregation in 1968 and 1972 in Each Region

	Within-District			Between-District		
	1968	1972	Change	1968	1972	Change
	(1)	(2)	(3)	(4)	(5)	(6)
United States	.63	.37	−.26	.32	.36	+.04
New England	.35	.33	−.02	.25	.31	+.06
Middle Atlantic	.43	.43	.00	.38	.44	+.06
Border	.48	.44	−.04	.48	.48	.00
Southeast	.75	.19	−.56	.18	.22	+.04
West South Central	.69	.48	−.21	.32	.37	+.05
East North Central	.58	.57	−.01	.30	.32	+.02
West North Central	.61	.56	−.05	.35	.39	+.04
Mountain	.49	.25	−.24	.15	.17	+.02
Pacific	.56	.42	−.14	.30	.34	+.04

the decreases in overall segregation, among those districts that do show a decrease, are somewhat less than changes in within-district segregation. This reflects the fact that while there were reductions in segregation within districts, due to desegregation policies, there were at the same time increases in segregation between districts, due primarily to the movement of white students to districts with few blacks.

This counterbalancing increase in segregation can be seen more directly by examining the within- and between-district segregation in 1968 and 1972 in each region. . . . As Table 11 shows, the within-district segregation has declined in every region except Middle Atlantic, where it remained constant, while the between-district segregation has increased in every region except Border, where it remained constant. In 1968, the within-district segregation was greater than the between-district segregation in every region; by 1972 the between-district was greater than the within-district in three of the nine regions. Thus the segregation that reflects residential separation into different school districts shows a steady increase throughout the country. . . .

Within- and Between-District Segregation in Metropolitan Areas

Another way of seeing what is happening in school segregation in the largest metropolitan areas is to examine trends in the segregation between different school districts in the metropolitan area. Most large cities have a separate school district from that of the surrounding suburbs (although many districts in the South are countywide). And just as there is racial segregation due to blacks and whites attending different schools in the same district, there is racial segregation due to blacks and whites living in different districts. Although the former (within-district segregation) has been reduced in a number of cities, especially in the South, the latter (between-district seg-

TABLE 13

Black-White Segregation Among Schools Within Central Cities and Districts in the Metropolitan Area

	1968		1972		Projected* 1976
	Within	Between	Within	Between	Between
New York	.47	.28	.48	.34	.41
Los Angeles	.86	.26	.80	.28	.31
Chicago	.86	.40	.87	.48	.55
Philadelphia	.64	.39	.70	.44	.48
Detroit	.66	.47	.64	.57	.67
Houston	.89	.15	.74	.26	.37
Baltimore	.71	.38	.69	.42	.46
Dallas	.91	.16	.72	.26	.36
Cleveland	.85	.43	.87	.47	.51
Wash., D.C.	.53	.66	.47	.59	.52
Memphis	.92	.04	.79	.05	.06
Milwaukee	.76	.15	.76	.21	.27
San Diego	.66	.06	.55	.07	.07
Columbus, O.	.60	.12	.58	.14	.16
Tampa	.78	.01	.03	.01	.01
St. Louis	.82	.47	.85	.54	.61
New Orleans	.72	.24	.61	.32	.41
Indianapolis	.67	.19	.57	.25	.31
Boston	.60	.21	.64	.28	.34
Atlanta	.85	.36	.63	.51	.65
Denver	.69	.21	.33	.26	.31
San Francisco	.38	.40	.08	.46	.52

*Projections are simple linear projections, which over small ranges and in the absence of sharp actions, such as large-scale desegregation over the whole metropolitan area, are sufficient for rough projections.

regation) has been increasing in each of the metropolitan areas containing the 22 largest central city districts except for Washington, D.C.

Table 13 compares the within-district and between-district segregation in each of the 22 largest central city districts and their metropolitan areas in 1968 and 1972.[17] In addition, the trends in between-district segregation exhibited from 1968 to 1972 are projected forward to 1976 in a simple linear projection. The data show that already in 1972, the between-district segregation is substantial in many of these metropolitan areas; for example, it is greater than .40 in nine of them. In Washington, D.C., and San Francisco, it exceeds the segregation within the central city district itself. Furthermore, the projections of these trends to 1976 show that it may be expected to grow substantially in many metropolitan areas. And in two metropolitan areas in addition to Washington and San Francisco—Detroit and Atlanta— it will exceed the within-district segregation of these cities (assuming that the latter does not change).[18] These projections indicate that the segregation of the future in metropolitan areas is as much a matter of segregation between districts as it is a matter of segregation within districts.

The Washington metropolitan area, as the one metropolitan area in which between-district segregation is decreasing, is especially interesting, because it illustrates the kind of process that may be expected to occur in many metropolitan areas as an outgrowth of present patterns of within-district school desegregation, and continuing residential segregation. Washington schools became almost completely racially homogeneous (6% white in 1968, and 3% in 1973), with the between-district segregation of whites and blacks increasing (highest among all these cities in 1968 and 1972), until finally the between-district segregation had nowhere to go but down. This pattern, of course, involves the central city first turning nearly all black before there is reduction of the city-suburb segregation.

All the changes described so far suggest a strong individual response to school desegregation on the part of families, especially where desegregation has been great. Direct evidence, however, lies in the tendency of white families to move when desegregation occurs, either to a district with fewer blacks, or to a district in which there is greater segregation—in either case, keeping the proportion of black schoolmates for its children low. What do the data show about the movement of white children out of the central city districts when desegregation occurs?

The Size of Individual Segregating Responses to Desegregation

It is clear from the preceding sections that there is a segregating process occurring through individual movement, primarily of white families, from schools and districts in which there is greater integration or a greater proportion of blacks, to schools and districts in which there is less integration or a smaller proportion of blacks. The consequences of this, of course, are to partially nullify the effects of school desegregation as carried out by various governmental or legal agencies.

What is not yet clear is whether desegregation itself induces an increased movement of whites from the desegregated district. This is a difficult but important question to answer, because desegregation in particular school districts is a direct outcome of social policy or legal rulings, and it is important to ask whether there are indirect consequences of desegregation itself which partly nullify it, and if so, what the size of this response is under various circumstances.[19]

The question is difficult because casual observation shows that desegregation has evoked differing reactions in different cities, and because desegregation has taken place in very different settings. For example, in many areas of the South, school systems are countywide, encompassing both a city and the surrounding suburbs. Leaving a desegregated system in that setting entails leaving the public school system itself, or a rather distant move (unless adjacent counties have also desegregated, which was a common occurrence in the early 1970's in the South). This, of course, is more difficult than a move to a separate predominantly white suburban school system, which is the common pattern in the North. Another variation is in city size, which creates nearly a qualitative difference in the character of desegregation. For full-scale desegregation in a large city entails mixing student populations that are much more socially distinct and more residentially separated than in small cities.

Additional complications include these:

a. Most desegregation in this period took place in the South, so that except as there was a similar response in those few places in the North that did desegregate, the generalization of results to northern cities must remain a question.

b. There was a general loss during this time of whites from central cities, a loss which preliminary analysis indicates is greater as the size of the city is greater, and as the proportion black in the city is greater.

c. The available data show simply the student populations of each race for each of the six years, 1968–73, so that only changes in student populations are directly measured. This is not exactly the same as movement, although something about net movement of a racial group out of the district's schools can be inferred from these measures of gain or loss.[20]

d. If there is a loss of whites when desegregation occurs, it is not clear what the time progression of this loss is. When does it begin? Does it continue, and accelerate as the proportion white in the schools declines, or is it a one-time response which does not continue once the degree of desegregation is constant? Or does it in fact reverse itself, with whites returning to the district's schools a year or so after they have desegregated? Initial observation of particular cities which have fully desegregated suggests that a loss due to desegregation begins in the *same* year that desegregation takes place, but its subsequent course is less clear. Using these indications from individual cities, we will first attempt to examine the loss of whites in the same year that desegregation occurs.

These difficulties are not overcome simply, but the data are extensive, showing racial composition of schools over each of the six years 1968–73.[21] The cities to be examined are divided into two groups because of the indications that response to desegregation differs considerably in very large cities from the response in smaller ones: 1) twenty-one of the twenty-three largest districts in the country classified as central-city districts;[22] 2) forty-six of the next forty-seven largest central-city districts.[23]

These cities are divided into two groups because the response to desegregation appears, as indicated above, different in the largest cities from smaller ones. In analyzing the question of how loss of white students is related to desegregation, we will first examine the loss that is related to reduction in segregation in the same year. The measure of segregation used is the standardized measure r_{ij} presented in earlier sections.[24]

In this analysis, all years are taken together (that is, Δr_{ij} in 68–69 is related to change in whites in 68–69, Δr_{ij} in 69–70 is related to change in whites in 69–70, etc.) in an equation as follows:

$$(4) \qquad \frac{w_t - w_{t-1}}{w_{t-1}} = a + b_1 \, \Delta r_{t,t-1} + b_2 \, p_{bt-1} + b_3 \, \ln N_{t-1}$$

where:

w_t is number of white students in the system in year t
r_t is the standardized measure of segregation in year t
p_{bt-1} is the proportion black in the system in year $t-1$
N_{t-1} is the number of students in the system in year $t-1$

The analysis is carried out for t = 69, 70, 71, 72, 73. They are taken together to obtain an average effect over the five years, because among the 22 cities, massive desegregation in any one year in one city can distort results for that year. The two additional variables of proportion black in the system and number of students are included because these variables appear to be related to loss of whites from the system independently of the change in segregation.

Note that the independent variable measuring change in segregation $\Delta r_{t,t-1}$, is just that. It is not a measure of a particular form of change in segregation, such as busing, nor even of a desegregation policy. Change in r can occur through individual movement of black or white students; and certainly the slight upward movement of segregation (as measured by r) in some northern cities is just that. However, these individual movements make only small differences in r over any year. Large negative values for Δr are due to desegregation policies instituted in that city. Although the term "desegregation" to a civil rights lawyer may mean only the move to full racial balance in all schools, it is important to remember that the desegregation variable used in this analysis refers to a reduction of any size in the index of segregation.

The results of the analysis are presented in Table 14. The table presents the coefficients to the above equation for the largest 21 central-city systems and the next 46, along with standard errors of the coefficients and amount of variance accounted for. To gain some sense of the magnitude of the effects represented by these coefficiants, we can express what the expected yearly rates of loss of white students would be in various circumstances. It is important to remember that these are *average* effects, which differ from city to city, as will become apparent in subsequent analysis.

1. For a city with the average number of students, with no blacks and no reduction in segregation, the expected loss per year is:
   a. Largest 21: (gain of) 0.9% of whites present at beginning of year (average number of students is 169,000)

TABLE 14
Regression Coefficients for Analyses of White Student Loss to Central Cities

	Largest 21		Next 46	
Equation 1				
ΔR	.279	(.062)	.056	(.026)
Prop. black	−.133	(.028)	−.090	(.014)
ℓn N	.000	(.008)	−.042	(.010)
Constant	.013		.452	
R^2	.290		.260	
Number of Observations	(105)		(226)	

Including inter-district segregation in SMSA, and interaction of desegregation with South:

	Largest 21		Next 46	
Equation 2				
ΔR	.199	(.156)	−.148	(.137)
Prop. black	−.044	(.039)	−.035	(.016)
ℓn N	.066	(.008)	−.041	(.010)
R SMSA	−.165	(.050)	−.110	(.021)
ΔR × S	.143	(.170)	.242	(.137)
Constant	−.059		.438	
R^2	.360		.350	

Including interactions of desegregation with proportion black and inter-district segregation, and also including South as a dummy variable:

	Largest 21		Next 46	
Equation 3				
ΔR	−.459	(.184)	−.349	(.151)
Prop. black	.051	(.037)	−.026	(.019)
ℓn N	.003	(.006)	−.039	(.009)
R SMSA	−.210	(.044)	−.102	(.025)
ΔR × South	.148	(.198)	.244	(.145)
ΔR × Prop. black	1.770	(.307)	.511	(.215)
ΔR × R SMSA	.561	(.494)	.894	(.314)
South	−.006	(.010)	−.002	(.006)
Constant	−.039		.414	
R^2	.600		.400	

    b. Next 46: 1.2% of whites present at beginning of year (average number of students is 58,000)

2. Additional expected loss if the city is 50% black:
    a. Largest 21: 6.8% of whites present at beginning of year
    b. Next 46: 4.5% of whites present at beginning of year

3. Additional expected loss if the city experiences a decrease of .2 in the index of segregation in that year:[25]
    a. Largest 21: 5.6% of whites at beginning of year
    b. Next 46: 1.1% of whites at beginning of year

4. Additional expected loss if a city was twice its size:
    a. Largest 21: 0% of whites present at beginning of year

b. Next 46: 2.9% of whites present at beginning of year

Taking the first three losses together, the expected loss of whites from a city system with 50% blacks would be:

For the largest 21:
  with reduction of .2 in segregation: (−) 0.9% + 6.8% + 5.6% = 11.5%
  with no change in segregation: (−) 0.9% + 6.8% = 5.9%
For the next 46:
  with reduction of .2 in segregation: 1.2% + 4.5% + 1.1% = 6.8%
  with no change in segregation: 1.2% + 4.5% = 5.7%

These results suggest that the impact of desegregation is quite large for the largest 21 districts, of the same order of magnitude as other effects; but that for the next 46 cities, the impact is much less, considerably smaller than that due to other factors. (The average loss of whites per year in the largest 21 cities was 5.6% of those present at the beginning of the year, and in the next 46, 3.7%.) It should be remembered also that this is an effect for the year of desegregation only; we do not yet know about subsequent effects.

But how does a decrease of .2 in the segregation index compare to the actual largest declines that occurred in segregation in these cities in any single year? One way to get a sense of this is, as stated earlier, from the fact that in a city with .5 blacks in the schools, an increase of 10% blacks in the average white child's school is equivalent to a decrease of .2 in the segregation measure. To give another sense of the magnitude of a change of .20, the cities among the 21 largest districts are listed below in which a reduction in segregation of .10 or more occurred in any single year, together with the year it occurred:

City	Year	Reduction in Segregation
Houston	69–70	.11
Dallas	70–71	.19
Memphis	72–73	.48
Tampa	70–71	.52
Indianapolis	72–73	.18
Atlanta	69–70	.11
	72–73	.15
Denver	68–69	.22
San Francisco	70–71	.16

Eight of the 21 cities underwent a reduction in segregation of .1 or more in any single year, and three a reduction of .2 or more (and seven of them underwent a reduction of .2 or more over the total period 68–73). Among the next 46, 13 underwent a reduction of .2 or more over the whole period, and 10 of these a reduction of .4 or more. Many cities, of course, underwent no desegregation at all, and their segregation indices remained approximately constant, or increased.

A next step which can be taken (or two steps at once) is to attempt to consider two more factors which differ among cities which have experienced desegregation, factors which may affect the rate of loss of whites. One is location in the South or North. This factor we do not expect to affect the *general* loss of whites, but only their loss when desegregation occurs. Thus we can ask what is the effect of desegregation of .2 for southern cities, and what is the effect for northern cities? Second, cities differ in the degree to which a suburban alternative is available. Some cities, either because the school district encompasses all or most of the metropolitan area, or because the rest of the metropolitan area is about the same racial composition as the central city, have no such available havens. Thus we can ask how the loss of whites is affected by the racial disparity between city and suburbs, or what we have called in an earlier section, the between-district segregation.

A regression equation which includes these two variables gives results as indicated in Table 14, which allow the following estimates.

Estimated increase in loss of whites in one year as a function of reduction of .2 in index of segregation:

	South	North
Largest 21	6.8%	4.0%
Next 46	1.9%	*

*No reliable estimate for the North can be made since the correlation between Δr and $\Delta r \times$ South is .983 (i.e., nearly all changes in segregation occurred in the South in these 46 cities). See footnote 26 for further discussion.

These results show that indeed there has been a greater loss of whites when desegregation has taken place in large southern cities than when it has taken place in large northern cities, with the estimate nearly twice for the southern cities what it is for northern ones. For the smaller cities, there is a smaller loss for the Southern cities though no effect can be estimated for the North in these smaller cities.

For this analysis with the two additional variables, we can also ask what differences in loss of whites are associated with a difference between 0 and 50% black in the city schools and a difference between 0 between-district segregation and .4 between-district segregation.

Estimated increase in loss of whites in one year as a function of 50% black in city school district and between-district segregation of .4:

	50% Black	Between-district Segregation of .4
Largest 21	2.2%	6.6%
Next 46	1.7%	4.4%

The estimates show that the loss which was earlier seen as resulting from the proportion black in the city can in fact in considerable part be accounted for by the between-district segregation, which is a function of the *difference* between proportion black in the city and that in the suburbs. Thus the frequent observation that the loss of whites from central-city school systems depends on the existence of suburban systems with high proportions of whites is certainly confirmed by these data. Note, however, that this is a *generally* greater loss of whites under such conditions, not related to the period of desegregation. The question of whether there is additional loss at the time of desegregation can be answered by a further analysis, to which we now turn.

In this analysis, we include not only the possibilities that have already been examined, but three others as well:

a. The possibility that there is a generally different loss rate of whites from central cities in the South than in the North, in the absence of desegregation
b. the possibility that desegregation produces different rates of loss when the proportion black in the city differs (interaction between proportion black and change in segregation)
c. the possibility that desegregation produces different rates of loss when the inter-district segregation differs

The estimates of these effects can best be expressed as the total estimated loss rates under different illustrative conditions.[26] We will consider what the loss rates would be for the average size district in the South for each group of cities where the reduction in segregation is .2, as in earlier illustrations. Estimates are given for various combinations of proportion black in the central-city district, ranging from .25 to .75 and between-district segregation ranging from 0 to .4.

The tabulation below shows the estimated loss rates under these various illustrative conditions.

Between-district Segregation	Largest 21 Proportion Black			Next 46 Proportion Black		
	.25	.50	.75	.25	.50	.75
0	2%	10%	17%	3%	6%	9%
.2	9	16	24	8	11	15
.4	15	23	30	14	17	20

These estimates are for a city in the South. In the North the losses at the time of reduction in segregation are estimated to be 3.6% less in the largest 21 cities with no reliable estimate possible in the next 46. . . . It should be recalled that more desegregation took place in the South, so that the estimates are less reliable for northern cities. It should also be noted that some combinations of proportion black and between-district segregation are impossible or quite unlikely, such as .25 proportion black and .4 between-district segregation, or .75 black and 0 between-district segregation.

The most striking from these illustrative estimates are two effects. One is the large increase in the effect of desegregation on rate of white loss as the proportion black in the district increases. This effect exists in both size cities, though it is more pronounced in the largest 21. There is a similarly large increase in the effect of desegregation on white loss if there are suburban alternatives, as measured by a high value for between-district segregation. In this case, the estimated augmentation effect is high both for the smaller cities and for the large ones. . . .

A more careful statistical examination may be made by introducing into the regression equation a dummy variable for each city. Since in equation (4) there are five observations for each city, the degrees of freedom in the equation are $5n - n - 3$.

This analysis makes a somewhat different comparison than the previous ones. In those analyses, districts which have desegregated are compared with those that have not, to discover the effect of desegregation on loss of white students to the system. In this analysis, by contrast, we compare districts that have desegregated with their own expected rates of loss in the absence of desegregation, to discover any additional loss of whites due to desegregation. This is obviously a much more stringent test because it controls for the general characteristics of each city. The equations used in the analysis include proportion black, logarithm of number of students, and between-district segregation, with the addition of a dummy variable for each city. The results of the analysis give coefficients for Δr of .262 (.057) for the largest 21 city districts, and .098 (.025) for the smaller cities.[29] These coefficients correspond closely to those found in earlier equations, indicating that the estimate of the average additional loss rate during desegregation is a stable one, and not due to uncontrolled characteristics of the cities.

Finally, it is possible to carry out a full analysis of covariance, in which we can not only control for the characteristics of the individual cities, but also estimate the loss rate under desegregation for each city which underwent substantial desegregation.[30] These estimates are probably as close as we can obtain to the actual effects of desegregation on white loss in the year of desegregation. They show that the estimated white loss does vary considerably from city to city, and that the average loss rate specified earlier obscures very different loss rates in different cities. Table 17 shows the estimated loss rate in the year of desegregation if Δr were .2, for all cities listed earlier which underwent desegregation of .1 or more in a single year. These rates must still be regarded as only estimates because there are other things varying concurrently with desegregation. For three of these, proportion black, between-district segregation, and size of district, the equation has controlled the general effects; but the specific effects of each of these variables (as well as others) may differ from city to city. Nevertheless, these figures do indicate where the losses due to segregation are especially great, and where they are small. . . .

TABLE 17
Estimated Additional Loss of White Students in Specified Cities (Loss during desegregation in cities which had a Δr in one year of $-.1$, beyond general loss of whites in those cities. Desegregation assumed is $\Delta r = -.2$.)

City	Estimated Loss as a Percent of White Students Present at Beginning of Year
Houston	9.1% (gain)
Dallas	7.9%
Memphis	15.6%
Tampa	2.6%
Indianapolis	6.7%
Atlanta	16.7%
Denver	4.0% (gain)
San Francisco	5.1%
Average	5.2%

Note: Professor Reynolds Farley (personal communication 10 September, 1975) has pointed out to us that Houston, Dallas, Memphis, and Denver annexed substantial amounts of territory during the period 1970–73, so that the losses for those cities may be underestimated due to an undetermined number of white children added through annexation. Thus the apparent gains for Houston and Denver may well be due to annexation.

Altogether then, what does this analysis of effects of desegregation in cities indicate? Several results can be specified with some assurance:

1. In the large cities (among the largest 22 central city school districts) there is a sizeable loss of whites when desegregation takes place.
2. There is a loss, but less than half as large, from small cities. These differences due to city size continue to hold when the reduced opportunity of white flight into surrounding school districts in the smaller cities is taken into account.
3. The estimated loss is less in northern cities which have undergone desegregation than in southern ones.
4. In addition to effects of desegregation on white loss, both the absolute proportion of blacks in the central city and their proportion relative to those in the surrounding metropolitan areas have strong effects on loss of whites from the central-city district.
5. Apart from their general effect on white loss, a high absolute proportion of blacks in the central city and a high difference in racial composition between the central-city district and the remaining metropolitan area both intensify the effects of desegregation on rates of white loss.
6. When general rates of white loss for individual cities are taken into account, the desegregation effects still hold to about the same degree as estimated from comparisons among cities.

. . .

8. The effect of desegregation on white loss has been widely different among different cities where desegregation has taken place.

. . .

All this leads to general conclusions consistent with those from earlier sections of this examination: that the emerging problem with regard to school desegregation is the problem of segregation between central city and suburbs; and in addition, that current means by which schools are being desegregated are intensifying that problem, rather than reducing it. The emerging problem of school segregation in large cities is a problem of metropolitan area residential segregation, black central cities and white suburbs, brought about by a loss of whites from the central cities. This loss is intensified by extensive school desegregation in those central cities, but in cities with high proportions of blacks and predominantly white suburbs, it proceeds at a relatively rapid rate with or without desegregation.

Notes

. . .

2. A different consequence may be of legal interest: the degree to which segregation resulting from action of any level of government (thus failing to provide equal protection under the 14th Amendment) is eliminated. Still other consequences are of interest to particular groups, and these may depend on the particular way that segregation or integration arises. For example, if either segregation or integration is achieved through assignment of children to schools at some distance because of their race, then the parents affected may feel a greater deprivation of rights than in the case when such assignment does not occur, even if the school's racial composition does not differ. However, a study of the kind carried out here cannot examine these consequences.

3. The OCR surveys measure enrollments of the following categories: Blacks, American Indian, Oriental, Spanish Surnamed Americans, and Other. White non-minority and undesignated minority groups are included in the category "Other."

. . .

10. Several regions have been reclassified, because the character of racial segregation has differed within the region. Hawaii and Alaska have been separated as "outlying" states from the Pacific region; and the South Atlantic and East South Central have been combined and redivided into Border (Delaware, Maryland, West Virginia, Kentucky) and Southeast (all others in these two regions). In all tabulations beyond Table 2, the Outlying states, Hawaii and Alaska, are dropped, because as Table 2 shows, there is no black-white segregation in their schools, and the number of blacks in those states is very small.

. . .

13. These 22 largest central city school districts are classified according to 1972 enrollment and an Office of Education metropolitan status classification. They represent 22 of the 23 largest central city districts; Albuquerque is excluded (the 22nd largest) because it is not among the largest 50 cities in total population.

. . .

15. As suggested in the elementary-secondary comparisons [not included here], the indirect effects in the form of residential movement can also have their effects

on segregation within districts. The only portion of the indirect effects that the present analysis can measure is that which has its effect on segregation between districts.

. . .

17. Data are available, as in other tables, for 1973 for these central city districts, but cover only some of the non-central city districts in 1973. Thus 1972 comparisons must be used.

18. Of course, desegregation within Boston in 1974 and in Detroit in 1975 reduces sharply the within-district segregation in those cities.

19. There have been several studies of the effect of school segregation on the loss of white children from the desegregating school system. In an attitude survey of parents in eight Florida countywide desegregated school districts, one group of authors (Cataldo et al., 1975) concluded that when the racial composition of schools is less than 30% black, almost no whites leave; but beyond 30% a higher proportion leave. Mercer and Scout in a comprehensive (as yet unpublished) survey of white school population changes in California districts between 1966 and 1973 found no relation between population changes and the amount of desegregation undergone in the district. Charles Clotfelter (1975), in contrast, shows that desegregation in Mississippi had a significant effect on private school enrollment, an effect that increased with increasing proportions of blacks in the schools. Reynolds Farley (1975) used the same OCR data used in our analysis, but only up to 1972. He found no relation of school integration to white population loss for 125 cities with 100,000 or more population and at least 3% blacks, and also for the largest northern and southern cities. His methods differ, however, from our own in several respects, particularly in our year-by-year examination contrasted to his five-year examination.

20. Fertility changes among whites also affect the change in numbers of white children in the schools. Fertility of whites in the years preceding this period was declining, which leads to a general decline in white student populations. This affects the constant term in the regression equations, but not the indicated effects of desegregation, unless the decline in white fertility was by some change greater in those cities that desegregated. The covariance analyses even controls for that possibility (see p. 000).

21. Schools are not identified each year in a way that makes possible tracing changes in individual schools.

22. Washington, D.C., which has only about 3% white, is excluded because it is already racially homogeneous. Albuquerque, the 22nd largest central-city district, was excluded because the city of Albuquerque is not among the first 50 in population. Size of central-city district corresponds reasonably well to size of city, but there are some discrepancies. This set of districts included 19 of the largest 21 cities in the country by the 1970 census (excluding only San Antonio and Phoenix). In addition, it includes Denver (the 25th largest), Atlanta (the 27th largest), and Tampa (the 50th largest). The latter is a county-wide school district, which accounts for the large district size relative to city size. In preliminary analyses, only the largest 20 central-city districts were included, excluding Denver and San Francisco. However, because Denver and San Francisco were two of the few northern cities to undergo extensive desegregation during the period 1968–73, they have been included.

23. Richmond, Va., which annexed some suburban districts in the same year it underwent extensive desegregation, was excluded. It was not possible to tell from Richmond the exact size of white loss from the original district, although the loss in years subsequent to the annexation shows that it was substantial. Memphis also had annexation, but its size was affected only slightly, so it was not excluded.

24. It seems likely that the tendency of white families to leave the system is related not to a change in the "index of segregation," but to a change in the proportion of blacks in their child's school. Thus a change in the unstandardized measure of earlier sections, s_{ij} (the proportion of black children in the average white child's school), should be more directly related to loss of whites than is r_{ij}. However, the unstandardized measure is affected by the number of white children in the system, and thus any analysis including it must relate the change in s_{ij} in the *previous* year to the loss of whites in a given year. A discussion in Appendix 3, however, indicates how one might use the change in s_{ij} as a determinant of loss of whites in the same year. The relation between the size of a change in s_{ij} and the corresponding change in r_{ij} depends on the proportion black in the system. When it is .5, which is about average for the largest 22 central-city districts, then the change in r_{ij} is twice the change in s_{ij} (since $r_{ij} = (p_j - s_{ij})/p_j$). It is because both the numerator and denominator of the formula for r_{ij} are affected by loss of whites to the system that r_{ij} in a given year is approximately independent of loss of whites in that year.

25. A decrease of .2 in the index of segregation is approximately equal to an increase of 10% in the black schoolmates of the average white in the system if the proportion is .50.

26. The individual coefficients from Table 14 if interpreted alone without combining both the interaction terms and the main effects are not meaningful. Thus the negative sign on the coefficient for Δ r is not itself interpretable, without the compensating positive coefficient of Δ rx proportion black. Even so, particular combinations of values for the variables would show results that would seem unlikely on their face (for example, integration at very low proportions black apparently bringing about a small gain in proportion of whites in city schools, rather than a loss, or increased proportion black apparently bringing about a small gain as well). This is probably due to misspecification of the equation—for example, some nonlinearity in effect of proportion black, not allowed by the equation as specified, or to a tendency of two highly correlated variables to have coefficients that polarize, due to minor sampling fluctuations. (See "Instabilities of Regression Estimates Relating Air Pollution to Mortality," Gary C. McDonald and Richard C. Schwing, Technometrics. Vol. 15, No. 3, Aug. 1973.) Finally, there is the fact that some coefficients would give meaningless values of rate of loss (e.g., over 100%) for extreme values of the independent variables (e.g., Δ r = 1 and proportion black = 1.0). This is due to a deliberate misspecification of the equation. The appropriate dependent variable would have been logarithm of (whites in year t/whites in year t−1), rather than (whites in t − whites in t−1)/ (whites in t−1). The latter was used because it gives almost the same results as the former, and the coefficients are more directly expressible as additions to a given rate of loss.

. . .

29. R^2 in these equations are .65 and .60 respectively.

30. This analysis is carried out by an equation with Δr (change in segregation), dummy variables for each city, and interactions between the city dummy variable and Δr. The coefficient for each city is the same as the sum of the coefficients for Δr and the interaction term.

References

1. Cataldo, Everett; Giles, Michael; Athos, Deborah; and Gatlin, Douglas, "Desegregation and White Flight." *Integrateducation*, 13 (January-February, 1975).

2. Clotfelter, Charles T. "School Desegregation, 'Tipping,' and Private School Enrollment." *Journal of Human Resources* (Forthcoming).
3. Farley, Reynolds. "Racial Integration in the Public Schools, 1967 to 1972: Assessing the Effects of Governmental Policies." *Sociological Focus*, VIII (January, 1975).
4. McDonald, Gary C., and Schwing, Richard C. "Instabilities of Regression Estimates Relating Air Pollution to Mortality." *Technometrics*, XV (August, 1973).

13

Presentation to the Massachusetts Legislature
March 30, 1976

I want to express my pleasure at being here to address you, along with my surprise at being invited to do so. This is not the surprise of an academic scholar in being taken seriously by persons who make decisions and take action, for scholars have in recent years come to be taken very seriously in current affairs. It is rather surprise at your creation of a direct dialogue unmediated by television, newspapers, newsmagazines, or even written research reports, between those who make policy and one who carries out research which is relevant to that policy. This is a rare occasion, one which few legislatures bring about, and I want to commend the legislature of Massachusetts for doing so.

The occasion, I will assume, reflects the depth of your concern with the problem of school desegregation, the problem of bringing about an integrated society, and the problem of bringing justice and equity to all citizens of Massachusetts. I will do my utmost to respond with the seriousness and responsibility which that concern warrants.

What I will try to do in this session is to first indicate the goals that are intended to be achieved in school desegregation, then to present some research results that are relevant to certain of these goals, next to lay out what I feel are the necessary requirements for a viable policy of school integration, and finally to indicate the kinds of policies that meet those requirements. I will not, despite what the Boston Globe has to say, recommend to you specific courses of action, such as still another compulsory busing plan. I trust that the Globe will report correctly what I have to say today; but even if it does not, the dialogue today is a direct one.

The first goal in school desegregation is that of achieving equal protection under the law for all children regardless of race. This means, since the landmark 1954 *Brown* decision in the U.S. Supreme Court, the elimination of *de jure* segregation, that is, the elimination of dual school systems where they exist, and the elimination of official practices by school systems which bring about segregated schools. A second goal, related to the first, but distinct from it, is the goal of increasing the educational gains of disadvantaged children, particularly minority children, black, Spanish American, and others. This goal came to be linked to school desegregation by research results, which showed that disadvantaged children achieved more highly on standardized tests in schools that had a middle class majority. The best known of this research, usually referred to as the "Coleman Report," was carried out by myself and others in the U.S. Office of Education under the Civil Rights Act of 1964. Since school desegregation has become widespread, a large amount of additional research on this topic has been carried out. I will mention briefly some of the results of that research later.

A third goal in school desegregation is that of helping to achieve an integrated society, one in which racial distinctions play a smaller part than at present, and in which a person's skin color is not an overriding social characteristic. This too is related to the first goal, but goes beyond it. It was the main impetus behind the decision to desegregate in the 1960s by school boards in many smaller northern systems which had not practiced *de jure* segregation, but had residential segregation which led to extensive segregation in the schools. Examples are: Evanston, Illinois; White Plains, New York; Ann Arbor, Michigan; and Berkeley, California.

All three of these goals are important ones for our society to achieve. But it is important to keep in mind these distinct goals of school desegregation for three reasons. First, although they appear at first glance compatible, it turns out that they are not always so, and that sometimes actions taken to achieve one are harmful to the others. Second, the instruments of government that are appropriate to each of these goals are somewhat different. The courts are the appropriate instrument, or at least the instrument of final resort, for the first; school authorities and teachers are the appropriate instruments for the second, with possible aid from legislative actions; and school boards, state legislatures, and the Congress are appropriate instruments for the third. Finally, research results are differentially applicable to the three goals. They are not directly applicable to the first. Research results on what happens to children educationally, particularly disadvantaged minority children, under conditions of school segregation and desegregation are of course directly relevant to the second goal. And research results on how school desegregation affects the broader integration of society are relevant to the third goal. In particular, the effects of school desegregation on demographic changes which may strengthen or weaken the integration of society are relevant.

With these distinctions in mind, I will review briefly research results that are relevant to the second and third goals, for it is these two goals which actions of this legislature might help achieve.

The Effects of School Desegregation on
Achievement of Disadvantaged Minority Children

The so-called Coleman Report, published in 1966 under the Civil Rights Act of 1964, showed that disadvantaged children performed better on standardized tests in schools that were predominantly middle class, and that middle class children did not perform worse in schools with substantial proportions of disadvantaged children. Since there are too few middle class minority children to bring about predominantly middle class schools without racial desegregation, this result has direct implications for desegregation, implying that desegregation would improve the performance of blacks without lowering that of whites.

This result was subject to some questioning and some reanalysis. Questions concerned the possible selectivity of disadvantaged children in middle class schools, since most of the integration existing at that time was that due to residential proximity of blacks and whites. And the reanalysis showed that some portion of the apparent effect vanished when stronger controls for the social backgrounds of children were taken into account.[1] Nevertheless the research results remained, and were widely used in support of school desegregation.

Since that time, there have appeared results on the actual effects of school desegregation on achievement in particular school districts, which are more directly relevant to the issue. In general, these results can be summarized by saying that achievement benefits of school desegregation for blacks are sometimes found, sometimes not, and where they are found, are generally small, much smaller than would have been predicted from the Coleman report. David Armor, in a study of the Metco plan in the Boston area in 1972, and a review of other studies, found no benefits. Nancy St. John, in summarizing the effects for a large number of individual desegregation studies, finds erratic and small positive effects. Since her review, some other research has been similarly disappointing. An extensive study of long-term system-wide desegregation in Riverside, California finds no achievement increases, a study of Pasadena arrives at similar conclusions, and a study of busing in Waco, Texas shows negative effects.[2] A very recent analysis of National Assessment results, released on March 17, shows what appears to be a beneficial result: although there are declines in achievement for nearly all groups throughout the country in recent years, black children in the Southeast have *increased* achievement in science since 1969. This period has been the period of greatest desegregation in the South. But the further analysis shows that this increase has been in schools that have remained all-black, just as in the integrated schools. Thus an explanation other than the racial composition of the school is necessary for these encouraging results.[3]

Altogether, the current evidence indicates that the presumed benefits of school desegregation for black achievement are sometimes present, but not uniformly so, and are small when they are found. Thus the earlier hope that school desegregation would constitute a panacea for black achievement, or contribute substantially to the goal of increasing black achievement, appears to have been misplaced.

Similarly, most of the studies mentioned earlier have found that the psychological effects (such as effects on self-esteem) and the attitudinal effects (such as interracial attitudes) of school desegregation are not uniformly in a positive direction, and are sometimes negative. Altogether, I believe we can say from the research results on the educational effects that school desegregation is seldom harmful (though where there is extensive turbulence, the short-term effects may be educationally harmful to both blacks and whites), sometimes beneficial, but not sufficiently so that school desegregation can be a major policy instrument for increasing black achievement and self-esteem.

The Demographic Effects of School Desegregation

Now I would like to turn to research results relevant to the third goal of achieving social integration. The effects that have been most extensively studied are the effects of desegregation on the racial stability of the schools, and most particularly on the loss of whites from the schools. The questions are: does this effect exist? if so, under what conditions? and what are its long-term consequences for the integration of the schools and of society?

The answers to these questions are fairly complex. First of all, it has been shown that in many small systems, when the proportion of black children in the system is not large, especially in the North and West, but also to a considerable extent in the South, desegregation does not have strong effects on loss of whites, and in fact, any effects are difficult to detect statistically. The fact that this holds true even in the South has meant that Southern desegregation, primarily in 1970, has made its schools the least segregated in the nation. Several studies have shown the absence of sta-tistically observable effects in the North and West. Jane Mercer found this in California, and Christine Rossell found this in the North generally.[4] However, when the proportion of black children is high, then even in small districts, system-wide desegregation does have very strong effects on loss of whites from the public schools. This has been observed only in the South, for it is only there that small school systems have high proportions of blacks. Charles Clotfelter found in a study of desegregation involving system-wide racial balance in Mississippi counties that as the percentage of black children increased from 40% to 80%, the percentage of whites leaving those districts and enrolling in private schools increased from about 20% to about 90%.[5] And Luther Munford found, in another Mississippi study, that as the percentage of black children increased from 40% to 90% the percentage of whites who left the public schools in the first year increased from about 5% to about 90%. For every 10% increase in proportion of black children in those schools, an additional 16% of white children left the schools.[6] In a study of Florida countywide desegregation, Michael Giles and his associates showed that when the percentage of black children was below about 30%, the loss of whites was small. In some smaller districts in the North such as Pasadena, California and Pontiac, Michigan, where the proportion of black children was substantial then there has been substantial loss of whites as well.

I should point out that these results do not imply that whites will always escape a circumstance in which the schools are majority black. In the neighborhood in which I live in Chicago, the school has been a majority black school with a stable integrated population for 15 years. But such patterns of integrated school stability depend upon integrated neighborhood stability, they depend on continuous efforts by blacks and whites working together, and are seldom achieved by administrative or judicial fiat.

When we turn to desegregation in large cities, the picture includes an additional complexity, that is, the existence or absence of predominantly white suburbs outside the district which is desegregating. A few large cities, primarily in the South, have county-wide school districts, including all or nearly all the suburbs in the metropolitan area. These cities include Tampa, St. Petersburg, and Miami, in Florida; Charlotte, North Carolina; and Nashville, Tennessee. In these county-wide systems, all with a small pro-portion of black or other minority population, the loss of whites is not large (averaging about 5% in the first year of desegregation), and for those located in areas which are experiencing a population boom, as in Florida, the loss appears to be confined to the first year, with succeeding years showing the population gains characteristic of the region as a whole.

The situation, however, is quite different in central city school districts, surrounded by predominantly white suburban school districts. This is char-acteristic of most large cities in this country, and particularly so in the large cities of the East and Midwest. It is true to a lesser extent for medium-sized cities. Desegregation in such cities brings about a substantial loss of whites in the first year, and a continuing loss beyond the first year. The results of my own research over the past year show this. As an example, for the nine largest central-city school districts which underwent substantial desegregation between 1968 and 1974, I examined the loss of whites in years before, during and after desegregation. Two years before desegregation, the average loss was 4.1%; one year before, it was 4.8%. In the year of desegregation, it jumped to 12.4%, almost three times as great. In the four years following desegregation, it went down, but not to the pre-desegregation level: to 7.0%, 6.7%, 10.1%, and 8.1%.

In a similar tabulation, David Armor has examined these losses for the 16 cities in this country which have the following characteristics: in all of them, desegregation occurred through court order; all were in 1968 20,000 or larger in number of students; all have substantial suburbs for whites to move to, and all had a percentage of black children in the range of 20% to 50%. There was an overlap of only four cities between the nine I just described and Armor's 16. Armor found an average loss of 2% per year in the two years before desegregation, 10% in the year of desegregation and the year after, and an average loss of 7% per year in the next two years, the second and third years following desegregation. Although the cities were largely different ones, those results correspond closely to my own.

These results are serious in their demographic consequences for our large cities: for with blacks constrained within the city both by economics and by suburban residential discrimination, and whites given an additional incentive to leave by desegregation measures in the central city, the metropolitan area becomes composed of black schools in the city and white schools in the suburbs.

Even more generally, it is important to see those results in the context of broader patterns of migration that are occurring in this country. There are two major components to the current migration patterns. One is to the South and Southwest, to the "sun belt" as it has recently been called, and the other is away from major metropolitan centers. For the first time in history, the metropolitan area population, not just the central city population, has begun to decline. The movement is a movement of the segment of the population that is white, middle class, and young, the segment with most mobility. Whether this is labelled escapism, or whether it is seen as an attraction for the natural environment, it is there, and it affects most greatly the large, older urban centers of the Northeast and Midwest. They are no longer attractive to many of the young most able to move. And their moves increase the separation of blacks and whites, as they increase the decline of our older metropolitan areas.

If these trends were not serious enough, there is another aspect of the desegregation effects I have described earlier: these effects are only for the "average" city which has undergone desegregation. In a city with a high proportion of black children, then desegregation, even when it is less than full-scale racial balance, brings about a much larger loss of whites than in a city with a low proportion of blacks. For example, I carried out a statistical analysis of desegregation in the largest central cities, and my estimates show that when there is an amount of desegregation that is sufficient to bring about a 9% loss in the first year in a district with a 25% black school population, that same amount of desegregation would bring about a 24% white loss in the first year if the district were 75% black rather than 25%. For an extreme example, in Detroit last summer, there was a court case for school desegregation. Detroit had a 75% black school system last year. The plaintiff's desegregation plan was one to create racial balance, within about 5%, in all Detroit schools. The estimates I just described, based upon large central-city desegregation which occurred between 1968 and 1973, would lead to the prediction that if the plaintiff's plan of full-scale racial balance had been adopted (which it was not) Detroit's schools would be 95% black today, that is nearly all black central-city schools and nearly all white suburban ones.

When the proportion of black children is substantial, but smaller than .75, such sharp consequences are not immediate; the effect is a snowballing one: after some whites leave, the proportion of black children is greater, leading still more whites to leave.

Boston presents an example, though far from the most extreme, of what happens when extensive desegregation is imposed in a central-city school district. In the five years before desegregation, there had been a loss of approximately 4.5% of whites per year. In 1974, when desegregation took place, there was a loss of 16.1%, over three times as great. And in 1975, the additional loss, using figures for December 31, 1975, is 15.5% if students are kept on the rolls who never came to school throughout the fall. If they are not included, the figure is even worse, a loss of 18.9% of the 1974 white enrollment—or altogether, in two years, a loss of 32% of the 1973 white enrollment, almost one-third. This had the effect of reducing the non-Spanish white student population in Boston from 57% to 41% in two years.

Altogether, then, when we look at the effects of school desegregation for the third goal, the goal of achieving social integration in America, the results are mixed. If we look at small school districts, rural areas, and countywide metropolitan districts, then extensive school desegregation, even compulsory racial balance, has not led to social segregation through a loss of whites from the schools—so long as the proportion of black children in the schools is low. Because it has not led to demographic instability, it has probably been beneficial, in both the short run and the long run, to the goal of social integration. But at the other extreme, that is in large cities, with available suburbs, and with a moderate to high proportion of black children, school desegregation, in particular compulsory racial balance, has proved disastrous to social integration, by greatly accelerating the loss of whites from the cities, and leading to racially divided metropolitan areas, with a black central city and white suburbs. The extent of this impact is not yet evident, because it is a snowballing effect, which has had only a short time to operate. But it is a policy that, carried out in the name of accomplishing the first goal of desegregation, that is, elimination of *de jure* segregation, acts to defeat the third goal, the goal of achieving social integration. If this policy of racial balance, ordinarily imposed by a court order, is required to overcome *de jure* segregation, then we confront an insoluble dilemma: an action necessary to bring about equal protection under the law for blacks and whites has the overall effect of defeating social integration among blacks and whites. However, I believe the dilemma to be a false one: that seldom if ever is compulsory racial balance in a large school system necessary to overcome *de jure* segregation. Rather, straightforward elimination of *de jure* segregation in large cities would constitute primarily a redrawing of school attendance zones to eliminate gerrymandering, and would have little impact, one way or another, on the third goal of achieving integration. That goal must be achieved by much more long range policies, involving residence at least as much as schools, policies that recognize both the needs and desires for ethnic community and those of ethnic integration. The achievement of that third goal in our metropolitan areas must involve a variety of policies, including those that attract middle class whites into the city, and those that make the suburbs available to blacks commensurate with their rising incomes.

This is not by any means to say that imposing racial balance in city schools is the only policy that has led to increasingly black central cities and white suburbs. Freeway construction, FHA mortgage policies, the inability to control crime, and other policies have been responsible as well. But there is probably no single action that has had as strong and immediate an effect in removing whites from already substantially black central cities than the policies of racial balance in the schools, where those policies have been put into effect in large central cities.

These various research results raise finally the question of what should be the characteristics of school desegregation policies if the three goals, elimination of *de jure* segregation, benefitting achievement of disadvantaged children, and achieving social integration, are to be realized. First, I believe it must now be recognized, although I did not at one time believe this to be so, that school desegregation is not a central instrument for achieving the second goal. It is neither necessary nor sufficient for improving the achievement of disadvantaged children. Imaginative and varied patterns of interaction with children from other social classes and ethnic groups can be an important and valuable element in education, but to paraphrase Wilson Riles, Superintendent of Schools in California, it is not necessary for a black child to sit next to a white child in order to learn.

Second, the first goal, of eliminating *de jure* segregation, should be recognized for what it is, and as quite separate from the goal of achieving racial integration in society. Elimination of *de jure* segregation, properly done, will in large cities neither greatly aid nor greatly harm the racial integration of the society. By itself, it cannot be an important instrument for the latter goal in large cities where blacks and whites are largely separated by residence. When it has been used as such, it has helped defeat, rather than achieve this third goal, as I have indicated in the statistics I presented.

Third, the third goal, achieving an integrated society, is one for which government policies can be decisive, but only if the policies recognize that they require active support and implementation by ordinary families, of all racial groups: families whose actions and attitudes in the long run will determine the success of the policies. These policies must, by their very nature, be carried out primarily by legislatures, for most are outside the reach of the courts, and beyond the scope of local jurisdictions.

What I would like to suggest, then, are certain requirements that school policies should meet if they are to aid in achievement of the goal of achieving a racially integrated society.

1. Any policy should insure equal treatment for all children, regardless of race, ethnicity, or social origin.

2. Any policy designed to aid in achieving an integrated society should be one which facilitates and encourages social integration of whites, blacks, and other minorities, and one which prevents exclusion by one group of members of another; but it should allow members of each group to be in minority or majority situations. It is not an appropriate aim of policy, for example, to "eliminate racially identifiable schools," which is a euphemism for eliminating all-black schools.

3. Any policy should not by design or consequence be punitive on families or children, whether in the name of redressing past wrongs or for other

purposes. Much of the error in school desegregation policy has been the result of an unarticulated punitiveness which has no place in achieving positive social goals.

4. If a policy imposes additional constraints in order to increase the degree of racial integration in schools, it should impose those constraints on schools or school districts, and not on families or children, through arbitrary school assignment. To do the latter creates an incentive for those with money to leave the school system, either for private schools, for the suburbs, or for another metropolitan area altogether, and a disincentive for persons to move into the area. A policy should attempt to achieve integration through *increasing* the options available to families and children, not through restricting options. Such an increase is especially important for blacks and other minorities, and for low-income families, for their residential options have been severely limited through residential discrimination or economic constraints.

5. Any policy must not treat differentially city and suburbs, despite the fact that there are different school systems involved. To do so increases the relative attractiveness of the suburbs for middle class families, especially whites, and directly defeats the goal of social integration of blacks and whites.

These requirements for a policy are, taken together, quite restrictive. They imply that no political subdivision below the state can take appropriate integrative action—not a city, not a suburb, for integration must involve the metropolitan area as a whole. Thus they imply that a state legislature is one of the few arms of government that can take appropriate action. And they imply that whatever policies a legislature does impose cannot assign children to specific schools distant from their home, that is, cannot involve compulsory busing.

I will describe a policy that meets these requirements, to illustrate what I feel is a feasible school desegregation policy. I am not recommending such a policy to you, because it would be presumptuous of me to tell you what should be done in Massachusetts.

A policy which meets these criteria would be one of educational entitlements: each child in a metropolitan area would be entitled to attend any school in the metropolitan area, whether it is in his school district or not, so long as it does not have a higher proportion of his own racial group than the school to which he would be assigned on the basis of residence. With this entitlement would go the provision of transportation, so that the plan sounds like a "voluntary busing plan across school district lines." But it is not that, for each family and child would be able to choose either his neighborhood school or nearly any other school in the district. Every school would be required to accept out-of-attendance-zone students up to something like 15% of its total student population, a percentage small enough so that double shifts would not be required, but large enough to provide a wide opportunity for choice. State aid to education would necessarily be modified in such a way that a child's per-pupil expenditure followed him to his new district. The plan would be most important for blacks and low income families, who are excluded by economics or discrimination from certain residential areas. But it would not by any means be a one-way movement, because especially at the high school level, the city can offer specialized schools and alternative schools that a suburb cannot, schools which can attract young people from the suburbs. The plan could be described as one in which every school in the metropolitan area becomes a magnet school, for each school would be required to attract its student body. It is this aspect of such a plan, incidentally, that often makes school administrators uncomfortable with it: it is much easier to assign captive student bodies to schools than to compete for students.

Obviously, such a school desegregation plan will not "eliminate racial segregation" in the schools of the metropolitan area. But to do that is, as I have said, a wholly inappropriate and even racially discriminatory goal. It would weigh heavily upon black children, for each black would be in an extreme minority; neither blacks nor Spanish-Americans could choose to be in a school where they were in a racial majority.

This sketches the outlines of a plan which would meet the criteria that I believe are necessary if school desegregation is to aid the goal of stable racial integration in the society. It is not the only such plan, and school desegregation is not the only kind of policy that can aid integration. But it is one policy that I believe would do so. I should mention as an aside that an important litmus test of any school desegregation policy you might develop, to determine whether its principle is a sound one, is that it be equally effective if the racial composition of the metropolitan area were reversed. If it would not, then the principle on which it is based is likely an unsound one.

I will conclude by expressing my belief that not only is it desirable for state legislatures to develop creative policies that move toward the goal of a racially integrated society; it is important that they do so. For it is in the absence of such policies that plaintiffs have often felt, and understandably so, that only be redefining *de jure* segregation in a very inclusive way, and only by use of the courts, could any progress toward the third goal be made. As I have indicated by the statistics I have given, those actions have in the large cities taken us instead farther from that goal rather than closer to it. It thus becomes especially important for state legislatures to initiate those policies that will aid stable social integration, and will make their cities and metropolitan areas more attractive places for families of all groups to live and raise their children.

Again, I want to express my pleasure at being here, and to commend you for creating occasions such as this, in which there can be a direct dialogue between those who make policies and one who carries out research relevant to those policies.

Author's Addendum, October 1989

Additional data prepared for, but not presented at, the legislative session give a further insight into the effect of proportion black in the schools

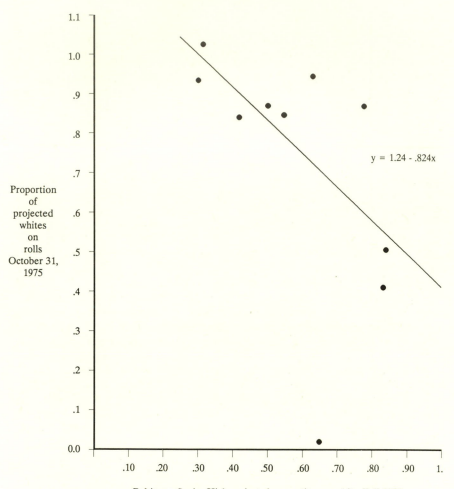

Baltimore Senior High projected proportion nonwhite, Fall 1975

FIGURE 1   Relation Between Projected Proportion White and Proportion of Projected Whites on Rolls in Baltimore Senior High Schools, Fall 1975, Following Initiation of a Busing Plan

following a desegregation reorganization on loss of whites. These data, shown in Figures 1 and 2, consist of the projected proportion nonwhite in Baltimore junior and senior high schools in Fall 1975, following school reorganization to bring about integration, and the proportion of whites assigned to those schools who were actually enrolled on October 31, two months after the plan was put into effect. As Figures 1 and 2 show, the loss is very dependent on the racial composition of the school. For schools projected to be 30% black, there was essentially no loss. For senior high schools projected to be 70% black, only 65% of whites remained. This meant that the actual racial composition of the two schools (assuming that

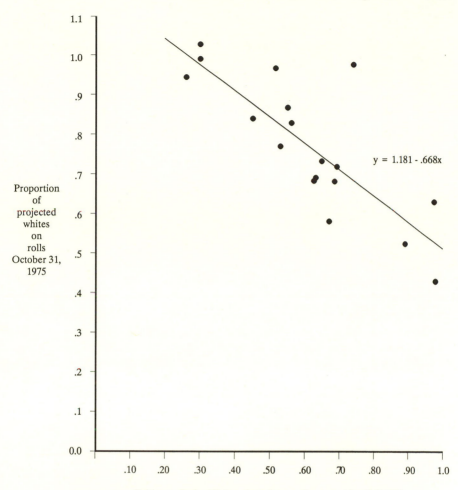

Baltimore Junior High projected proportion nonwhite, Fall 1975

FIGURE 2 Relation Between Projected Proportion White and Proportion of Projected Whites on Rolls in Baltimore Junior High Schools, Fall 1975, Following Initiation of a Busing Plan

all black students projected to enroll actually did so) would be not 30% and 70%, but 30% and 78%.

Notes

1. See Marshall Smith, in F. Mosteller and D. Moynihan, *On Equality of Educational Opportunity*, Random House, 1972.

2. See David Armor, "The Evidence on Bussing," *The Public Interest*, Summer, 1972, pp. 90–126; Nancy St. John, *School Desegregation*. New York: Wiley, 1975; *Desegregation: A Longitudinal Study*. Ralph Gerard and Norman Miller, Plenum Press,

1975, and Lawrence Felice, "Mandatory Bussing and Minority Student Achievement: New Evidence and Negative Results." Unpublished paper.

3. See National Assessment of Educational Progress, "Science Achievement: Racial and Regional Trends, 1969–73." March 17, 1976.

4. See Christine Rossell, "School Desegregation and White Flight," *Political Science Quarterly*, 1976, Vol. 90, pp. 675–695, and Jane Mercer, and Terrence Scout, "The Relationship between School Desegregation and Changes in the Racial Composition of California School Districts, 1966–73." 1974.

5. Charles Clotfelter, "School Desegregation, 'Tipping,' and Private School Enrollment," *Journal of Human Resources*, VII, 1976, pp. 29–50.

6. Luther Munford, "Desegregation and Private Schools," *Social Policy*, 1976, Vol. 6, No. 4, pp. 42–45.

14

Destructive Beliefs and Potential Policies in School Desegregation

We have come to a point now at which it is possible to be sober, straightforward, and realistic about school desegregation in major metropolitan areas. In particular, three major beliefs about segregation and integration in education have finally been shown to be incorrect. With the destruction of these beliefs (each of which, as it played a part in social policy, employed some amount of wishful thinking), it becomes possible to point to policies that are not doomed to failure from the beginning.

It is useful to indicate just what these wrong beliefs have been and to proceed from there.

I. Beliefs Perpetuating Harmful Desegregation Policies

First, it was once assumed that official elimination of school segregation, whether by establishment of dual school systems in the South or by gerrymandering and other school district actions in the North, would eliminate all, or nearly all, racial segregation in the schools. This romanticism may have been held by some of the Supreme Court justices in the Brown decision; but whether it was held by those jurists or not, it was widely held by other persons, who saw the courts' elimination of *de jure* segregation as identical to elimination of racial segregation in the schools. In many rural and small-town districts in the South, this became fact, not fiction. But any knowledge of urban areas—of the residential segregation that develops in urban areas along ethnic, income, and racial lines—leads immediately to the recognition that most urban area segregation, whether ethnic, class, or race, is due to residential patterns. The Supreme Court has now recognized this as well;

Reprinted with permission from John W. Smith, ed., "Detroit Metropolitan City-Suburban Relations," *Occasional Papers of the Henry Ford Community College*, no. 3 (June 1979), pp. 5–12. Copyright © 1979 by the Henry Ford Community College Board of Trustees.

in recent rulings on cases in Austin, Texas, and Dayton, Ohio, the High Court ruled that sanctions against an unconstitutional segregating activity must be limited to the extent of the violation—that the particular violation cannot be taken as cause for branding as unconstitutional all racial segregation in the city's schools.

The implication of this recognition—that urban populations are residentially separated by ethnicity, class, and race—is that eliminating unconstitutional "official" segregation through the courts will not eliminate most of the segregation that these areas exhibit. This is especially evident now, as white exodus to the suburbs has produced a situation in which most of the largest central-city school systems are majority black, while the surrounding ring remains predominantly white. Such segregation did not arise by official action, unless one wants to argue that the actions of the courts in ordering racial balance became "official segregating acts" because they resulted in whites leaving the city; yet this black city-white suburb form of segregation is the most important form in most major metropolitan areas.

The further implication of recognizing the fiction as a fiction is that policies to reduce racial segregation in urban areas can no longer use what once appeared to be the instant solution: immediate elimination of segregation through court order in the city. Instead, more difficult actions, carried out through other agencies of government and employing the active cooperation of blacks and whites, are necessary. But before discussing such policies, it is useful to turn to the second fiction.

It was once assumed that integration—at least in majority middle-class white schools—would automatically improve the achievement of lower-class black children. I hasten to say that it was research of my own doing that laid the basis for this second assumption. That research, carried out under the Civil Rights Act of 1964 and completed in 1966, showed that lower class black children in majority middle class white schools scored better on standardized tests than did other children like them in all-black schools. And it showed further that there was little decrement in the achievement of whites in integrated schools. I, among others, argued that this meant integration would bring about achievement benefits. Arguments of this sort were used in a number of school desegregation cases, and such an argument helped lead Judge Roth to his decision in the Detroit case, which was later overturned by the Supreme Court.

However, it has not worked out this way in many of the school desegregation cases reviewed since completion of that research. Some cases appear to show slight gains, others show no effects, still others record slight losses in achievement. Some of the cases most carefully studied over a period of years following desegregation, such as Pasadena and Riverside, California, show no achievement effects, and even reversals. Thus, what once appeared to be fact is now known to be fiction. School desegregation, as it has been carried out in American schools, generally does not bring achievement benefits to disadvantaged children. It probably is true that desegregation under optimal conditions will increase their achievement. But that is not the point: very likely any school changes, under optimal conditions, will have this effect. What we must look for is the effect on disadvantaged children that occurs under the variety of conditions in which desegregation actually is carried out.

This recognition of the actual effects of desegregation on achievement carries with it the implication that no longer should we look solely, or even primarily, to racial balance in the schools as the solution to inequality of educational opportunity. Inequality of opportunity is not something to be easily overcome. If we are looking for policies to help bring about equality of educational opportunity, it is necessary to broaden our horizons. If we are looking for reasons to implement policies of racial balance in the schools, we must look further.

Third, it was once assumed that policies of radical school desegregation, such as a busing order to create instant racial balance, could be instituted; and that the resulting school populations would correspond to the assignments of children to the schools—no matter how much busing and regardless of the number of parents who objected to the school assignments. It is now evident, despite the unwillingness of some—researchers and others—to accept the fact, that extensive losses of white students from large central cities take place when desegregation is implemented in those cities. To be sure, those losses are extensive only when the proportion of blacks in the city is high, or when there are predominantly white suburbs to flee to, or both. But again, this is not the point. One of these two conditions holds in all large American cities; and in most, both conditions hold.

Several policy implications follow from recognition of this fact. One should have been seen all along and no longer can be ignored: that the enrollment of a child in a given public school is not determined by the government. It is a joint result of the government's decision that makes school assignments and of the parents' decision on whether to remain in the same residential location, whether to send their child to a private school, or whether to move into one school district or another if the family is moving into a metropolitan area. The fact that the child's enrollment is the result of a joint operation of these two decisions means that government policies, to be effective, must anticipate parental decisions and that the government must obtain the active cooperation of parents in implementing school policy.

A second, more powerful, implication is that no appreciable school desegregation within a major American city can ignore the suburbs and expect to remain stable. School desegregation that provides an incentive for whites to go to the suburbs—as do all busing plans to achieve integration within a city—is inherently unstable. It is most unstable when there are extensive white suburbs and a high proportion of blacks in the central city, a condition that exists in most large cities. And those few large American cities without a high proportion black (Seattle, Washington, for example), also happen to be those where the ease of movement to the suburbs with little increase in commuting is greatest.

A third implication is that no school desegregation can be carried out, whether it includes the suburbs or not, if it imposes an extreme burden upon parents or children; if it does, resourceful parents will find a way to improve their situation. They may choose to send their children to private schools, as many have done. Or they may choose to move beyond the reach of the policy; for example, countywide desegregation in Louisville, Kentucky, has led surrounding counties to become among the fastest growing in the nation.

The implication for positive policy is that any desegregation that is to remain stable must begin with a plan that involves the metropolitan area as a whole and which outweighs coercive qualities with attractive ones. Many school policy makers and many courts, still operating under the fiction that constitutionality requires racial balance, have not recognized this; harmful school desegregation policies are still being implemented in American cities. Seattle, for example, is engaging in a plan which will almost certainly be unstable. And just recently the Illinois Board of Education, overlooking the suburban haven altogether and ignoring Chicago's extensive set of Catholic schools, declared Chicago's plan for voluntary student transfers inadequate because it did not meet a state requirement that all schools in a district be within 15 percent of the district racial composition. But the Illinois Board is only one of many such bodies still living with the romantic fiction that a government plan of student assignment will result in enrollments matching that assignment. Like many others, the Illinois Board is deluding itself with the notion that such mandates do no harm to the long-term chances for integration in a metropolitan area.

This set of three incorrect beliefs has led to harmful and destructive school desegregation policy in the past. But in the absence of these beliefs, one might argue that the ground is cut out from under school desegregation policy—that these beliefs have been necessary to the development of positive policy toward reducing racial segregation in the schools. Indeed, it seems clear that this is why those beliefs have been clung to for so long by so many, and why some still hold to them despite all evidence to the contrary. Does not the exposure of these beliefs as incorrect undercut desegregation policy generally?

II. Beliefs Undercutting Positive Policies

But another set of beliefs, also incorrect, has prevented access to other avenues of desegregation policy. Just as the former beliefs have sustained policies that have been largely harmful to desegregation—and to schooling—in large metropolitan areas, this second set of beliefs has prevented the development of policies that might be helpful to desegregation and education.

First, it has been assumed that lower class black parents, when provided with an opportunity for choice in education, will not use it; and that if they do, will not use it wisely. This belief, in part, is a conceit of the educational professionals, who believe they know better than parents or children what is good for children. In part it reflects a lack of trust by black leaders in the intelligence and interest in education of their constituents.

In part it betrays an arrogance on the part of the white liberal, who believes that he knows what is best for dependent or disadvantaged populations; they should be given benefits but should never be given a choice.

Black families, lower class as well as middle class, have given ample evidence that this belief is wrong. On all surveys of interest in education, interest has been higher among blacks than among whites. College attendance comparisons between black children and white children having parents on comparable economic and educational levels show that the black children are more likely to attend; in fact, the proportion of all eighteen- and nineteen-year-olds in school is now higher among blacks than whites.

Evidence of an active exercise of choice by black parents was apparent even in the "freedom of choice" desegregation plans initiated for a time in the South. Although roadblocks were often put in the way of black parents who chose to send their children to a previously white school, they did so choose, and in large numbers, where the plans were administered honestly.

The most explicit evidence of choice and interest, however, lies in the widespread use of Catholic schools by central city black parents. These parents, mostly non-Catholic and mostly poor, have increasingly turned to the parochial schools as a means of escape from the low educational standards, disorder, physical danger, and moral risk they see in the public schools to which their children have been assigned. In many large cities a substantial number of black parents manage to save the few dollars a week necessary to send their children to a parochial school.

The implication of all of this is that desegregation plans dependent on choices exercised by black parents will not flounder because of parental failure to exercise those choices intelligently. A variety of plans that depend on wise choices exercised by black parents can be considered, then, in planning school policy.

Second, the belief has been held that an all-black school is inherently bad. Thus, one criterion used by courts in determining the acceptability, or success, of desegregation plans has been whether all "racially identifiable" schools have been eliminated. Here, "racially identifiable" has always been used to mean all-black schools, never all-white schools.

The belief in the inherent inferiority of an all-black school has a curiously racist flavor. It originated, however, in an attempt by courts to establish a criterion for deciding whether a school district in the South that had maintained a dual system had in fact eliminated its dual system. In such a context, and in localities where little residential segregation existed, this rule of thumb was a reasonable one; the breakdown of reason came in elevating this rule-of-thumb criterion to a principle for judging the quality of the school. The error implicit in considering the all-black school to be inherently inferior is perhaps a corollary to the mistaken belief that extensive achievement benefits spring from school integration. When the latter belief is shown to be wrong, the incorrectness of the former almost directly follows.

It is reasonable to trace one source of the error to a confusion, which still persists in the minds of many, between (1) a school that was all black because the black students lived in the ghetto or in a dual system situation and had no opportunity to choose another school to attend, and (2) a school that was all black despite the fact that its students could choose to attend other schools. The latter choice, unfortunately, is still rare in most cities, but a black school that thrives in its presence is obviously not an inferior school. It is a school to which parents freely choose to send their children.

There have been, and there are, all-black schools that are excellent schools by any standard. Thomas Sowell, a black economist at UCLA, has identified striking examples of black high schools that have graduated men and women who went on to become outstanding in the world of public affairs, the professions, and government. As another criterion, numerous all-black elementary schools can be cited in which achievement levels are above grade level, using national norms.

Recognition that all-black schools are not inherently inferior has important implications. Perhaps the most significant is the realization that the ethnically and culturally pluralistic society of the United States has room for schools of all sorts: schools which are racially integrated, certainly; but also schools that are all black, just as there are schools that are all white. What is essential, as I indicated earlier, is that if a child is in an all-black school, it should be because he wants to be there and his parents want him to be there, not because it is the only school that he has a reasonable chance to attend.

Third, it has been assumed that a child's right to equal educational opportunity ends at the school district boundaries. This belief is based on the long-honored practice of states in delegating to localities (cities, towns, townships, sometimes counties) the control and operation of schools in those localities. But according to the Constitution of the United States, education is the responsibility of the states; and however a state has chosen to delegate that responsibility, a child in the state has a claim upon the state to provide him with educational opportunity. What this means specifically is that the educational opportunities of a child in Detroit or Chicago should not be limited by the boundaries of Detroit or Chicago. He or any child in a metropolitan area should have the right to choose to attend any school within reasonable distance—not, of course, to escape an integrated school, but to escape the constraints on his schooling that are imposed by his residence.

Upon recognition of the errors of the two sets of beliefs about school desegregation, what kinds of policies become feasible and desirable to examine? Does the recognition that attempts at desegregation thus far have been based on erroneous beliefs leave, in fact, any possible policies for the integration of schools?

III. Alternative Policies

The answer is that we have a remarkable choice of workable alternative policies. These would be wholly unlike the racial-balance policies currently being imposed through compulsory busing in some cities, and proposed for others. The alternatives would attach far higher significance to parental choice than do present desegregation policies. The aims would be fundamentally different: not to "eliminate segregation," but to provide opportunity for every child and to facilitate long-term stability in the integrated school. The aims of the policy would recognize the diversity of schools that would result: some black, some white, some integrated. The assurance that equal opportunity is in fact being provided would lie not in an artificial numbers game, with children moved like pawns on a chessboard, but in the range of opportunities available to every child.

A number of policies fit the various criteria I have described. As the criteria indicate, they have a number of elements in common. But the way these elements are achieved, and in fact the resulting patterns of school attendance, could differ widely. I will describe a few possible policies, for only by looking at concrete policies can we get a feeling for the joint implications of abandoning the six mistaken beliefs that I have described above. The policies differ in character, but they all contain some properties in common. First, their goal is not the elimination of all racial imbalance in schools. Rather, it is to provide a complete, full opportunity for a child to free his attendance at school from constraints imposed by his residence and to facilitate school integration, which has been discouraged by a variety of factors ranging from residential ghettoization to the fears of white parents as they confront the possible effects of busing policies.

Second, these proposed policies are based upon interaction between governmental decisions and parental decisions, and not upon the assumption that governmental decisions are the determining factor. All of the policies I shall describe provide a greater degree of parental choice than is currently the case in most cities, and any governmental decisions are designed to make those parental choices lead not to segregated schools but to schools that show a higher degree of integration than at present.

Third, because the policies I shall describe do not maintain the fiction that the segregation they are attempting to reduce is unconstitutional, and because these policies are not coercive, they do not elevate school district boundaries to the status of exclusion barriers. In short, they do not treat suburbs as havens, protected by boundaries; instead, they allow parental choice to range beyond the confines imposed by residence.

The policies I will describe are not exhaustive; rather, they illustrate how, if we abandon the fictions held for so long, a variety of policies is possible.

1. Interdistrict Voluntary Transfers

Wisconsin has embarked on an extraordinarily sensible policy: to allow, not require, children in a metropolitan area to transfer not merely to another school in the district, but to another school in the metropolitan area outside their districts—so long as they do not, by this move, increase the racial imbalance in the school.

A child in Milwaukee, for example, can choose to attend a school outside of Milwaukee, so long as he does not increase racial imbalance by doing so; and the state will compensate the district into which he transfers for the extra costs of the extra pupil. This transfer plan is not the only way such an opportunity can be realized. The essential point is the recognition that a state has the responsibility to provide its citizens educational opportunity—and that it fails its responsibility when it allows a local district to exclude children who do not live within district boundaries. The state, of course, must foot the bill to the locality for entering students, and the locality must have the right, within reason, to limit the number of students entering from outside. But this does not negate the state's responsibility to the children who reside within it.

The implications of abandoning the belief that the child's educational opportunities end at school district boundaries are, of course, profound. This does not imply abandonment of local control over the content of education, as it is now practiced, nor that the state has the right to order a family's children to attend a school in another district. It does imply, however, a limitation on the locality's control of who else may attend schools in that locality. In particular, it means that a suburb does not have an inherent right, except as the state gives it that right, to prevent a reasonable number of children from the city, whose educational opportunity is limited by the constraints of their place of residence, from attending school in that suburb, rather than in the city. Another way of looking at the matter is that parents who can afford to do so should have the right to choose their child's school by their choice of residence, but they should not have the right to exclude others by use of school district boundaries as barriers.

In general, a policy of this sort would allow families to make their choice of school independent from their choice of residence, with reasonable transportation expenses provided. State funds would necessarily follow the child, so that the financial burden upon the receiving district would not increase. Each school necessarily would be able to limit the number of students coming in; for example, no transferring child need be accepted if the proportion of his or her race had reached the average proportion of the metropolitan area as a whole, or if the school's capacity was exceeded. But below that point, the receiving school would not have the right of rejection.

All that is necessary for establishment of such a policy is a decision by the state legislature. This is not to suggest that such a policy would be easy to institute, because suburbs—and their legislative representatives—are likely to oppose it. For them, desegregation has been a fine policy so long as it's been the other fellow's district that was desegregated. But, as the example of Wisconsin already shows, it is not a policy impossible to pass. And as that example will show in the longer run, it is a policy that can lead to improved schools in both suburbs and city. For example, I suspect that a set of specialized high schools in the central city, attended voluntarily by both blacks and whites, will emerge from such a policy.

These schools will offer technical programs or programs in the arts that cannot be duplicated in any suburban schools. It would be overly optimistic to believe that this could occur soon; but it would be unfair to future generations of children not to provide a structure within which such educational excellence could grow.

2. Vouchers for Education

Perhaps the simplest, cleanest, and most straightforward way to provide equal educational opportunity, independent of race, residence or wealth, would be to give every child a voucher or entitlement, to be used in any accredited school, public or private. Such a plan, which has recently been proposed in MIchigan as well as in other states, does not immediately exhibit its potential for encouragement of school integration. But that potential can be realized quickly if the vouchers are worth more in integrated schools. This means that integrated schools would have somewhat higher expenditures, a somewhat richer program, than non-integrated schools. Such a policy of course, would be objected to by some; but it is hard to see the merit of such objections, for any child, if the parents so chose, could attend an integrated school and receive the richer offerings. No one would be excluded by reason of race or any other attribute—except his preference for a segregated school. If he were to choose such a school, he would pay in the form of a somewhat less rich educational program.

3. A System of Incentive Combined with Choice

A third variation in policy is one that focuses on direct incentives for attendance in an integrated school. The policy, which has been proposed by a Cincinnati school board member, John Rule, is to reward children and parents for the child's attendance at an integrated school. The rewards would be in the form of post-secondary tuition, so that, for example, attendance at an integrated school for twelve years would result in four years of college or other post-secondary tuition—one year for each three years in an integrated school.

Again, some will object to such a policy. But do the objections have merit? Do we want integrated schools or not? And who are expected to be the primary beneficiaries of integrated education? Possibly the children, but just as possibly the larger society, through the increased cohesion and social integration of the society as a whole. If it is the latter, the larger society that is the primary beneficiary, then the larger society should bear the cost of integration—a cost which is measured by the amount of benefit necessary to provide for families, white and black, in order to achieve the degree of integration desired.

Other policies, of course, exhibit the properties I described earlier; these are just a sample. They show that integrated education does not depend on romanticized distortions. Once we shed these beliefs—the mistaken beliefs on which desegregation policy has rested in the past—and those other beliefs that have stifled new ideas that could aid integration, it becomes possible to take the long, hard road toward achieving an integrated society.

*   *   *

Questions from the Audience

Q. What was your reaction to a plan for having parents choose to send their child to a close public school in another district, with the state picking up the tuition?

A. The voucher plan I described provides the child with an entitlement to attend a school, whether it's a school run by the public system or by a non-public system, rather than to provide hiim simply with the services of his own district's public school, which is what we do now. Implicit in what I said is that I think such a policy would have the kinds of benefits I described if it also contains the other aspects that I described. I can't say that I would favor the policy as the most desirable one, but I certainly think that such a policy is very much worth trying. It's not going to result in an emasculation of the public school system; I don't think this could occur very easily. What it would do is provide for children—and this is the central point that we have to remember—to provide for children and their parents the kind of opportunity that they don't now have unless they have money.

Q. With respect to the sliding voucher that's worth more in an integrated school, I immediately jump to the conclusion that you mean race. But does that also include ethnic, class and religious differences?

A. No, it means only race, because the reason for the sliding scale is the richer program then possible in a racially integrated school. Collectively, we've decided as a society that integration is better for black children or white children, or that it's better for society as a whole. Now if we believe that racial integration is better for society as a whole, and if we can achieve it only through coercion—which, as we've seen, has all sorts of ways of not working—or through incentives, then we ought to do it through incentives. I don't think the same kinds of problems exist with regard to other distinctions, such as religious distinctions, in today's society. I think that two hundred years ago some of the same kinds of problems did exist with regard to religious distinctions. One of the reasons why we have as strong a constitutional clause as we do with regard to separation of Church and State in education is because the founding fathers at that time sensed the danger of a religious cleavage in the schools. I think, in some sense, that this has abated; but in a sense the possibility of racial isolation of the schools poses a comparable danger.

Q. Just what class were you speaking of when you said that proportionally the number of blacks eighteen to nineteen years old attending college was higher than that for eighteen- to nineteen-year-old whites?

A. *I didn't say exactly that. I said the proportion of blacks eighteen and nineteen attending school was higher. Now some eighteen- and nineteen-year-olds are attending high school and some are in college, so it's a mixed group. A survey by the United States Bureau of Census in 1977 showed for the first time that the proportion of eighteen- and nineteen-year-old blacks in school, either in high school or college or other post-secondary schools, was higher than that of whites. Now, as I say, I have to clarify that, because it is in part due to fewer occupational opportunities for blacks than whites. Nevertheless, the result does hold. Looking at all the country as a whole, there is a higher proportion of eighteen- and nineteen-year-old blacks in school than whites.*

Q. You mean in terms of proportion?

A. *Yes.*

Q. In your addressing us today, you've been speaking much about race. When you spoke about the voucher system in an integrated school, especially in view of the reality of Southwest Detroit, I am wondering where and how the integration of race, when we speak of race, begins and ends. In that part of the city there are Hispanics, there are Arabs, there are blacks, there are whites. Would you address that whole thing about race, the separating or moving out of the black and white?

A. *That's an important question. Despite my response earlier to the question of class distinctions or religious distinctions, I think that essentially what the society has to do or what it has done to find distinctions that are currently covering most problems from the point of view of possible societal isolation of subgroups. I think society clearly has concluded that it's not just a black-white separation that can threaten the solidarity of the society and the integration of the society, but that there's also an Hispanic-white and an Hispanic-black separation that can foster the same problems.*

Q. Contd. The very interesting thing you just said—about Hispanic "whites" as well as the Hispanic "blacks" is true with the Puerto Ricans. There is that mixture; but within, let's say, the last ten years the desire of the Hispanic, especially the Mexican, has been to be designated not as white, but as brown. How are you going to fit us in there? We do want our history, our culture; it's not a "white" culture.

A. *In some sense, the points you just made in regard to the Hispanic population are among the things that begin to make it very apparent that the age of complete racial balance of minorities and majorities in every school is an inappropriate goal; it does not allow for the possibility of developing some kind of cultural identity, a black cultural identity, a Spanish cultural identity, which can exist in an essentially single race school.*

Q. contd. Then you run into another problem, especially in Southwest Detroit and in a lot of Southwestern states: one identity, but what about that one-language thing? With the bilingual education being so pertinent, should a person choose to go to a school in Dearborn when he has the educational availability of a school that may be in the middle of Detroit?

A. contd. You bring up too many problems. It's true that these are problems and they have to be addressed; but as I said, you bring up too many all at once. I think I'll just have to beg off that one for the moment. I've thought about that one, and as you say, it is a serious problem.

Q. As an observer of American history, I see our society as seemingly leaning toward the right. Do you think it is possible that desegregation and integration will ever come about in the United States of America? In the schools or anywhere else?

A. I think it is possible. If I had to characterize the principal mechanisms through which I think it will occur, they are really very different from those we've talked about today. The principal mechanisms through which I think it will occur are not within the schools, despite the fact that the kinds of policies I described are very important. Instead, I think the principal mechanism lies in jobs; that is, jobs of a sort that blacks never had the opportunity to have before, jobs which make for a much larger black middle class population than ever existed before. Second, new urban areas will be established which are defined as neither black nor white, but which have a kind of possibility to become integrated in ways that are much more difficult in already existing areas. For example, there's a new city in Maryland, Columbia, Maryland, and Reston, Virginia. Columbia, Maryland, is about 50-50 black and white. It's also 50-50 black and white not residentially block by block, but house by house. These are mostly single family dwellings. It's very residentially integrated. I think that has come about through the existence of middle class income for blacks and also because it is a new city built without the pattern of racial succession which ordinarily occurs in older residential areas. Another thing I think we need to look at is this: Where did segregation of ethnic groups in the central cities of the United States decline? Segregation declined not in the first generation, not as long as the groups continued to live and work in the same places, but in the move from the city to the suburbs. When that move took place, the Poles were moved closer to the Hungarians than they ever were before, and the Italians became interspersed more than they had been before. I think we can see the same kinds of patterns evolving between blacks and whites. It's not in the same location that one creates residential integration, it's in the move out.

Q. Here we have come upon the socio-economic factor, with Columbia, a new city, as a microcosm of urban America. But I'm speaking of a larger community, and I'm not particularly speaking of those of us who "have"; I'm speaking of the have-nots. What is going to happen to them?

A. Well, I think that is certainly a serious problem, but that's not the problem you asked me to address at the outset. The question you asked me at the outset had to do with black-white integration, not with social class integration. I think in the long run, as you suggest, social class integration is going to be the serious problem of the United States. Incidentally, one thing that I'm reminded of with regard to your question having to do with language: about twelve years ago, I was in a discussion with French-Canadian and English-Canadian friends, and I said, "The United States is going to solve its black and white problems before Canada is going to solve its French-English problems." I still think that's going to be the case and the reason why is because language is more powerful than race.

Q. Did I understand you to say that governmental action has not played a significant role in residential segregation?

A. No. I just said that the major portion of segregation in the city is residential segregation, and that although the major portion of residential segregation may be facilitated by governmental action it is due primarily to individual choice. I don't mean to say that there haven't been governmental actions, actions by local governments as well. For example, the FHA program had the effect of creating differential opportunities outside the city and increasing the racial isolation between black cities and the suburbs. So I do think that oftentimes government facilitates certain things; nevertheless, in this case the principal source of the problem—residential segregation—was individual choice.

Q. The major problem as perceived by some caucasian integrationists is the different attitudes toward school integration by the leaders of the Afro-American community. I would appreciate it if you would comment now, and I'd be very happy to hear from members of the audience later on, as to suggestions that would be helpful either from studies you know about or your own experiences or philosophy for dealing with Afro-American community leaders who might respond to your talk about black cultural identity, although that sounds disturbingly like a cover word for resegregation or something like that.

A. I'm not sure of the import of your question, but I do think that there is within any black group a kind of ambivalent stance on the part of some black leaders with regard to racial identity of schools and integrated schools. One can build a kind of cultural identity in the school in which a particular group is in a majority; that's not possible with a group dispersed as a minority. That's one of the reasons why I think it a peculiar notion that racially identifiable schools must be eliminated. But I think perhaps in the discussion later this evening, some of the points of view you raised questions about might come out.

Q. You mentioned the active cooperation of parents in establishing new school policies. Does this imply active participation of parents in thinking of the regional programs in the City of Detroit? Would you comment on the possible worthwhileness?

A. Certainly one of the things that has been learned about successful and unsuccessful school desegregation, primarily in the South, is that the more parental involvement there is, the more school desegregation works. One of the greatest barriers is the parental generation, of course, rather than the children's generation. And it's a barrier because parents don't know what goes on in the schools.

Q. I believe you mentioned specialized high schools offering technical programs that will likely be found in the central city and attended by both black and white students based on their individual choice. Does this mean we can look forward to schools built in the future that will address the changing functions of the city? And if so, does this mean we can look forward to a possible emergence of high schools and post-secondary institutions that will have increased prestige in serving the needs of the total community?

A. I think yes to both of those questions. If one looks at the emerging functions of the city, it's clear that they include cultural activities and educational activities. If one looks, for example, at the specialized schools of New York City—the High School of the Performing Arts and other high schools emphasizing music and art—all of those schools provide extremely important opportunities for young people in the city. If the right context is established, schools will come to reflect a kind of division of labor, perhaps between suburbs and the city. I'm not talking about the immediate future, but the longer term future, with specialized and elite schools in the city attended by both black and white and general high schools outside of the central city attended by both black and white.

Q. contd. By long-range do you mean something in the range of ten years or so?

A. Yes, I mean something in the range of ten years. I think it will certainly begin before that time in some cities, but I don't think we'll see it very evident before ten years from now.

15

The Role of Incentives
in School Desegregation

Since the *Brown* decision of 1954, there have been sharp changes in both the goals of school desegregation and the means used to achieve these goals. Yet many discussions of school desegregation ignore these changes, which are of obvious importance in informing future desegregation policies. This inattention to the past is especially disorienting because ends and means have moved in opposite directions. That is, ends have moved away from those having a constitutional justification through the Fourteenth Amendment on equal protection toward those that have weaker justification. At the same time, means of desegregation have come to be considerably more coercive, possibly appropriate to constitutionally justified ends but not to those with lesser justification.

It is useful (even if somewhat oversimplified) to think of the history of school desegregation since 1954 as comprising two periods: the first stage, from 1954 to the late 1960s; and the second stage, the period since then.

The Ends in *Brown* and the Period Following

In the first stage, that is, at the time of the *Brown* decision and for a number of years after that, the sole end of desegregation (indeed, the very *meaning* of desegregation) was abolishing state-created segregation of the schools in order to provide blacks the same range of educational opportunity available to whites. This meant eliminating the dual school systems in the South and creating unitary systems. At first, this had no relevance at all for schools in the North, which had not had a history of dual systems; but a sufficient number of segregating actions by school boards in the North were found to show that some desegregating actions were necessary there as well. However, since these latter findings arose during the second stage of school desegregation, there has been a confusion about the ends of desegregation, both in the courts and outside.

But this gets ahead of the story. Let us turn to the second stage of school desegregation, beginning in the late 1960s.

The Ends of School Desegregation Since About 1970

In the late 1960s there emerged a new set of ends of desegregation and, as a result, an almost unnoticed redefinition of desegregation. The clue is provided by a term that appeared at about that time, "affirmative integration." There was a move away from the goal of eliminating state-imposed segregation to eliminating all segregation, whether it resulted from individual actions of families or from state action. Stated differently, the goal shifted from eliminating state-imposed segregation to instituting state-imposed integration, by creating a numerical racial balance throughout the school system.

What brought about this curious change? It is a change, of course, that was not agreed to by all, but a change initiated by desegregation protagonists and then to a considerable extent accepted by the courts. Because the issues were shaped by the protagonists (for it was they who brought the cases and designed the arguments contained in the briefs), their redefinition came to shape the course of desegregation policy.

There are at least two causes for the transition from first-stage ends to the more encompassing second-stage ends, one somewhat more justifiable than the other.

The first and less justifiable cause can be termed organizational preservation. This process can be illustrated by an organization in which it was studied in detail, the March of Dimes (Sills, 1957). The original goal of the March of Dimes organization had been to eliminate polio. But with the advent of the vaccine, polio *was* virtually eliminated. So what could the March of Dimes do with the experience and momentum of its enormous volunteer staff and small full-time staff? It did not go out of business when its goal was accomplished. Rather it found a new goal, which allowed it to remain in operation: elimination of birth defects.

The point is that when the original *Brown* goal was achieved (as it essentially was in 1970, except in some large cities in the South), the organizations that had carried the desegregation fight forward found it necessary to take on a new goal, just as the March of Dimes did when polio was eliminated. The goal was that of eliminating all segregation, not merely that resulting from state action.

The second cause for the shift indicates why the new goal was not wholly unreasonable. To indicate what that cause is requires examining briefly the origins of American public education. Public education in America has a history unlike that in any country in Europe. European education was, from the outset, two-tiered: one set of schools for the elite, another for the masses. This dual school system took different forms in England, France, Germany, and elsewhere. But everywhere, whether in the lycée, gymnasium, grammar school, or other form, it was marked by richer, more academic, and more intensive curricula and a longer period of schooling for children of the elite.

American public education was, however, from its beginning a single system, founded on the ideology of a single "common school" that children of all economic levels and all groups would attend. Only in the South was there a parallel to the dual school systems of Europe, and that duality depended on racial distinction. Everywhere else there was a single system, with only minor aberrations. For example, the East Coast, mimicking Europe and always less egalitarian than the rest of the country, maintained and still maintains a number of private schools for the elite; throughout other parts of the country private secondary academics were numerous seventy-five years ago, but vanished when public secondary schools came into being. Another aberration has been the religious schools, primarily Catholic. But because Catholics have seldom been an economic elite in American communities, Catholic schools have not constituted a separation of the elite from the masses. And finally, the ideal of the common school was always realized more fully in towns, small cities, and rural areas than in large cities.

The general idea of the common school did not mean, of course, that schools were fully egalitarian. Within the school, children from lower socioeconomic groups were likely to fare less well; the general social structure of the community impressed itself on the functioning of the school. Nevertheless, the difference between these schools and the class-stratified schools of Europe was marked, just as the general assumption of equal opportunity of America was markedly different from the European assumption that every man had his station.

However, there have been changes, economic and technological, that undermine the idea of the common school and the underlying idea of equal opportunity through education. The technological changes have been in transportation, principally the automobile, whose existence has made possible the physical separation of work and residence by rather long distances. The economic changes have stemmed from a general increase in affluence, which allows families (given that the car frees them from living near work) to choose where they will live and to repeat that choice several times during their lifetimes as their economic conditions change. The result has been communities far more economically homogeneous than before World War II, and suburbs that differ sharply in economic level from one another as well as from the central city. Racial segregation by residence has also become more feasible than in the past and maintains itself despite sharp reductions in racial prejudice and discrimination in all walks of life.

The effect of this residential fractionation along economic and racial lines is felt in the schools. Although residence and workplace are no longer tied together for the adult members of the family, residence and schooling are tied together for the family's children. This is in part because of the naturally smaller radius of movement that young children have—making the "neighborhood school" a likely institution, while the "neighborhood office" or the "neighborhood factory" is not—and it is in part because of school policies. These policies characteristically limit the child to attendance at a particular school within the school district, the one into which he is zoned by his residence. This is often the closest school (his "neighborhood school"); if not, it is at least one of the closest.

With families sorting themselves out residentially along economic and racial lines, and with schools tied to residence, the end result is the demise of the common school attended by children from all economic levels. In its place is the elite suburban school (in effect a homogeneous private school supported by public funds), the middle-income suburban-school, the low-income suburban school, and central-city schools of several types—low-income white schools, middle-income white schools, and low- or middle-income black schools.

The effect on racial segregation in the schools of this reduction of economic and technological constraints on residence has been great. The existence of black ghettos in large cities has meant all-black schools in those ghettos, a segregation not imposed by the state but by the residential choices of white families with the money to implement their preferences. And, as Thomas Schelling shows, it requires only a very small preference for same-race neighbors to produce a high degree of residential segregation, if there are no economic or other constraints on moving (Schelling, 1978, ch. 4).

It is this situation that desegregation protagonists, having largely overcome state-imposed segregation, began to attempt to undo in the late 1960s. An indication of the new philosophy can be seen in the legal arguments used for the first time in the city-wide busing cases such as Charlotte-Mecklenburg and Denver. These were cases in which there was obviously affirmative integration, designed to overcome much more than state-imposed segregation. One element in the legal arguments that won these cases was that black children learned better in schools that were majority white schools, an argument that had not been used during the first stage of school desegregation, and one that bears no relation to removal of state-imposed segregation.

Are the Second-State Ends Wrong?

In the case of the March of Dimes, the new goal taken on by the organization (elimination of birth defects) was no less meritorious than the old one (elimination of polio), though it commanded considerably less public attention and support. What can be said about the new goal of desegregation action that arose in the second stage?

I believe the situation is similar. The new goal of overcoming the segregation that results from unconstrained residential choice is based on the same foundations as the goals behind the early American ideal of the common school for all—the creation of a single, unified nation by bringing together its children in school, regardless of race, religion, ethnicity, or class.

There is, however, a difference between the first-stage goal and the second-stage goal that is fundamental for the means used to achieve them. The first-stage goal concerns protection of the individual against discriminatory actions by the state and its agencies. It is not a goal designed to produce a particular social configuration in the schools, but rather one directly related to constitutional guarantees provided to all citizens. The second-stage goal, in contrast, *is* designed to produce a particular social configuration in the schools. It does not derive from constitutional guarantees, but from a sense of what a "good society" should be like. It may be more important in achieving the good society than is the narrower constitutional goal of the first stage. But somewhat different means are required to achieve it. And it is not and never has been in American society, an overriding goal to be achieved at any expense. The common school of the American ideal had to compete with other goals in society: the right of people to live where they wish, schools as an integral part of the communities they serve, and others.

Means Appropriate to Second-Stage Ends

One can say, as a constitutional lawyer would, that when the goals change from those involving constitutional guarantees to those involving social configurations that can help bring about the good society, the appropriate locus of action shifts from the court to other arenas. Those arenas may be the legislature, the school board, the city council, or non-governmental groups (for example, groups that establish integrated private schools for the socialization benefits they bring to black and white children). But the court is not one of them.

There is a more fundamental reason different means are necessary to reach this new, more encompassing goal. If a social arrangement (such as dual school systems before 1954 in the South) is the result of an action of an agency of the state, then that agency may be the defendant in a court case, and, if the case is won by the plaintiff, the defendant may be ordered to undo its offending action. Since there is a particular offending action, or set of actions, the court may oversee or police the undoing.

When the social arrangement is not the result of state action, but is the joint result of a multitude of individual residential decisions, each wholly legal, and many taken for admirable reasons (such as the decisions by many—civil rights leaders and desegregation fighters included—to move to a location where their children can attend a good school), then there is no proper defendant for a court case, nor even the basis for a court case. When a court case *is* initiated to overcome such segregation, with the city school system as defendant, as has occurred in many cities since about 1970, the results are peculiar. If the city loses the case, it is ordered to undo the segregation that exists, ordinarily through compulsory busing to achieve racial balance. When it complies, the outcome is simple, straightforward, and predictable: the same elements that brought about the segregation in the first place, individual residential and private-school decisions, will do so again. Sometimes this process occurs through a rapid evacuation, as in

Boston or Memphis, sometimes through a long and steady one, as in Denver and Dallas. Resegregation, of course, arises because the means used are wholly inappropriate to the goal: an agency of the state is required to undo actions not of its own, but of individual families—actions that are not subject to legal assault in the first place.

There are paradoxical consequences of this use of inappropriate means for achieving the second-stage goals. Legal action requires an agency of the state to be the defendant; that agency, if it is to be found guilty, must be the one responsible for students of both races (ordinarily a central-city school district). Those whose residential decisions brought about the segregation in the first place—individual white families—have a simple strategy in response. They need only move their residence or their children to a school distsrict without responsibility for large numbers of black students—and thus one that cannot be found guilty of segregating actions. This is precisely what they do, and they do so in large numbers when the "remedies" imposed are severe, such as busing their children to a different part of the city.

One might ask just how the pursuit of desegregation arrived at such an incongruity between ends and means. The answer involves many details of the way desegregation was pursued in the South, the transition from desegregation in the South to desegregation in the North, and the openings provided by the courts to continue use of the original means to accomplish new ends. The story of that process of transition and development cannot be pursued here. Rather, it is important to ask what means are appropriate to the new ends when those that are in current use are self-defeating.

First, of course, is the question of whether the ends of the common school, the unitary socialization experience provided by the common school, and the contribution this makes to society's integration are important to pursue. Members of the society will disagree about this; but much of the disagreement arises because the means used intrude on other values that may be strongly held (such as individual liberty). There is little disagreement with the ends themselves, only with their position in a hierarchy of social goals. And one of the safeguards that exists when these ends are pursued by appropriate means is that, because their accomplishment necessarily implies the assent of parents and children, black and white, the means are themselves self-policing. If they intrude little on other deeply held values, they will be effective; if they intrude too much, they will be ineffective and self-defeating, as in the case of court-order-induced white flight.

To develop a general idea of the means appropriate to the second-stage goals, it is useful to consider a small book by Charles Schultze (1978), chairman of the Council of Economic Advisers, based on the Godkin Lectures he presented at Harvard University in 1976. While at the Brookings Institution several years ago, Schultze held a seminar devoted to the same topic as the lectures. The seminar, lectures, and book all grew out of his experience as director of the Office of Management and Budget during the Johnson administration, when it was still the Bureau of the Budget. The general thesis is this: Government policy often produces the opposite of what is intended because of a failure to recognize the simple fact that persons, or local governments, or business firms, on whom a policy has its impact, themselves have goals that are different from those of the government. When a new policy is instituted, they will continue to work toward their own goals, viewing the official policy as a constraint or obstacle to accomplishing them. Thus policies often result in an outcome far from, and in some cases even *opposite* to, that intended by the policymakers. An example Schultze gives is the 1972 Water Pollution Act regulating the discharge of effluents into streams. He writes, "The very nature of the controls discourages pollution-reducing technological change. The 1983 criteria base effluent limits on 'best available technology.' But will firms in polluting industries sponsor research or undertake experimentation to develop a new means of reducing pollution still further if its very availability will generate new and more stringent regulations? The entire approach," he continues, "provides strong and positive incentives for polluters to use the legal system to delay progress toward effective cleanup" (p. 53). In this way, Schultze suggests, policymakers can thwart their own intent by not recognizing that there is an active party at the other end of the policy. What Schultze describes can be summed up in what we might term Schultze's Law: If a social policy does not actively employ the interests of those on whom it has an impact, it will find those interests actively employed in directions that defeat its goals.

Unfortunately, school desegregation policy in large cities is a case that Schultze can add to his list. Two kinds of consequences of school desegregation policy have been examined in some detail. One is the effect of desegregation efforts *within* a school district on the degree of segregation *between* districts. For large cities desegregation within the central city seriously increases the segregation between city and suburbs. In a striking recent case, the city of Boston lost 16 percent of its white students in 1974 when a busing plan was put into effect, and 19 percent the next year when its "Phase II" went into effect. In 1978 extensive desegregation in Los Angeles led to massive white flight, that is, segregation between the city of Los Angeles and its suburbs. The segregation that occurs is long-distance residential segregation, deeper and more difficult to overcome than segregation within a city. This is no accident, for those who are escaping the consequences of a policy they do not like make sure they are more difficult to reach the next time. In Los Angeles and other large cities, school desegregation has helped bring about a ghettoization of the city. We have, then, a prime example of Schultze's Law. Desegregation policies have been made with the simplistic assumption that racial composition of schools can be fixed by school assignment—that children and families are like pawns on a chessboard, and will stay where they are put. They do not, and the result is a tragic confirmation of Schultze's Law.

Another example of Schultze's Law can be found in the effect of desegregation on achievement. In 1966, the National Center for Education Statistics in HEW produced a report titled *Equality of Educational Opportunity*. It showed that disadvantaged black children achieved better in schools that were predominantly middle-class (which meant in effect majority white) than in homogeneous lower-class schools. The implication was the desegregation should lead to higher achievement of black students.

Since then the effects on achievement of black students of the desegregation of the late 1960s and early 1970s have been examined. A large number of desegregated school districts have been studied. The most recent review of these studies, by Crain and Mahard (1979), reports nineteen studies showing increased black achievement, twelve showing reduced achievement, and ten showing no effect at all. Among the studies in northern districts, there were in fact *more* showing reduced achievement than increased achievement. These results were reported despite the fact that Crain and Mahard were themselves interested in showing how desegregation could be beneficial for black achievement. Another review carried out earlier by St. John (1975) shows roughly similar results. The precise numbers are unimportant; what is important is that the premise based on the research results reported in *Equality of Educational Opportunity*, that there would be *generally* beneficial effects on achievement, has not been realized.

I do not believe that this nullifies the earlier research results, which show the potential that desegregation has for increasing achievement of the disadvantaged. What it *does* show is that, *as it has been carried out* in the past ten years, school desegregation has realized that potential too seldom. Again we have an illustration of Schultze's Law: A policy intended to increase achievement for black students has, in a large number of districts (if we are to generalize from this sample), decreased it instead; in others it has had no effect on achievement.

Why? Why the difference from the results reported in *Equality of Educational Opportunity?* I believe that again there has been a failure to recognize that the consequences of policies depend on the goals—and in turn on the responses—of those who are affected by them. We know little, in this case, about what caused the decreases in achievement. We do know that in many cases desegregation was implemented with little attention to its possible consequences in increasing disorder, conflict, and absence from school. Instead, attention was concentrated on the right numbers of the right colored bodies at specified schools, in order to comply with a desegregation edict that addressed itself to numbers alone. And the school system, including teachers and other staff, has only a limited amount of attention to allocate. If that attention is focused primarily on compliance with a court's edict or HEW administrative orders, then it must be less focused on educational goals.

In both ways I have shown, the means used to bring about school desegregation have illustrated Schultze's Law by defeating ill-conceived policies. One must then ask, What kinds of policies in school desegregation would not be defeated by Schultze's Law? The first part of the answer is to recognize that the movement in the direction of the second-stage goal does not necessarily involve overcoming all segregation. "Elimination" of every all-black school in a city need no longer be the criterion for success of the policy. There is a place for integrated schools, for all-black schools, for all-Spanish schools, for all-Chinese schools, for all-white schools, under a single criterion: that every child has the full right and opportunity, unconstrained by residence or race or transportation costs, or by artifical school district boundaries, to attend the school of his or her choice. The principle that ought to hold is that a child and his family have the right of choice of school, within or outside the district of residence, but that the school does not have the right to exclude the child.

If the second-stage goal of school desegregation is, as I have suggested, good though not overriding, it should be encouraged. To encourage or increase racial integration of schools beyond that which free choice would bring about—that is, to move in the direction of the second-stage goals— it is important to attend to Schultze's Law, and actively employ the interests of all those on whom the policy has an impact. This means actively using the interests of school administrators, teachers, and both black and white parents and children. There are a number of current and proposed policies that engage the interests of one or more of these groups for their success, and the use of incentives is what Schultze's Law implies.

Incentives for Integration

Magnet Schools and Other Increases in School Attractiveness

One general class of incentives not usually seen as such is the creation of magnet schools, which have some special characteristics that others do not have, sometimes including extra funds. Some magnet schools have curricula that include offerings not provided at other schools, such as special programs in music or foreign languages. In many respects, although the term "magnet" is new, the idea is old, perhaps best realized in some of the specialized high schools of New York City. In some integration plans (Boston, for example), there is an attempt to combine compulsory racial balance with the incentives provided by magnet schools, by designating certain schools as magnet schools but requiring a certain racial composition of the student body.

Incentives to School Districts or Schools

One incentive system that has been used to facilitate transfers across school district lines includes a financial incentive to the sending district and one to the receiving district for students who choose to transfer across school district lines. This plan is employed in Wisconsin for cross-district transfers. In practice, it is used mainly for black students transferring from Milwaukee to suburban school districts. In this case, both the Milwaukee district and the suburban district receive a payment from the state for the child who is transferring.

When we consider the possibility of such transfers, it appears that both kinds of incentives are necessary. If the receiving district is not to have an extra burden, the state should pay the costs of the transferring child, which include both the state aid ordinarily provided on a per-pupil basis and the portion of expenditures that are provided from local taxes (since the entering child's family does not pay local taxes in the district). And if the sending district is not to suffer, it will need at least a portion of the state aid that would have come to the district if the student had continued in school within it.[1]

Incentives to Schools in Conjunction with Voucher Plans

Voucher plans, in which a child brings a voucher to the school he chooses to attend, can be accompanied by incentives of various sorts. One that has been suggested is to have the voucher from a child who is in a minority in the school redeemable by the school for a greater amount of money than the voucher provided by a child who is in the majority in the school. This would create an incentive for the principal (and for the teachers, if they could participate in the extra benefits) to have a school that is racially heterogeneous, since it would mean greater school resources. Such proposals have not progressed very far, because they depend upon the existence of choice of school by children and their parents through a voucher or entitlement plan, and no such plans have been adopted.

Conclusion

The incentives I have discussed do not, of course, exhaust the possibilities for policies that actively employ the interests of affected parties in bringing about their success. But I believe the principle is clear.

Policies in this class are highly constrained, both in the means they use and in the degree of integration they can bring about. Yet they are the only kind of policy compatible with the second-stage goals. They do not suffer the serious defect of the unconstrained policies designed to achieve instant racial balance through compulsory busing. That defect, of course, is in accord with Schultze's Law—unconstrained policies exacerbate the very problem they are designed to cure.

Note

1. There are two conflicting considerations that determine whether the sending school district is financially better or worse off if it loses a child and the state aid that accompanies the child. One is that, because such transferring students are sparsely strewn throughout the district, loss of one or a few children from the school system affects costs very little, but reduces income by the amount of state aid for those students that is no longer provided. (State aid is, on the average, more than 40 percent of school expenditures, while federal aid is about 9 percent.) The opposing consideration is that there is a reduction in the number of pupils without a reduction

of the local tax base, so that the same local taxes provide more money per pupil after the transferring children have left.

References

Crain, Robert, and Rita Mahard. 1979. Desegregation and academic achievement. In *New Perspectives on School Integration*, ed. M. Friedman, R. Meltzer, and C. Miller. Philadelphia: Fortress Press.

St. John, Nancy. 1975. *School Desegregation: Outcomes for Children*. New York: Wiley Interscience.

Schelling, Thomas C. 1978. *Micromotives and Macrobehavior*. New York: W. W. Norton.

Schultze, Charles. 1978. *The Public Use of Private Interest*. Washington, D.C.: Brookings Institution.

Sills, David, L. 1957. *The Volunteers*. New York: Free Press.

PART FOUR

Public and Private Schools

American education is and has been overwhelmingly public education. Throughout this century, the percentage of American children in private schools has remained at about 10 percent of the total school population, and most of those children have been in Catholic schools. Despite the lack of growth in the percentage of students in private schools, perceived problems with the public schools have focused increased attention on private schools. It is in part this increased attention, and the fears for the future of the public schools it has generated, that was responsible for the furor generated by the 1981 report by Sally Kilgore, Thomas Hoffer, and me on public and private schools (published as a book in 1982). Apart from the protective reaction on behalf of public schools, there was also a reaction to the apparent absurdity of comparing the effectiveness of public and private schools when there were so many selective forces at work giving them different student populations. There was the further apparent absurdity of claiming that the private sector did not contribute to racial segregation in the schools, even though it was evident that some white parents used private schools as havens from school desegregation.

However, these apparent absurdities are not quite so absurd upon further examination. Perhaps the public school havens from desegregation in the suburbs were more important and more extensive than the private school havens. And, perhaps schools in the private sector brought about more contact between blacks and whites—that is, more racially mixed schools—than did the average public school in those metropolitan areas. Thus, the question of the private sector's overall impact on school racial integration is more complex than it first appears.

Similarly, studying the relative effectiveness of public and private schools may not be so absurd. Studying growth in achievement over a two-year period eliminates much of the difference due to initial self-selection. Statistically controlling background characteristics eliminates more. By finding public-private differences in achievement growth in some academic areas but not in others, it became evident that the differences involved something more than self-selection. The finding that these differences correspond to differences in the courses students take strengthens the evidence that more is involved. Testing for a creaming effect and finding none strengthens it even more.

Of course, the results reported in Chapters 16–18 do not resolve the controversy. Yet after this work appeared in the early and mid-1980s, other studies using differing data and some studies using data from different countries began to show confirming results, particularly about the effectiveness of religiously based schools.

The value of this work, however, does not lie merely in its demonstration of the academic effectiveness of private-sector schools. It lies in what it can demonstrate that is of value for schools in general. A part of what is valuable is the information such work provides about the *sources* of school effectiveness. The research of Part 2, together with other research carried out in the 1960s and 1970s, showed the ineffectiveness of factors traditionally measured as aspects of schools that bring about achievement. The research of the 1980s has begun to locate factors that are important in bringing about achievement. These factors include, not surprisingly, the kind of coursework a student takes. That raises other questions: Why is there variation in the courses that comparable students take? Why, in the 1970s, was there such a decline in the number of students taking foreign languages and college preparatory mathematics in the public schools? Why was there not a comparable decline in Catholic schools?

These questions, however, go beyond Part 4. The chapters of Part 4 present research results, including both the differential effects of the different sectors on achievement and some of the proximate factors responsible for those differences. The further questions raised by these results are left until Part 5.

16

Quality and Equality
in American Education
Public and Catholic Schools

The report, "Public and Private Schools," of which I was an author, has raised some questions about certain fundamental assumptions and ideals underlying American education.[1] In this article, I shall first describe briefly the results that raise these questions. Then I shall examine in greater detail these fundamental assumptions and ideals, together with changes in our society that have violated the assumptions and made the ideals increasingly unattainable. I shall then indicate the negative consequences that these violations have created for both equality of educational opportunity in U.S. public schools and for the quality of education they offer. Finally I shall suggest what seems to me the direction that a new set of ideals and assumptions must take if the schools are to serve American children effectively.

A number of the results of "Public and Private Schools" have been subjected to intense reexamination and reanalysis. The report has occasioned a good deal of debate and controversy, as well as a two-day conference at the National Institute of Education and a one-day conference at the National Academy of Sciences, both in late July. Part of the controversy appears to have arisen because of the serious methodological difficulties in eliminating bias due to self-selection into the private sector. Another part appears to have arisen because the report was seen as an attack on the public schools at a time when tuition tax credit legislation was being proposed in Congress.

I shall not discuss the controversy except to say that all the results summarized in the first portion of this article have been challenged by at least one critic; I would not report them here if these criticisms or our own further analyses had led me to have serious doubts about them. Despite this confidence, the results could be incorrect because of the extent of the methodological difficulties involved in answering any cause-and-effect question when exposure to the different treatments (that is, to the different types

Reprinted with permission from *Phi Delta Kappan*, vol. 63, no. 3 (November 1981): 159–164.

of schools) is so far from random. Most of my comparisons will be between the Catholic and the public schools. The non-Catholic private schools constitute a much more heterogeneous array of schools; our sample in those schools is considerably smaller (631 sophomores and 551 seniors in 27 schools), and the sample may be biased by the fact that a substantial number of schools refused to participate. For these reasons, any generalizations about the non-Catholic private sector must be tenuous. Fortunately, the principal results of interest are to be found in the Catholic schools.

There are five principal results of our study, two having to do with quality of education provided in both the public and private sectors and three related to equality of education.

First, we found evidence of higher academic achievement in basic cognitive skills (reading comprehension, vocabulary, and mathematics) in Catholic schools than in public schools for students from comparable family backgrounds. The difference is roughly one grade level, which is not a great difference. But, since students in Catholic schools take, on the average, a slightly greater number of academic courses, the differences could well be greater for tests more closely attuned to the high school curriculum. And the higher achievement is attained in the Catholic schools with a lower expenditure per pupil and a slightly higher pupil/teacher ratio than in the public schools.

The second result concerning educational quality must be stated with a little less certainty. We found that aspirations for higher education are higher among students in Catholic schools than among comparable students in public schools, despite the fact that, according to the students' retrospective reports, about the same proportion had planned to attend college when they were in the sixth grade.

The first two results concerning equality in education are parallel to the previous two results; one concerns achievement in cognitive skills and the other, plans to attend college. For both of these outcomes of schooling, family background matters less in the Catholic schools than in the public schools. In both achievement and aspirations, blacks are closer to whites, Hispanics are closer to Anglos, and children from less well-educated parents are closer to those from better-educated parents in Catholic schools than in public schools. Moreover, in Catholic schools the gap narrows between the sophomore and senior years, while in the public schools the gap in both achievement and aspirations widens.

It is important to note that, unlike the results related to educational quality, these results related to equality do not hold generally for the public/private comparison. That is, the results concerning equality are limited to the comparison between public schools and Catholic schools. Within other segments of the private sector (e.g., Lutheran schools or Jewish schools) similar results for educational differences might well hold (though these other segments have too few blacks and Hispanics to allow racial and ethnic comparisons), but they are not sufficiently represented in the sample to allow separate examination.

The final result concerning educational equality is in the area of racial and ethnic integration. Catholic schools have, proportionally, only about half as many black students as do the public schools (about 6% compared to about 14%); but internally they are less segregated. In terms of their effect on the overall degree of racial integration in U.S. schools, these two factors work in opposing directions; to a large extent they cancel each other out. But of interest to our examination here, which concerns the internal functioning of the public and Catholic sectors of education, is the lesser internal segregation of blacks in the Catholic sector. Part of this is due to the smaller percentage of black students in Catholic schools, for a general conclusion in the school desegregation literature is that school systems with smaller proportions of a disadvantaged minority are less segregated than those with larger proportions. But part seems due to factors beyond the simple proportions. A similar result is that, even though the Catholic schools in our sample have slightly higher proportions of Hispanic students than the public schools, they have slightly less Hispanic/Anglo segregation.

These are the results from our research on public and private schools that raise questions about certain fundamental assumptions of American education. Catholic schools appear to be characterized by *both* higher quality, on the average, *and* greater equality than the public schools. How can this be when the public schools are, first, more expensive, which should lead to higher quality, and, second, explicitly designed to increase equality of opportunity? The answer lies, I believe, in the organization of public education in the United States, and that organization in turn is grounded in several fundamental assumptions. It is to these assumptions that I now turn.

Four Basic Ideals and Their Violation

Perhaps the ideal most central to American education is the ideal of the common school, a school attended by all children. The assumption that all social classes should attend the same school contrasted with the two-tiered educational systems in Europe, which reflected their feudal origins. Both in the beginning and at crucial moments of choice (such as the massive expansion of secondary education in the early part of this century), American education followed the pattern of common, or comprehensive, schools, including all students from the community and all courses of study. Only in the largest eastern cities were there differentiated, selective high schools, and even that practice declined over time, with new high schools generally following the pattern of the comprehensive school.

One implication of the common-school ideal has been the deliberate and complete exclusion of religion from the schools. In contrast, many (perhaps most) other countries have some form of support for schools operated by religious groups. In many countries, even including very small ones such as the Netherlands and Israel, there is a state secular school system, as well as publicly supported schools under the control of religious groups. But the melting-pot ideology that shaped American education dictated that there would be a single set of publicly supported schools, and the reaction to European religious intolerance dictated that these be free of religious influence.[2]

The absence of social class, curriculum, or religious bases for selection of students into different schools meant that, in American schooling, attendance at a given school was dictated by location of residence. This method worked well in sparsely settled areas and in towns and smaller cities, and it was a principle compatible with a secular democracy. Two factors have, however, led this mode of school assignment to violate the assumptions of the common school. One is the movement of the U.S. population to cities with high population densities, resulting in economically homogeneous residential areas. The other is the more recent, largely post–World War II expansion of personal transportation, leading to the development of extensive, economically differentiated suburbs surrounding large cities.

The combined effect of these two changes has been that in metropolitan areas the assumptions of the common school are no longer met. The residential basis of school assignment, in an ironic twist, has proved to be segregative and exclusionary, separating economic levels just as surely as do the explicitly selective systems of European countries and separating racial groups even more completely. The larger the metropolitan area, the more true this is, so that in the largest metropolitan areas the schools form a set of layers of economically stratified and racially distinct schools, while in small cities and towns the schools continue to approximate the economically and racially heterogeneous mix that was Horace Mann's vision of the common school in America.

In retrospect, only the temporary constraints on residential movement imposed by economic and technological conditions allowed the common-school ideal to be realized even for a time. As those constraints continue to decrease, individual choice will play an increasing role in school attendance (principally through location of residence), and the common-school assumption will be increasingly violated. Assignment to school in a single publicly supported school system on the basis of residence is no longer a means of achieving the common-school ideal. And, in fact, the common-school ideal may no longer be attainable through *any* means short of highly coercive ones.

The courts have attempted to undo the racially segregative impact of residential choice, reconstituting the common-school ideal through compulsory busing of children into different residential areas.[3] These attempts, however, have been largely thwarted by families who, exercising that same opportunity for choice of school through residence, move out of the court's jurisdiction. The unpopularity and impermanence of these court-ordered attempts to reinstitute the common school suggest that attempts to reimpose by law the constraints that economics and technology once placed upon school choice will fail and that, in the absence of those naturally imposed constraints, the common-school ideal will give way before an even stronger ideal—that of individual liberty.

It is necessary, then, to recognize the failure of school assignment by residence and to reexamine the partially conflicting ideals of American education in order to determine which of those ideals we want to preserve and which to discard. For example, in high schools distinguished by variations in curriculum—one form of which is a type of magnet school and another form of which is the technical high school—a more stable racial mix of students is possible than in comprehensive high schools. As another example, Catholic schools are less racially and economically segregated than are U.S. public schools; this suggests that, when a school is defined around and controlled by a religious community, families may tolerate more racial and economic heterogeneity than they would in a school defined around a residential area and controlled by government officials.

A second ideal of American education has been the concept of local control. This has meant both control by the local school board and superintendent and the responsiveness of the school staff to parents. But these conditions have changed as well. The local school board and superintendent now have far less control over education policy than only 20 years ago. A large part of the policy-making function has shifted to the national level; this shift was caused primarily by the issue of racial discrimination, but it has also affected the areas of sex discrimination, bilingual education, and education for the handicapped, among others. Part of the policy-making power has shifted to the school staff or their union representatives, as professionalization and collective bargaining have accompanied the growth in size of school districts and the breakdown of a sense of community at the local level.

The loss of control by school boards and superintendents has been accompanied by a reduced responsiveness of the school to parents. This too has resulted in part from the breakdown of community at the local level and the increasing professionalization of teachers, both of which have helped to free the teacher from community control. The changes have been accompanied and reinforced by the trend to larger urban agglomerates and larger school districts. And some of the changes introduced to overcome racial segregation—in particular, busing to a distant school—have led to even greater social distances between parent and teacher.

A result of this loss of local control has been that parents are more distant from their children's school, less able to exert influence, less comfortable about the school as an extension of their own child rearing. Public support for public schools, as evidenced in the passage of school tax referenda and school bond issues and in the responses to public opinion polls, has declined since the mid-1960s, probably in part as a result of this loss of local control. Even more recently, in a backlash against the increasingly alien control of the schools, some communities have attempted to counter what they see as moral relativism in the curriculum (e.g., the controversy over the content in *Man: A Course of Study*) and have attempted to ban the teaching of evolution.

Technological and ecological changes make it unlikely that local control of education policy can be reconstituted as it has existed in the past, that is, through a local school board controlling a single public school system and representing the consensus of the community. Individuals may regain such local control by moving ever farther from large cities (as the 1980 census shows they have been doing), but the educational system as a whole cannot be reconstituted along the old local-control lines. Again, as in the case of the common-school ideal, present conditions (and the likelihood that they will persist) make the ideal unrealizable. One alternative is to resign ourselves to ever-decreasing public support for the public schools as they move further from the ideal. Another, however, is to attempt to find new principles for the organization of American education that will bring back parental support.

A third fundamental assumption of American public schooling, closely connected to local control, has been local financing of education. Some of the same factors that have brought about a loss of local control have shifted an increasing portion of education financing to the state and federal levels. Local taxes currently support only about 40% of expenditures for public schooling; federal support amounts to about 8% or 9% and state support, slightly over half of the total. The shift from local to state (and, to a lesser extent, federal) levels of financing has resulted from the attempt to reduce inequalities of educational expenditures among school districts. Inequalities that were once of little concern come to be deeply felt when local communities are no longer isolated but interdependent and in close social proximity. The result has been the attempt by some states, responding to the *Serrano* decision in California, to effect complete equality in educational expenditures for all students within the state. This becomes difficult to achieve without full statewide financing, which negates the principle of local financing.

Yet the justification for student assignment to the schools within the family's taxation district has been that the parents were paying for the schools *in that district*. That justification vanishes under a system of statewide taxation. The rationale for assignment by residence, already weakened by the economic and racial differences among students from different locales, is further weakened by the decline in local financing.

A fourth ideal of American public education has been the principle of *in loco parentis*. In committing their child to a school, parents expect that the school will exercise comparable authority over and responsibility for the child. The principle of *in loco parentis* was, until the past two decades, assumed not only at the elementary and secondary levels but at the college level as well. However, this assumption vanished as colleges abdicated the responsibility and parents of college students shortened the scope of their authority over their children's behavior from the end of college to the end of high school.

Most parents, however, continue to expect the school to exercise authority over and responsibility for their children through the end of high school. Yet public schools have been less and less successful in acting *in loco parentis*. In part, this is due to the loss of authority in the society as a whole, manifested in high school by a decreasing willingness of high school-age youths to be subject to *anyone's* authority in matters of dress and conduct. In part, it is due to the increasing dissensus among parents themselves about the authority of the school to exercise discipline over their children, sometimes leading to legal suits to limit the school's authority. And, in part, it is due to the courts, which, in response to these suits, have expanded the scope of civil rights of children in school, thus effectively limiting the school's authority to something less than that implied by the principle of *in loco parentis.*

There has been a major shift among some middle-class parents—a shift that will probably become even more evident as the children of parents now in their thirties move into high school—toward an early truncation of responsibility for and authority over their adolescent children. This stems in part from two changes—an increase in longevity and a decrease in number of children—which, taken together, remove child rearing from the central place it once held for adults. Many modern adults who begin child rearing late and end early are eager to resume the leisure and consumption activities that preceded their child-rearing period; they encourage early autonomy for their young. But the high school often continues to act as if it has parental support for its authority. In some cases it does; in others it does not. The community consensus on which a school's authority depends has vanished.

An additional difficulty is created by the increasing size and bureaucratization of the school. The exercising of authority—regarded as humane and fair when the teacher knows the student and parents well—comes to be regarded as inhumane and unfair when it is impersonally administered by a school staff member (teacher or otherwise) who hardly knows the student and seldom sees the parents. Thus there arises in such large, impersonal settings an additional demand for sharply defined limits on authority.

This combination of factors gives public schools less power to exercise the responsibility for and authority over students that are necessary to the school's functioning. The result is a breakdown of discipline in the public schools and, in the extreme, a feeling by some parents that their children are not safe in school. Again, a large portion of the change stems from the lack of consensus that once characterized the parental community about the kind and amount of authority over their children they wished to delegate to the school—a lack of consensus exploited by some students eager to escape authority and responded to by the courts in limiting the school's authority. And, once again, this raises questions about what form of reorganization of American education would restore the functioning of the school and even whether it is possible to reinstate the implicit contract between parent and school that initially allowed the school to act *in loco parentis.*

The violation of these four basic assumptions of American education—the common school, local control, local financing, and *in loco parentis*—together with our failure to establish a new set of attainable ideals, has hurt both the quality and the equality of American education. For this change in society, without a corresponding change in the ideals that shape its educational policies, reduces the capability of its schools to achieve quality and equality, which even in the best of circumstances are uncomfortable bedfellows.

Next I shall give some indications of how the pursuit of each of these goals of quality and equality is impeded by policies guided by the four assumptions I have examined, beginning first with the goal of equality.

The organization of U.S. education is assignment to school by residence, guided by the common-school, local-control, and local-financing assumptions, despite those elements that violate these assumptions. In a few locations, school assignment is relieved by student choice of school or by school choice of student. But, in general, the principle observed in American education (thus making it different from the educational systems of many countries) has been that of a rigid assignment by residence, a practice that upholds the common-school myth and the local-control and local-financing myths.

It is commonly assumed that the restriction of choice through rigid assignment by residence is of relative benefit to those least well off, from whom those better off would escape if choice were available. But matters are not always as they seem. Assignment by residence leaves two avenues open to parents: to move their residence, choosing a school by choice of residence; or to choose to attend a private school. But those avenues are open only to those who are sufficiently affluent to choose a school by choosing residence or to choose a private school. The latter choice may be partially subsidized by a religious community operating the school, or, in rare cases, by scholarships. But these partial exceptions do not hide the central point: that the organization of education through rigid assignment by residence hurts most those without money (and those whose choice is constrained by race or ethnicity), and this increases the inequality of educational opportunity. The reason, of course, is that because of principles of individual liberty, we are unwilling to close the two avenues of choice: moving residence and choosing a private school. And although economic and technological constraints once kept all but a few from exercising these options, that is no longer true. The constraints are of declining importance; the option of residential change to satisfy educational choice (the less expensive of the two options) is exercised by larger numbers of families. And in that exercise of choice, different economic levels are sorted into different schools by the economic level of the community they can afford.

We must conclude that the restrictions on educational choice in the public sector and the presence of tuition costs in the private sector are restrictions that operate to the relative disadvantage of the least well off. Only when these restrictions were reinforced by the economic and technological constraints that once existed could they be regarded as effective in helping to achieve a "common school." At present, and increasingly in the future, they are working to the disadvantage of the least well off, increasing even more the inequality of educational opportunities.

One of the results of our recent study of public and private schools suggests these processes at work. Among Catholic schools, achievement of students from less-advantaged backgrounds—blacks, Hispanics, and those whose parents are poorly educated—is closer to that of students from advantaged backgrounds than is true for the public sector. Family background makes much less difference for achievement in Catholic schools than in public schools. This greater homogeneity of achievement in the Catholic sector (as well as the lesser racial and ethnic segregation of the Catholic sector) suggests that the ideal of the common school is more nearly met in the Catholic schools than in the public schools. This may be because a religious community continues to constitute a functional community to a greater extent than does a residential area, and in such a functional community there will be less stratification by family background, both within a school and between schools.

At the same time, the organization of American education is harmful to quality of education. The absence of consensus, in a community defined by residence, about what kind and amount of authority should be exercised by the school removes the chief means by which the school has brought about achievement among its students. Once there was such consensus, because residential areas once *were* communities that maintained a set of norms reflected in the schools' and the parents' beliefs about what was appropriate for children. The norms varied in different communities, but they were consistent within each community. That is no longer true at the high school level, for the reasons I have described. The result is what some have called a crisis of authority.

In our study of high school sophomores and seniors in both public and private schools, we found not only higher achievement in the Catholic and other private schools for students from comparable backgrounds than in the public schools, but also major differences between the functioning of the public schools and the schools of the private sector. The principal differences were in the greater academic demands made and the greater disciplinary standards maintained in private schools, even when schools with students from comparable backgrounds were compared. This suggests that achievement increases as the demands, both academic and disciplinary, are greater. The suggestion is confirmed by two comparisons: Among the public schools, those that have academic demands and disciplinary standards at the same level as the average private school have achievement at the level of that in the private sector (all comparisons, of course, involving students from comparable backgrounds). And, among the private schools, those with academic demands and disciplinary standards at the level of the average public school showed achievement levels similar to those of the average public school.

The evidence from these data—and from other recent studies—is that *stronger academic demands and disciplinary standards produce better achievement.* Yet the public schools are in a poor position to establish and maintain these demands. The loss of authority of the local school board, superintendent, and principal to federal policy and court rulings, the rise of student rights (which has an impact both in shaping a "student-defined" curriculum and in impeding discipline), and, perhaps most fundamental, the breakdown in consensus among parents about the high schools' authority over and responsibility for their children—all of these factors put the average public school in an untenable position to bring about achievement.

Many public high schools have adjusted to these changes by reducing their academic demands (through reduction of standards, elimination of competition, grade inflation, and a proliferation of undemanding courses) and by slackening their disciplinary standards (making "truancy" a word of the past and ignoring cutting of classes and the use of drugs or alcohol).

These accommodations may be necessary, or at least they may facilitate keeping the peace, in some schools. But the peace they bring is bought at the price of lower achievement, that is, a reduced quality of education.

One may ask whether such accommodations are inevitable or whether a different organization of education might make them unnecessary. It is to this final question that I now turn.

Abandoning Old Assumptions

The old assumptions that have governed American education all lead to a policy of assignment of students to school by place of residence and to a standard conception of a school. Yet a variety of recent developments, both within the public sector and outside it, suggest that attainment of the twin goals of quality and equality may be incompatible with this. One development is the establishment, first outside the public sector and then in a few places within it as well, of elementary schools governed by different philosophies of education and chosen by parents who subscribe to those philosophies. Montessori schools at the early levels, open education, and basic education are examples. In some communities, this principle of parental choice has been used to maintain more stable racial integration than occurs in schools with fixed pupil assignment and a standard educational philosophy. At the secondary level, magnet schools, with specialized curricula or intensive programs in a given area (e.g., music or performing arts), have been introduced, similarly drawing a clientele who have some consensus on which a demanding and effective program can be built. Alternative schools have flourished, with both students and staff who accept the earlier autonomy to which I have referred. This is not to say, of course, that all magnet schools and all alternative schools are successful, for many are not. But if they were products of a well-conceived pluralistic conception of modes of secondary education, with some policy guidelines for viability, success would be easier to achieve.

Outside the public sector, the growth of church-operated schools is probably the most prominent development, reflecting a different desire by parents for a nonstandard education. But apart from the religious schools, there is an increasingly wide range of educational philosophies, from the traditional preparatory school to the free school and the parent-run cooperative school.

I believe that these developments suggest an abandonment of the principle of assignment by residence and an expansion of the modes of education supported by public funds. Whether this expansion goes so far as to include all or part of what is now the private sector or is instead a reorganization of the public sector alone is an open question. The old proscriptions against public support of religious education should not be allowed to stand in the way of a serious examination of this question. But the elements of successful reorganization remain, whether it stays within the public sector or encompasses the private: a pluralistic conception of education, based on "communities" defined by interests, values, and educational preferences rather than residence; a commitment of parent and student that can provide the school a lever for extracting from students their best efforts; and the educational choice for all that is now available only to those with money.

Others may not agree with this mode of organizing education. But it is clear that the goals of education in a liberal democracy may not be furthered, and may in fact be impeded, by blind adherence to the ideals and assumptions that once served U.S. education—some of which may be unattainable in modern America—and by the mode of school organization that these ideals and assumptions brought into being. There may be extensive debate over what set of ideals is both desirable and attainable and over what mode of organization can best attain these ideals, but it is a debate that should begin immediately. Within the public sector, the once-standard curriculum is beginning to take a variety of forms, some of which reflect the search for a new mode of organizing schooling. And an increasing (though still small) fraction of youngsters are in private schools, some of which exemplify alternative modes of organizing schooling. These developments can be starting points toward the creation of an educational philosophy to guide the reorganization of American schooling in ways fruitful for the youth who experience it.

Notes

1. The other two authors are Thomas Hoffer and Sally Kilgore. A first draft of "Public and Private Schools" was completed on 2 September 1980. A revised draft was released by the National Center for Education Statistics (NCES) on 7 April 1981. A final draft is being submitted to NCES this fall. A revised version of the April 7 draft, together with an epilogue and prologue examining certain broader issues, is being published this fall by Basic Books as *Achievement in High School: Public and Private Schools Compared*.

2. It has nevertheless been true that in many religiously homogeneous communities, ordinarily Protestant, religious influence did infiltrate the schools. Only since the Supreme Court's ban on prayer in the schools has even nonsectarian religious influence been abolished.

3. The legal rationale for these decisions has been past discriminatory practices by school systems; but, in fact, the remedies have constituted attempts to overcome the effects of residential choice.

17

Predicting the Consequences of Policy Changes
The Case of Public and Private Schools

Segregation and Private Schooling

A major policy issue in American education over a long period of time has been the role of private schooling. In the United States, as in most countries, private schools existed before public schools. However, the early development of public schools, together with the use of the public school as a melting pot for the diverse cultures of immigrants, has led to a particularly strong "common school" tradition in the United States. Today, only about 10% of American children attend schools other than those of the single public school system. Unlike some countries, including Israel, religious education and schools operated by religious groups are wholly outside the public system, and unsubsidized by the state.

In the private sector, by far the largest number of schools are those sponsored by religious bodies, and of those, the largest number are Catholic, with about two-thirds of the total private school enrollment. Baptist schools are next in size, but with only about one-twentieth of the Catholic enrollment, and then Jewish schools, with about half the enrollment of the Baptist schools. However, from every religious group, including Catholic, a much larger number of children attend the public schools than attend private schools.

The 90:10 balance between public and private schools has not changed radically over the years. However, two developments have acted in recent years to affect the balance. First, the cost of education, including private education, has risen faster than the cost of living, leading to a slow decline in the proportion of students in private schools. The rise in cost has been especially great in Catholic schools, where the inexpensive services of nuns

Reprinted with permission from James S. Coleman, *Evaluating the Welfare State: Social and Political Perspectives* (San Diego, Calif.: Academic Press, 1983), pp. 273–293. Copyright © 1983 by Academic Press, Inc.

and priests as teachers have been largely replaced by the more expensive services of lay teachers. This has led to a near-crisis in Catholic education, with the closing of many schools.

The second factor affecting the balance between public and private education has acted in the other direction. The level of dissatisfaction of parents and students with public schools has grown in recent years. This has been due to a number of factors, most prominent of which has been a general sense of lack of order, discipline, and attention to fundamentals in education, generating a "back to the basics" movement in education, as well as a shift by some parents to private schooling for their children. In addition, several recent policies in education, most at the federal level, and most prominently desegregation actions which have radically affected the organization of schools, have led to a flight from the public schools into private schools. School desegregation has led to so-called white flight which is mostly to suburban public schools, but in some part to private schools. However, there has been "black flight" as well, with black parents using the private schools to insulate their children from the general disorder and disarray of some ghetto public schools.

These two factors, one leading to lesser and the other to greater private school enrollment, have resulted in three things: first, a slight increase in the proportion of students in private schools, despite the increasing costs; second, pressures, primarily by government agencies, to send children who have fled desegregation back to public schools, and third, pressures, primarily from parents who are using or want to use private schools, for some kind of government aid or subsidy to private education. These last two pressures are in direct opposition to each other, an opposition that showed itself most strongly in an enormous public response to a recent proposed ruling from the Internal Revenue Service that would require private schools to maintain a degree of racial balance in order to continue their tax status.

The arguments of opposing government barriers to private schooling have been primarily those of individual liberty to raise children without direct state intervention, supplemented by the argument that religious freedom implies an alternative to state secular education. The further argument that private education should be facilitated by some sort of state subsidy is based primarily on the issue of double taxation. That is, parents of children in private schools argue that they pay twice for education—once through taxes to provide free public education, and once through tuition for their own children's schooling. This argument is particularly strong for religious schools: If the state supports only nonreligious education, this discriminates, it is argued, against those parents who want to raise their children in a religious setting.

At different times, different issues have been central to the arguments against facilitating private schooling or for barriers to private schooling. The earliest issue was that of economic or social class segregation, with the rich seen as separating themselves from others through the use of private schools. Then was added the issue of religious segregation, with Catholic schools seen as a dividing influence, separating Catholics and non-Catholics in America. Further, any governmental encouragement, facilitation, or support of religious schools would go directly against the constitutional requirement of separation of church and state. Finally, the private schools have more recently been seen as a haven for whites fleeing desegregation, and thus making school integration more difficult to achieve.

The arguments opposing governmental barriers to private schools should, if all else were constant, be controlling, for they are based on widely held and constitutionally protected values of individual freedom. But if the charges that private schooling promotes segregation are true, then all else is not constant, since that violates other widely held or constitutionally protected values. It is here that social policy research can be of aid, because the amount of truth in these charges is at base a factual question. It is possible, by use of research data, to see just what the economic, religious, and racial differences are between the public schools and the private schools, and to see what the degree of segregation is within each of these sectors on each of these dimensions. Using such information, it is possible to go a step further—by making certain assumptions—to see how this degree of economic, religious, and racial segregation in the United States would be different if the public schools were the sole educational sector, that is, if private schools did not exist. With a slightly different set of assumptions, it is possible to take an additional step, to ask how a specific policy change would be expected to affect the degree of segregation along these dimensions. The policy change most directly addressable with the data at hand is one that would increase family income by a given amount at each income level, thus increasing their ability to afford a private school for their children. A closely related, but more likely policy change would be the reduction of the cost of a private education by providing tax credits, tuition vouchers, or something similar.

These hypothetical situations, such as elimination of the private schools or reduction of the cost of private schools, are beyond description because implicitly they ask a question of cause and effect: What would be the effect of a certain kind of policy change? As with all questions of cause and effect, they can be answered only with uncertainty, because they are questions about not what *is*, but *what would be*. Despite this uncertainty, they may still provide those who are interested in policy better information than they would otherwise have about the potential effects of policy change.

The Current Status: Segregation Between
and Within Public and Private Sectors

The first evidence regarding the directly factual question is shown in Tables [1], [2], and [3]. In all three of these tables, the private school sector is broken into two groups: the Catholic schools which account for two-thirds of private school students, and the other private schools, including

TABLE [1]
Percentage of Students from Various Backgrounds in Public and Private Schools

Response to BB101 " ... the amount of money your family makes in a year."	Public	Catholic	Other private	U.S. total
$6,999 or less	7.7	2.4	2.9	7.2
$7,000–11,999	12.5	6.3	6.3	11.9
$12,000–15,999	17.2	12.8	11.5	16.7
$16,000–19,999	19.0	17.3	15.2	18.7
$20,000–24,999	18.0	20.7	16.3	18.1
$25,000–37,999	14.6	20.4	15.0	15.0
$38,000 or more	11.1	20.1	32.8	12.4
Total	100.1	100.0	100.0	100.0

TABLE [2]
Percentage of Catholics and Non-Catholics in Public, Private and Other Private Schools

	Public	Catholic	Other private	U.S. total
Catholic	31	91	17	34
Non-Catholic	69	9	83	66
Total	100	100	100	100

both schools affiliated with religious groups and those that are independent of any religious affiliation.[1]

Table [1], on the oldest question of private school economic segregation, shows that there is some economic difference between students in public schools and those in either Catholic or other private schools. The question is, just how great is this difference? Is it sufficiently great to be economically divisive, or not? The question is not easily answerable, but there is another step that could be carried out to get some idea about the degree of economic segregation between public and private schools. This is to compare the degree of economic segregation within the public school sector with that between the public sector and either of the private sectors, or between the public and the two private sectors taken together. However, such a comparison might be misleading. It would show a lower degree of economic segregation between any pair of sectors than between schools within any one of them; but since schools are relatively small units, whereas the sectors are very large, we would expect the heterogeneity within each sector to moderate the segregation between them. Nevertheless, it is worth noting that the between-sector economic segregation is much smaller than the between-school segregation within any sector, though this need not be true, as we shall see in the case of religious segregation.

In the case of the religious distribution of students in schools shown by Table [2], there is a sharp difference between the three sectors. Thus it

TABLE [3]

Percentage of Hispanics, Non-Hispanic Blacks, Non-Hispanic Whites in Public, Catholic, and Other Private Schools

	Public	Catholic	Other private	U S . total
Hispanic	7	7	5	7
Non-Hispanic black	14	6	3	13
Non-Hispanic white	78	87	92	80

appears that there is some basis for the argument that private schools tend to separate children of different religious groups into different schools. It is true, on the other hand, that 81% of all Catholic children in these years of school (sophomore and senior) are in public school, with only 17% in Catholic schools.

Thus, I think it is reasonable to say that as matters stand now, given the existing financial and ecological barriers to attendance of nonpublic schools, the private sector does not constitute a threat to social integration on religious grounds, and arguments to further restrict private schools on this basis are misplaced.[2]

At the same time, the religious difference between the sectors means that if the financial and ecological barriers were removed, we cannot say what fraction of parents of the 81% of Catholic children now in public schools would shift to Catholic schools nor what fraction of parents of the children from other religious groups now in the public sector would choose schools affiliated with their own religious group, rather than public schools or other private schools. There would almost certainly be an increase in religious segregation, for some parents of children now in the public schools would choose schools affiliated with their religious group. What is not known is just how many would do so. The large size of the state secular school system in Israel is clear indication that even without the financial barriers, many parents in Israel choose a secular education; and one can suppose this would also be so in the United States.

Altogether, then, the evidence undermines arguments for further restricting private schooling through federal policy on grounds of religious segregation. On the other hand, reducing the existing barriers is almost certain to increase religious segregation, but the data are silent on just how much it would do so.

Table [3] shows the distribution of students in each of the three sectors according to three racial and ethnic categories: students of Hispanic background (i.e., the Caribbean, Central and South America), non-Hispanic blacks, and non-Hispanic whites. Hispanics are very close to the same proportion in each sector, from a high of 7% in the public sector to a low of 5% in the other private sector. Blacks, however, are only about half as numerous in Catholic schools as in public schools, and only about half as numerous in other private schools as in Catholic schools. The non-Hispanic whites constitute the remainder in each sector, ranging from a low of 78% in the public sector to a high of 92% in the other private sector.

Again, as in the case of religious segregation, it is clear that for the country as a whole the private schools do not constitute a threat to the racial integration of schools, since a vast majority of whites attend public schools, as do most blacks. There are communities in which this is not so, particularly in some rural areas of the Deep South, where racial integration of schools led whites to set up private schools that are all white or nearly so, and where the public schools thereby became predominantly black. Existing federal policy requires such schools to be nondiscriminatory in order to maintain their tax exemption, and there are continuing arguments over whether additional federal policies can be introduced to aid racial integration without infringing on the individual freedom of parents to send their children to private schools.

Despite the contributions of private schools to racial segregation in certain localities, the small size of the private sector, together with the fact that it is not homogenously non-Hispanic white, undercuts arguments that federal (as opposed to local) policies to restrict private schools are warranted on the basis of their contribution to racial segregation. This does not negate the need for federal policies targeted to those localities in which the existence of private schools clearly does contribute to segregation, so long as it does not differentially restrict the civil liberties of parents who live in those localities.[3]

All this leaves aside, of course, the question of just what degree of racial segregation there is *within* the private sector, or the Catholic and other private sector conducted separately; for if such internal segregation were pronounced, it could constitute a means by which private schooling contributed to racial segregation in education. It is to that question that I now turn, examining also the analagous question for economic and for religious differences.

Internal Segregation in Public, Catholic, and Other Private Sectors

Until now, the examination has been confined to the differences in composition between sectors. But this is only part of the question of the possible segregating effect of private schools. The other part concerns the distribution of students with different economic, religious, racial, or ethnic backgrounds *within* each of these sectors. To compare sectors according to their internal segregation requires a measure of segregation: the measure I use is based on the proportion of whites (using the example of black-white segregation) in the average black's school, compared to the proportion in the sector as a whole.[4] The measure is 1.0 if there is complete segregation, and 0 if every school in the sector has the same proportions of the two

TABLE [4]
Economic, Religious, and Racial Ethnic Segregation Within the Public Sector, the Catholic Sector, and the Other Private Sector

	Public	Catholic	Other private	Total private
Segregation between children from families with incomes over $20,000 and those from families with incomes under $12,000	.20	.16	.16	.16
Segregation between Catholic and non-Catholic children	.21	.15	.27	.56
Segregation of Hispanics and non-Hispanic whites	.30	.25	.55	.35
Segregation of blacks and whites	.49	.32	.21	.34

groups in question. Values for this measure in each of the areas of potential segregation are given in Table [4]. Values are also calculated for the private sector considered as a whole, not separated into Catholic and other private schools.

Table [4] shows that the internal segregation of these sectors differs considerably among areas and among sectors. Economic segregation is least of all the areas. Religious segregation is low within each of the sectors considered separately, but when the private sector is considered as a whole, it has the highest value in the table. This suggests that if all children attended private schools chosen by them and their parents, these schools would show an especially high degree of religious segregation. Racial segregation is indicated as the greatest internal segregation in the public schools. Whether the private schools are considered as two sectors or one, the are considerably less internally segregated than the public schools. The same is not true for segregation between Hispanics and non-Hispanic whites; it is lowest in the Catholic schools, but higher in the other private schools.

Altogether, no overall statements can be made about the relative internal segregation of the private and public sectors. The private sector considered as a whole is very religiously segregated—far more than the public sector. On the other hand, the black-white segregation is by far highest in the public sector. A marginal expansion of the private sector would mean students were moving into: (a) slightly less economically segregated schools; (b) much greater religiously segregated schools; (c) slightly greater Hispanic-Anglo segregation; but (d) considerably lower racial segregation.

The Predicted Impact of a Policy Change Facilitating Private Schools

It is possible to go a step further. There has been much discussion of what the impact would be of making private education less burdensome financially. One proposal, nearly passed in Congress, was to provide tax credits of up to $500 for school tuition. Another widely discussed proposal is that of an educational voucher to allow all children to choose freely among private and public schools.[5]

Some have argued that such changes as this would differentially benefit the white upper middle class, who use private schools more. It would, in this view, extend still further the creaming process which leaves the poor and minorities in the public schools. Others argue that such measures would place private schooling in the reach of those who cannot now afford it, and thus differentially benefit minorities and those less well-off financially.

With these data, it is possible to predict which students would be recruited into private schools by a reduction in the financial burden (although it would be a less direct reduction than that in either of these policy proposals). In particular, we know for each income level the proportions of students from a given group (say Catholics, or blacks) in private schools. This tells us the income elasticity of private schooling for each of these groups. Thus one can predict what would be the recruitment into private schools from each group if there were a change which increased income by a fixed amount for all, or the defection from private schools if income were reduced by a fixed amount for all. I will ask the former question with respect to whites, blacks, and Hispanics: Suppose income were increased by $1000 for all, for example, by a tax rebate or by a general increase in the standard of living; would this mean that racial segregation between public and private schools would be increased, by increasing the flow of white children into the private schools? Or would it mean that racial segregation between these sectors would be decreased, by bringing more black and Hispanic children into the private schools?

This question can be answered by use of two items of information: the number of Hispanics, blacks, and non-Hispanic whites in the public school sector at each income level; and the increment in proportion in private schools per $1000 income increase of income level for each group. The latter is shown in Figure [1] for the Catholic schools, and Figure [2] for the other private schools.

Figure [1] shows that the increase in proportion of students attending Catholic schools with income increase (the slope of the curve) is greatest for Hispanics. It is greater for whites than for blacks at low income levels, but, somewhat surprisingly, greater for blacks than for whites at high income levels. Figure [2] shows that for all three racial and ethnic groups, the increment in proportion attending other private schools, is lower than for Catholic schools, except at the highest income levels for non-Hispanic whites. The curve is especially flat for blacks, except at the upper extreme of income.

Using the numbers of students from each of these three groups at each income level together with the information provided in Figures [1] and [2] gives the information in Table [5].

The results of this hypothetical experiment are rather interesting. First, only a very small proportion of public school students—less than .5% of any of the three groups—would shift. Second, and somewhat surprising,

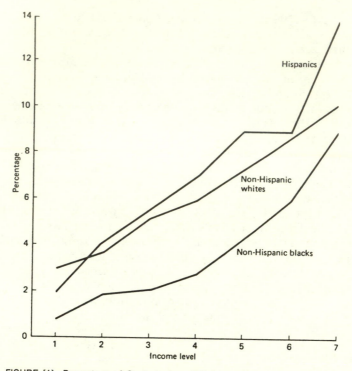

FIGURE [1] Percentage of Students from Differing Income Levels in Catholic Schools by Race and Ethnicity

the greatest shift would come among the Hispanics. Third, in both the private sectors, the racial and ethnic composition of those shifting (third column) includes more minorities than does the current composition of those schools. Fourth, among those shifting into the Catholic sector, there is a higher proportion of minorities (third column, .12 + .12 = .24) than in U.S. schools as a whole (fifth column, .13 + .07 = .20); but this is not true in the other private sector (.03 + .07 = .10).

Altogether, what can be said in response to the question I posed is that the racial segregation between the public and the private schools as a whole would be reduced by such a change, because the proportion of minorities among those coming into the private school is somewhat greater than the proportion already in these schools—and that this comes about primarily through the shifts of minorities (especially Hispanics and higher-income blacks) into the Catholic schools. Thus the common belief that policies encouraging attendance at private schools would increase segregation is not at all supported by these data, since the data indicate that for Catholic schools, which constitute two-thirds of the private sector, both blacks and Hispanics will respond to financial incentives to as great or greater a degree

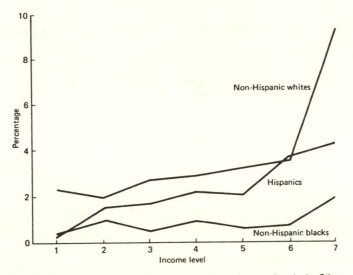

FIGURE [2] Percentage of Students from Differing Income Levels in Other Private Schools by Race and Ethnicity

as whites will, and that both parts of the private sector would come to have higher proportions of blacks and Hispanics than they now do.

It would be preferable to predict the results of a different policy, such as a tuition tax credit, say of $500. Such a credit would have the effect of reducing the tuition for private schools by $500 divided by the number of children the family has in school. To make such a prediction, information on price elasticity of private schooling for each of these groups, rather than income elasticity, would be necessary. By making some heroic assumptions, one might be able to use these data to estimate something about the effect of such a policy. However, I will not do so here, because the assumptions appear to be rather strong.

We now turn to the second policy issue directly related to private schools. This has to do with the maintenance of discipline and order, and its effects.

Discipline, Order, and Private Schooling

Many parents who withdraw their children from public schools to enroll them in private schools say they do so because of the greater degree of discipline and order in the private schools. This is most often stated with respect to Catholic schools, and it appears to be an especially common reason for the use of Catholic schools by black families in the ghetto.

Several questions related to policy arise. One is the descriptive fact: Are the Catholic and other private schools better disciplined and more orderly than the public schools? The second is a question of cause: If there is such a difference, what is it due to? What are the constraints under which public

TABLE [5]

Predicted Numbers of Students Shifting to Catholic and Other Private Schools with $1000 Increase in Family Income[a]

	Predicted number	Proportion of those in public school	Proportion of those shifting	Present composition sector	U.S.
To Catholic schools					
Non-Hispanic whites	8,221	.0025	.76	.87	.80
Non-Hispanic blacks	1,308	.0025	.12	.06	.13
Hispanics	1,281	.0035	.12	.07	.07
Total			1.00	1.00	1.00
To other private schools					
Non-Hispanic whites	5,595	.0017	.90	.92	.80
Non-Hispanic blacks	204	.0004	.03	.03	.13
Hispanics	401	.0011	.07	.05	.07
Total			1.00	1.00	1.00
Total					
Non-Hispanic whites	13,816	.0043	.81	.89	.80
Non-Hispanic blacks	1,512	.0029	.09	.05	.13
Hispanics	1,682	.0046	.10	.06	.07
Total			1.00	1.00	1.00

[a]Predicted numbers shifting to Catholic and other private schools were calculated as follows: $Nijp \times Sij$, where $Nijp$ is the number from racial or ethnic group i in income level j in public schools (sophomore and seniors combined) and Sij is, for racial or ethnic group i at income level i, the estimated change in proportion in Catholic or other private schools with increment of $1000 in income. Sij is calculated for each income level as follows (income in thousands of dollars).

level 1 (below 7)	$(P_2 - P_i)/5$
level 2 (7–12)	$\frac{1}{2}[(P_2 - P_1)/5 + (P_3 - P_2)/4.5]$
level 3 (12–16)	$\frac{1}{2}[(P_3 - P_2)/4.5 + (P_4 - P_3)/4.0]$
level 4 (16–20)	$\frac{1}{2}[(P_4 - P_3)/4 + (P_5 - P_4)/4.5]$
level 5 (20–25)	$\frac{1}{2}[(P_5 - P_4)/4.5 + (P_6 - P_5)/9]$
level 6 (28–38)	$\frac{1}{2}[(P_6 - P_5)/9 + (P_7 - P_6)/12]$
level 7 (above 38)	$(P_7 - P_6)/12$

The second column, proportion of those in public school, is obtained by taking the total number of sophomores and seniors in public school, subtracting out the number who did not report family income (and thus were not used in the above calculations), and dividing this into the predicted number shifting.

schools are operating, or what are the different value premises in public schools, that lead them to exercise less discipline than do private schools? The third is a question of effect: If there is greater discipline in private schools, does this affect, positively or negatively, learning?

The first question of fact can be addressed directly with the social policy research data at hand. In principle, the second question can also be answered by research data, and is important to address because it may point to some of the sources of malaise affecting the public schools. But it cannot be addressed from data at hand, and would require specially designed research.[6]

TABLE [6]
Five Measures of Disciplinary Standards and Demands, and of Teacher Interest, in Public, Catholic, and Other Private Schools[a]

	Proportion responding as indicated		
	Public	Catholic	Other private
Rules about student dress			
Sophomore report	.42	.97	.69
Administrator report	.51	1.00	.70
Students held responsible for property damage school			
Sophomore report	.64	.77	.71
Administrator report	.96	.90	1.00
Effectiveness of discipline "excellent" or "good"			
Students	.42	.74	.62
Fairness of discipline "excellent" or "good"			
Students	.38	.50	.49
Teachers interest in students "excellent"			
Students	.11	.25	.38

[a] Student report for the last three items are averages of sophomore and senior reports. Reports by students at the two grade levels are quite consistent.

The third question can be addressed with these survey data, subject always to the uncertainties about answering any question of cause and effect.

The Current Status: Discipline and Order in Public and Private Schools

The question of whether there is greater discipline and order in private schools than in public schools can be divided in two: (*a*) Are there different disciplinary standards and demands in the private sector?; (*b*) Are there differences in student behavior in the public and private sectors? The demands and the behavior are, of course, interdependent. But it is useful to examine them separately. Table [6] shows several measures of disciplinary standards, demands by the school, and teacher orientation to students. Some of the information is from reports by the schools, and some is from reports by students.

Table [6] shows some sharp differences, and some similarities, between the educational sectors. According to either sophomore reports or administrator reports, only about half as many (or less) public school students as those in Catholic schools are subject to rules about student dress; virtually all Catholic schools have such rules. The other private schools are about halfway between the public and Catholic schools. As for rules about accountability for property damage, administrators everywhere uniformly report that students are held accountable; but between 23% (in the Catholic sector) and 34% (in the public sector) of sophomores report otherwise. Presumably in some schools such accountability exists in name but is not practiced. Public and private sectors do not differ greatly here.

However, when students are asked how effective the discipline is, those in public schools are much less likely to report that it is excellent or good; again, as in dress rules, the other private schools are between the Catholic and public schools, though closer to the former. In fairness of discipline as reported by students, the Catholic and other private schools are alike, and better than the public schools. This is somewhat paradoxical, for the public schools are under a number of legal and administrative constraints imposed by state and federal government beyond those imposed on the private sector, to ensure fairness of discipline; yet they are regarded by their students as being less fair than the private sector schools.

Perhaps the most striking difference is in the students' belief about their teachers' interest in them: Fewer than half as many in public schools report teachers' interest as excellent, compared to students in Catholic schools, and fewer than a third as many, compared to those in other private schools.

There are, then, some rather clear differences in disciplinary standards and in teachers' relations to students in the public and private sectors, even though these measures provide only imperfect indicators of those differences. The Catholic schools have, as is popularly believed, the strongest discipline, and the other private schools appear to have teachers who show the greatest interest in students. (This last may be due to size differences: the average public high school in the United States has 758 children, the average Catholic school has 454, and the average other private school has 103.)[7] According to student reports, the public schools have the weakest and the least fair discipline, and the weakest relation between students and teachers. It is probably also true that, as in the examination of segregative tendencies of private schooling, local comparisons would show greater public-private differences than those found here, for most Catholic schools, and many if not most other private schools, are located in urban areas, where problems of discipline in the public schools are greatest.

There are some measures of student behavior that can help answer the second half of the first discipline question (that is, do the students in private schools behave better than those in public schools?) by showing how student behavior differs in the different sectors. Again, these are imperfect measures, for they address only a few selected aspects of student behavior. The results for three sectors are shown in Table [7].

Table [7] shows three different sources of information about student behavior: students' reports about themselves, reports by school administrators, and (sophomore) student reports about the behavior of the student body. By all three sources, there are considerable differences between the public schools and the two private sectors. The largest differences are in the administrators' accounts and the sophomores' reports about the student body. Again, this is possibly due to size differences, since the occurrence of some individual behavior problem, all other things constant, is twice as

TABLE [7]

Selected Measures of Student Behavior Related to Disciplinary Standards and Demands, in Public, Catholic, and Other Private Schools

	Public	Catholic	Other private
Students' reports of own behavior			
Average number of hours per week spent on homework	3.7	5.3	5.9
	Percentage giving indicated response		
Never absent except when ill	26	41	34
Never cut classes	58	82	65
Never late to school	39	45	32
Administrators' reports			
Absenteeism is "serious or moderate problem".	57	15	14
Cutting classes is "serious or moderate problem"	37	5	0
Drug or alcohol use "serious or moderate problem"	49	26	18
Vandalism of school property "serious or moderate problem"	25	14	12
Sophomore reports on student body			
"Students often don't attend school"	46	8	16
"Students often cut classes"	62	16	26
"Students often talk back to teachers"	43	23	22
"Students often get in fights"	27	9	6
"Students don't obey teachers"	30	15	13

likely in a school that is twice as large. But taken all together, the data are consistent and striking: Both the Catholic and other private sectors have far fewer behavior problems than do the public schools. The evidence is that a disciplined and ordered classroom is much more likely in these schools than in the public schools.

These differences make especially important the investigation of the second question posed earlier, which I indicated could not be addressed here: Which of the additional constraints imposed on public schools or which of the value differences among public school staffs, are most responsible for the differences in discipline?

It is clear from the data examined already that the answer to the first question is strongly affirmative: The Catholic and other private schools are better disciplined and more orderly than the public schools. The disciplinary standards and demands imposed are stronger, and the students behave better; and, as suggested earlier, the differences would probably be even more striking if they were examined within local areas, since most Catholic schools and many other private schools are located in urban areas, where disciplinary standards have characteristically been hard to maintain in recent years.

But this leaves open the answer to the third question, that is, Just what difference does it make? If it makes no difference in school outcomes, then little importance can be attached to variations in discipline and order; but if it does make a difference then variations between public and private sectors are important. There have been several recent studies, mostly qualitative, which suggest that structure, discipline, and order in schools has a positive effect on achievement. It is to this question that I now turn.

The Predicted Impact of Changing the Levels of Discipline in the Schools

Throughout this section, I have raised the question of what factors are responsible for the discipline differences that are found in the public and private schools. Although I have not been able to answer that question, it is possible to raise a complementary question: Suppose the public schools were able to achieve the levels of discipline and order that exist in the Catholic or other private schools. What differences would it make for the basic skills achievement of their students? Thus, as in the first half of the chapter, we can ask what is the predicted impact of a policy change. We do not know what specific policies would be affected studying the question, but we do know that there are such policies—for there are schools in the public sector that have as high, or even higher levels of discipline and order as the average Catholic school or other private school. It is exactly this fact which provides the tool for predicting what impact those policies would have.

Achievement scores in vocabulary, and mathematics were obtained for each student on subtests which were identical for sophomores and seniors. Thus it is possible to estimate a least squares regression equation, using public school students only, in which measures of the students' behavior are taken as the predictors. In estimating such an equation, background characteristics of the student are included, so that effects of differences in background do not masquerade as effects of differences in behavior (since it is only the behavior, not the backgrounds, that can be controlled by school policy). The regression coefficients for the behavior measures give an estimate of the effect of each on achievement. Then multiplying these coefficients by the differences in mean behavior levels between Catholic and public schools—or other private and public schools—will give the predicted gain in achievement that would occur by maintaining student behavior in these three areas at the level of that in the Catholic or other private schools. Table [8] shows the results of this analysis.

Table [8] shows modest but not inconsequential gains by reducing absenteeism, lateness, and cutting classes to the level of that in Catholic schools, and small gains by reducing it to the level of that in other private schools. Comparing the gains to the sophomore-senior differences in achievement shows that the gains by a change to the Catholic level are about .2 of a grade level in vocabulary, and .5 of a grade level in mathematics. The predicted gains by a change to the other private level are much smaller, about 8% in vocabulary, 12% in mathematics.

TABLE [8]
Predicted Achievement Gains in Public Schools if Individual's Absenteeism, Lateness and Cutting Classes Were Same as that in Private Schools[a]

| | Total items | Public school means | | Predicted gain from reducing absenteeism, lateness, cutting classes to the level of | |
		Sophomore	Senior	Catholic	Other private
Vocabulary	8	3.7	4.5	.06	.03
Mathematics	18	9.4	10.6	.28	.07

[a] Regression equation includes student's absenteeism, lateness, cutting classes, and also father's education, mother's education, race, if Hispanic, family income, and grade level. Predicted gain is determined as the sum of products of regression coefficients of each of the three behavior measures multiplied by the difference in means between Catholic and public or other private and public schools. r^2 in the two equations is .191, .201.

TABLE [9]
Predicted Achievement Gains in Public Schools if Discipline and Order Were Same as That in Private Schools, Holding Constant Student's Own Absenteeism, Cutting Classes, and Lateness[a]

| | Total items | Public school means | | Predicted gain from maintaining discipline at the level of | |
		Sophomore	Senior	Catholic	Other private
Vocabulary	8	3.7	4.5	−.01	.22
Mathematics	18	9.4	10.6	.30	.78

[a] Regression equation includes four school-level measures of discipline, and school-level measures of absenteeism and cutting classes. In addition, it includes individuals absenteeism, cutting classes, lateness, father's education, mother's education, race, Hispanic, family income, and grade level. Predicted gain is determined as the sum of products of regression coefficients for school level measures multiplied by difference in means between Catholic and public or other private and public schools. r^2 for the two equations is .203, .217.

But this considers only gains to the student from reducing his or her *own* level of absenteeism, lateness, and cutting classes. There are also possible gains due to a reduction in the general level of disorder in the school.

The second, environmental, component of the impact of discipline on achievement may be assessed by adding to the above equation school level measures. Controlling on the student's own behavior and background it is possible to predict the impact on achievement if the level of discipline in the schools were maintained at the level of that in Catholic or other private schools. The results of these calculations are shown in Table [9].

These predictions show, except for vocabulary at the Catholic discipline level, an even stronger effect than the effect of reducing the student's own absenteeism, lateness, and cutting classes, and in general a greater effect by moving to the private school level of discipline than that of the Catholic schools. (This is because the estimated effect of these areas of behavior in which the other private schools are better than the Catholic schools is

TABLE [10]
Predicted Total Gains in Grade Levels of Achievement in
Public Schools by Maintaining Same Discipline Levels as
in Private Schools

	Grade level gains	
	Catholic	Other private
Vocabulary	.13	.65
Mathematics	.95	1.39

especially great.) The environmental gains predicted by moving to the Catholic levels of discipline are no gain in grade levels for vocabulary and .5 grade level for mathematics. By moving to the other private levels of discipline, the predicted gains are about .5 a grade level for vocabulary, and 1.3 grade level for mathematics.

These two components of the effect of a greater degree of discipline in the public schools are independent and can be added,[8] giving overall effects of maintaining the discipline which characterizes the average Catholic and other private school shown in Table [10].

These effects are substantial indeed, and give special force to the question that this research is not able to show what the factors are that prevent public schools as a whole from maintaining a higher level of discipline. The results indicate that if that discipline could be instituted (as it, of course, already is in some public schools) then students in public schools would stand to gain considerably in achievement of basic skills.

Conclusion

I have attempted in this chapter to show both substantive results relating to social policy affecting public and private schools in the United States and to indicate a general strategy in the use of policy research. The substantive conclusions have been stated earlier so I will just summarize the general strategy illustrated in the two analyses.

In a variety of ways, a research methodology for social policy research that is distinct from the research methods in social science disciplines has slowly begun to emerge. The analysis described in this chapter is an attempt to contribute to that methodology. Many aspects of the analysis use statistical research methods designed primarily to answer social scientific questions. At one point, however, in each of the analyses carried out here, a different kind of question was asked. The general character of the question was, What would be the predicted effect if a certain policy were instituted? This question requires taking an analysis one step beyond that demanded by a social scientific question, which ordinarily asks about causes. It requires first establishing a framework in which the causal relevance of the factors controlled by a proposed policy is established, and then examining the predicted change in one or more outcome variables when values of those factors are varied.

In the first analysis, this meant first establishing the causal relevance of income for private school enrollment for Hispanics, non-Hispanic blacks, and non-Hispanic whites. In the second, it meant establishing the causal relevance of the student's own behavior (absenteeism, lateness, cutting classes) and of the level of discipline in the school. Then, in the first case, the analysis involved changing income by $1000, to examine the effect on the racial composition of public and private schools. In the second case, it involved changing the level of discipline in the school, and the levels existing in the average Catholic and other private schools were used as convenience values at which to establish the new levels. This allowed predicting the change in basic skills achievement that would occur if such a policy change were brought about.

Before concluding, it is important to recognize the uncertainty that is present in any analysis involving causal inferences and predictions. Policy research of this sort cannot give conclusive answers to questions about the effects of particular policy changes. It can express its results in a form that is particularly relevant to policy—which is what I have attempted here— but, like predictions of policy effects based on other grounds, it constitutes only an aid to reduce the uncertainties that attend policy changes.

Notes

1. All data reported here are taken from a survey of high school sophomores and seniors in a random sample of 1015 high schools throughout the United States. The analyses reported are drawn from a larger report (Coleman, Hoffer, and Kilgore 1982).

2. It may be, of course, that there are communities in which most Catholics attend Catholic schools, and non-Catholics attend public schools. If there are such communities, then the existence of a private sector may contribute to religious divisiveness in the community. This cannot, however, be sufficiently widespread to justify further barriers to private schooling through federal policy.

3. A comparison is instructive here. The existence of public schools that are nearly all white in suburban districts of central cities with large proportions of blacks clearly contributes to the segregation of black and white school children. Yet, federal policy, including court rulings, has not imposed restrictions on those districts in the absence of a finding of intent to discriminate.

4. This measure is constructed as follows: If P is the proportion of whites in the sector as a whole, P_k is the proportion of whites in school k, and n_k is the number of black students in school k, then

$$s_{bw} = \frac{\sum_k n_k P_k}{\sum_k n_k}, \text{ and } r_{bw} = \frac{P - s_{bw}}{P},$$

where r_{bw} is the index used, and s_{bw} is the proportion of whites in the average black's school.

5. A Gallup poll taken in November 1980 asked a national sample about attitudes toward a voucher plan. Vouchers were favored by 47% and opposed by 42%, with 11% undecided. The support has increased from about 40% in the early 1970s. (*Cincinnati Enquirer,* December 19, 1980).

6. During the design period for this research, a representative of the American Federation of Teachers recognized the importance of such information, and suggested the inclusion of questions in the school questionnaire, such as "How many days in the past month has the principal been in court?" The question was designed to show the greater constraints on public school principals for due process in student expulsions, as well as other legal constraints. But such questions do not really provide the right information, for it may take only one or two such cases in a school district to change the levels of discipline imposed throughout the system.

7. These sizes are based on high school students only, in those schools with grades other than high school.

8. Strictly speaking, the two effects to be added should both be calculated from the second equation, which contains both the student's own behavior measures and those of the school as a whole. This however, would make only minor differences in the predictions.

References

Coleman, J., Hoffer, T., and Kilgore, S. *High school achievement.* New York: Basic Books, 1982.

Coleman, J.S., Kelly, S., and Moore, J. 1975. *Trends in school segregation, 1968–1973.* Washington: The Urban Institute.

Cincinnati Enquirer. December 19, 1980. Gallup report, pc-16.

18

Achievement Growth in Public and Catholic Schools

THOMAS HOFFER, ANDREW M. GREELEY, AND JAMES S. COLEMAN

Introduction

After the first data collection of the High School and Beyond (HSB) study of sophomores and seniors in American high schools in 1980, we reported the results of studies that compared the effects of public and private schools on achievement. Two of us (Coleman and Hoffer) examined the differential effects of Catholic schools, other private schools, and public schools on the student population as a whole (Coleman, Hoffer, and Kilgore [CHK], 1982b); and one (Greeley) focused upon the differential effects of Catholic and public schools on black and Hispanic students (Greeley, 1982).

These analyses not only examined somewhat different questions but also used somewhat different methods and measures. The conclusions, however, were consistent: Both analyses found that Catholic high schools are more effective than public high schools. The Greeley analysis found that the advantage of Catholic-school attendance is especially pronounced for black and Hispanic students. The CHK analysis found that the average effect of Catholic schools is about one grade level in mathematics, vocabulary, and reading comprehension. Consistent with the Greeley analysis, CHK also found that the Catholic-school effect is somewhat larger for minority and lower-SES students.

These results were strongly challenged. Apart from the spontaneous reaction of persons concerned with protecting the public schools, a number of social scientists came to the public schools' defense. Critiques of the CHK analysis can be found (together with replies by CHK to these critiques) in the *Harvard Educational Review* (November 1981) and in two issues of *Sociology of Education* (April/July 1982 and October 1983). These critiques

---

Reprinted with permission from *Sociology of Education*, vol. 58, no. 2 (April 1985): 74–97.

of the CHK analysis also implicitly (and in some cases explicitly) criticized the Greeley analysis, for the results of our two analyses were consistent, though carried out independently.

Data from a second time point, the spring of 1982, are now available, thus allowing us to examine changes among the 1980 sophomores over a two-year period. These data are especially interesting, because they include scores on achievement tests that were given to sophomores in 1980 and again to seniors in 1982, making it possible to examine achievement growth over the junior and senior years of high school.

The new data make possible an unusual event in social science: They allow us to test a set of quantitative inferences about institutions with data generated by those institutions after the initial inferences have been made. To what degree are the original inferences correct? To what degree are certain of the critics correct in arguing that there is little or no differential effect of Catholic and public schools on achievement?

In pursuing these questions jointly, we confront a serious problem: The Greeley analysis and the CHK analysis used somewhat different methods, treated the sample somewhat differently, and asked related but not identical questions. These variations in technique were useful in the cross-sectional analysis, because the consistency of the results across variations in method indicated some robustness of the inferences. However, for testing the inferences with longitudinal data, these variations can become problematic. Definitions and procedures necessitate some arbitrary decisions, ways of approaching a problem differ, and styles of reporting results and pursuing a sequence of findings differ. To resolve each of these differences by compromise would be to lose many of the virtues of the two approaches. Therefore, to compare the longitudinal and cross-sectional results of both analyses, it appears most sensible to carry forward both techniques.

The next section is a longitudinal extension of the Greeley (1982) analysis, and the section following that is a longitudinal extension of the CHK (1982b) analysis. There are two modifications: (1) Although the Greeley cross-sectional analysis used unweighted data, the longitudinal extension uses data weighted to represent the U.S. student population; and (2) although the CHK cross-sectional analysis compared both Catholic schools and other private schools to public schools, the longitudinal analysis is limited to Catholic schools because of the small size and heterogeneity of the sample of non-Catholic private schools.

The final section of the article examines the consistencies and inconsistencies between the two analytical sections and draws together the results from both approaches. It also examines studies by Alexander and Pallas (1985) and Willms (1985) and discusses the points of convergence and divergence between their results and those presented here.

1. Longitudinal Extension of the Greeley Analysis

In this section, we extend the analysis begun in Greeley (1982). The methodological skepticism of that study is retained: We assume the presence of a school effect only after we have attributed as many school-related differences as possible to differences in individual and family input and only when we can link the residual difference to actual school programs and policies. We therefore attribute to student-input variables, as opposed to school-effect variables, such influences on academic performance as the students' college plans, which might themselves be the result of their school experience.

The objections to our earlier reports can be summarized as follows:

1. Any apparent effects are merely the result of a higher learning curve for Catholic-school students, due to selection.
2. The effect of Catholic schools is confined to the most able students and to those from homes where there is strong motivation and support for academic achievement.
3. Catholic schools seem to have an effect because they eliminate their disciplinary problems by expelling them from the school.
4. The effect of Catholic schools is confined to the students whose parents have made repeated decisions to send them to Catholic schools.
5. The apparent effect of Catholic schools disappears when track assignment is controlled, because most Catholic-school students are assigned to an academic track.
6. The differences between Catholic- and public-school outcomes cannot be linked to specific institutional policies and programs.

The first objection is addressed in section 2, the extension of the CHK analysis. In that analysis, it is shown that when senior test scores are regressed upon sophomore test scores and background variables, two areas of achievement, science and civics, show *no* significant Catholic-school effect. The other five tests, however, show highly significant effects (see Tables 2.2 and 2.3). If the apparent Catholic-school effect were due to selection, it would be uniform over all areas of achievement. But as the tables show, it is not.

In this section, we will bring evidence to bear on objections 2 through 6. First we will determine the indices of the presence or absence of an effect.

In the 1982 HSB follow-up study, seniors were given the same achievement tests that they were given as sophomores in 1980. Thus, one can measure an individual student's improvement (or lack of improvement) on the same test two years later. In principle, three different findings regarding the Catholic-school advantage in test scores between the sophomore and senior years are possible:

a. The difference in test scores between Catholic- and public-school students may diminish. Perhaps the public schools work more effectively with their students once the problem students have dropped out.

TABLE 1.1
Average Sophomore and Senior Test Scores for Public- and Catholic-School Students

Test	Public			Catholic			Catholic Advantage (col. 6–col. 3)
	Sophomore 1	Senior 2	Difference 3	Sophomore 4	Senior 5	Difference 6	
Reading	6.97	8.21	1.24	8.67	10.34	1.67	0.43
Vocabulary	8.74	10.88	2.14	11.24	13.82	2.58	0.44
Math1	10.39	11.90	1.51	13.54	16.06	2.52	1.01
Math2	2.61	3.01	0.40	3.44	4.06	0.62	0.22
Writing	8.51	10.22	1.71	10.62	12.50	1.88	0.17
Total	37.22	44.22	7.00	47.51	56.78	9.27	2.27
Science	9.13	10.09	0.96	10.14	11.30	1.16	0.20
Civics	4.62	5.73	1.11	5.53	6.61	1.08	−0.03
Total	13.75	15.82	2.07	15.67	17.91	2.24	0.17

    b. The difference between Catholic- and public-school students may not change. In the sophomore year, Catholic-school students had almost seven more correct answers on the achievement test (a summary of reading, vocabulary, math, and writing test scores). A continuation of that difference, indicating no relative increase or decrease in the Catholic-school advantage, would suggest that there was no sector effect between the sophomore and senior years and that the difference measured in the sophomore year may have been an ability difference rather than a sector difference.

    c. The difference in test scores between Catholic- and public-school students may increase, indicating the presence of a sector effect beyond family and individual input influences.

To measure the *change* in school effects between the sophomore and senior years, we use the sophomore test score as a surrogate for ability, motivation, knowledge, industry, and other related variables. That part of the sophomore achievement difference that is due to prior school effects rather than to student input is taken as given.

Alexander, Pallas, and Cook (1981:619) discuss the use of endogenous measures of ability and find that they "behave much like pre-determined measures." While they prefer temporally prior ability measurement, they are willing to settle for cross-sectional ability measurements to investigate school-process effects. They take it for granted that temporally prior ability measurement is a highly effective technique for controlling input variables in order to measure a possible school-process effect.

To simplify the analysis in this section, we constructed a composite achievement variable by summing the scores from five of the tests.[1] Science and civics were excluded, because we found that the Catholic-school effect was confined to the other five tests (see Tables 2.2 and 2.3). As Table 1.1 shows, the third possibility discussed above—a relative increase in the Catholic-school advantage between the sophomore and senior years—is confirmed. The combined test score of the public-school students increased from 37.22 to 44.22, while the test score of the Catholic-school students

TABLE 1.2

Catholic-School Advantage in Test-Score Increase between the Sophomore and Senior Years, by Background Status

	Catholic Advantage	Sample Size	
		Public	Catholic
By SES			
Lower quartile	2.37	4,096	311
Middle quartile	1.68	7,736	992
Upper quartile	1.86	3,390	736
By minority status			
Minority	3.94	4,108	664
White	1.76	11,269	1,394
By sophomore test scores			
Lower quartile	2.65	3,410	215
Middle quartile	3.47	7,762	1,095
Upper quartile	1.16	4,205	748
By sophomore year suspension			
Was not suspended	2.04	13,316	1,820
Was suspended	2.97	1,302	162

increased from 47.51 to 56.78. Thus, between the sophomore and senior years, the Catholic-school advantage in vocabulary, reading, math, and writing increased from 10.29 correct answers to 12.56—an increase of 2.27 items. Note that this is not a repetition of the sophomore finding. For the purposes of this analysis, the sophomore standing is taken as the starting point. Thus, we find not a sustained Catholic-school advantage—the second of the three possibilities outlined above—but an increased Catholic-school advantage. This 2.27-item increase in the Catholic-school advantage over public school is the principal dependent variable for the rest of this analysis.

Objection 2: The effect of Catholic schools is confined to the most able students and to those from homes where there is strong motivation and support for academic achievement. The notion that it is only the advantaged or especially the advantaged who benefit from attending Catholic secondary schools is widespread. Even Catholic-school teachers and administrators frequently lament that they are not really helping the poor. But as Table 1.2 shows, they really are helping the poor. The evidence directly contradicts the conventional wisdom about the differential effectiveness of Catholic schools: It is the most disadvantaged Catholic-school students who are the most likely to profit from attending Catholic secondary schools—i.e., those from low socioeconomic backgrounds, members of the black or Hispanic communities, those with low sophomore test scores, and those who start off their high school careers with disciplinary problems.

Note that one of the results of this concentration of the sophomore-to-senior Catholic-school advantage among the disadvantaged is what CHK have called the common-school effect. The philosophy of American public education has always been that it is the role of the common or public school to produce greater social equality, to minimize the differences that exist among population groups. However, we found that the difference between minority and nonminority students in public schools was not only larger than it was in Catholic schools, it *grew* between the sophomore and senior years by 1.3 items for the five tests. In the Catholic schools it *declined* by 0.9 items for the five tests. Thus, it is the Catholic schools that are more likely to have a common-school effect.

Objection 3: Catholic schools seem to have an effect because they eliminate their disciplinary problems by expelling them from the school. This objection is often heard from public-school administrators, but it has also been made by academic critics of our earlier analyses, who sometimes regard it as self-evident. However, the evidence from the HSB data, although indirect, does not support this objection. Among students who reported that they had been suspended during their sophomore year, those in the Catholic sector were more likely to be in the same school as seniors than those in the public sector (63 percent to 56 percent). (Retention rates for students without disciplinary problems were 78 percent in the public schools and 87 percent in the Catholic schools.) Moreover, as Table 1.2 shows, Catholic-school students who had disciplinary problems as sophomores showed greater sophomore-to-senior advantage in test-score improvement over their public-school counterparts than those who did not have sophomore disciplinary problems. Thus, students who are disadvantaged by discipline problems, like students with other disadvantages, benefit even more from the last two years of a Catholic school than students who do not have discipline problems.

The Catholic school's ability to retain its disciplinary problems is not a private-school phenomenon. The other private schools in the HSB sample retained only 38 percent of their sophomore disciplinary problems (and 66 percent of their students without disciplinary problems).

Objection 4: The effect of Catholic school is confined to the students whose parents have made repeated decisions to send them to Catholic schools. It is possible to measure, at least in some fashion, parents' decisions to send a young person to Catholic school. One can determine how many years of Catholic education a student has had and hypothesize that each year's decision to pay the substantial extra cost of a Catholic-school education is some measure of parents' seriousness about educational outcome. Of course, such a determination excludes all effects of previous Catholic-school attendance on sophomore scores.

As Table 1.3 shows, there is a Catholic-school advantage in sophomore-to-senior gains for all students, regardless of minority status and previous Catholic schooling. There is a slightly lower estimated Catholic-school advantage for white students who had no Catholic elementary school, and there is a significantly lower advantage for minority students who had no Catholic elementary school; but for both groups, the Catholic-school advantage is present.

Objection 5: The effect of Catholic schools disappears when track assignment is controlled. Some of the critics of the previous NORC research have assumed

TABLE 1.3
Catholic-School Advantage in Test-Score Increase between
the Sophomore and Senior Years, by Minority Status and
Number of Years in Catholic Grammar School

	Catholic Advantage	Sample Size	
		Public	Catholic
White			
0	0.90	10,162	173
1–7	1.13	703	415
8	1.16	404	806
Minority			
0	2.53	3,805	117
1–7	4.79	243	262
8	4.02	60	285

that academic-track assignment is a surrogate measure of ability (see Peng and Fetters, 1981; Goldberger and Cain, 1982). They note that Catholic-school students are much more likely to be in the academic track than in general or vocational tracks and thus are likely to have higher ambitions and greater ability than public-school students. These critics argue that track assignment is independent of sector and that taking track assignment into account explains the differences between Catholic-school and public-school outcomes.

In fact, a control for track assignment does reduce the difference in achievement growth between Catholic- and public-school students by about half: The overall Catholic growth advantage of 2.3 is reduced to 1.1 among academic-track students and to 1.5 among nonacademic-track students. These figures indicate, however, that the Catholic-school advantage is *not* eliminated and that it is *not* confined to the academic track. Indeed, even though Catholic-school students in the nonacademic track are a much smaller part of the Catholic educational enterprise, they have a greater sophomore-to-senior advantage over their public-school counterparts than do the students in the academic track.

Equating the Catholic growth advantages that remain after controlling for track assignment with the extent of the Catholic effect is tantamount to assuming that track is determined prior to enrollment—i.e., that track has the same explanatory status as family background. It is certainly reasonable to hypothesize, however, that school sector influences track assignment independently of family background. Table 1.4 indicates that such a sector influence is in fact very substantial: Controlling for SES and sophomore achievement, we find that Catholic-school students, on the average, are 22 percent more likely to be assigned to an academic track (averaging all nine differences in Table 1.4). These results show that there is a strong effect of Catholic-school attendance on curriculum assignment.

Objection 6: The differences between Catholic- and public-school outcomes cannot be linked to specific institutional policies and programs. This objection

TABLE 1.4

Percent Assigned to Academic Track in Public and Catholic Schools, by Parents' SES and Sophomore Achievement (sample sizes in parentheses)

Type of School and Parents' SES[b]	Sophomore Achievement[a]		
	Low	Middle	High
Public			
Low	12	22	49
	(2,221)	(2,493)	(498)
Middle	15	29	62
	(1,925)	(5,136)	(2,358)
High	19	45	80
	(308)	(1,804)	(2,039)
Catholic			
Low	18	47	74
	(82)	(211)	(75)
Middle	36	59	80
	(146)	(651)	(353)
High	39	81	91
	(36)	(394)	(395)

[a] The measure of sophomore achievement is a standardized composite of the six achievement-test scores collapsed into the lower, the middle two, and the upper quartiles (HSB codebook variable BYTESTQ).
[b] The measure of parents' SES is the HSB codebook composite (FUSESQ) collapsed into the lower, the middle two, and the upper quartiles.

is based on the assumption that for comparable students, the demands of public and Catholic schools are the same or, if not the same, are unrelated to achievement. But as Table 1.5 shows, Catholic-school students are much more likely than public-school students to study five or more hours a week; and this propensity to study is true for both white and minority students in both the academic and the nonacademic tracks.

Moreover, Catholic-school students in both tracks are much more likely than public-school students to take advanced courses in mathematics, though not in science (see Table 1.5). The differences in mathematics are especially great among minotiry students in the nonacademic track: Minority Catholic-school students in a nonacademic track are nearly twice as likely to take second-year algebra and almost three times as likely to take geometry. This advantage, however, largely vanishes in science courses. The experience of being in a nonacademic track is obviously very different in Catholic and in public schools, especially for minority students. The payoff in Catholic-school attendance in mathematics is greater for minorities than for non-minorities, greater for those in the nonacademic track than for those in the academic track. In other words, the common-school effect is especially strong for the multiply disadvantaged.

TABLE 1.5
Percent of Students in Public and Catholic Schools Completing Homework and Advanced Coursework, by Track and Race-Ethnicity

| | Nonacademic Track | | | Academic Track | |
	White	Minority		White	Minority
Public					
Homework[a]	17	18		44	39
Advanced courses					
Algebra I	71	57		97	86
Algebra II	30	25		80	63
Geometry	38	25		88	66
Trigonometry	10	6		56	32
Physics	9	14		40	25
Chemistry	19	16		71	50
Sample size (average)	7,890	3,790		5,240	1,410
Catholic					
Homework[a]	31	24		51	54
Advanced courses					
Algebra I	94	76		98	96
Algebra II	57	45		83	80
Geometry	73	65		94	93
Trigonometry	25	15		63	53
Physics	11	11		35	26
Chemistry	30	21		69	60
Sample size (average)	405	212		1,065	503

[a] Five or more hours per week.

It is now possible to sort out the influences that might account for the apparent Catholic-school effect in the sophomore-to-senior test-score change. In general, there are three different sets of variables that could enter into the Catholic-school outcome: (1) measured background variables, to which we attribute family and student characteristics, which are independent of the school; (2) measured school variables; and (3) residual variables, which are unmeasured background or school variables. We use multiple-regression analysis, in which variables are entered into an equation in a specific causal order. By using this technique, we are able to account for portions of the Catholic-public difference in test-score gain, showing for each new variable the amount of explanation it adds to that provided by the prior variables. In the analysis, the measured background variables are used to account for whatever variance they can; then, the measured school variables are added to account for some part of the remaining variance. The remaining unexplained difference between Catholic and public schools in the sophomore-to-senior test-score change is attributed to the unmeasured residual variables. Note that in the logic of this approach, no effect that can be explained by a background variable is attributed to a school variable, and any effect that cannot be explained by either the school variables or the background variables is considered unexplained and is *not* regarded as a school effect.

Table 1.6 is a verbal specification of the model. It describes each variable in the regression equation and how that variable is measured. Eight different background variables are included in the model: (1) the sophomore test score, which is used to measure ability, motivation, knowledge, and previous education; (2) parents' education, occupation, and income, which is specified by a composite SES scale; (3) student's race; (4) student's Hispanic ethnicity;

TABLE 1.6
Theoretical Model to Explain Catholic-School Advantage in Test-Score Increase Between the Sophomore and Senior Years

---

A. Background variables
1. Ability, motivation, knowledge, and previous education (sophomore test score)
2. Parents' education, occupation, and income (SES scale)
3. Student's race (0–1)
4. Students' Hispanic ethnicity (0–1)
5. Parents' decisions to send student to Catholic school (number of years of Catholic grammar school student attended)
6. Parents' plans for student's further education (father's plans)
7. Parents' participation in school activities (Is parent a school volunteer?)
8. Student's college plans (Does student plan to attend a four-year college after graduation?)

B. School variables
1. Track assignment
2. Number of advanced courses student has taken (three variables: semesters of English courses taken between 10th and 12th grade; sum of [0–1] responses to whether advanced mathematics courses taken; and sum of [0–1] responses to whether advanced science courses taken [see Table 1.5 for list of advanced math and science courses])
3. Extent of discipline problems in the school (sum of responses to five variables measuring the extent of the following problems: students not attending school, cutting classes, talking back to teachers, not obeying instructions, and fighting with one another)
4. Amount of time spent on homework (hours per week)

C. Residual variables
Statistically significant unexplained variance that cannot be attributed to school or background as we are able to measure them

---

(5) parents' decisions to send the student to Catholic school, which is specified by the number of years of Catholic grammar school the student attended; (6) parents' plans for student's further education (specified by father's plans; if mother's plans are entered into the equation, there is no change in the variance explained); (7) parents' participation in school activities; and (8) the student's own college plans, specified by whether s/he plans to attend a four-year college after graduation.

Four different school variables are included in the model: (1) the student's track assignment; (2) the number of advanced courses the student has taken; (3) the extent of discipline problems in the school (based on the student's report); and (4) the number of hours the student spends on homework each week.

In Tables 1.7 and 1.8, we apply the model stated in Table 1.6 to the sophomore-to-senior test-score difference between Catholic- and public-school students to see what part of the Catholic-school advantage may be assigned successively to background, school, and residual components. Thus, the model in Table 1.7 represents eleven different regression equations. When sophomore-to-senior gain is regressed on Catholic-school enrollment, the Catholic-school advantage is 2.19 correct answers. When sophomore achievement is added to the equation to control for students' initial levels of achievement, the Catholic-school advantage increases to 2.67.[2] Then, when socioeconomic status, race, and Hispanic ethnicity are added, the difference diminishes to 2.17 correct answers. When the number of years in Catholic grammar school is added to this set, the difference diminishes to 1.57 correct answers, and so on.

In brief, of the 2.19-item Catholic-school advantage in test-score increase, approximately 50 percent (or one correct answer) can be explained by

TABLE 1.7
A Model to Explain Catholic-School Advantage in Test-Score
Increase Between the Sophomore and Senior Years

	Catholic Advantage
Catholic advantage in sophomore-to-senior gain	2.19
A. Net of sophomore achievement	2.67
+	
Socioeconomic status, race, ethnicity	2.17
+	
Years in Catholic school	1.57
+	
Father's college plans for respondent	1.39
+	
Parents' participation in school	1.33
+	
Respondent's own college plans	1.08
B. Track	0.41
+	
Advanced coursework	0.04
+	
Disciplinary climate	−0.42
+	
Time spent on homework	−0.49
Sample Sizes	
Public 15,377	
Catholic 2,058	

Catholic students' higher levels of individual and family background, and 1.08 remain unexplained. When track and advanced coursework are taken into account, the difference is diminished to 0.04; and when discipline and homework are added, the difference falls below zero. In other words, about one half of the sophomore-to-senior Catholic-school advantage can be explained by background; the other half is related to things that occur in the school, measured here by curriculum assignment policies, advanced coursework, homework, and discipline climate.

In Table 1.8, the same explanatory model is applied to minority students, to students who were in the lower two quartiles in sophomore test scores, and to low-SES students. For all these students except the minorities, the residual differences are statistically insignificant, and half or more of the explained Catholic advantage can be accounted for by the set of school-experience variables.

We have no explanation for the substantial unexplained advantage of minority students in Catholic schools ($b = 2.16$, $t = 2.4$), and further analysis of the issue is beyond the scope of this article. For now, it is sufficient to note that the much higher probability of academic-track assignment, the more rigorous coursework demands, and the greater number of hours spent on homework explain a large share (1.7 items) of the background-adjusted difference.

TABLE 1.8

Model to Explain Catholic-School Advantage in Test-Score Increase Between the Sophomore and Senior Years, by Minority Status, Sophomore Test Score, and Parents' SES

	Minority Respondents[a]	Low-Score Respondents[b]	Low-SES Respondents[b]
Catholic advantage in sophomore-to-senior gain	3.94	3.58	1.90
A. Net of sophomore achievement	4.82	3.91	2.43
+			
Socioeconomic status, race, ethnicity	4.26	3.01	2.27
+			
Years in Catholic school	4.42	2.48	1.75
+			
Father's college plans for respondent	4.32	2.24	1.48
+			
Parents' participation in school	4.31	2.18	1.47
+			
Respondent's own college plans	3.87	1.87	1.27
B. Track	2.90	0.91	0.64
+			
Advanced coursework	2.34	0.01	−0.02
+			
Disciplinary climate	2.26	−0.10	−0.36
+			
Time spent on homework	2.16	−0.25	−0.47
Sample sizes			
Public	4,108	7,181	8,043
Catholic	664	686	729

[a] Blacks and Hispanics.
[b] Lower two quartiles on HSB composite variables.

Critics argue that the amount of time spent on homework and the number of advanced courses taken are not school-effect variables. They contend that even after all the background variables specified in the model have been controlled, homework and advanced coursework are the result of the student's personality and unmeasured background variables, not school demands. But since homework and advanced coursework account for the sophomore-to-senior Catholic-school advantage net of all the prior background variables, we can at least presume that they are school-effect variables.

We can examine indirectly whether greater academic effort in the Catholic school can be attributed to the demands of the school or to the demands of the student's personality. If the difference in effort were due to personality differences, then we would expect the Catholic-public difference to be small when track and college plans are taken into account, especially because Catholic schools put into an academic track students who in public schools would be in a general or vocational track. Yet the differences remain, and the greatest difference between Catholic- and public-school students in the number of advanced courses taken is found precisely among those students who have the least motivation for taking such courses—namely, students in the nonacademic track (see Table 1.9). Moreover, the greatest difference between Catholic- and public-school students in the number of hours spent on homework is not among those in the academic track but among those in the nonacademic track. It seems reasonable to conclude from Table 1.9 that the differences between Catholic- and public-school students in these two variables, particularly in the amount of time spent on homework in

TABLE 1.9
Number of Advanced Courses Taken and Hours Spent on Homework, by Track and College Plans

	Nonacademic Track		Academic Track	
	Does Not Plan to Attend College	Plans to Attend College	Does Not Plan to Attend College	Plans to Attend College
Public				
Number of advanced courses taken	1.6	2.7	3.5	4.6
Hours spent on homework per week	2.9	4.0	4.6	6.1
Catholic				
Number of advanced courses taken	2.6	3.7	3.8	4.7
Hours spent on homework per week	3.7	5.4	5.1	6.8

TABLE 1.10
Recreational Patterns of Students in Public and Catholic Schools, and Correlations of Recreational Variables with Advanced Coursework Factor

	Public	Correlation with Advanced Coursework Factor	Catholic	Correlation with Advanced Coursework Factor
Percent watching T.V. three or more hours per day	36	−.16	31	−.15
Percent dating weekly	61	.07	60	.01
Percent talking to friends daily	76	−.07	83	−.08
Percent driving around daily	25	−.07	24	−.10

the nonacademic track, are the result not of differences in students' ambitions but of differences in the demands of public and Catholic schools.

This inference is strengthened when we examine out-of-school behavior. As Table 1.10 indicates, Catholic-school students do not seem to be any more serious outside school than their public-school counterparts, even when we do *not* take into account student's track assignment, background, and college plans. There are no important differences between the students in T.V. watching, dating, talking to friends, or driving around in automobiles. These results, taken together with those somewhat lower correlations of Table 1.9, suggest that Catholic-school students take more demanding courses not because they are more serious about school but because their schools require them to do so.

The results reported in Tables 1.7 through 1.10 strongly support the proposition that the test-score advantage of Catholic-school students arises from a specific school effect over and above any family or student-input effect, and that the school effect can be attributed to school policies and programs—i.e., placement of students into an academic track, demands for more homework, requirements for more advanced courses, and (less importantly) greater disciplinary stability.

2. Longitudinal Extension of the CHK Analysis

It is difficult to draw inferences about differential effects of different institutions on achievement using nonexperimental data, because selection into an institution is not random; it is determined by factors that may affect achievement. Thus, elimination of apparent institutional effects that are spurious—i.e., a result of selection—is the most important task. In our earlier analysis, we were forced to use family-background characteristics as statistical controls; but additional information is available in the 1982 data, and it is now possible to use the 1980 sophomore scores as statistical controls. Thus, we can examine growth in achievement in the public and private sectors over the two-year period. In such analyses, the student's sophomore score is a statistical control on the senior score; therefore, the hypothesis that differences (in either direction) are due to selection is more difficult to maintain.

The most straightforward inference is that differential change is due to differences in the two school environments to which students are exposed. This is expressed in equation (1), which gives predicted senior achievement as a function of sophomore achievement and school sector:

$$\hat{y}_2 = a + b_1 y_1 + b_2 x, \tag{1}$$

where $\hat{y}_2$ is predicted senior achievement score, y_1 is sophomore achievement score, x is school sector (0 = public, 1 = Catholic), b_1 is the effect of sophomore score on senior score, and b_2 is a preliminary measure of the effect of Catholic school on senior score. This same equation can be rewritten to show the predicted growth in achievement from sophomore to senior year:

$$\hat{y}_2 - y_1 = a + (b_1 - 1)y_1 + b_2 x. \tag{2}$$

Equation (2) makes clear that the effect of the Catholic school expressed by b_2 is an effect on *growth* in achievement over the two-year period. Table 2.1 reports the Catholic-school increments in growth for the six tests that were given to students in their sophomore and senior years. These increments are values of the coefficients b_2 in equation (1) or (2). The table shows estimates of substantial Catholic-school effects. Column 5 shows that on average, Catholic-school students gained 0.8 to 1.7 grade equivalents more than public-school students in the two-year period.

A better understanding of achievement growth for low- and high-achieving students can be obtained by examining the average senior achievement levels for students with given sophomore achievement levels. Figures 1 and 2 show the average senior scores on the vocabulary and mathematics tests for students classified according to their sophomore scores. For example, public-school students who got 12 vocabulary items correct as sophomores got an average of 13.8 correct as seniors; Catholic-school students who got 12 correct as sophomores got an average of 14.6 correct as seniors.

Figures 1 and 2 show that Catholic-school students at almost all levels of sophomore achievement outperformed public-school students when they were seniors. The sector differences in mathematics are about the same

TABLE 2.1
Estimates of Catholic-School Effect on Achievement Growth in Six Tests (standard errors[a] in parentheses)

	1	2	3	4	5
					Catholic Increment as Grade
		Average Number	Average		Equivalent
	Number	Correct in	Growth	Catholic	(col. 4)/
	of	Public School	in	Increment	[.5(col. 3)]
Test	Items	at Sophomore Level	Public School	in Growth	
Reading	19	9.3	1.00	0.66 (.121)	1.3
Vocabulary	21	11.0	1.75	0.72 (.119)	0.8
Mathematics	38	19.1	1.46	1.24 (.192)	1.7
Writing	17	10.5	1.31	0.64 (.114)	1.0
Science	20	11.2	0.79	0.37 (.109)	0.9
Civics	10	5.9	0.84	0.33 (.079)	0.8

NOTE: The test scores reported here and in the remaining tables of section 2 are the numbers of items correctly answered. As in section 1, all analyses use the sample weights (HSB codebook variable PNLTSTWT).
[a] Standard errors are adjusted for an assumed design effect of 1.5. This adjustment is carried out throughout section 2.

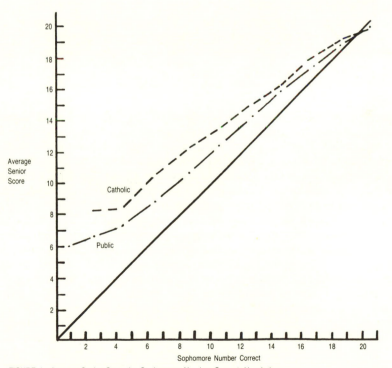

FIGURE 1 Average Senior Score by Sophomore Number Correct: Vocabulary

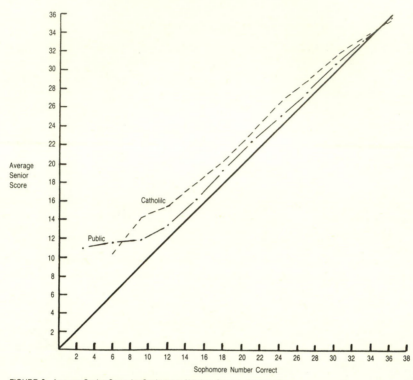

FIGURE 2   Average Senior Score by Sophomore Number Correct: Mathematics

magnitude as the sophomore-to-senior gain for public-school students (i.e., the vertical distance from the public line to the main diagonal), and about two-thirds that magnitude in vocabulary.

This analysis controls for initial achievement and thus controls for the effect of selection on achievement at grade 10; but it is possible that it does not also control for an effect of selection on *growth* in achievement. Put another way, public-school and Catholic-school students not only experienced different school environments over the two-year period, they also experienced different home environments. Two students who had different home environments over this period, like students who had different school environments, can be expected to show differential gains.

Consequently, we augment the analysis shown in equation (1), Table 2.1, and Figures 1 and 2 by incorporating family-background characteristics. Expressed as an extension of equation (2), the equation is

$$\hat{y}_2 - y_1 = a + (b_1 - 1)y_1 + b_2 x + b_3 z, \tag{3}$$

where z is a vector of family-background characteristics, and b_3 is a vector

TABLE 2.2
Estimates of Catholic-School Effect on Achievement Growth of Average Public-School Student in Six Tests, Controlling for Family Background (standard errors in parentheses)

Test	Average Number Correct in Public School at Sophomore Level	Average Growth in Public School	Catholic Increment in Growth	Catholic Increment as Grade Equivalent
Reading	9.3	1.00	.53 (.15)	1.1
Vocabulary	11.0	1.75	.70 (.14)	0.8
Mathematics	19.1	1.46	.78 (.24)	1.1
Writing	10.5	1.31	.73 (.13)	1.1
Science	11.2	0.79	.10 (.14)	0.3
Civics	5.9	0.84	.14 (.09)	0.3

NOTE: See note to Table 2.1.

of coefficients expressing the effect of family background on achievement growth over the two years.

In the base-year study, we found considerably greater family-background effects in public schools than in Catholic schools. Thus, in the analysis reported here, we have again allowed for the interaction of family background and school sector by regressing senior achievement on sophomore achievement and family background separately for public- and Catholic-school students.[3]

The present analysis includes five more measures of individual background than the base-year analysis. These additional measures are (1) region of the country, (2) respondent's sex, (3) whether or not the respondent had college plans in the 9th grade, (4) whether or not the respondent was handicapped (according to self-description), and (5) urban/rural residence. These measures of individual background are included in addition to the background variables used in the base-year analysis. The individual measures of income, parents' education, and household possessions we used in our base-year analysis are replaced here by a single SES composite variable, which also includes some additional variables that our base-year models excluded: father's occupational status and four additional household possessions. The composite, which is included in the public-use data sets, was constructed by standardizing each of the individual component variables and averaging the sum of the components. Ten measures of background, which we used in the base-year analysis, but which we did not include in the SES composite, are also used in the present analysis.[4]

Results of the analysis are presented in Table 2.2. This table shows that when family background is controlled, the Catholic increment is somewhat reduced (compare Table 2.1) but remains substantial for four of the six tests. For science and civics, the estimated increments are much smaller and not statistically significant. The lack of a substantial Catholic-school effect in science, which was also found in the earlier analysis of sophomore test data, provides an indirect confirmation of a Catholic-school effect in the other areas, operating through the greater academic demands placed on Catholic-school students. As we showed with the sophomore data (Coleman and Hoffer, 1983:226), Catholic-school students in both academic and general tracks take considerably more specialized mathematics courses (second-year

TABLE 2.3

Estimates of Catholic-School Effect on Achievement Growth of Average Catholic-School Student in Six Tests, Controlling for Family Background (standard errors in parentheses)

Test	Average Number Correct in Catholic School at Sophomore Level	Predicted Growth in Public School	Catholic Increment in Growth	Catholic-School Effect as Predicted Public-School Grade Equivalent
Reading	10.7	0.93	.42 (.10)	.9
Vocabulary	13.1	1.66	.44 (.09)	.5
Mathematics	22.1	1.72	.68 (.15)	.8
Writing	12.1	1.22	.35 (.08)	.6
Science	12.0	0.83	.10 (.09)	.2
Civics	6.6	0.73	.10 (.06)	.3

NOTE: See note to Table 2.1.

algebra, trigonometry, geometry, calculus) than public-school students, though this is not true for chemistry and physics.

The estimated Catholic-school increments shown in Table 2.2 are for students with initial achievement and family background comparable to that of the average public-school student. Because this analysis included inter-actions between sector and family background and between sector and initial achievement, the increments may differ for other students. Table 2.3 presents the estimated Catholic-school effect for students with initial achievement and background comparable to that of the average Catholic-school student. As the table shows, the increments for the average Catholic-school student are smaller, because this student is closer to the ceiling on the achievement tests (see Figures 1 and 2). Equivalently, the Catholic-school effects are more pronounced for students from lower socioeconomic backgrounds or with lower initial achievement than they are for students from higher socioeconomic backgrounds or with higher initial achievement. This phenomenon is analyzed in some detail below; for the present, it is sufficient to note that the general results shown in Tables 2.1 and 2.2 hold: There are strong positive Catholic-school effects in reading, vocabulary, mathematics, and writing (at least four standard error differences) and weak and statistically insignificant effects in science and civics.

Differential Effects of Background Between Sectors: The Common-School Effect

An important subsidiary issue to the assessment of overall sector effects is how the relationship of student background to achievement varies between sectors. In the base-year analysis, we found that socioeconomic background, race, and ethnicity tended to be more weakly related to achievement in the Catholic schools than in the public schools. This finding led us to conclude that the Catholic high schools more closely approximate the common-school ideal than do the public schools. Critics attacked this conclusion, arguing that low-SES and minority students in Catholic schools exceed their public-school counterparts in initial achievement more than high-SES and white students do.[5] For example, if only the most able lower-SES students enrolled

TABLE 2.4

Sector Differences in Estimated Effects of Background and Sophomore Achievement Variables on Senior Achievement (standard errors of differences in parentheses)

Test	Black	Hispanic	SES	Sophomore Achievement
Reading	−.57	−.38	.32	−.020
	(.47)	(.34)	(.15)	(.026)
Vocabulary	−.52	−.67	.22	.061
	(.44)	(.32)	(.15)	(.023)
Mathematics	−.25	−1.02	.03	0
	(.76)	(.56)	(.25)	(.024)
Writing	−.49	−.72	.12	.083
	(.28)	(.29)	(.13)	(.024)
Science	.16	−.14	−.07	.050
	(.43)	(.32)	(.14)	(.028)
Civics	−.29	−.04	.12	.032
	(.28)	(.20)	(.10)	(.031)

NOTE: Sector differences are obtained by subtracting the Catholic regression coefficients from the public coefficients. The regressions include the school-level means of the four individual-level variables shown in this table.

in Catholic school, then the apparent effect of SES would be lower in the Catholic sector. This assumption can now be tested. With test performance measured at two points in time, we can statistically control for sophomore achievement (i.e., initial achievement) when examining senior achievement.

The method used here to test for the presence of a common-school effect differs somewhat from that used in the original analysis. The present analysis constitutes a more stringent test: It examines the relative effects of race, ethnicity, and SES *within* school in the two sectors. Thus, differences in achievement growth due to enrollment in schools with different average SES, racial, or ethnic compositions are statistically controlled. Though the effects of these variables on between-school differences in growth represent an important issue (addressed at a later point in this article), the effect examined here is only the within-school component of the overall effect.

To estimate the within-school differentiating effects of race, ethnicity, and SES on achievement growth, senior achievement in each of the six areas is regressed on individual and school mean[6] measures of race and ethnicity, the codebook SES composite, and sophomore achievement, separately by sector. Table 2.4 presents the sector differences in the within-school regression coefficients for these variables. The table indicates that the effects of race, ethnicity, and SES are generally lower in the Catholic schools. The coefficients for race in the Catholic schools are much lower than those in the public schools, except in science. The average difference over all six tests is about one half of the average public-school coefficient. Hispanics are even more advantaged in the Catholic schools than blacks. The average difference over the six tests is over 60 percent of the average public-school coefficient. The effects of SES are also smaller, on average, in the Catholic schools, though the average difference is not as large and there is a reversal in science.

The existence of a common-school effect can be seen in another way as well: Just how much, in the two sectors, does senior achievement depend on sophomore achievement? The greater this dependence, the more a student whose achievement is low as a sophomore is "locked into" low performance. This may occur through tracking into different programs or through grouping into homogeneous sections, or it may occur because few demands are placed on low-performing students, and they are simply passed through the system. The fourth column of Table 2.4 shows the sector differences in the within-school regression coefficients for sophomore achievement-test scores. For four of the six dependent variables, the regression coefficients show that senior achievement is less dependent on sophomore achievement in the Catholic schools than in the public schools. In reading, the senior test score is more dependent on the sophomore score in the Catholic sector, and in mathematics the dependency is equally strong in both sectors.

However, a second question arises when we compare the dependence of senior achievement on sophomore achievement in each sector. Does the relative advantage of some portions of the student body occur at the expense of the other portions? That is, in this case, do the higher-achieving students in Catholic schools gain *less* than their counterparts in public schools?

The dependence of senior performance on sophomore performance can be seen graphically in Figures 1 and 2, which show average senior achievement as a function of number of items correct on the sophomore test. These graphs show that the greater sophomore-to-senior growth among Catholic-school students holds for students at all levels of sophomore achievement. (The other four tests, not presented in graphs, show the same result.) This suggests that the pronounced advantages of lower-achieving Catholic-school students do not result in higher-achieving students learning less than they would in the more differentiated public schools.

In summary, these results generally support our original common-school hypothesis: The differentiating effects of race and ethnicity are consistently less in the Catholic schools than in the public schools. The effect of SES on achievement growth is also lower in Catholic schools, though the Catholic-school superiority is somewhat less pronounced. We have also addressed the common-school hypothesis by asking whether senior achievement is more or less dependent on sophomore achievement in the Catholic schools, and we have shown that the differentiating effects of Catholic-school attendance tend to be lower in this respect as well. While the statistical significance of the sector differences is low for most of the comparisons shown in Table 2.4, the consistency of the Catholic-school advantage is strong support for the common-school hypothesis.

Comparing Students with Equal Propensities for Catholic-School Enrollment

Rosenbaum and Rubin (1983) have proposed a stronger test for elimination of selectivity bias than the linear-regression methods used above. They point

TABLE 2.5
Catholic-School Effect on Senior Achievement, by Propensity Quintile

Test	Quintile				
	1	2	3	4	5
Reading	.318	.631	.444	.134	.358
	(.469)	(.343)	(.266)	(.241)	(.189)
Vocabulary	.402	.613	.555	.045	.410
	(.508)	(.338)	(.255)	(.216)	(.164)
Mathematics	.634	.751	.642	.765	.665
	(.736)	(.566)	(.425)	(.371)	(.296)
Writing	.856	.490	.557	−.091	.335
	(.496)	(.339)	(.243)	(.201)	(.155)
Science	−.714	.292	−.172	−.027	.085
	(.439)	(.314)	(.235)	(.208)	(.194)
Civics	.182	.247	.124	−.020	.015
	(.317)	(.230)	(.165)	(.142)	(.108)
Approximate sample size[a]					
Public	3,323	3,052	3,087	2,964	3,061
Catholic	119	223	328	417	845

NOTE: Catholic-school effects are estimated from pooled regressions of senior achievement on sophomore achievement, race, Hispanic ethnicity, composite SES, number of rooms in the home, number of siblings, and the sector dummy.
[a] Cases with missing values on one or more of the variables used in the logistic regression were deleted from the analysis. The sample sizes shown here are averages across the six tests of the numbers of cases with no missing values.

out that fewer assumptions are made (for example, the assumption of linearity in effects of background variables) if comparisons are limited to those persons who are comparable in their propensity to be selected into the treatment. The method entails a two-step process. First, each student's propensity to be enrolled in a Catholic school is estimated. Second, the achievement of public- and Catholic-school students who have the same propensity to be in a Catholic school is compared.[7] In practice, the sample is divided into propensity-score quintiles, and comparisons are made within each quintile. If the sector differences are similar in each quintile, then we can infer that the overall sector effects are in fact applicable for students from all backgrounds. If these differences are approximately the same as the Catholic-school effect measured with a linear-regression model, the assumptions implicit in that analysis are confirmed.

Our analysis includes such a test. First, we determined each student's propensity for or probability of Catholic-school enrollment, based on a logistic regression.[8] Then, following the recommendation of Rosenbaum and Rubin (1983), we stratified the sample into quintiles of the propensity score and estimated Catholic-school effects within each of these homogeneous groups.[9]

The results of this analysis are shown in Table 2.5. Reading across the rows of the table from the lowest propensity quintile (i.e., those students who are least likely to enroll in Catholic school) to the highest propensity quintile, there does not appear to be any strong pattern of increase or decrease in the estimated Catholic-school effects. The estimates of the Catholic-school advantage in mathematics are the most stable, fluctuating little between the first and fifth quintiles. In reading, vocabulary, and writing—the other three areas in which the overall estimates indicated substantial sector effects—the estimates tend to be quite stable and in the expected direction in the first, second, third, and fifth quintiles, but they are sharply lower in the fourth quintile. The reasons for this estimated drop in verbal achievement gains—a drop that is not at all present in mathematics—are not clear; but the quintiles on both sides of this quintile give confidence that the effects are not confined to those students with especially high or low likelihoods of enrolling in a Catholic school.

Table 2.5 indicates that the overall sector effects on achievement estimated in earlier tables are found within homogeneous subsamples defined in terms of propensity for Catholic-school enrollment. Moreover, in the two areas of achievement in which we found no overall sector effects—science and civics—the absence of effects holds across the stratified sample. (The sole exception to this latter generalization is found in the large, but insignificant, negative effect of Catholic-school attendance on science achievement among those students who are least likely to attend Catholic school—the first propensity quintile.)

Rates of Learning and Forgetting

Figures 1 and 2 show that in both sectors, the absolute gains differed for students at different levels of initial achievement, and it is useful to understand why the higher-achieving students gained less. It is possible to understand the process if we conceive of each item separately and if we think of the student in either of two states for each item: knowing the answer or not knowing it. The principal process over the period of two years is a learning process; but there is also a forgetting process for those items that have been learned. For example, a sophomore who correctly answered 35 out of 38 items in mathematics could forget 35 items and learn only 3 by the time s/he was a senior, while another sophomore who correctly answered only 1 item could forget only 1 item and learn 37. Thus, the overall process of change can be represented as follows:

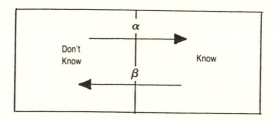

For each item, there is a learning rate, α, from not knowing to knowing, and a forgetting rate, β, from knowing to not knowing. If, for simplicity, we assume that all items are alike, that the learning and forgetting rates are constant over time, and that these rates are the same for all students in a given sector, then it is possible to estimate the values of α and β in the public and Catholic schools. If $p_i(0)$ is the proportion of items that student i knows at the sophomore year, and if $p_i(t)$ is the proportion student

TABLE 2.6
Estimated Learning and Forgetting Rates in Public and
Catholic Schools

	Learning Rates		Forgetting Rates	
Test	Public	Catholic	Public	Catholic
Reading	.088	.121	.035	.022
Vocabulary	.093	.165	0	.047
Mathematics	.041	.070	.004	−.008
Writing	.141	.230	.019	.017
Science	.101	.154	.043	.055
Civics	.251	.352	.080	.099

NOTE: The rates are calculated using estimates of *a*
and *b* derived from bivariate regressions of senior
achievement on sophomore achievement run separately for each sector.

i knows at the senior year, then with the above assumptions, $p_i(t)$ is related
to $p_i(0)$ by an especially simple relation:

$$p_i(t) = a + bp_i(0), \qquad (4)$$

where *a* and *b* are functions of α, β, and *t*.[10]

We derived the learning and forgetting rates reported in Table 2.6 by
estimating *a* and *b* for Catholic and public schools through linear regression
and then by estimating α and β from these (see footnote 10). Of course,
these estimates depend on the model used and on the assumptions underlying
it. One particularly strong assumption is that all students have the same
learning and forgetting rates. Since they do not, the model may not fit the
data, as is shown for Catholic-school students in mathematics, where the
forgetting rate is negative, an impossibility under the assumptions of the
model.

Despite the assumptions on which they are based, these estimates give
some further insight into the differences between the two sets of schools,
because they are based on changes in individuals, not merely on changes
in each sector. The results show that although Catholic-school students had
higher forgetting rates on three of the six tests, they had consistently higher
learning rates than public-school students—roughly one and one-half times
higher. This means that those who did not know an item were much more
likely to learn it in Catholic schools than in public schools, although the
retention was no greater, in general, in Catholic schools than in public
schools.

By abandoning the assumption that rates are alike for all students in
each sector, we can calculate more precise learning and forgetting rates for
particular subsets of students. If rates differ for different students, and if
the differences depend on family background, then a portion of the public-
Catholic difference in learning rates is due to differences in average family

backgrounds in public and Catholic schools. It turns out (see Coleman, 1981: Ch. 3) that if family-background characteristics contribute additively to the learning rate (and correspondingly subtract from the forgetting rate), an appropriate way to estimate the differences in learning and forgetting rates between public and Catholic schools net of family-background differences is simply to extend equation (4) to multiple regression. This was carried out earlier in the analysis leading to Tables 2.2 and 2.3.[11] Although we will not carry out those calculations here, the regression coefficients on which Tables 2.2 and 2.3 are based could be used to estimate these rates.[12]

Growth Rates Compared to Pseudogrowth Estimated in the Base Year

None of the effects estimated in this analysis until this point can be directly compared with those obtained in the cross-sectional analysis, since that analysis estimated effects on the *level* of achievement obtained, and the analysis reported here estimates effects on *growth* in achievement. However, in the cross-sectional analysis, sophomore-to-senior learning rates were estimated by comparing sophomores' and seniors' scores on three subtests, in reading, vocabulary, and mathematics. The actual learning rates of the 1980 sophomores between their sophomore and senior years can be compared to these imputed learning rates. This provides the closest approximation to a direct test of the estimates in the cross-sectional analysis using the longitudinal data.

Because of noncomparability of the cohorts in the cross-sectional analysis, it was not possible to estimate true learning rates. Therefore, we estimated three rates under different assumptions in an attempt to bracket the true rates. The rates may be expressed as the rate in a learning equation:

$$\frac{dp}{dt} = q\ (1-p), \tag{5}$$

where p is the probability that the item is answered correctly, dp/dt is the change in this probability, and q is the learning rate, expressed as the probability that an item will be learned in a year, given that it is not already known. This is a simplification of the process described in the preceding section; it ignores the forgetting process, which cannot be estimated by comparison of cohorts, as was necessary with the cross-sectional data.

The rates estimated from raw and background-adjusted scores are favorable to the public sector and are probably overestimates of the true rates. Those estimated from the dropout-adjusted scores are favorable to the Catholic sector and are probably underestimates of the true rates. From these estimates, it was inferred that in vocabulary and mathematics, Catholic-school students showed unambiguously higher learning rates than public-school students. In reading, however, there was ambiguity, since the public-sector rates were higher according to one set of estimates, and the Catholic-sector rates were higher according to another. It is these imputed learning rates to which the

TABLE 2.7
Estimated Learning Rates from 1980 Cross-Sectional Data
Using Sophomore and Senior Scores on Subtests and from
Longitudinal Data Using Full Tests

Test	Public	Catholic
Reading		
Cross-sectional		
Raw scores	.11	.10
Background-adjusted	.09	.09
Dropout-adjusted	.06	.07
Longitudinal	.05	.09
Vocabulary		
Cross-sectional		
Raw scores	.10	.13
Background-adjusted	.08	.12
Dropout-adjusted	.05	.10
Longitudinal	.10	.14
Mathematics		
Cross-sectional		
Raw scores	.08	.08
Background-adjusted	.05	.06
Dropout-adjusted	.02	.05
Longitudinal	.04	.06

actual gains in achievement of the 1980 sophomores in public and Catholic schools can be compared.

Using the results presented in Table 2.2, it is possible to estimate the learning rate q, net of family background, for students with a family background like that of the average public-school student, now based on actual changes in achievement rather than on the cohort comparisons estimated with the cross-sectional data. Furthermore, although the learning model estimated here is simpler than that of the preceding section because it assumes a zero forgetting rate, it does control for family-background differences that affect the learning rate. The estimated rates are shown in Table 2.7, along with the earlier estimates.[13]

The learning rates estimated from the longitudinal data correspond very well to those estimated from the cross-sectional data. The cross-sectional estimates for vocabulary and for the Catholic-public difference in reading appear to be too low; otherwise, the correspondence appears quite good. Thus, the longitudinal data confirm this aspect of the cross-sectional analysis, though they indicate that the Catholic-school effects may have been underestimated.

Sector Effects on School Experiences Related to Achievement

Up to this point, we have identified sector effects on achievement only residually, as the differences in achievement growth that remain after controlling for influences external to the schools. The argument for positive effects of Catholic-school attendance can, of course, be strengthened if we identify the ways in which Catholic schools generate the estimated advantages. This longitudinal extension of the CHK analysis corresponds to the examination carried out in section 1 under objection 6.

In the base-year analysis, we identified, on theoretical grounds, two analytically independent mechanisms through which Catholic schools may realize their students' estimated gains: academic demands and disciplinary standards. After controlling for family background and other extrascholastic influences, we found that Catholic-school students took more mathematics and foreign language courses and spent more time on homework than public-school students. We also found that Catholic schools had lower rates of absenteeism and class cutting and that Catholic-school students had more favorable perceptions of their school's disciplinary climate (CHK, 1982b:Table 6–20). To test the hypothesis that the sector differences remaining after controlling out-of-school influences can be explained by these sector differences in academic demands and disciplinary standards, we regressed achievement on both the background and the school-experience measures and standardized the regression equations to obtain predicted achievement levels. The standardization procedure was designed to estimate how much the average student in one sector would achieve if s/he attended a school with the same academic demands and disciplinary standards that the average student in the other sector experienced. The results of this procedure indicated that public-school students would generally achieve at levels comparable to their Catholic-school peers if public schools maintained the same academic demands and disciplinary standards as Catholic schools (CHK, 1982b: Table 6–21).

The models estimated here differ in two respects from those estimated in the base-year analysis. Critics of our earlier work argued that if Catholic schools increase individual students' achievement, they do so not because of school policies but because of the higher initial achievement and social backgrounds of the other students in the school (McPartland and McDill, 1982). To test for this possibility, we estimated the sector effects on school aggregate student achievement and background and the effects of these compositional variables on senior achievement. A second criticism of our original work concerned our exclusion of students' curriculum program from the analysis. Therefore, we included a measure of program enrollment, which we treated as endogenous to sector as well as to student background and sophomore achievement.

The estimation procedure employed here consists—as in the base-year analysis—of two steps. In the first step, we estimated the effects of school sector on the school-experience variables for students with the same background and sophomore achievement as the average public-school student. In the second step, we regressed senior achievement on the full set of background and prior-achievement variables and the school characteristics and experience variables. We then standardized these regression results to the background of the average student in the public sector and to the predicted levels on the school-experience variables for the same type of student in the Catholic sector.

TABLE 2.8

Predicted Levels of School-Experience Variables, Standardizing to Average Public-School Sophomore Achievement and Background (standard errors of differences in parentheses)

	Public	Catholic	Catholic Advantage
Average sophomore achievement			
Reading	9.25	10.27	1.02
Vocabulary	11.01	12.47	1.46
Mathematics	19.08	21.33	2.24
Writing	10.48	11.63	1.15
Science	11.15	11.83	0.68
Civics	5.91	6.47	0.56
Average SES (composite)	−0.04	0.27	0.31
Proportion Hispanic	0.12	0.12	0
Proportion black	0.12	0.07	−0.05
Proportion with 8th-grade college plans	0.59	0.76	0.17
Probability of being in academic program	0.37	0.61	0.23 (.023)
Hours of homework per week	4.00	5.01	1.01 (.220)
Semesters of coursework since sophomore year			
English literature	3.64	3.85	0.21 (.056)
Foreign languages	1.10	1.43	0.33 (.100)
Mathematics	2.37	2.67	0.30 (.076)
Science	2.03	2.13	0.10 (.085)
History/social studies	3.10	3.29	0.19 (.086)
Advanced coursework			
Honors English (0–1)	0.27	0.22	−0.04 (.025)
Number of advanced math courses[a]	2.08	2.74	0.66 (.054)
Number of advanced science courses[b]	1.34	1.54	0.19 (.042)
Attendance			
Absenteeism[c]	2.45	2.18	−0.27 (.063)
Cut class sometimes (0–1)	0.40	0.23	−0.17 (.023)
Perceived student behavior[d]			
Absenteeism	1.61	2.25	0.64 (.012)
Cutting class	1.55	2.30	0.75 (.024)
Students fighting	2.09	2.54	0.46 (.012)
Students threatening teachers	2.84	2.94	0.10 (.004)

[a] Sum of responses to five dichotomous items asking student whether or not s/he has taken Algebra I, Algebra II, geometry, trigonometry, and calculus.
[b] Sum of responses to three dichotomous items asking student whether or not s/he has taken biology, chemistry, and physics.
[c] Ordinal variable ranging from 1 (never absent) to 7 (21 or more days absent); refers to the first semester of the 1981–82 school year.
[d] These items ask students to rate the seriousness of the problems in their schools. Responses range from 1 (often happens) to 3 (rarely or never happens). School-level averages of the items are used in this analysis.

The results of the first step of this procedure are presented in Table 2.8. The figures in the "public" and "Catholic" columns are the predicted levels of each of the school-experience variables for a student with background and sophomore achievement equal to that of the average public-school student. The figures in the "Catholic advantage" column are simply the differences between the sectors' predicted levels of the school-experience variables. These results indicate that Catholic-school students generally have substantial advantages compared to their public-school counterparts on these measures of school characteristics and experiences that are presumed to contribute to achievement. The Catholic-school effects on other student characteristics are treated here as evidence of sector selectivity plus, in the case of school-aggregate sophomore test scores, the effect of sector prior to the sophomore year. Selectivity is a much less likely explanation for the remaining advantages displayed in the table. When background and soph-

TABLE 2.9
Achievement Differences Between Public and Catholic Schools Due to Differences in School Functioning, for Students
Similar to the Average Public-School Student

	Reading	Vocabulary	Mathematics	Writing	Science	Civics
Background and sophomore achievement composition of school	.022	.076	.131	.033	−.025	.073
Academic program	.185	.179	.201	.127	.113	.134
Hours of homework per week	.037	.039	.065	.039	.025	.034
Academic coursework	−.023	−.018	.927	−.022	.282	.010
Discipline	.011	.007	.056	.042	.019	.015
Perceived student behavior	−.018	.131	.084	.038	−.017	.024
Total accounted for	.21	.41	1.46	.26	.40	.29
Total to explain (from Table 2.2)	.53	.70	.78	.73	.10	.14

omore achievement are controlled, we find that Catholic-school students complete more homework and coursework in academic subjects, show lower rates of absenteeism and class cutting, report that various discipline problems are less serious in their schools, and are about 23 percent more likely to be enrolled in an academic program.

To determine the extent to which these Catholic-school advantages account for sector effects on achievement, it is necessary to estimate the effects of the school-experience variables on achievement. This was done by regressing each of the six achievement tests on the full set of individual and school-aggregate measures of background and sophomore achievement and the school-experience variables shown in Table 2.8. The figures in the "Catholic advantage" column were then multiplied by these regression coefficients. The results of these multiplications using the public-school regressions are displayed in Table 2.9. The figures in each row of the table indicate the amount of improvement (or decline, when the comparative sign is negative) that public-school students could be expected to realize on each achievement test if they were at the same level on the row variable or sets of variables as their Catholic-school counterparts. For each test, then, the sum of the row components provides an estimate of the total amount of improvement that public-school students would realize if they had the same school experiences as Catholic-school students. This total can be compared with the estimated sector effects from Table 2.2 in order to obtain an idea of how adequate our explanatory effort has been.

The results shown in Table 2.9 indicate that the explanatory success is in fact limited. Of the four areas of achievement that show substantial sector effects—reading, vocabulary, mathematics and writing—only in mathematics is there a sector difference on these explanatory variables that can fully account for the observed sector effect. The reason for the model's success with mathematics is the exceptionally large effect of advanced mathematics coursework coupled with the substantial positive effect of Catholic-school enrollment on the numbers of these courses that students take. In contrast to this pattern, the effects of English and foreign language coursework on verbal achievement are much smaller, and Catholic-school effects on courses completed in these areas are relatively slight and even negative in advanced English studies.

Despite the limited success of the explanatory effort, certain points are worth noting. Table 2.9 indicates that the less-restrictive academic-program entry criteria in Catholic schools promote higher achievement. The greater amount of time spent on homework and lower rates of absenteeism in the Catholic schools also improve achievement in each of the six areas. Limitations notwithstanding, then, these findings suggest avenues through which student achievement can be improved in the public schools.

3. Comparison of the Analyses

In sections 1 and 2 of this article, we extended the Greeley (1982) and CHK (1982b) cross-sectional analyses of the 1980 HSB data using the achievement-test results from the 1982 follow-up study. We used the same methods in these longitudinal extensions that we used in the earlier cross-sectional analyses. This results, of course, in some differences in presentation, and it is useful to discuss the differences in the methods and the consistency of the results.

Differences in Method

The extension of the Greeley analysis in section 1 is largely based on a combined test score, which includes reading, vocabulary, mathematics (both parts), and writing and excludes science and civics, which were found to be little affected by Catholic-school enrollment. The combined score is based on formula scores for individual tests. The extension of the CHK analysis in section 2 treats each of the six tests separately. The score on each test is simply the number of items correct.

The regression analysis reported in section 1 (Tables 1.7 and 1.8) is based on pooled samples of public- and Catholic-school students, and the analysis reported in section 2 is stratified by sector. The stratification procedure allows the effects of the independent variables to vary by sector, while pooling without including explicit interaction terms constrains the effects to be equal. Since the advantages of Catholic-school attendance are greatest for students from lower socioeconomic backgrounds, the section 1 estimates are probably somewhat low for these students and somewhat high for students from higher socioeconomic backgrounds.[14] There are various other methodological differences between the sections, but these are apparent in the presentations and need not be mentioned here.

Consistency of Results

Both analyses found the same relative Catholic-school advantage on the achievement tests, and Table 1.1 and nearly all the tables in section 2 show that Catholic-school effects in science and civics are negligible. This same absence of effects was found at the sophomore level in an earlier study (Coleman and Hoffer, 1983:226).

However, when we compare Tables 1.7 and 2.2, we find an apparent inconsistency in the results of the two analyses. In Table 2.2, the total

Catholic increment in growth for the four tests (excluding science and civics) after family background is controlled is 2.74 (the sum of the four increments in the penultimate column of the table). The corresponding figure from Table 1.7 is 1.08, before track is included. This inconsistency, however, is at least partly due to the allowance in section 2 for interaction with family background, which shows that the Catholic-school effect differs for students with different backgrounds. (For the average Catholic-school student, the effect, from Table 2.3, is 1.89.)

We can also compare Table 1.2 and Table 2.4. In Table 1.2 the Catholic-school advantage is shown for several groups, including those differing in socioeconomic status and minority status. Table 2.4 shows the different effects of race, ethnicity, and SES on achievement in public and Catholic schools. If the differences between public and Catholic schools are added for the four tests, we see that the *differential* advantage of Catholic-school attendance is 1.83 for blacks and 2.79 for Hispanics. In Table 1.2, the differential advantage for minority students is 2.18. The correspondence is rather good. On the other hand, Table 1.2 shows a reasonably strong differential effect for students of low socioeconomic status, while Table 2.4 shows a weaker SES effect. Table 2.4 shows a consistent differential effect for students with low sophomore test scores, which is consistent with Table 1.2, although quantitative comparisons are not possible.

The analysis in section 1 is somewhat more successful in the search for characteristics that differentiate public and Catholic schools and that might account for the Catholic-sector effect (see Tables 1.7, 1.8, 2.8, and 2.9). This appears in part to be due to the explanatory power of the advanced coursework variables and to the lack of sector interactions with background and schooling variables in the section 1 analysis. There are, of course, a number of additional aspects of the analyses that treat different questions and thus cannot be compared. The above comparisons indicate reasonable consistency despite the different methodological tools used and thus indicate the robustness of the results.

Comparison with Alexander and Pallas

Alexander and Pallas (1983, 1985) also analyzed the data from the 1980 HSB study and the 1982 follow-up but found small or negligible Catholic-school effects on achievement.

There is a fundamental methodological difference between Alexander and Pallas's (1985) analysis and the analyses presented here: They adjusted the test-score correlations—but no other correlations—using reliabilities that were estimated by other investigators who analyzed the same data. The adjustment is not trivial: It increases the correlation between sophomore and senior tests, which is already high, to a very high level.

Given this difference, what do Alexander and Pallas find? Their principal result is expressed in their Table 2, which presents Catholic-school effects as fractions of a year's growth. A comparison with our analysis in section

TABLE 3.1

Catholic-School Effect for Average Public-School Student, from Table 2.2 and Alexander and Pallas (1985: Table 2)

Test	From Table 2.2	From Alexander and Pallas, Table 2
Reading	1.1	0.5
Vocabulary	0.8	0.7
Mathematics	1.1	0.8
Writing	1.1	0.6
Science	0.3	0.3
Civics	0.3	−0.1

2 is possible, using fractions of a year's growth from Table 2.2. The comparisons are given in Table 3.1.

Some of Alexander and Pallas's results are very close to ours, although their estimates for reading and writing are considerably below our estimates. They summarize the differences they find, excluding civics, as "about two thirds of a year's growth." Our estimate, excluding science and civics, is about a year's growth.

The issue, however, is not two thirds of a year's growth versus a year's growth. Alexander and Pallas argue that either difference is quite small— less than 0.1 standard deviation. What they neglect to recognize is that this extra year's (or two thirds of a year's) growth occurs over the two-year period. Thus, according to our estimates in section 2, the average public-school student is only learning at about two thirds of the rate at which his counterpart in a Catholic school is learning. In other words, the public-school student is learning two grade equivalents in two years, while the Catholic-school student is learning three grade equivalents.

To be sure, the average growth in either school is small relative to individual differences in performance. But we do not abandon schooling for that reason. If it is to be argued, as Alexander and Pallas do, that the extra benefit of Catholic school as measured by these tests is small, then it can be said that the extra benefit of the last two years of high school is small. It should be noted that part of the reason Alexander and Pallas find the Catholic-school effect particularly small is that they fail to recognize that it is a differential growth between grades 10 and 12, not the *total* Catholic-school effect. They compare it to the effect found in the cross-sectional analyses at grades 10 and 12 as if it were a measurement of the same effect. But it is clearly not that; it is an additional effect *beyond* the 10th grade. The cross-sectional estimates were estimates of the cumulative effect up to grade 10 or grade 12.

Alexander and Pallas also fail to find a general common-school effect. Both sections 1 and 2 of this article show the strength of that effect, and the analyses in section 1 document it in great detail. The very simplest of analyses (see Figures 1 and 2) show that the extra gains in Catholic schools are especially great among the students who are low achievers in their sophomore years. Other simple comparisons show it as well. For example, the variance in achievement within Catholic schools went *down,* rather than up, for three of the tests (vocabulary, writing, civics), while it went up for all six tests in the public schools. Of the eighteen correlations of race, Hispanic ethnicity, and socioeconomic status with the six achievement tests, nine went down in Catholic schools, while only three went down in the public schools.

In the face of all this evidence, Alexander and Pallas's analysis shows no consistently higher relation of race, Hispanic ethnicity, or socioeconomic status to achievement in the public sector than in the Catholic sector. Indeed, their regression coefficients (Alexander and Pallas, 1985: Table 4) show a *lower* relation of achievement growth to these three background characteristics. How can this be? The answer appears to lie in the "correction" of correlations for reliability, which they carried out before any regressions were done. This operation raised the sophomore-senior test correlations in the public sector to extremely high levels, leaving very little variance to be explained by any other variable. This correction has a major effect on the results: In four of Alexander and Pallas's regression analyses, the multiple R^2 in the public schools, when only three additional variables were used, was greater than .9; in our analyses (and in Willms's [1985]), the multiple R^2 ranged from around .4 to around .7. Thus, it is no wonder that Alexander and Pallas's regression coefficients for race, Hispanic ethnicity, and socioeconomic status are especially small in the public sector and highly variable in both sectors. This correction also presumably accounts for the deviation of their estimates of a Catholic-school effect from ours in Table 3.1.

Comparison with Willms

Willms (1982, 1985) also examined the effects of schooling on achievement using the 1980 and 1982 HSB data and, like Alexander and Pallas, concludes that no substantial Catholic-school effects are present. His analysis is similar to our analysis in section 2, but it differs in certain methodological and interpretive points. The principal interpretive difference lies in Willms's use of the posttest variance as a standard of comparison for Catholic-school effects. Our criticisms of Alexander and Pallas's reliance on this standard are applicable to Willms's study as well.

The principal methodological differences are twofold. First, Willms uses sophomore test scores in reading, vocabulary, and basic mathematics (28 of the 38 items) as ability controls in all regressions, along with the sophomore score for the test being examined and background characteristics. This may capture sophomore achievements that affect growth on the other three tests.

Second, Willms relies on estimates from single regressions for all students, rather than separate regression equations for public- and Catholic-school students. This forces the relation of all other statistical controls to be alike for Catholic and public schools. In one analysis, he introduces interactions between the Catholic sector and the other statistical controls but dismisses

TABLE 3.2

Comparison of Sector Effects in Equations With and Without
Additional Statistical Controls for Reading, Vocabulary, and
Mathematics (standard errors in parentheses)

Test	Without Added Controls (from Table 2.2)		With Added Controls	
	Items	Grade Equiv-alent	Items	Grade Equiv-alent
Reading	.53	1.1	.35	0.7
			(.14)	
Vocabulary	.70	0.8	.66	0.8
			(.14)	
Mathematics	.78	1.1	.70	1.0
			(.24)	
Writing	.73	1.1	.62	0.9
			(.12)	
Science	.10	0.3	−.10	−0.3
			(.13)	
Civics	.14	0.3	.04	0.1
			(.09)	

NOTE: Values of R^2 in the public sector in each of
these equations range from .40 (for civics) to .72 (for
mathematics) and exceed those reported in Willms
(1985:Table 7), where comparisons are possible, so
our estimates of effects are not due to less-effective
statistical controls.

his results because the interaction terms appear to add little explanatory
power to the model.

The effect of each of these differences is to lower the estimated Catholic-
school effects. The inclusion of the additional sophomore tests as controls
is a defensible strategy; however, as we have noted, the only possible
drawback of our strategy of allowing for sector-by-background interactions
is that it can reduce the efficiency of the estimates.

To assess the consequences of additional controls for sophomore achievement for our results, we added them to the analysis that generated the
estimates in Table 2.2. The results are presented in Table 3.2. Inclusion of
the additional controls used by Willms does reduce the estimated sector
effects, but not by much. All four of the tests for which statistically significant
differences were found continue to show significant differences. The conclusions of our analysis are not affected by the inclusion of these additional
controls.

Conclusion

The results we have shown make it difficult to beliefe that the impact
of Catholic school on sophomore-to-senior achievement growth is no greater

or only trivially greater than that of the average public school. As we stated above, if one concludes that these differences in growth are trivial, one must also conclude that the growth in achievement in the last two years of high school is trivial.

American educators and educational researchers typically assume that Catholic schools are academically inferior to public schools. They attribute this inferiority to larger classes, less-professional teacher training, more limited resources, smaller per-pupil costs, and religious narrowness, which they believe restricts thought and imagination. To show that Catholic schools, for all their apparent weaknesses, are not worse than public schools may not be too unsettling. But to suggest, as we have, that in terms of academic outcome they might be somewhat better is such a reversal of the conventional wisdom that one might well expect intense debate. How could schools that have always been thought to be somewhat less effective be more effective, and how could schools thought to undermine the American ideal of the common school somehow be closer to that ideal than the public schools?

Because Catholic schools compete with free public schools for their students, some see our earlier results as divisive and harmful to the public schools. Two points should be made in response to this. First, the greater effectiveness of the Catholic schools, which must compete, against strong economic odds, for students, suggests that a little competition might not be harmful for American public schools. The special success Catholic schools have had with the disadvantaged provides added confirmation, because it is the public schools these students attend that come closest to having a captive audience.

Second, our results provide some basis for policies that might benefit achievement, whether in the public or private sector. Despite the somewhat different approaches of our two investigations, there is convergence in the explanation for the differential effectiveness of Catholic and public schools. Although the analyses do not fully account for the differential effects, there is consistency in the results. Catholic schools place in an academic track many students whose sophomore achievement would relegate them to a general or vocational track in public schools. Catholic schools demand more homework and advanced coursework, especially from those who are disadvantaged in one way or another and especially from those who are not in the academic track. These differences are also consistent with the common-school findings of both analyses: Catholic schools are especially beneficial to the least-advantaged students—the minorities, the poor, and those whose initial achievement is low. For these students, the lack of structure, lower demands, and lower expectations found in many public schools are especially harmful.

Our analyses show that those public schools that make the same demands as the average Catholic school produce comparable achievement. This point has frequently been overlooked in the present controversy. The difference in average scores between Catholic- and public-school students reflects the lower demands of many public schools. In the one area in which Catholic schools do not make coursework demands greater than the average public school—i.e., science—there is no Catholic-school effect.

There is, of course, a remaining question: Why are Catholic schools able to make more demands on their students? But we can just as well ask, Why are some public schools unable to make such demands? International studies, which show that greater demands are made in nearly all developed countries, make the question even more pointed (see Husén, 1967). Indeed, the difference between Japanese and American public schools makes the Catholic-public sector differences pale by comparison. The question of how American public schools can modify their policies in this direction, though it is beyond the scope of this article, is quite pertinent to both educational research and educational policy.[15]

Notes

1. As in Greeley (1982), the achievement-test scores analyzed in this section are formula scores. However, direct comparison with cross-sectional analysis is not possible, because the current analysis is based on weighted data.

2. This increase in the Catholic-public difference results from the ceiling effect—i.e., the expected gain is less when initial achievement is high. Thus, the Catholic gain was depressed more than the public gain because sophomore achievement was higher.

3. We do not understand why Goldberger and Cain (1982) vehemently object to our allowance for interaction effects.

4. The ten additional background measures are (1) number of siblings, (2) rooms in household, (3) whether both parents or guardians are present in household, (4) whether mother worked before respondent was in elementary school, (5) whether mother worked while respondent was in elementary school, (6) extent to which respondent talks to parents about personal experiences, (7) whether father expected respondent to go to college when respondent was a sophomore, (8) whether mother expected the same, (9) Hispanic ethnicity, and (10) race. The HSB codebook names for the full set of background variables we used are as follows: RACE (respondent's race and Hispanic ethnicity), BYSES (parents's SES), FY106 (number of siblings), BB103 (rooms in household), BB036b–e (presence or absence of both parents), BB037b&c (mother working or not working when respondent was young), BB047g (extent respondent talks to parents), BB050a&b (parents' educational expectations for respondent), SCHREGN (region of the country [3 dummy variables]), FY100 (rural/small town/suburb/city residence [3 dummy variables]), SEX (respondent's sex), FY103a–g (whether or not respondent is handicapped), BB068b (whether or not respondent planned to go to college in 9th grade).

5. This criticism could not, however, explain why the effect occurred only in the Catholic schools, not in the other private schools, where socioeconomic background is as highly related to achievement as it is in the public schools. It is logically possible for the public sector to show lower effects of school-average SES, race, and ethnicity, and thus to compensate for the within-school common-school effects found in the Catholic schools. However, we have carried out those analyses and do not find such effects.

6. Individual students' values for the independent variables are removed from the computation of their respective school means. The mean values thus represent averages for each individual's schoolmates.

7. See Rosenbaum and Rubin (1983) for details. If certain variables within a quintile remain related to achievement, a within-quintile regression may be carried out to control for their effects.

8. Students' propensities for Catholic-school enrollment are estimated by a logistic regression of sector (Catholic = 1, public = 0) on the set of background measures used in the base-year analysis (substituting the composite SES measure for parents' education and income and household possessions) plus a composite measure of sophomore achievement. Because our analysis of sector entry in the base year found that the relationships of background to entry varied for white, black, and Hispanic students (CHK, 1982b: Ch. 3), the logistic regression was fit on a stratified basis. Propensity scores (in the form of probabilities of Catholic enrollment) were then obtained for each student.

9. As indicated in footnote 7, relations of background to achievement remaining within quintiles can be controlled by within-quintile regression analysis. To determine which variables required further adjustment, we carried out a sector-by-quintile analysis of variance for each of the twelve predictor variables. We found that significant main and interaction effects of sector within quintiles remained for sophomore achievement, SES, rooms in household, number of siblings, race, and Hispanic ethnicity. Consequently, we controlled for these variables in within-quintile regressions of senior achievement, which we used to obtain estimates of the Catholic-sector effects.

10. The process is described by the equation $dp/dt = \alpha (1-p) - \beta p$. Solving this for $p(t)$ gives

$$p(t) = p(0)e^{-(\alpha + \beta)t} + \frac{\alpha}{\alpha + \beta}\left[1 - e^{-(\alpha + \beta)t} \right].$$

This equation has the same form as equation (4), where

$$b = e^{-(\alpha + \beta)t}$$

and

$$a = \frac{\alpha}{\alpha + \beta}\left[1 - e^{-(\alpha + \beta)t} \right].$$

If we take $t = 2$ years, then

$$\alpha = \frac{-a \log b}{2(1-b)}$$

and

$$\beta = -\alpha - \tfrac{1}{2} \log b.$$

See Coleman (1968, 1981:Ch. 3) for further discussion.

11. Because forgetting rates are quite small relative to learning rates, the assumption that background factors subtract an amount from the forgetting rate equal to the amount they add to the learning rate is probably a poor one. A multiplicative model, as well as other variations, is discussed in Coleman (1981:Ch. 3).

12. The transformations necessary to obtain α and β in Catholic schools for students with backgrounds comparable to some standard background, such as the average public-school student's background, are as follows:

$$\alpha = \frac{(a_c + \sum_{k=2}^{m} b_{kc}\overline{X}_{kp}) \log b_{lc}}{2n(b_{lc}-1)}$$

and

$$\beta = \tfrac{1}{2}\log(b_1 -\alpha),$$

where b_{kc} is the kth regression coefficient in the Catholic-school equation, n is the number of items in the test, b_{lc} is the regression coefficient for the sophomore test, and $\overline{X}_{kp}$ is the average value for background characteristics k for public-school students.

13. The estimate is made by integrating equation (5) to give

$$q = -\tfrac{1}{2} \log \left[\frac{1-p(t)}{1-p(0)} \right].$$

Given the numbers of items in each of the tests (column 1 of Table 2.1), $p(t)$ for public- and Catholic-school students are obtained from the figures displayed in Table 2.2.

14. A major contention of some critics of the CHK analysis (see Goldberger and Cain, 1982) is that pooled regressions rather than separate public and private regressions are warranted. We have demonstrated the weakness of that contention elsewhere (CHK, 1982a). In the analyses reported here, we use both techniques and show that the effects occur with either.

15. One possible explanation advanced by Greeley is that Catholic schools did not abandon stringent academic demands in the late 1960s and early 1970s in the name of social relevance, as did some public schools, because they were not so well connected into the network of professional educational fashions and because they lacked the resources and the flexibility to search for relevance.

References

Alexander, K. L. and A. M. Pallas. 1983. "Private schools and public policy: New evidence on cognitive achievement in public and private schools." Sociology of Education 56:170–82.

_____. 1985. "School sector and cognitive performance: When is a little a little?" Sociology of Education 58:115–28.

Alexander, K. L., A. M. Pallas, and M. A. Cook. 1981. "Measure for measure: Ability data in school process research." American Sociological Review 46:619–32.

Coleman, J. S. 1968. "The mathematical study of change." In H. M. Blalock and A. B. Blalock (eds.), Methodology in Social Research. New York: McGraw-Hill.

_____. 1981. Longitudinal Data Analysis. New York: Basic.

Coleman, J. S. and T. Hoffer. 1983. "Response to Taeuber-James, Cain-Goldberger and Morgan." Sociology of Education 56:219–34.

Coleman, J. S., T. Hoffer, and S. Kilgore. 1982a. "Achievement and segregation in secondary schools: A further look at public and private school differences." Sociology of Education 55:162–82.

———. 1982b. High School Achievement. New York: Basic.

Goldberger, A. S. and G. G. Cain. 1982. "The causal analysis of cognitive outcomes in the Coleman, Hoffer and Kilgore report." Sociology of Education 55:103–22.

Greeley, A. 1982. Catholic High Schools and Minority Students. New Brunswick, NJ: Transaction.

Húsen, T. (ed.). 1967. International Study of Achievement in Mathematics: A Comparison of Twelve Countries. New York: Wiley.

McPartland, J. M. and E. L. McDill. 1982. "Control and differentiation in the structure of American education." Sociology of Education 55:77–88.

Peng, S. and W. Fetters. 1981. Review of Draft Report of Minority Students in Catholic Secondary Schools by Andrew Greeley. Washington, D.C.: National Center for Education Statistics.

Rosenbaum, P. and D. Rubin. 1983. "The central role of the propensity score in observational studies for causal effects." Biometrika 70:41–55.

Willms, J. D. 1982. "Achievement outcomes in public and private schools: A closer look at the 'High School and Beyond' data." Stanford Institute for Research on Educational Finance and Governance.

———. 1985. "Catholic-school effects on academic achievement: New evidence from the High School and Beyond follow-up study." Sociology of Education 58:98–114.

PART FIVE

Families and Schools, Achievement and Equality

Schooling outside the home has always had a complex relation to the interests of the family. On the one hand, schooling has provided a service for the family by providing training and knowledge that parents had neither the time (after the Industrial Revolution had removed the man's work from the home, and a son's training could no longer occur as a by-product of his father's work), nor, in most cases, the knowledge or background to provide. At their best, schools do for children what most parents never do.

At the same time, schools are instruments of the larger society and are sometimes used by the larger society in ways inimical to the family's interests or values. They promote a single national identity, language, and culture, often undermining ethnic identities of the parents. Schools may teach values or orientations that conflict with those held by parents—as occurs, for example, when a child from a family in which the Bible is interpreted literally learns evolutionary theory in school. Schools provide environments in which children may get into trouble, learn bad habits, or be victimized by other children. Schools constitute systems that always seem to generate, among some fraction of children in them, poor performance, failure, and loss of self-esteem.[1]

From the school's perspective, the family is sometimes an ally but often a nuisance. The school has a set of goals, and the family's activities often impede the achievement of those goals: The farm family may keep children at home to help with chores; the affluent family may take children on vacation trips during the school year. Parents create problems for the school when they intervene in its treatment of their children and when they contest its authority.

There are changes in schools, communities, and families that affect the nature of the difficulties they pose for one another. Schools have become more professional and more bureaucratic, making them more distant from the communities they serve. Teachers often are not from the community, thus reducing the multiple contacts parents once had with teachers to a single, weak, and short-term relation. Communities built around neighborhoods have declined in strength and given way to aggregations of households whose contacts with each other are minimal.

Families, however, have changed most. Children are no longer intrinsic to the household but constitute a luxury that increasing numbers of households forgo. (In 1880, less than 30 percent of households in the United States had no children under eighteen; in 1980, 65 percent of households had no children under eighteen; see Chapter 21.) The change in the adult composition of the household is even more striking and more rapid as divorce becomes more common at all socioeconomic levels. For children born between 1950 and 1954, 19 percent of white children and 48 percent of black children have lived some portion of their years before age eighteen without one or both natural parents; for children born in 1980, 70 percent of whites and 94 percent of blacks will have lived a portion of their years before age eighteen without one or both natural parents. Currently, of all first marriages, two-thirds can be expected to disrupt (Martin and Bumpass 1989:49). If the problem of the school a hundred years ago was the resistance of strong and inwardly focused families to the school's goals, the problem of today is the passivity of families too weak, broken, or unstable to support the school in its task. The decline in school achievement that has occurred in the United States since the mid-1960s has been seen as a deficiency of the schools. It might, however, be more a result of deficiencies in families as children experience the consequences of marital disruption and other problems of the modern family.

An examination of the functioning of families and the role of children within the family, both as it has occurred in the past and as it exists now, will give a perspective on the relation between family and school that will be most beneficial to children and the kind of relation we can expect in the future. The three chapters of Part 5 are directed to that end.

Notes

1. One social scientist argues persuasively that schools *create* the problem of "stupidity," by the very nature of their activities and evaluations. See Dexter (1964).

References

Dexter, Lewis. 1964. *The Tyranny of Schooling*. New York: Basic Books.
Martin, Teresa C., and Larry L. Bumpass. 1989. "Recent Trends in Marital Disruption." *Demography* 26:49.

19

Schooling and Equality

The ideal of equal educational opportunity is one that has come to be increasingly widely held throughout the world. In highly developed nations and in less developed nations, the ideal is expressed often and with vigor. If there is any theme in eduation more dominant than any other in nations throughout the world, it is this theme of equal educational opportunity for all children within a nation. In every nation, there is a general recognition, in the government and in the populations, among educational professionals and among lay persons, that the ideal is far from being realized. Yet the demand for equality of opportunity is a strong and widely shared one.

It was not always so. In the early years of public education in Europe, there was no thought of equal educational opportunity. The educational system followed the pattern of the class structure, with a low-level common school attended for a brief period by children of commoners, and an elite tier for those from higher backgrounds and destined for higher occupations. And since schooling was a local community activity, each community determined its own level of educational effort, with no thought of equality between communities. In America, without the background of a feudal class structure, the ideal of the single common school for all was present from the beginning of public education; but the local community responsibility for and authority over education meant that there was never a conception that all children throughout the nation were entitled to an equal educational opportunity. It is still the case in America that legal requirements for equalizing educational opportunity are limited to within each of the fifty states. In less developed countries, where state-provided public education is rather recent, the educational system seldom encompasses all children, and ideals of equal educational opportunity are even farther from realization.

Yet the ideal is an exceedingly strong and widely held one. Why is it that the ideal has gained such strength, in diverse countries throughout the world? What are the social conditions that have brought demands for equality into being? And given that the ideal is strong, just how does a nation's educational system go about providing equal opportunity in education?

Reprinted with permission from T.J.H.M. Eggen, ed., *Open Session IEA General Assembly 1983* (Enschede, Neth.: Twente University of Technology, 1983), pp. 85 and 87–90.

As it will turn out, answers to these last two questions are related. The provision of something approaching equal educational opportunity differs in different circumstances. A nation with one kind of social and economic structure can approach equal educational opportunity in a very different way than can a nation with a different social and economic structure. . . .

An appropriate conception of formal schooling is one that does recognize the sociale structural sources of unequal opportunities, and sees the school as an institution that in some fashion complements that structure. In this conception, it is not the school itself which provides educational opportunity, but the school in conjunction with existing institutions in the fabric of society, particularly the family.

Once this is recognized, then a further recognition must follow: Since social structures, and in particular families, are very different under different societies, the school must do different things in different societies. A single conception of the school suitable for all social structures is inappropriate. And a single conception of how schools can equalize educational opportunity is equally inappropriate.

Very roughly, three broad phases may be distinguished in the state of a nation's economy and social structure. Parallel to these are three broad phases in the state of a family's economic and social conditions. Thus whatever the phase for a nation as a whole, for example, Phase 2, there will nevertheless be in it some families that are at Phase 1, and some at Phase 3.

I will outline each of these phases, and attempt to give for each a sense of the role of schooling in the equalization of educational opportunity. I distinguish these three phases because in each, the family has a certain set of interests in its children that shape the way it acts toward its children and thus set the environment that the school confronts.

Phase 1: The Exploitation of Children's Labor

What I will call Phase 1 is an economy in which most households are at or slightly above a subsistence level. An economy based largely on subsistence farming is the most widespread example, though extractive economies in general, in which most occupations are in the primary economic sector, fit this phase, as do village-based societies in which most households are engaged in herding. In such social structures, households directly produce most of what they consume; economic exchange and division of labor are minimal.

In such societies, the labor of children is useful, both because in the diversified activities of the household, there are always tasks that children can carry out, and because the economic level of the household is sufficiently low that the effort of all is needed. Children are not costly to the family because food is ordinarily produced at home. Families have many children, and exploit their capacity for labor, with little regard for the impact of this upon the children's opportunities. Families have narrow horizons, are inwardly focused, and base little interest in or resources for extending their children's horizons broadly.

In an economic and social structure of this sort, the principal role of the school is in protecting children from exploitation by the family, and in providing a broadening influence beyond the family's horizons. The family constrains and limits the child; the school breaks some of these bonds and reduces the constraints. The school often stands, in such a setting, in an antagonistic position to the family, for the interests of the two often conflict. The school is the liberator of the child from the exploitative grasp of the family.

Yet nations whose economies and social structures are of this sort are the poorest, so that the economic resources necessary to provide educational opportunity are most limited. The nation's capability of providing a strong school system to oppose the constraining force of the family is weakest. Consequently, it is in this phase that educational resources are ordinarily most unequally distributed, between rich and poor villages, or between rich and poor regions. Educational opportunity depends largely on the opportunity provided by the family and the immediately surrounding area.

In this phase, the tangible educational resources, textbooks, teachers, classrooms, libraries, are in short supply. Consequently it is in such societies that these input facilities make most differences in educational outcomes. One can well say that for a nation in Phase 1, equalization of educational opportunity is most dependent on tangible educational resources. In this phase, the first definition of equal educational opportunity, in terms of input resources, is most relevant, since variations in educational opportunity depend most on variations in these resources.

Phase 2: Children as Investments for the Family

A post-agricultural, urban, industrial society, engaged largely in manufacturing and some commerce I will call Phase 2. Here the economy is an exchange economy, most labor is performed in full-time jobs, and the family's economic needs are provided mostly through the exchange of wages for goods. Children's labor is no longer needed for the household's economy, and there are fewer possibilities for productive work of children within the household.

In such a society, the family continues to have a strong interest in children, for a more long-range goal. Children are the carriers of the family across generations from the past into the future, and investment in children is an investment in human capital for the family's future. A large number of children is no longer valuable for this purpose, but high investments in each one, to increase the status position, economic position, and social respectability of the family in the next generation is.

This change in the family's interest in children has many implications. One is a decline in the birth rate. Another is an increase in the demand for universal education and for equal educational opportunity. The quantity of children is no longer valuable to the family, but the quality of their preparation and training is.

The family is no longer the school's antagonist, but is its most important ally. The family creates a strong motivation for schooling in its children, for the school's goals for the children coincide with the interest of the family.

High academic achievement is to be expected from children whose families are in Phase 2, and high academic achievement in the nation as a whole when the nation is in Phase 2. Family and school are reinforcing each other's actions toward high achievement.

Phase 3: Children as Irrelevant

An advanced industrial society (what Daniel Bell has called a post-industrial society) or a welfare state with a high degree of affluence I will call Phase 3. In this phase, the family's central role in the economy has vanished, and the family itself has become a kind of appendage to the economic structure. It is an institution relevant to consumption, but no longer to production. Its functional role has been reduced to that of childrearing.

The family's central place in the economy and society has been taken over by large corporate bodies—industrial and commercial corporations. As the economic functions of the family are withdrawn to other institutions, the family loses much of its raison d'être, and begins to disintegrate. It is no longer an institution spanning generations, but forms anew with each generation, so the family's interest in children to carry the family into the future declines. The stability of marriages (and thus of households) declines, as the multi-generational family is no longer present to restrain its members from individualistic solutions at the expense of the family.

In such circumstances, we can expect that families would make fewer investments in children, would press strongly toward academic achievement, and would support the goals of the school less completely than in Phase 2. The evidence concerning these actions is not clear. In the United States and some countries in Europe, which are closest to Phase 3, there is an even stronger demand for equal educational opportunity, and more resources invested in education than in the earlier period of Phase 2. But families have shifted much of the responsibility for financing higher education to the government. Parents spend less time with children, and children less time with parents in whole-family settings. Leisure activities instead take place in age segregated settings: cocktail parties for the adults, rock concerts for the youth. Increasing numbers of children are abandoned, run away from home, or become addicted to drugs, and an increasing number of the children of divorce are unwanted for custody by either mother or father. Yet all these statistics involve a minority of children. At the same time, there is a strong professed interest of parents in their children's educational development.

My own assessment of the trends in the United States is that there is, as one would expect, lesser investment in children than was true thirty or forty years ago, and that the evidence will soon begin to show this more clearly. If I am correct, this means that the school loses much of the active support it had during Phase 2, and that the motivation to achieve which families impart to their children is less frequent. The school's task, in this condition, comes to be one of supplying not only the resources for learning, but also taking active responsibility for bringing about learning. The school, under these conditions, comes to take over some of the functions which the family once provided, but which it no longer provides.

If this picture is a correct one, it accounts for an otherwise puzzling result: Although in less developed countries there is a strong relationship between the tangible school resources in a region or locality or a school and the level of academic achievement of the students in that region, locality, or school (controlling on family backgrounds of the students), this relationship vanishes or is sharply reduced in highly developed countries. The achievement attributable to the school itself in highly developed countries is almost independent of the level of tangible school resources provided by the community or the nation. The achievement is not independent of the way the school is organized, the disciplinary constraints it imposes on students, and the academic demands it makes on them. But a school with excellent physical resources, laboratories, books, and teacher qualifications, a school with high per pupil expenditures, does not produce high achievement if these less tangible organizational elements are missing.

If the picture I have given is correct, the highly developed countries are moving into Phase 3, in which tangible school resources are in oversupply, not only in the school itself, but in the home, through television, and quite generally throughout the society. The student motivation to learn, which was provided by families in Phase 2, is now problematic. With these tangible resources in oversupply, an increase or decrease of 50% in the school resources does not make much difference in achievement, though it did when these countries were in Phase 1 and Phase 2, and these resources were in short supply.

What is in short supply in the affluent Phase 3 is not these tangible resources, but the motivations that strong families, interested in investing time, effort, and attention in their children, provided in Phase 2. The schools that are most effectvie in this third phase are those that are able to supply the intangible qualities that impel students to take full advantage of the opportunities provided by the tangible resources. The school, in Phase 3, is one of many elements competing for the attention and interest of children and youth, and what cannot be taken for granted are the motivational forces that direct attention and interest toward school learning, rather than toward the other attractive competitors for this attention and interest.

Conclusion

What, then, does provision of educational opportunity consist of? All that I have described above implies that it consists of different things when the social and economic conditions of the nation differ. When a nation is in Phase 1, it consists of the provision of tangible resources for learning, plus legal and other constraints on families' exploitation of their children, so that children are free to take advantage of these resources. Some caution must be introduced here, however, because the mere provision of educational opportunity through formal schooling in an economy with an occupational structure that requires the old skills is harmful to both the child's and nation's future. It has drawn children away from the old skills without being able to make use of the new ones. The activities that were economically helpful to the household were also inculcating certain narrow skills that the child could use as he or she replaced father or mother in the next generation, and the school's influence undercuts the learning of these.

In Phase 2, the nation's task in providing educational opportunity is the simplest: mere provision of the tangible resources of formal schooling. This, combined with the motivation that families—acting in their own interest—provide gives an effective educational opportunity. And insofar as these resources are provided in different schools with some approximate degree of equality, the nation is providing an effective educational opportunity that is a strong influence in the direction of equal opportunity.

In Phase 3, the school's task in providing educational opportunity becomes more complex, as described earlier, and is no longer satisfied by the provision of tangible school resources. The full scope of the task is unclear, and I suspect that it will be some time before we learn just how it can be best accomplished. The school's role expands, the possibilities for greater equality of opportunity increase as the power of families declines; but the possibilities for educational mediocrity increase as well. Altogether it is part of a structure of society that is only beginning to unfold, and one about which we have much to learn.

20

Schools and the Communities They Serve

Some variations among schools affect their operations, yet seldom play a part in school policies. I will examine one such crucial variation in this article. First, however, let me describe schools in two communities with which I am familiar, to give a sense of the kind of comparisons I plan to make.

The first community is in the heart of Appalachia. It lies in Tucker County, West Virginia, a rural and mountainous region largely covered by forest. The county has only one town of any size: Parsons, the county seat, population 1,937. Tucker County has one high school, one vocational high school, and several elementary schools.

I am most familiar with the community served by one of the elementary schools, a school with three teachers and five grades. The first and second grades are together under one teacher, grades 3 through 5 are together under another, and there is one head teacher—though the grade combinations vary each year, depending on the size of the age groups. The teachers live in the local community. Parents know them well, both directly and through the extended network of kinship, friendship, and work relationships that pervades each of the communities served by the school and connects these communities.

The father of some of the children work in the mines; some have farms (not productive enough to make a living), which they combine with other jobs, such as driving a school bus; some are engaged in such community services as operating a gas station and general store or delivering mail. In Parsons, the county seat, the jobs are more diversified—insurance agent, barber, bank teller, state or county employee. Some of the men receive unemployment compensation, and a few families are on welfare; until the mines reopened a few years ago, many more were. One man, who had children late in life by an Indian woman he brought back from Mexico,

Reprinted with permission from *Phi Delta Kappan*, vol. 66, no. 8 (April 1985): 527–532.

draws disability compensation for injuries suffered in the mines. A number of the older men in the community receive black lung compensation.

Because many of the fathers work near home and because the men often work around the house, yard, and garden, they see their children a lot when the children are not in school. They sometimes play with the younger children, but the form of interaction changes when the children reach age 8 or 10. The fathers' activities are physical and often outdoors, and the boys (and some of the girls) tag along. The boys often emulate their fathers, whether riding four-wheelers or motorcycles, drinking beer, trying to chew tobacco, or hunting raccoons.

Most of the mothers do not work outside the home, but some do, in the local shoe factory or in clerical jobs in the county seat. Many of the grandparents of schoolchildren live in the community, as do many of their aunts, uncles, cousins, and other relatives. Few parents have gone beyond high school, and many never completed high school. Most of the children will not go beyond high school, but some will—and most of those who do so will leave the county because of the absence of work other than the sorts of jobs described above. Thus depleted, the next generation that remains in Tucker County will continue to consist primarily of high school graduates and dropouts.

The weekly newspaper published in the county seat usually contains extended news about children in school: competitions for queen of the county fair and for homecoming queen and for the queen's court (which includes grade school children), or football games, or car accidents involving local teenagers, or accounts of local boys' scrapes with the law.

These communities in Tucker County, and the schools that serve them, are the residue of a segment of rural America that now represents only a tiny fraction of the country.

The second community is also unusual, though in many respects it could hardly be more different from the one I've just described. This community is Hyde Park–Kenwood, which surrounds the University of Chicago. Nearly three-fourths of the faculty members of the university live in Hyde Park or Kenwood, within a mile of the university. Many walk or ride bicylces to work; those who come by car drive only a few blocks.

The Hyde Park community has several public elementary schools, three private schools (two of them affiliated with religious groups), and one university laboratory school. There is a single large public high school and a private high school, the laboratory school. I am most familiar with the laboratory elementary school and will focus on it.

This school, with three or four classes per grade level, is larger than the one in Tucker County. Many of the teachers live in Hyde Park or Kenwood, and some are affiliated with the university community. Some parents know their children's teachers outside school, but most do not. They do know them by reputation, through the extended network of friendship, neighborhood, and work relations that binds Hyde Park and Kenwood. Kinship networks are largely missing, though there are examples of family "dynasties" with members involved in University of Chicago schools through virtually their whole lives. The most prominent are Edward and Julian Levi, brothers who were first enrolled in the laboratory nursery school and who have recently retired as president of the university and professor of law at the university.

One or both parents of most children in the lab school work at the university, either as faculty or staff members. Younger children are often brought to school on foot by fathers or mothers on their way to work at the university. Others live in Hyde Park (or adjacent Kenwood) and are connected to the university community only by friendship relations and neighborhood associations. A few live outside the Hyde Park–Kenwood area and are not connected to these networks at all.

More of the lab school mothers than the Tucker County mothers are employed outside the home, many at the university. The lack of an extensive network of kinship relations means that there are few family gatherings at which gossip flows about children, teachers, and school; but there are many social gatherings at which such gossips flows.

Nearly all the students at the lab school will go on to college, and many will obtain advanced degrees. A few of those will remain in the community, but most will leave. In contrast to the residents in the Tucker County communities, their families will be succeeded by others from outside the community, similar in education and lifestyle but geographically mobile.

An incident in each of these two schools will facilitate further comparisons.

Event 1. On the first day of school in Tucker County, a fourth-grader reported to her mother that her sister (a first-grader who is shy and verbally backward) cried most of the time, and that the head teacher, Mrs. X, yelled at her, which made her cry even more. The mother called the first-grade teacher and asked her about it, then called two friends and talked to them about Mrs. X.

The next day, the fourth-grader reported that much the same thing had happened. Again, the mother talked to friends about the events. On the third day the mother went to the school, confronted Mrs. X, and discussed her first-grade daughter. By the weekend, the daughter seemed to have accepted school; she had stopped crying, and Mrs. X had stopped yelling. Nevertheless, at a barbecue on Saturday of that week, most of the gossip among the mother and three other women (two whose children had attended the school and one whose child would enter school the next year) was about the school and the teacher—with occasional remarks from one of the men, who knew and didn't like Mrs. X's husband.

Event 2. Last spring, a faculty member at the University of Chicago realized that his son, who was then in nursery school, was due to be placed in one of the lab school kindergarten classes. He talked to a colleague in his department, who said vehemently, "Don't let him be put in Mrs. A's class. She is terrible for boys who don't do just what she expects." The colleague's son had had that same teacher and had adjusted to school only after being moved to another class. When the father spoke to a second

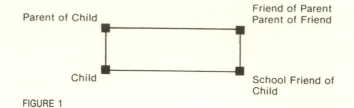

FIGURE 1

colleague whose two sons had attended the school, he heard a similar story about Mrs. A.

Then the mother talked to some friends and heard a slightly different story about Mrs. A: that she was strict, demanding, and not good for children (especially boys) whose progress was slow. The parents then talked at length to Mrs. B, their son's nursery-school teacher, who had followed the progress of many of her former students in Mrs. A's classes. They also talked to other nursery-school parents whose children were friends of their son. Based on Mrs. B's comments, the set of parents decided collectively to have their children placed in Mrs. A's class. The friends all began kindergarten in Mrs. A's class—but their parents remained especially attentive because of the warnings they had heard.

I could list additional events, but these two are sufficient to introduce the explicit comparisons I wish to make. I am suggesting that—despite the enormous differences between these two communities, between the probable futures of the children who live in them, and between the schools that serve them—there are strong similarities. I also wish to suggest that most public schools in the United States differ sharply from these two schools and are becoming more different all the time.

What makes these two schools similar and distinguishes them from most U.S. schools is the strength of the functional communities they serve. The Tucker County school serves a functional community built around kinship, residence, church, and work. The Hyde Park school serves a functional community built primarily around work and residence.

Perhaps the most important property of these functional communities (for my purposes here) can, without too much distortion, be expressed in a single sentence: *A child's friends and associates in school are sons and daughers of friends and associates of the child's parents.* This property is expressed in Figure 1. In contrast, a diagram representing the *absence* of a functional community that spans generations (Figure 2) does not show this kind of closure.

The two events I described, involving the Tucker County first-grader and the Hyde Park kindergartner, make it evident that something very like the type of closure shown in Figure 1 was critical to the actions taken by the parents. Without the closure, in a social structure like that shown in Figure 2, the Tucker County mother would not have had the information that reinforced her views and encouraged her to go to the school and talk to

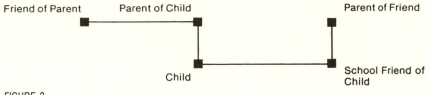

FIGURE 2

the head teacher. She would have been forced to rely on her individual resources, and for most parents these are not sufficiently strong to impel actions of the sort she took. The intimidation of the school is far too strong.

The diagram is not precisely accurate in the Tucker County case, since some of the friends on whom the mother depended were not parents of friends of her daughter, but parents whose children had been in the same social context—in the same school with the same teacher. The same holds true in the second example: the two colleagues with whom the Hyde Park father discussed the kindergarten teachers were not parents of his son's friends, but parents who sons had been exposed to those teachers.

Nevertheless, with this minor caveat, the general principle stands. In these functional communities, the social structure characteristic of parents and children exhibits *intergenerational closure* of the sort shown in Figure 1. In school settings not embedded in functional communities, the social structure of the community fails to exhibit such closure, thus cutting off the information flow that strengthens and supports parents in their school-related activities. Information flow of the sort exhibited in these events is not the only—nor perhaps even the most important—type of feedback or support provided to the parent by a functional community with closure of the sort shown in Figure 1. In such a community, the parent need not depend only on the child for information about the child's behavior, both in and out of school. The parent has additional channels: through the friends and acquaintances of the child, then to the parents of those children, and back to the parent. The parent has an informal network of sentinels—each imperfect but, taken together, capable of providing a rich store of information about the child's behavior and even capable of exercising discipline in lieu of the parent. In the absence of this closure, the last link of the feedback chain is missing, and there are no sentinels on whom the parent can rely. The child's behavior can remain unnoticed and unattended by adults whom the parent knows, and the parent is again unsupported—in negotiations not with the school but with the child.

It may well be this consequence of the decline of intergenerational closure—the inability of a community of parents to establish and enforce norms of behavior for their children—that has made schools so difficult to govern in recent years. If so, the prognosis for school administration is not good, for the decline shows no sign of reversal.

Another consequence of closure within the functional community is the possibilities it creates for personal relations between a child and an adult other than the child's parents. In Tucker County, a grandfather may help his grandson raise a calf for 4-H, or a man whose own sons are grown may introduce his neighbor's son to the complexities of trapping. There is no shortage of youth leaders. In Hyde Park, there is less such interest, but there is some. A faculty member will hire a colleague's teenage daughter or son as a research assistant, or a runner whom a faculty member knows at the fieldhouse will teach his friend's son about training to become a competitive runner.

In a structure without closure (Figure 2), a child's principal relations with adults are—except for teachers—with his or her own parents. There is little reason for another adult to take an avuncular interest in the child's friends. Indeed, any such interest is suspect, given the potential for exploitation, sexual or otherwise.

Throughout American society, there has been for some years a decline in the number of volunteer youth leaders (e.g., scoutmasters or boys and girls club leaders); currently, there is increased alarm about sexual exploitation of children by adults. If my analysis is correct, both of these phenomena are a consequence of the decline of functional communities with intergenerational closure.

It is also important to point out some other consequences of functional communities characterized by a social structure with intergenerational closure— but consequences that are inimical to equality of opportunity. A social structure with closure facilities the development of *reputations;* in a structure without closure, reputations are nonexistent. And in a social structure with intergenerational closure, there is the *inheritance* of reputation. An example from Tucker County illustrates this well. The man with the Mexican-Indian wife and the back injury from working in the mines, whom I'll call Jack, had a reputation as a ne'er-do-well. He lived with his wife and two children in a two-room shack surrounded by broken-down cars. His children went to school, of course, though they very likely did not receive much support and encouragement at home. And because everyone knew the father, that is, because of the intergenerational closure of the community, the father's reputation descended to his son.

The son left school early, got a girl pregnant, and has moved with her into a trailer. He's something of a hell-raiser and appears likely to turn out like his father. It is difficult to know to what extent the son's career in school and since is due to his home environment and to what extent his inherited reputation itself had an impact within the school. But suppose for a moment that Jack and his wife, while otherwise no different, had provided an exemplary environment for doing homework and fulfilling school requirements. The reputation would still have been inherited by the son, and it would still have been a difficult impediment to overcome.

This kind of inheritance of reputation exists to a lesser extent in Hyde Park, both because the community has less intergenerational closure and because of egalitarian values held by many Hyde Park residents. Yet the feedback channels do exist, and there is some inheritance of reputation—

more than in a suburb characterized by anomie. As a result, some children go through school with a subtle advantage. A child of a distinguished professor inherits a portion of the parent's reputation, a legacy that the child of an ordinary member of the community lacks.

This impediment to equal opportunity is not a new one; indeed, it has been documented in studies such as *Middletown*, by Robert and Helen Lynd (1929) and *Elmtown's Youth*, by A.B. Hollingshead (1949). What has *not* been generally noted is that the inheritance of reputation depends on a social structure with intergenerational closure, that such structures also bring benefits, and that such structures are vanishing from U.S. society. (Richard Hoggart, in *The Uses of Literacy* [1957], an examination of working-class neighborhoods in the urban North of England, is one of the few who had documented the benefits of this closure.)

Indeed, some of the benefits of these social structures are particularly important for disadvantaged children. One of the major changes that rural migrants to city ghettos or slums experience is the loss of the functional community that has aided in disciplining their children and keeping them out of trouble. Such a loss is especially severe for families with meager economic and personal resources. Jack's son, for instance, may have been branded by his father's reputation, but he has also been kept out of some trouble by community sanctions that would be missing in modern urban or suburban areas.

More generally, we might conjecture that the strong collective resources provided by communities with intergenerational closure (whether in ethnic urban neighborhoods or in rural ares) were important for the extraordinary social and intellectual development that occurred in the first half of the 20th century among Americans who parents had few personal resources. Today, a variety of changes have broken that closure. Consequently, the two schools I've described (one public and one private) and the functional communities surrounding them are atypical.

To be sure, some communities have many of the characteristics I have attributed to functional communities, but many forces act to weaken them. Most fathers work outside the communities in which their children attend school, and an increasing number of mothers do also. Friends and associates are increasingly drawn from the workplace rather than from the neighborhood. Work- and residence-based ties have been eroded, as the men who were once their foundation have gone to work outside the community. Neighborhood-based associations are weakened, as the women who were once their foundation enter the labor force. Geographic mobility reduces the proximity of grandparents, uncles, aunts, and cousins in the lives of the children.

School policies at all levels—federal, state, and local—have also weakened the community in which the school is embedded. These policies have included school consolidation (designed to introduce "efficiencies of scale") and those kinds of school desegregation that have been explicitly designed to break the neighborhood/school connection. Policies of increasing school size and reducing school grade-spans have had similar effects.

The overall impact of all of these changes, some technological in origin and some political, has been to destroy the networks of relations that once existed in geographic neighborhoods and linked these neighborhoods to the schools within them.

Residential Proximity and Functional Communities

The functional communities that once existed in the U.S., communities within which public schools were embedded, were defined geographically. There were *neighborhoods*, characterized by rich textures of interpersonal relations and by the kind of intergenerational closure that is still found in Tucker County and, to a lesser extent, in Hyde Park. But, though functional communities built on a residential base have largely vanished, the public schools continue to be organized on a residential base.

Some private schools in the U.S. are created by functional communities that are not residentially based. Most of these schools are religious, but some, like the University of Chicago Laboratory School, have a different institutional base.

A smaller number of private schools, largely concentrated in the Northeast, have traditionally been based on functional communities defined by a geographically dispersed but socially connected social elite. Many of these schools no longer have this closure; instead, they are attended by children whose parents are not only geographically dispersed but also have no functional connection. Thus it may be that, though some private schools exhibit higher levels of intergenerational closure than can be found in public schools, others exhibit the very lowest levels of closure.

However, much opposition to private schooling has been based on the exclusionary and separatist consequences of intergenerational closure not based on residential communities. The ideology of the common public school has been based on the premise that a school serving a residentially defined community provides a much more democratic and socially integrating form of intergenerational closure—bringing together children of different religions, different social classes, different ethnic groups, and thereby bringing their families closer together—than does a school serving a community based on ethnic, religious, or social-elitist connections.

In general, this premise has been a sound one. In recent years, however, the residential community has ceased to be a functional community except in such unusual instances as Tucker County or Hyde Park. Furthermore, the separation of work and residence has destroyed the democratic and integrating character of schools based on residental proximity. Residential areas are quite homogeneous both in income and in race.

The recency and gradualness of the demise of residential communities as functional communities have generally obscured the fact that functional communities are an important social resource, not least because of the possibility they create for intergenerational closure, connecting communities of adults to communities of children. Thus social policy persists in opposing schools serving communities based on anything but residence, on much the same grounds as in the past. There is little recognition of the imporant fact that breaking down the intergenerational closure of non-residence-based communities does not lead to more democratic and integrated functional communities, but to racially and economically homogeneous schools without the strength that can be provided by an adult functional community.

The issue of the organization of education, then, has come to be a different one than in the past. The issue now is whether the benefits of intergenerational closure provided by schools serving non-geographically-defined communities outweigh the separatist tendencies inherent in such communities. Or, to put it differently, the issue is whether the value of this social resource—the intergenerational closure provided by schools serving functional communities—is sufficiently great to outweigh the costs of such schools to broader social assimilation.

A New Range of Policies

The general decline of functional communities in American society and the loss of intergenerational closure that has attended this decline make the question of how best to organize education much more difficult to resolve than when functional communities were abundant. Once the issue is seen in the context in which I have presented it here, then a broader range of policies in the organization of education becomes evident. It may be possible to organize schools so that the social costs brought about by technological change are mitigated without reimposing all the costs that resulted from our old social structure.

Some institutions designed to strengthen intergenerational closure have long existed. Parent/Teacher Associations certainly have this aim. In some cases, they are able to reinstitute links between parents that afford a degree of intergenerational closure. In many cases, however, parents have too few daily, informal contacts to sustain these links. Some principals and teachers have attempted to bring together parents for ad hoc meetings when an issue or crisis arises in the school (e.g., drug abuse or suicide). Crises of this sort can sometimes establish ties between parents that persist, even in the absence of regular contact. Thus school crises, if they mobilize parents in any collective fashion, can leave as residue a set of relations that aid the school, the parents, and their children in the future.

The fact that intense common experiences create enduring ties suggests other possible policies. Some private schools (and, less often, public schools) use events sponsored by parents as a means of raising money; this type of event can strengthen parental links. Recognizing this, school administrators can initiate events and activities designed specifically to bring together parents of children in the school. Many administrators know that, by creating collective strength among parents, they create a force that can be a nuisance; less often do they recognize that this collective strength can be a resource that both eases their task of governing a school and benefits the children who attend it.

There are more fundamental changes that can help achieve intergenerational closure. The most direct approach would be to reopen the question of organizing publicly supported schools by residential proximity. As I have indicated above, the assumptions on which that model of school organization is based no longer hold, except in isolated instances outside metropolitan areas. Yet the pattern of school organization continues to exist.

When that question is reopened, one way of answering it would be to search for those functional communities that still remain in the highly individualistic society that the United States has become. Religious association continues to be a basis for functional communities for some, for whom religious observance, religious affiliation, and activities related to religion are important enough to play a part in everyday life. For some of these persons, private schools run by their religious groups create intergenerational closure. This suggests a reexamination of the uniquely American policy of refusing public support for privately organized schools.

Another basis for functional communities for much broader sets of adults is the workplace of either or both parents. Increasingly, adults' friends are drawn from the workplace rather than from the neighborhood. It follows that a natural way to reestablish intergenerational closure is to organize schools by workplaces. (The University of Chicago Laboratory School is an illustration; however, that school exists only because the university performs research and teaching related to education.) Schools based at the workplaces of parents, whether in a steel mill or in an office building downtown, constitute a sharp departure from neighborhood-based schools. But this model has the potential to partially reconstitute the intergenerational community that no longer exists in the neighborhood and, furthermore, to cut across racial and economic lines.

*　　*　　*

The changes in school policy that I have suggested indicate some of the ways in which school reorganization might help to reunite the communities of children and youth with the adult community. These are not the only possible policy changes. Yet they serve to open these questions for discussion, so that we may examine potential ways of reconstituting intergenerational closure without reintroducing the social costs that have traditionally accompanied it.

Schools have long been based on the premise of strong families and strong functional communities of families. Now that the functional communities of neighborhood have withered and families themselves are increasingly fragile, it may be that the goals of schools can best be aided by policies that build upon and strengthen those links that exist among families.

21

Families and Schools

The earliest of the English private schools, which are called "public" schools, was Winchester, which began in the 14th century. These elite boarding schols, supported by endowments and by tuition fees from parents, came to be known as "public" schools in contrast to the other principal means of schooling, which was the private tutor. For all children other than those of the elite, schooling was even more fully lodged in the family. It was schooling via the household's productive activities and via a system in which children and youth learned trades, other than that of their household, in nearby households.

For the upper status family, the private tutor was an appendage to the family who provided instruction within the context of the household. The boarding school, which transferred these activities from the household to a setting which brought together and taught boys from many families, constituted a sharp disjunction. But even though Winchester began in the 14th century, mass state-supported schooling did not begin until the late 19th and early 20th centuries.

Thus, throughout the history and prehistory of the human race, mass formal schooling occupies less than a century, a period that is minuscule in the history of mankind. For most of society's children and youth, formal schooling hardly existed until this century: Children grew up in the context of the household and the neighborhood. All the activities and facilities for training that would prepare them for adulthood took place within the household or in easy distance from it. A child, as it grew, would slowly move into those activities, with training being almost wholly confined to "on-the-job-training," and the job being closely linked to household activities. For many children in the traditional sector of the third world, the activities of the household and the village still constitute their school.

In this paper, I want to describe changes that have occurred in the relation between family and society, and suggest consequences of those changes for the family's capacity to raise its children. The implications for schooling are of course extensive, for school as we conceive of it implies family as we

Reprinted with permission from *Educational Researcher,* vol. 16, no. 6 (August/September 1987): 32–38.

conceive of it. Yet family as we conceive of it no longer corresponds to family as it now exists.

Transformation of the Household

What has happened over the past two centuries to change the context of childrearing? One way of describing the change is as a change in the locus of dominant activities in society. Until this century, the principal economic activities were within the household and the surrounding neighborhood. The economy was a subsistence economy, with families producing for their own use a far wider range of goods than they obtained by exchange—and most of what they obtained through exchange was from the local area. With few exceptions, economic enterprises that employed others were outgrowths of household production, had their basis in the family, and were located near to it. The whole structure of social and economic organization has as its basic building block the family.

That changed, with the change accelerating from the latter half of the 19th century. The central element in that change was the movement of economically productive activities outside the household. The new activities were, in their early stages proximate to the household, but became increasingly distant from it. This distance implied the removal of men's labor from the household and from close proximity to it. Men left the farm, or the neighborhood shop, and went away to the office or factory. An indicator of this change is the percentage of men in the labor force who are in agriculture, for agriculture is the principal occupation carried out at home. As Figure 1 shows, in 1810, it was 87%; by 1900, it had declined to 42%; and, by 1980, to 3%.

This change could be described by its technical component, as it ordinarily has been, in all that is implied by the term Industrial Revolution. It could, however, be described by its social structural component, creation of a structure of productive social activities that was independent of the household. The law recognized the social structural change from an early period, defining a new kind of legal agent: a "fictional person," as it was called, for it had no natural person as its head. It was a corporate body with a life of its own: free-floating in society, legally "owned" by a set of shareholders, but with a legal personality distinct from any of them. This new kind of person in society is the modern corporation. The French have an apt name for it, "société anonyme," an anonymous society. I call it a corporate actor. The name is not important. What is important is that it *is* an actor in society, it does *not* derive from the family, and it has come to play an increasingly central role in the functioning of society.[1]

The movement of men's work out of the household was paralleled by another change, the growth of public schooling. As men ceased working in or near the home, there came to be a social investment in a new, "constructed" institution, the school. Although the complex of changes that led to public schooling cannot be easily separated, certainly the father's leaving home-

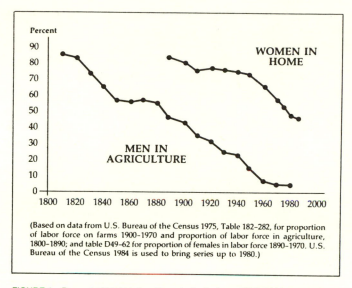

FIGURE 1   Percent of Male Labor Force in Agriculture, 1810–1982, and Percent of Women Not Employed in Paid Labor Force, 1890–1982

based employment, where his sons could learn adult's work from him, for externally based (and ultimately corporation-based) employment, was a nontrivial element.

Since the period in which work outside the household replaced the family in the father's daytime life, there have been extensive further changes. One of the most striking has been the movement of women's work from inside the household to outside. Figure 1 also shows, parallel to the men's percentage in agriculture, the percentage of women not in the paid labor force, that is, in the household during the day. The woman's presence in the household during the day in the 1980s is just about like that of the man's in the 1880s.

The family has become, as corporate actors have swallowed up an increasingly large fraction of first men's, and then women's activities and attention, a kind of backwater in society, cut off from the mainstream. But, although this world of corporate actors has come to be critical for adults, removing first fathers and then mothers from the household during the day, children remain outside it—as do the old, the sick, and all those whom we call "dependent." It is useful briefly to focus on dependency and its locus, because it can help us to see more clearly the essential character of the change that has crept up on us.

A Change in the Locus of Dependency

In the old social structure, dependency was not a public phenomenon. The streets of New York and Philadelphia were not populated with homeless men and women, and foster care institutions were not populated with children who had two live and healthy parents. Dependency was absorbed by the family and its extensions. Families took care of their aged; unmarried men and women lived in the households of their married siblings, as aunts and uncles; and children were fully ensconced within the household.

In short, *the household was the principal welfare institution of society.* Beyond the household were the extended family and kin group, and they constituted the secondary, or backup welfare institution in society.

That has changed. Many of the welfare activities of the family are no longer carried out within it. Welfare has moved outside the extended family, into the larger society. It has not moved to the corporation, to which the household's economic activities migrated, but to the state.

The sources of the family's incapacity to serve as the principal welfare institution of socity are several. One of the most recent is the increasing distribution of income away from households that have children or other dependents. Once wages replaced household production for the prototypical household, the wage-earner's income was distributed, via the household budget, to nonwage earners within it: children, spouse, and possibly adult dependents, such as parents of husband or wife. But this distribution depends on dependents and incomes being similarly distributed across households.

At the time this country was founded, this was more or less true. The few historical studies indicate that only between 15 and 20% of households had no children under 18 within them. The most recent census data show that currently about 65% of households are without children under 18. Figure 2 shows how that percentage has increased over the last hundred years of the nation's existence and shows that much of the increase has come in recent years. The implication is obvious; if households are without children, they ordinarily do not redistribute the household's income to children.

The family as a welfare institution also depends upon the pattern of incomes being distributed across households. But households have diverged: An increasing proportion of households has no earnings, and an increasing proportion has income from two wage earners but no children.[2] The latter phenomenon is sufficiently common that an acronym has been coined; DINKs, *Double Income, No Kids.* The result is a correlation between household income and number of dependents that moves in a negative direction: Adults in a portion of the nation's households are occupied with having children, and adults in another portion of households are occupied with making money; but increasingly, households are specializing in one of these two activities. A result is that the income available to children, relative to that available to adults, declines. The decline has recently been especially rapid: Between 1970 and 1980, children under 5 became the age group in the population with the highest percentage in poverty (Preston, 1984). In this ten-year period, the percentage rose from 16 to 24%.

We might conclude that this specialization, this division of labor, is merely an instance of the general movement toward division of labor that the Industrial Revolution and its accompaniment, the modern corporation brought.

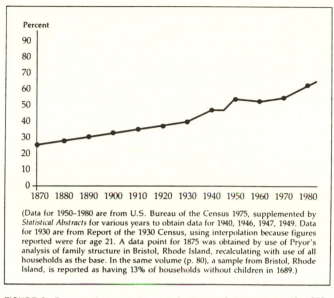

(Data for 1950–1980 are from U.S. Bureau of the Census 1975, supplemented by *Statistical Abstracts* for various years to obtain data for 1940, 1946, 1947, 1949. Data for 1930 are from Report of the 1930 Census, using interpolation because figures reported were for age 21. A data point for 1875 was obtained by use of Pryor's analysis of family structure in Bristol, Rhode Island, recalculating with use of all households as the base. In the same volume (p. 80), a sample from Bristol, Rhode Island, is reported as having 13% of households without children in 1689.)

FIGURE 2   Percent of Households in U.S. Without Children Under 18, 1870–1983

As economists have been fond of pointing out since Adam Smith's famous illustration of the manufacture of pins, division of labor ordinarily increases efficiency. And if the transfer of income to dependents can take place, not within the household, but between households through taxation, with government taking the role of chief welfare institution of society, all would appear to be well.

There are, however, problems with the proposition as it affects the raising of children. One is the inefficiency created by the roundabout transfer through a government bureaucracy. A more important problem is that governments are not very good at humane welfare, as is exhibited by foster care or mental health institutions (See Testa & Wulczyn, 1980; Hugi, 1983). Still another, and perhaps the most intractable, is the extraordinary difficulty government has in providing welfare to dependents without creating an incentive for dependency. This is an incentive which increases the very dependency it sets out to alleviate.[3]

The common examples of this incentive effect are the growth of Aid to Families with Dependent Children (AFDC), the abuse of the food stamp program, and a wealth of other means of exploiting government welfare. Some of these are important because of the incentive they provide for producing children in households that have only minimal resources to offer these children. But there is another, less evident, incentive effect which may be even more important. The division of labor between earning income and raising children is not merely a division of labor between households (the households of the DINKs and the households of the welfare mothers). It is a division of labor between households engaged in earning income and governments engaged in raising children.

Reduced Incentives for Parental Responsibility

Again one might think first of the extreme case, government foster care of children—an activity which has shown great growth in recent years (Testa & Wulczyn, 1980; Hugi, 1983). However, the incentive effects of this division go far beyond foster care; they involve incentives of all families with children, even those that would be regarded as most responsible. A variety of indicators shows the reduced incentive on the part of parents to take responsibility for their children.

Finances for College

Before the 1960s or 1970s, there was a general assumption that costs of college education were principally the responsibility of parents, aided, in some cases, by earnings of the student. Since that time, there has been a shift: Costs of college education are seen increasingly to be in part a governmental responsibility, through scholarship funds and subsidized loans, in part a responsibility of the student, through work and through incurring loans, and in lesser part a responsibility of parents. This change has arisen in part through increased government responsibility for equality of educational opportunity. The reduced assumption of responsibility by middle class parents provides a good example of the apparently inescapable effect: Governmental assumption of responsibility for persons in need creates increased need.

After-School and Summer Activities

There has been a growth in demand for full-day and year-round institutionalization of children, ordinarily in school or in school-related care. This demand has not been confined to lower classes, but has probably been greatest among middle class and upper middle class parents. The role of unstructured, home-based or neighborhood-based activities for children under the supervision of parents has declined, and the role of structured, school-based activities under the supervision of professionals has increased. A large part of this can be explained, of course, by the growth in single-parent households and in families where both parents work full time. But that growth itself reflects decreased responsibility for children and increased attention to self-fulfillment.

Parental Authority

Before the 1960s, parents continued to assume some authority over their children as long as the children remained in school, including college. Colleges operated under an assumption of *in loco parentis*, exercising parietal rules in dormitories and other regulations consistent with the presumption of a delegation of authority over children from parent to college administrators.

With parents' relaxation of authority over college-age children, colleges relaxed these rules. In 1975, a step in the same direction was taken at the high school level: The landmark Supreme Court case of *Goss vs. Lopez* gave children rights of due process before suspension by the school. It went almost unnoticed that this decision presumed that the issue was not between parents and schools, but between the child, as an autonomous agent with full civil rights, and the school.

Domains of Socialization

Parents have delegated an increasingly wide range of socialization activities to the school. Sex education, a part of the curriculum of many schools, is only the most obvious example. Others include afterschool activities that go considerably beyond the school's traditional tasks. Perhaps more important than parents' delegation of domains to the school is their turning over of curriculum decisions to their children. Powell, Farrar, and Cohen's *The Shopping Mall High School* (1985) describes the growth of a new kind of public high school in America. A proliferation of courses in the 1960s and 1970s has led to high school curricula in which students put together courses like items on a shopping list, often bypassing the more difficult college preparatory courses in foreign language, mathematics, and physical science. Such a cafeteria of courses is found, of course, in colleges as well; but there students are clearly no longer under parental authority. Its downward migration to high school is an indicator of downward migration of the point at which parental authority is relaxed.

Other Indicators

The extraordinary success of many first-generation Asian children in American schools is often seen to reside in strong families, highly oriented to academic success. But the obverse of this relative strength of the Asian family is the relative weakness of the non-Asian family. Beyond low levels of achievement, first observed in Scholastic Aptitude Test Score declines and in international comparisons of science and mathematics achievement (Husen, 1967; Comber & Keyes, 1973), a set of alarming behaviors among American youth can be linked to parental inattention: high levels of drug and alcohol use, illegimate births, and suicide. Each has multiple causes, but their rise suggests reduced levels of attention on the part of parents.

It was a French sociologist, Emile Durkheim (1951), who first showed the strong relation of suicide to social isolation. (He saw this isolation as resulting from "egoisme," which we would translate as individualism in society. The phenomenon is sometimes mistakenly described as "anomie," by which Durkheim meant something quite different, and, on the whole, less important.) The extraordinary increase in suicide rates among teen-agers in America would be regarded by Durkheim as an indicator of the growth in their social isolation. This social isolation is not a result of oppressive parenthood; it is a result of relaxed and inattentive parenthood.

Generally, in this century, there has been a drift downward in the age at which a young person achieves autonomy from parental authority. There have been conflicting trends which made this decline less rapid than it otherwise would be, trends such as later marriage, longer financial dependence of youth on parents, and a more extended period of education. Counter to these trends, which taken by themselves would lead to a lengthening period of subordination of youth lead parental authority, there has been a general decline in hierarchical authority throughout society, particularly in the family. This has not been a move from a hierarchical structure to a communitarian form, but a move away from strong relations of any sort.[4] The consequences for youth are a loss of parental claims of legitimacy in the exercise of authority over their teen-age children. The parental relation has moved in the direction of being a "friendship" relation rather than an authority relation. But the further consequence of that is a weakening of the intensity of the relation. For there is little occasion for building friendship across generations in modern Western society. The society is highly age-segregated in its leisure pursuits and its daily activities. A teen-ager has much more in common with another teen-ager, and middle-aged adult has much more in common with another middle-aged adult, than either has with the other. The rationale for an intense relation evaporates when the relation becomes an egalitarian one, for both parent and child have more rewarding alternative egalitarian relations with others their own age.[5]

To suggest, as Charles Murray (1984) has, that the rise in AFDC households is due to the incentive effects that are created by the existence of government-provided welfare is different from suggesting, as I am doing here, that the behavior of parents at *all* economic and educational levels in raising their children is subject to similar incentive effects. Confronted with the alternatives of contributing to their own self-development, an activity from which they can capture the benefits in terms of income or enjoyment, or investing in their child's future, an activity from which they can capture only a decreasing fraction of the benefits (as children less often care for aging parents, and as the notion of children carrying the family honor into the next generation fades), it is reasonable for them to opt for the former, and to shift the burdens of the latter activities to government.

The Interaction of Families and Schools

One might still argue that there is nothing wrong with this increased specialization or division of labor, where many households specialize in career development and earning income, while other households and government institutions specialize in childrearing. There are, however, some further disturbing facts. As the Equality of Educational Opportunity report of 21 years ago first made clear, variations among family backgrounds make more difference in achievement than do variations among schools. This does not imply that "schools don't make a difference." There is evidence that in the *absence* of schooling, children from whatever background learn very little of certain things, such as mathematics (see Coleman & Hoffer, 1987, p. 87). What it does imply is that schools, of whatever quality, are more effective for children from strong family backgrounds than for children from weak ones. The resources devoted by the family to the child's education interact with the resources provided by the school—and there is greater variation in the former resources than in the latter. The strategy of career-and-income oriented households in shifting burdens of childrearing onto the state, or onto schools, and supporting those activities through taxes or tuition, runs into this fact.

As the formal institutions of childrearing, schools and day care centers, are structured, they can provide a certain class of inputs into the socialization process. These inputs can be loosely characterized as *opportunities, demands,* and *rewards.* But a second class of inputs comes only from the child's closer, more intimate, and more persisting environment. These inputs can be loosely described as *attitudes, effort,* and *conception of self;* and the environment that most affects them is, for nearly all children, the social environment of the household. (For those few children in boarding schools, a portion of that environment may be found within the boarding school, which constructs for the child a temporary household.)

Thus, the division of labor that leads a household to concentrate in careers and income, while leaving to the school the tasks of socialization, merely results in an increase in the one set of inputs, the opportunities, demands, and rewards, while ignoring those which interact with them, the attitudes, effort, and conception of self.

If all this is so, then what can public policy do? To answer this question requires recognition of two points. First, schools constitute a *constructed* institution, a result of public policy, designed to complement the noncon-structed, spontaneous institution, the family, which has principal respon-sibility for childrearing. This implies that schools, to be effective, must change as families change, must be adjusted to the conditions of the institution they complement.

The second point that must be recognized in answering this question is that America is at a watershed for families as socializing institutions and, more generally, as welfare institutions, for their dependent young. Given current public policy and given current orientations among adults, many families at all social levels fail to provide an environment that allows their children to benefit from schools as they currently exist.

Social Capital

These two points taken together imply that more than minor modifications in schools are necessary if the children of America are to be properly served by the adult generation. To see what these changes might be, it is helpful to examine some results of recent research. The results are described more fully in *Public and Private Schools: The Impact of Communities* (Coleman & Hoffer, 1987). I mention here only what is necessary to give an understanding of a single concept, *social capital.* What I mean by social capital in the raising of children is the norms, the social networks, and the relationships between adults and children that are of value for the child's growing up. Social capital exists within the family, but also outside the family, in the community.

One example illustrates what I mean by social capital within the family and how it differs from the more common concept of human capital. A school district where children purchase textbooks recently found that some Asian families were purchasing two. Investigation led to the discovery that one book was for the mother, to enable her to better help her child succeed in school. The mother, uneducated, had little human capital, but her intense concern with her child's school performance, and her willingness to devote effort to aiding that, shows a high level of social capital in the family.

Beyond the family, social capital in the community exists in the interest, even the intrusiveness, of one adult in the activites of someone else's child. Sometimes that interest takes the form of enforcing norms imposed by parents or by the community; sometimes it takes the form of lending a sympathetic ear to problems not discussable with parents, sometimes volunteer youth group leadership or participation in other youth-related activities.[6]

In 1982, Hoffer and Sally Kilgore and I showed that, in 1980, students in Catholic and other private schools achieved at a higher level in tests of mathematics and verbal skills (but not in science) than did students from comparable backgrounds in public schools. The same tests were given two years later, in 1982, to students who had been sophomores in 1980, allowing an examination of growth in achievement over the two-year period.[7] But that is not the result to which I want to call your attention. Data were also obtained on who dropped out between 1980 and 1982. As Figure 3 shows, in the public schools, 14.3% of sophomores had left school without graduating by 1982; in the non-Catholic private sector, 11.9% had left; and in the Catholic sector, 3.4% had left, only a fourth to a third as many as in the other two sectors.[8]

Why was this? After extensive exploration, we concluded that unlike the achievement effects I referred to earlier, it was not the result of greater curricular demands or anything else *within* the school, but was due to a different relation of the school to the parental community. We concluded that the community surrounding the Catholic school, a community created by the church, was of great importance in reducing dropouts among students at risk of dropping out. In effect, this church-and-school community, with its social networks and its norms about what teenagers should and should not do, constituted social capital beyond the family that aided both family and school in the education of the family's children.

Furthermore, this social capital outside the family was of greatest value for children without extensive social capital in the home. For example, in the public schools, coming from the single-parent household increased greatly a child's change of dropping out of school: but in Catholic schools, a child

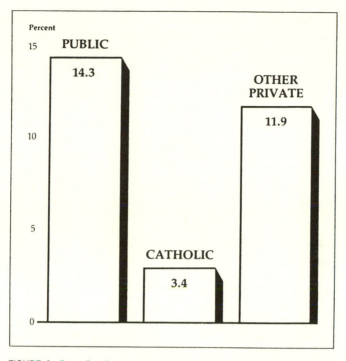

FIGURE 3 Drop Out Rates (spring of sophomore year to spring of senior year)

from a single parent family was no more likely to drop out than was a child from a two-parent family.

These effects were not merely due to religious observance; Catholic students in public schools who attended church regularly had considerably lower dropout rates than did Catholic students who never attended church, but the dropout rates for both were much higher than for their counterparts in Catholic schools.

What was equally striking was that this social capital did not exist in the nonreligious private sector, where the middle class dropout rate was substantial. In the independent private sector, most schools draw children individually from throughout the city; parents may share the same values, but often do not know each other and seldom constitute a community.

A critical test is provided by the non-Catholic religiously homogeneous schools that, like the Catholic schools and unlike the independent schools, are surrounded by a community. Among the non-Catholic religious schools, of which there were only eight (two Jewish, two Baptist, and four other Christian denominations), the dropout rate was virtually the same as in the Catholic sector (3.7%), suggesting comparable social capital in the religious communities surrounding these schools.

It was also possible to find public schools for which the social capital in the community surrounding the school was high; in these schools too the dropout rate was considerably lower than in the public schools without a strong community surrounding the school (see Carruthers & Coleman, 1987). But public schools with social capital in the neighborhood comparable to that surrounding the religious schools are infrequent.

Why is the extent of community, and the social capital it contains for the young, so much greater for the religious schools than for the public schools or the nonreligious private schools? We finally arrived at a provisional answer: Religious organizations are among the few remaining organizations in society, beyond the family, that cross generations. Thus, they are among the few in which the social capital of an adult community is available to children and youth.

The Erosion of Social Capital

The watershed referred to earlier can now be viewed differently: There has been, over the past twenty-five years, an extensive erosion of social capital available to children and youth, both within the family and outside it. Within the family, the growth in human capital is extensive, as reflected by the increased levels of educational attainment. But the social capital, as reflected by the presence of adults in the home, and the range of exchange between parents and children about academic, social, economic, and personal matters, has declined, at the same time that the parents' human capital has grown.

In the community outside the family, the erosion of social capital, in the form of effective norms of social control, adult-sponsored youth organizations, and informal relations between children and adults, has been even greater. The earlier migration of fathers from household and neighborhood during the day, and the very recent migration of mothers from the household into the labor force has meant reduced participation in community organizations, like the PTA, Scouting, and others. In addition, the society has been invaded by an advanced individualism, in which cultivation of one's own well-being has replaced interest in others. Indicators are the extensive growth in concern with one's health (jogging, health clubs, etc.), personal appearance, and career advancement.

Altogether, the social capital in family and neighborhood available for raising children has declined precipitously. The cost will, of course, be borne by the next generation, and borne disproportionately by the disadvantaged of the next generation—for the loss of social capital in the community hurts most the children with least human and social capital in their families.

An indirect and nonobvious implication of these results is that the strict separation of church and state, as practiced in America, has been harmful to the least advantaged and particularly harmful to children in the black community. This separation has prevented the school's making use of the social capital surrounding the church (an institution used more by those of low socio-economic status than those of high socio-economic status) to support the goals of the school. In many black communities, the most powerful community institution is the church; but schools cannot aid churches in aiding children, through, for example, joint after-school programs and youth organizations. Thus, the disadvantaged are harmed, and the black disadvantaged are especially harmed, by making impossible the use of the social capital that does exist in a setting where this capital is not abundant.

All this would not matter, of course, in a society in which social capital was abundant. In the past, many persons struggle to escape social norms of an oppressive closely knit community. But the world has changed: In the individualistic present, each narcissistically attends to self-development, with little attention left over for children, certainly not for others' children. It is very likely a reaction to this absence of community social capital that has led many inner-city black parents to send their children to Catholic schools and other black parents to establish, with a few friends, small *ad hoc* private schools. It is very likely a reaction to the same social changes that has led to the conservative Christian school movement, a movement in which parents are striving to recreate for their children's upbringing some of the social capital that once existed in local neighborhoods.

These are private responses. We may ask what are the public policy implications of the social changes that have resulted in a loss of social capital in the family and outside it?

Public Investments in Social Capital

The loss of social capital, inside and outside the family, has extensive implications for the structure of American childrearing. In effect, raising children once took place informally, as a by-product of other activities, in social institutions—the household, the extended family, and neighborhood-based organizations—that were held in place by these other activities. As the locus of the other activities has changed, the institutions have crumbled, and the by-product, childrearing, has crumbled along with them. The institutions that have replaced them (the offices and factories that have replaced households or neighborhoods as workplaces, the shopping malls and catalogs that have replaced neighborhood stores as places to shop, the cocktail parties and rock concerts that have replaced gatherings of extended families as leisure settings) are inhospitable to the relations between adults and children that constitute social capital for the children's growth.

This wholesale destruction of the institutional "underbrush" of society brings both danger and opportunity. One danger lies in the possibility that nothing will replace these informal institutions, and children will grow up in an environment consisting primarily of commercial recreation (music, clothes, thrill-generating activites) and populated primarily by other children. A second danger lies in the possibility that the old institutions will be replaced by consciously designed ones, but institutions inferior to those they replaced.

The opportunity lies in the possibility that new institutions, designed expressly for childrearing, can do so better than a system in which most childrearing occurred as a by-product.

To realize the opportunity rather than the danger, it is valuable to recall history: When men left the household in great numbers for daily work outside it, in the late 19th and early 20th centuries, an extensive public investment was made in a new form of social capital, mass public schooling. One might suggest that this newly created form of social capital was designed to replace the informal social capital that became unavailable to children when the father left the household for the factory or office.

A second major transformation of the household is now occurring, of perhaps even greater magnitude in the lives of children, as the woman leaves for the factory or office and as the neighborhood declines in strength. The parallel suggests a similar replacement of informal social capital, as a by-product of other activities, with a formal institution analogous to the school.

The general shape of the demand for a new institution is clear: It is a demand not for further classroom indoctrination, nor for any particular content, but a demand for child care: *all day, from birth to school age; after school, every day, till parents return home from work; and all summer.*

It is important, however, to look at something more than the explicit demand, because merely meeting the demand of parents may satisfy their needs without replacing the social capital that is important for children. Two points must be recognized. One is evident in the findings of *Equality of Educational Opportunity* on the importance of family background. As indicated earlier, an interpretation of these results is that the outputs of education result from the interaction of qualities the child brings from home—which can be loosely characterized as attitudes, effort, and conception of self—with qualities of the school. As the social capital in home and neighborhood shrinks, school achievement and other growth will not be increased by replacing these resources with more school-like resources— that is, those that produce opportunities, demands, and rewards—but by replacing them with resources which produce attitudes, efforts, and conception of self—that is, those qualities that interact with the ones provided by the school.

The second point is that some indication of what those resources must be like can be seen in the character of the currently eroding institutions that have provided the social capital in the past. Their essential qualities have been, I believe, attention, personal interest and intensity of involvement, some persistence and continuity over time, and a certain degree of intimacy.

Beyond these few statements about the nature of investments in social capital designed to bring greatest benefit, I am not prepared to go. But several points are clear. As we move toward a new structure of the household and neighborhood, new investments to provide social capital for the next generation are both in demand and socially desirable. These new institutions are analogous to the school, in that the demand for them arises as the mother leaves the household, just as the demand for mass schooling arose as the father left the household. Yet they cannot be like the school in the kinds of qualities they engender in children, for the social capital that is now eroding leaves a more fundamental vacuum. They must be institutions that induce the kinds of attitudes, effort, and conception of self that children and youth need to succeed in school and as adults.

Notes

1. A major difference between the Japanese corporation and that of Europe and America is that in the transition from feudalism to capitalism in Japan, the noble household remained more fully unscathed by revolution than in the West and served as the basis for the highly paternalistic Japanese corporation. Many welfare activities that are province of the State in the West are the province of the corporation in Japan. See Coleman (1982) for an examination of the new corporate structure of society.

2. In recent years, the inequality of household income has been increasing, as shown by the following statistics: In constant 1984 dollars, the percentage of household with incomes below $10,000 was 20.2 in 1970, 21.2 in 1984; and the percent with incomes of $35,000 or more was 21.6 in 1970, 28.1 in 1984. (U.S. Bureau of Census, 1985, Table 741.)

3. One might ask how families as welfare institutions manage to overcome this incentive effect. They do not do so perfectly, of course, as attested to by the classic case of the ne'er do well brother-in-law who continually sponges off the household. But the essential weapons available to microlevel institutions like the family, but less available to the government, are the weapons of shame, stigma, and other informal sanctions, which hold the incentive for dependency to a tolerable level. For a discussion of the relevance of stigma in reducing incentives for free rider behavior in government programs, see Coleman, 1982.

4. Hierarchy may have increased in occupations, as corporate employment has replaced self-employment for many. But within corporations, the amount of authority associated with hierarchy has declined greatly. The once-common "bull o' the woods" foreman, for example, is now a rarity in American manufacturing firms.

5. Once in awhile, this disparity can be overcome, as chronicled in *Zen and the Art of Motorcycle Maintenance*. But that book shows special circumstances: By making the motorcyle journey together, father and son cut themselves off from any other extended relationships and were thrust on one another. Apart from such special circumstances, parents and children are drawn off into their respective worlds, with their respective age-mates.

6. I recently observed an interesting illustration of this in a local volunteer swimming coach, a demanding martinet who imposes strong demands upon the flock of 5–15 years-old he coaches, but who pays them the great compliment of attention, respect, and high expectations. They respond with loyalty, extreme effort, self-discipline, and maturity. He is an important figure in their growing up. But his counterparts are not numerous in America today.

7. The results from the 1980 data were hotly debated; see especially various papers in *Sociology of Education* (1982, 1983, 1985). They are now generally accepted, after the analyses of the 1982 data.

8. These dropout rates do not include transfers, if the transfers were still in school elsewhere in 1982. Adding dropouts and transfers together, other private schools

were highest, and Catholic schools remained lowest. See Coleman and Hoffer, 1987, for elaboration.

References

Carruthers, B. & Coleman, J. S. (1987). *Legitimacy and social structure: Authority in high schools.* IL: University of Chicago.

Coleman, J. S., Campbell, E. Q., Hobson, C. J., McPartland, J., Mood, A. M., Weinfeld, F. D., & York, R. L. (1966). *Equality of educational opportunity.* Washington, DC: U.S. Government Printing Office.

Coleman, J. S. (1982). *The asymmetric society.* Syracuse, NY: Syracuse University Press.

Coleman, J. S. (1982). Income testing and social cohesion. In I. Garfinkel (Ed.), *Income-tested transfer programs: The case for and against* (pp. 67–88). New York: Academic Press.

Coleman, J. S., & Hoffer, T. (1987). *Public and private high schools: The impact of communities.* New York: Basic Books.

Coleman, J. S., Hoffer, T., & Kilgore, S. (1982). *High school achievement.* New York: Basic Books.

Comber, L. C., & Keeves, J. P. (1973). *Science education in nineteen countries.* New York: Wiley.

Durkheim, E. (1951). *Suicide.* New York: The Free Press.

Hugi, R. (1983). *Children and the state.* Chicago, IL: National Opinion Research Center, University of Chicago.

Husen, T. (Ed.) (1967). *International study of achievement in mathematics (Vol. 2).* Stockholm: Almquist and Wicksell.

Murray, C. (1984). *Losing ground.* New York: Basic Books, Inc.

Pirsig, R. (1974). *Zen and the art of motorcyle maintenance.* New York: William Morrow & Co., Inc.

Powell, A. G., Farrar, E., & Cohen, D. K. (1985). *The shopping mall high school.* Boston: Houghton Mifflin.

Preston, S. (1984). Children and the elderly. *Scientific American, 251,* (6), 44–49.

Pryor, E. J., Jr. (1972). Rhode Island family structure: 1875 and 1960. In P. Laslett (Ed.), *Household and family in past time* (pp. 571–589). Cambridge: Cambridge University Press.

Sociology of Education. (1982, April/July). *55,* (2/3); (1983, October). *56,* (4); (1985, April). *58,* (2).

Testa, M., & Wulczyn, F. (1980). *The state of the child.* Chicago, IL: National Opinion Research Center, University of Chicago.

U.S. Bureau of the Census. (1975). *Historical statistics of the United States colonial times to 1970.* Washington, DC: U.S. Government Printing Office.

U.S. Bureau of the Census. (1947, 1949, 1951, 1984). *Statistical abstract of the United States.* Washington, DC: U.S. Government Printing Office.

U.S. Bureau of the Census. (1985). *Statistical abstract of the United States, 1986.* Washington, DC: U.S. Government Printing Office.